PENGUIN BOOKS

1914–1918

Over the past twenty years Lyn Macdonald has established a reputation as a popular author and historian of the First World War. Her books are *They Called It Passchendaele*, an account of the Passchendaele campaign in 1917; *The Roses of No Man's Land*, a chronicle of the war from the neglected viewpoint of the casualties and the medical teams who struggled to save them; *Somme*, a history of the legendary and horrifying battle that has haunted the minds of succeeding generations; *1914: The Days of Hope*, a vivid account of the first months of the war and winner of the 1987 *Yorkshire Post* Book of the Year Award; *1914–1918: Voices and Images of the Great War*, an illuminating account of the many different aspects of the war; and *1915: The Death of Innocence*, a brilliant evocation of the year that saw the terrible losses of Aubers Ridge, Loos, Neuve Chapelle, Ypres and Gallipoli. Her most recent book is *To the Last Man: Spring 1918*, the story of the massive German offensive that broke the British line and almost broke the British Army. All are based on the accounts of eyewitnesses and survivors, and cast a unique light on the First World War. All are published in Penguin.

Lyn Macdonald is married and lives in London.

1914-1918
VOICES & IMAGES
of the
GREAT WAR

LYN MACDONALD

with research by Shirley Seaton

PENGUIN BOOKS

PENGUIN BOOKS

Published by the Penguin Group
Penguin Books Ltd, 80 Strand, London WC2R 0RL, England
Penguin Putnam Inc., 375 Hudson Street, New York, New York 10014, USA
Penguin Books Australia Ltd, 250 Camberwell Road, Camberwell, Victoria 3124, Australia
Penguin Books Canada Ltd, 10 Alcorn Avenue, Toronto, Ontario, Canada M4V 3B2
Penguin Books India (P) Ltd, 11 Community Centre, Panchsheel Park,
New Delhi – 110 017, India   .
Penguin Books (NZ) Ltd, Cnr Rosedale and Airborne Roads,
Albany, Auckland, New Zealand
Penguin Books (South Africa) (Pty) Ltd, 24 Sturdee Avenue,
Rosebank 2196, South Africa

Penguin Books Ltd, Registered Offices: 80 Strand, London WC2R 0RL, England

www.penguin.com

First published by Michael Joseph 1988
Published in Penguin Books 1991
12

Printed in England by Butler and Tanner Ltd, Frome and London

CONTENTS

1914

The Great War. Even the name is awesome. And its name had been fixed long before it happened. Those who studied the politics of power had seen it coming for a decade and it was an open secret that a 'great war' would one day be necessary to sort out the simmering quarrels and rivalries that were bubbling to the boil in Europe.

Germany had long been tempted to force war on France, her old defeated enemy, to settle old scores once and for all. Russia was apprehensive of the ambitions of Germany and Austria to increase their influence and control over the Baltic and the near east; France could not forgive Germany for the humiliation of defeat in 1871 and the annexation of her provinces of Alsace and Lorraine. Great Britain was disquieted by the rise of German militarism, by German colonisation of overseas territories and, not least, by her zeal in ship-building – the personal project of the Kaiser who made no secret of his desire, if not to consign Britannia to the depths, at least to rule beside her on the waves. By 1914 Germany was rich in warships and strong enough to challenge the supremacy of Britain's mighty navy, just as a burgeoning fleet of German merchant ships challenged Britain's trade routes to the Empire and the far-flung markets of the world.

Germany and Britain alike had enjoyed an unprecedented era of expansion and prosperity. But there was one vital difference. Germany's rulers believed that prosperity could only continue by the exercise of military might: Britain saw it rooted in a continuance of peace secured by the weapon of diplomacy – though 'gun-boat' diplomacy was not ruled out. Standing aloof from European squabbles, with all the confidence of wealth and power and the bulwark of her great Empire and Commonwealth to support her, in the sincere belief that British policies were unique in justice, wisdom and magnanimity, Great Britain stood proud, and a little apart from Europe, complacent in the role of elder statesman, peace-maker and peace-keeper. In the early years of the twentieth century the headline *Fog in Channel. Continent isolated* was not so funny as it appears in retrospect. In a sense it was an unconscious reflection of British aloofness and Britain's reluctance to become embroiled in a European war. Across the wide waters of the Atlantic the United States of America saw even less reason to take sides in a distant

---

quarrel which was no business of Uncle Sam's.

In the first fateful days of August 1914 when the war began, no one could have foreseen that by the end of it the whole world would have been drawn into conflict, that thrones would topple, that empires would vanish, societies crumble as the old order disappeared, that the world would never be the same again. That eight million young men would die. Regardless of nationality most died in the belief that they were fighting (as the British slogan had it) for 'Honour, Justice, Truth and Right'. Some had good reason to fight for Liberty. Such words rang hollow in the ears of the survivors, tempered by the experience of war, scarred by bereavement, numbed by remembered horrors. Innocence died in the trenches. People were doubtful now of old tenets, cynical of the long-accepted authority of Church and State, impatient of old barriers and divisions.

> ... At sermon-time, while Squire is in his pew,
>   He gives my gilded name a thoughtful stare;
>   For, though low down upon the list, I'm there;
> *'In proud and glorious memory'* ... that's my due.
> Two bleeding years I fought in France, for Squire:
>   I suffered anguish that he's never guessed.
> Once I came home on leave: and then went west ...
>   What greater glory could a man desire?

Thus wrote Siegfried Sassoon in November 1918 on behalf of the rank and file. Already the mills of change had begun to grind.

**BRITAIN'S ACTION
CHEERED BY CROWDS**

**Toronto Streets Thronged
When Declaration News Arrived**

Cheer after cheer from the crowds of people who had waited long and anxiously for the announcement of Great Britain's position in the present conflict in Europe greeted the news that the Mother Country had declared war against Germany.

Groups of men sang 'Rule Britannia', others joined in singing 'God Save the King'; some showed their sense of the seriousness of the situation by singing 'Onward Christian Soldiers'. A procession of men carrying Union Jacks and headed by fifes and drums marched up and down Bay Street and grew in numbers every moment.

The Mail and Empire, Toronto

But in August 1914 the doubts, the reappraisal and the questions were postponed. Patriotism was the watchword, hearts were high, Right was Might, and the young men who besieged recruiting offices from Ottawa to Auckland, Manchester to Melbourne, Oxford to Heidelberg, Vienna to Capetown, had one simple question to ask – 'How soon can we get to the front?'

No event in history has been so thoroughly documented as the Great War. Hundreds of millions of words were committed to paper – letters written to and from the Front, newspapers, propaganda, orders, reports, magazine articles, advertisements, passes, telegrams – poems that ranged from finely honed lines destined for publication to simple doggerel that had much in common with Norse sagas celebrating the exploits of fighting men a millenium before. There were songs, rousingly patriotic, mawkish or sentimental and a host of the wry bawdy parodies preferred by most soldiers of the line. There were diaries crafted with a high degree of literary skill or, scribbled in a pocket-sized 'Soldier's Diary', bald records of weather, (... *more sodding rain today!*) *fatigues* (... *out all night on a working party. And they call this Rest!*), letters and parcels received (... *4 letters recd. today and parcel from Mum – cake, smokes, sardines*), occasional entertainments enjoyed (... *walked to estaminet in Corbie. Bon time!*). All, in one way or another, reflect some aspect of the war and the manifold attitudes and experiences of the soldiers and civilians who endured it.

They also illuminate the mind of a generation and in them, taken as a whole, it is just possible to detect the first shiver in the sands that began to shift, almost imperceptibly, beneath the foundations of the old world that had seemed so solid and unchangeable to its inhabitants.

The words that follow have not been chosen necessarily on the grounds of literary merit – nor because they are brave or beautiful. Nor are they presented as a documentary history of the First World War. There are many gaps and omissions, little in the way of politics and, apart from Gallipoli, scant attention has been paid to theatres of war other than the Western Front. There are few literary gems, not much 'fine' poetry and not many of the 'great' names culled from the considerable literary heritage of the Great War. They have had their say. This is the turn of Tommy Atkins, Heinz Schmidt and Digger Smith, Bill Brown from Calgary, Jack Robinson from Christchurch, Joe Soap from Kansas. And this was their war.

Lyn Macdonald.
London, 1988.

MEDIATION OFFER REFUSED

WASHINGTON, *Monday*. Great Britain, France and Austria have declined to accept President Wilson's offer of mediation.

The Daily Telegraph

AUSTRALIA'S FIRST DRAFT

Splendid in physique, courage and patriotism, the first draft of the Australian Imperial Expeditionary Force for military service showed itself to the citizens of Sydney yesterday. The troops, whose very appearance carried conviction that they will acquit themselves well, wherever employed, were a fine, vigorous body of men, and as, to the accompaniment of rousing martial music, they steadily advanced from Moore Park to Fort Macquarie, for embarkation to Cockatoo Island, the citizens of Sydney poured forth in thousands to cheer them on their way and to wish them 'God-speed' in the enterprise which they have undertaken.

There was a great deal of rushing forward on the part of the crowd to say good-bye, but, quite properly, no one frowned upon it as a breach of discipline. Here were 'our boys' marching to the defence of the Empire, and everyone felt like shaking them by the hands.

Daily Telegraph, Sydney

FAREWELL!
THE ADVANCE GUARD
'GOD-SPEED AND A SAFE
RETURN'

Yesterday afternoon New Zealand, and Wellington more particularly, said farewell to its sons – the advance guard of many more – who are going to help the Empire in its time of stress. It was a hurried affair all through, but when the Empire calls, and there are enemies ever on the watch, there is need for hurry.

Five days after the call arrived from the heart of the Empire, a force of considerably over one thousand men, equipped substantially for special and arduous work, was ready to sail when the order came. On Wednesday the Moeraki and Monowai, laden with valuable human freight, carrying, too, all the necessary things of war, were taken into the stream, prepared at a moment's notice to sail for a region where it is essential the Union Jack should fly.

The New Zealand Times

INDIA'S PRINCELY AID

The House of Commons was aroused to a high pitch of grateful enthusiasm this afternoon by the reading of the Viceroy of India's telegram. It fell on the ears like a romance from the East, with all its variety, movement and colour. It was accepted as one of the finest tributes ever paid to the Imperial ideal. The rulers of the Native States, numbering nearly 700 in all, have offered their personal services and the resources of their States for the war.

The Times

AMERICAN ENTHUSIASM FOR BRITAIN
60,000 Volunteers.

According to Colonel Hughes, Minister of Militia, 60,000 citizens of the United States have offered to enlist in the Canadian Expeditionary Forces. These expressed the simple desire to fight for the British Empire. Application was even made in person to the Militia Department at Ottawa. Of course, no Americans could be enrolled.

The Times

For all we have and are,
For all our children's fate,
Stand up and take the war,
The Hun is at the gate!

Rudyard Kipling.

PRIVATE JACK COLE,
2nd Battalion,
The Worcestershire
Regiment.

Troops from the Aldershot Garrison were getting prepared for their annual furlough, but we had a rude awakening when the war clouds began to hover. Mobilisation on 4 August, 1914, and all leave cancelled. As Captain Whalley's batman I had just bought a new civilian suit, to go weekends to London's Union Jack Club, but had to pack it back home. In the meantime, all our red tunics, helmets and all unnecessary equipment was dumped. In our barrack room at Corunna Barracks we lined our blue walking-out hats on racks over our bed-cots, and wrote on them with chalk 'RIP'. Little did we know that RIP did come to thousands – not in Peace, but in Hell.

Diary of Lieutenant Henri
Desagneaux.

1 August, Saturday.
From the early hours Paris is in turmoil. The banks are besieged. At last at 4.15 in the afternoon, the news spreads like wild-fire, posters are being put up with the order for mobilisation on them! It's every man for himself, you scarcely have the time to shake a few hands before having to go home to make preparations for departure. At six in the morning, after some painful goodbyes, I go to Nogent-le-Perreux station.

Already you find yourself cut off from the world, the newspapers don't come here any more. But, on the other hand, how much news there is! Everyone has his bit of information to tell – and it's true! ... A squadron of Uhlans has been made prisoner; the 20th Corps is already in Alsace.

At last in the afternoon I catch the first train which comes along which is going no one knows precisely where, except that it is in the direction of the Front. The compartments and corridors are bursting at the seams with people from all classes of society. Morale is excellent, everyone is extraordinarily quiet and calm. Along the track at level crossings, in the towns, crowds singing 'La Marseillaise' gather to greet the troops.

The French women have set to it. They are handing out drinks, writing paper, and cigarettes. The general impression is the following: it's Kaiser Bill who wanted war, it had to happen, we shall never have such a fine opportunity again.

I was an apprentice for the decorating trade. The firm was John Barker & Son. Mr Barker sent decorators over to Paris in the winter to decorate two hotels and I was one of them. I went every year from 1910, and I made quite a number of friends there, lived amongst them. I had a chum who was an electrician. He said, 'Why not stop here this time and work for a French firm. You'll learn ever so many different ways in decorating, you'll earn a lot.' I said, 'All right,' and I did, so I was living in Paris when the war broke out. I worked with a French firm named Chablin, a one-man, very good firm, first class.

When the war started the French people all went crazy. I remember all along the boulevard Haussmann from the Opera House to the Place de la République there were thousands of men and women marching up and down shouting, '*A Berlin à Berlin.*' They were shouting all night long.

H. W. HOUGHTON,
2me Regiment,
French Foreign Legion.

On Sunday mornings I used to go to the Embassy Church, in the rue St Honoré, so I knew quite a few people there. The British Ambassador, Sir Francis Bertie, called a meeting of all British subjects. He wanted to form a Corps of British subjects living there. Lord Kitchener had so many recruits he said he couldn't do with us then, but the French Minister of War, Maginot, said, 'I can do with them, I'll have them.' We were sent to Toulouse where the 2nd Regiment of the Foreign Legion had arrived and we were incorporated into the 2nd Regiment of the Foreign Legion.

We got the full uniform the next day – a kepi, that was in scarlet and white, with a black peak – a sky-blue greatcoat which buttoned back from the waist. The idea was, in the desert, for them to walk without it flapping on their knees. Yellow epaulettes, scarlet pantaloons with little black leggings, and a white sash called a bandeau round the middle and that was it.

We went in the trenches in October, near Rheims. The cathedral was only a very short distance away, and the trenches ran from there, but there were not enough of us in those trenches to make a major attack, only local affairs.

The morale in the Foreign Legion was of a high order. The French Army itself was very patriotic, and so were these, there was no difference, even though there were foreigners in it. In fact, one of our Drill Sergeants in Toulouse was a German. He was quite ordinary, just like everybody else, but his drilling was absolutely severe. You had to do the very best and highest in drilling. It didn't seem to bother him that his country was at war. But he wasn't allowed to go to the trenches and they said he was very upset about that. In the Legion they didn't bother much who they were fighting. But that German Sergeant was the most efficient NCO. I ever met. If all Germans were like him I don't know how they came to lose the war.

◆

GERMAN MOBILISATION.

Germans who have served or are liable to serve, are requested to return to Germany without delay, as best they can.

For information they can apply to the German Consulate-General, 21a Bedford Place, Russell Square, London, WC.

R. L. Von Ranke
Consul (Acting Consul General)
London 3rd. August 1914

◆

LEUTNANT FRITZ NAGEL,
Reserve Feldartillerie Regiment Nr. 18

... On August 4, 1914, I presented myself to the army as a reservist and was told I now belonged to the Reserve Field Artillery Regiment Nr. 18, which was forming in Bahrenfeld near Hamburg, about 75 miles northeast of Bremen. Relatives were not allowed near the building where we had to assemble. As soon as I could I gave a message to a little boy so my family knew I would be shipped out to Bahrenfeld within the hour.

On August 6 I was issued my field grey uniform which I had never worn before. The colour was grey-green with dull buttons, the helmet was covered with a grey cloth so the ornaments would not glitter in the sun and the high riding boots were brown and very heavy. The whole outfit was heavy and ill-fitting.

All soldiers and most of the officers were reservists, but the commander, a first lieutenant soon to become a captain, was a regular army officer about 35 to 40 years old. Most of the NCOs were professionals.

In a few days serious training and the breaking-in of our battery started. It quickly became evident that the training of us one-year men had been quite insufficient and we soon became a pain in the neck to our top sergeant. I had saddled my horse during my one year's training only a dozen times and knew nothing about the little tricks of feeding and watering. As a result I was clumsy and slow. To handle one or two of these unbroken horses all day and night long and have everything ready to go, say at 4 a.m., was more than we one-year men could handle. During our service some soldier was ordered to do all of our heavy work while we were supposed to learn how to be efficient officers. But nobody trusted us yet with a command. This went on for some time. The top sergeant cursed and fussed with me, calling me a shirker and what-have-you. I made a big mistake by reminding him that I was not trained to do a common soldier's work. From that moment on he really gave me hell. I had to do more disagreeable work than anybody else, such as going on guard duty after a long, hard day. The other one-year men had been smart enough not to say anything, although they, too, were just about breaking down under the heavy physical work.

For instance, I did not have strength enough to pull the straps holding the saddle tight and the horses would blow themselves up in a sort of passive resistance. A regular soldier would give the horse a tremendous kick in the belly to let the air out. My kicks were so feeble they made no impression on my horse at all. I felt I could not last long with that sergeant breathing down my neck day and night. . . .

3 August, 1914 (Bank Holiday). I went to the City in case War was declared and anything of importance should have to be done. Although the Firm I am with is Belgian, the Representative Principal and many in the business were Germans. Some of them had already left for Germany to fight against us, but there were still several at the office who had not got the pluck to return and fight for their Country. As I write, I am pleased to say the Office is now clear of anything 'Germy' and none of the 'Germs' will ever set foot in it again if it is possible to avoid it.

7 August. I went with two colleagues from the office to the HQ of the Queen's Westminster Rifles. After waiting outside for two or three hours we struggled and pushed our way inside as soon as the door was

SERGEANT B. J.
  BROOKES,
1/16 Queen's Westminster
  Rifles,
(County of London
  Regiment).

opened. After much swearing outside the building, we were 'sworn in' and then waited in turn to see the Doctor. I passed as 'Fit' and was posted to E Company. It is a Territorial battalion, so we then paid our *entrance fee* (rather a good idea to pay to serve one's country!) and the receipt for this money permits free travelling even in civilian clothes.

TROOPER P. MASON,
9th (S) Battalion,
(Yorkshire Hussars
Yeomanry),
West Yorkshire Regiment.

I never said anything about enlisting when I went home that night and on the Sunday morning there was an OHMS envelope. I didn't open it. So when breakfast started Mother said, 'What's that? Get it opened.' I didn't want to open it but she insisted. The instructions were to report to the Drill Hall, Grange Road, Middlesborough. When I read that out, 'Jack,' she said to Dad, 'stop his gallop. He doesn't go! There's lots that will go before that boy goes.' So Dad said, 'Have you joined, Pete?' I said, 'Yes, Dad.' 'Well,' he said, 'this is a nice how-do-you-do.'

Then Mother started to get excited. She said, 'Stop his gallop, Dad. You see Chief Constable Riches. He's not going.' So Dad said, 'Well, just supposing, Pete, you came back with a leg or an arm off? Who wants you?' I said, 'Let me get there first, Dad, before I get back.' 'So,' he said, 'It's alright you talking like that but you don't know what you've done.' I said, 'But I do know what I've done.' 'Alright,' he said, 'if you've made your bed, you'll have to lie in it.' I said, 'I'll lie in it, Dad.' 'Well,' he said to Mother, 'there's no more to be said, Polly.' And that was the start.

2ND LIEUTENANT
J. MACLEOD,
3rd Reserve Battalion,
The Queen's Own
 Cameron Highlanders.

The Queensgate Hotel,
Inverness.
August 10th.

Dear Mother,

I had a very good journey, a very nice fellow from Tonbridge School, who is in a firm that supplies electric lights to railways, was the only other occupant of the compartment, though otherwise the train was crowded. On reaching Inverness, he took me to his hotel for a shave and wash-up. In this hotel I am now staying: it is clean, and very moderate – a temperance affair; it gives you high tea in the evening and no dinner. I never shaved so badly in my life, and got cut in five places. This was because the blades that I bought at Boots just do not fit. In spite of wounds I went to the Camerons' place. At first they were rather brutal, thinking me to be a German spy, I suppose, on account of my scarred face. They asked me a lot of questions to test my identity. Fortunately there was another old Rugbeian applying for a similar job. (I had met him before this painful interview in the Medical Officer's place, whither I was sent on arrival.) They turned me out of the room and sent for him, interviewing him separately. The result was that they suddenly turned friendly, and said that it was all right, *but*

(i) I would have to wait until I was gazetted, and as there was a rush on the Regiment, I might be gazetted to some other regiment, and therefore they would not tell me what kit to get;

(ii) I could not get any kit in Inverness; Edinburgh was the nearest place.

They advised me to go back to Cambridge, but that would be fearfully expensive, and cost about an extra £5. So I am going to write to the James' and ask them if they will put me up. I will let you know by wire where I am.
All love,
Jock

GUNNER R. ELWIS,
Royal Garrison
 Artillery.

There was such a rush for fellows to go in the Army that they'd had to get quite a number of officers in to deal with all these recruits. Even so, it was about two hours before my turn came. I was only eighteen and I didn't weigh very much – I didn't look very much like a soldier – I weighed 8 stone 11 lb., but I was passed. I was given a parcel of food and a railway warrant and we were taken down to Midland station and put on the train and instructed to report to the officer at Newhaven.
Anyway when we got down to Newhaven it was between nine and ten and a party of soldiers came to meet us, and we were taken up what seemed to me to be miles, up a long valley from the railway station. It was pitch dark and we didn't know where we were going. Anyway we

got to a place where there seemed to be a lot of tents and we were taken into a great big one, a marquee, with a long table down the middle and some forms and we were sat down and presently two fellows came with a big basketful of loaves which had been cut in two and another two men came down with a big dixie full of herrings and they plonked one of these herrings on half a loaf of bread and slapped the other half on the top of it and that was my supper.

As far as I could see in the night there must have been hundreds of tents and the Sergeant counted us out, there was twelve men put into each tent and he shoved us in. He said, 'There's some blankets there.' There was nothing on the floor, just the bare soil, and so we got down as best we could.

About six o'clock the next morning there was such a noise outside and then a fellow blew a trumpet and I had a feeling that must have been the Reveille. We got up. None of us had bothered about undressing. Some Sergeants came up then, 'Come on, fall in!' We didn't know what it was we'd got to fall into. It might have been the sea for all *we* knew!

CAPTAIN H. M. DILLON,
2nd Battalion,
The Ox & Bucks Light
Infantry.

Sunday, 9th August. 4th Day of mobilisation. During these last few days our reservists have fired 10 rounds on the rifle range, boots were oiled, and boots, caps etc which did not fit were changed. The OC gave our Colonel a £5 grant for each company. I spent this on nails for reservist's boots, buying dubbin to take out, also cotton wool, lint, boracic powder and tincture of iodine for sore feet, and clippers for hair.

◆ ◆

What's in the air? There's a murmuring note
Winding its way through a bugle's throat.
A sound in the distant far away,
Not very much in the air today.

SIR DOUGLAS HAIG.

The King seemed delighted that Sir John French had been appointed to the Chief Command of the Expeditionary Force. He asked me my opinion. I told him at once, as I felt it my duty to do so, that from my experience with Sir John in the South African War, he was certain to do his utmost loyally to carry out any orders which the Government might give him. I had grave doubts however, whether either his temper was sufficiently even or his military knowledge sufficiently thorough to enable him to discharge properly the very difficult duties which will devolve upon him during the coming operations with Allies on the Continent. In my own heart, I know that French is quite unfit for this great command at a time of crisis in our Nation's history.

◆

What's in the air that travels so fast
Following the sound of that bugle's blast?
A sinister note of war's alarms
Louder and clearer 'To Arms, To Arms'.

◆

On 12 August we moved out of barracks for the last time to Cowes where we embarked in two steam boats for Southampton. Large crowds assembled to see us off. As we moved out to the Solent, the Royal Yacht Squadron ran up a signal: 'Goodbye and good luck'. At Southampton we re-embarked on a P & O transport where we were packed like herrings. About 6 p.m. that evening we set sail, and it must have been a wonderful sight to see the convoy of ships passing down the Solent, past the forts and Spithead. We sat all through the night in darkness with a thousand thoughts of the future crowding through our brains. In order to relieve the monotony I started a bit of a singsong in the dark and we all sang the various musical comedy songs and kept cheery that way.

LIEUTENANT K. F. B. TOWER,
4th Battalion,
The Royal Fusiliers.

What's in the air? The soul-scaring tramp
Of armed soldiers marching to camp,
A rattle of bayonets, stern commands,
martial music from military bands.

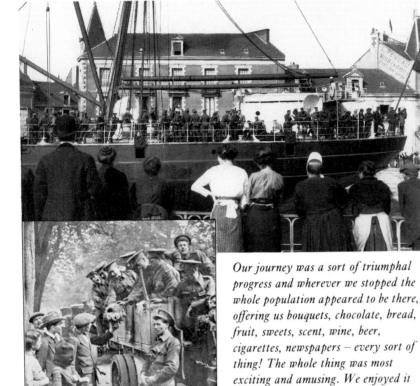

Arrived Havre. Curious to look down upon the quay and see the French faces. Everyone pleased to see us. The men have already discovered a language in which to speak and be understood. Consists chiefly, as far as I can see, in saying 'beer' and 'cigarettes'. Both words understood by the French, and of both articles no stint!

CAPTAIN C. J.
  PATERSON,
1st Battalion,
South Wales Borderers.

Our journey was a sort of triumphal progress and wherever we stopped the whole population appeared to be there, offering us bouquets, chocolate, bread, fruit, sweets, scent, wine, beer, cigarettes, newspapers – every sort of thing! The whole thing was most exciting and amusing. We enjoyed it immensely. Nearly every man was wearing a tricolour ribbon in his jacket or was waving a tricolour flag. Madame la République had truly taken Private Thomas Atkins to her heart!

LIEUTENANT CROSSE,
2nd Battalion,
The Ox & Bucks Light
  Infantry.

◆

*What's in the air? Oh, strategic plans,
And banquets for men in corned beef cans,
Oh yes, there's fever and dread disease
Mosquitoes, bluebottles, lice and fleas.*

◆

What's in the air? Loud thuds and wild yells,
Fire and flame and poison gas shells
Making a Hell of a world so gay,
Oh yes, there's more in the air today.

PRIVATE IVOR MORGAN,
16th Battalion (Cardiff Pals),
The Welsh Regiment.

'Do your duty bravely
Fear God
Honour The King'

Field Marshal Lord Kitchener

FOUR DAYS BATTLE

A BRILLIANT SERIES OF ENGAGEMENTS

CAPTAIN H. C. REES,
2nd Battalion,
The Welch Regiment.

22 August. The march to Peissant, with no knowledge of the enemy's whereabouts was not pleasant. We eventually arrived and found a squadron of French cavalry there and narrowly escaped fighting them in the dark. After both sides had decided that it was inadvisable to shoot

allies we turned our attention to local defence and billets, as it was then midnight. Unfortunately the inhabitants thought we were Germans. Eventually a shivering woman with a hurricane lantern, holding a small boy by the hand, was induced to come out and parley with Cocks, our chief French scholar. Cocks was apparently wildly excited and after saying a few words, suddenly let off his revolver and narrowly escaped shooting Somerset who was standing next to him! The woman rushed screaming into the house and bolted the door, leaving the hurricane lantern and a howling child on the doorstep. After unloading Cocks' revolver for him I started to find my way into the back of the house and promptly fell into the local stream from which I was ignominiously hauled out by the collar.

Before turning in I got a harrow from a neighbouring farm and planted it points uppermost in the middle of the road for the benefit of any stray German cavalry. I hadn't been in bed half an hour when I was woken up by the sergeant of the guard on my 'obstacle', to say that the owner of the harrow wanted it back! This was really the last straw! I told them both where to go.

23 August. I was out visiting my sentries in the woods about a thousand yards in advance of our position about 7 a.m. and was talking to an old Reservist, when we suddenly saw a horseman ride through the wood. He dismounted and tied his horse to a tree and advanced (about 300 yards from us) to the edge of the wood and stood looking at our position on the canal bank. My old Reservist said to me, 'Is that a German, Sir?' I said, 'Yes, I expect it is.' Whereupon he said, 'Shall I shoot him, Sir?' And I said, 'Yes, have a try.'

He picked up his rifle, took careful aim and fired. The man fell, and we walked over to look at him. He was a trooper of the famous Regiment of the Death's Head Hussars – the first German I had seen. So I took his horse and rode it back to our lines and made my report. I then returned to the sentries in front and before I got there I heard heavy rifle fire from our detachment on the main road. The next moment I saw a German officer with a heavy limp come running in my direction. I ran after him, and he held up his hands and shouted in English, 'I am Count von Arnim'. He was slightly wounded in the leg and was shivering with fright. It appeared he was one of an officers' Cavalry patrol who had ridden down the road and had been caught by the fire of our post on the road. They were all hit.

By this time the sun was getting quite hot. A gorgeous morning. The church bells were ringing and the Belgian peasants could be seen walking quietly to church. What a contrast! It seemed hardly believable that we were at war and that men had just been killed only a few yards away. I was just returning to my sentries when a terrific fire opened us from the woods to the north and my sentries came running in.

LIEUTENANT K. F. B. TOWER,
4th Battalion,
The Royal Fusiliers.

Shortly after this the enemy started to advance in mass down the railway cutting, about 800 yards off, and Maurice Dease fired his two machine-guns into them and absolutely mowed them down. I should judge without exaggeration that he killed at least 500 in the two minutes. The whole cutting was full of bodies and this cheered us all up. Soon, however, the enemy started debouching from the woods in all directions and we lay down and fired as hard and as fast as possible.

CORPORAL W.
HOLBROOK,
4th Battalion,
The Royal Fusiliers.

Bloody Hell! You couldn't see the earth for them there were that many. Time after time they gave the order 'Rapid Fire'. Well, you didn't wait for the order, really! You'd see a lot of them coming in a mass on the other side of the canal and you just let them have it. They kept retreating, and then coming forward, and then retreating again. Of course, we were losing men and a *lot* of the officers especially when the Germans started this shrapnel shelling and, of course, they had machine-guns – masses of them! But we kept flinging them back. I don't know how many times we saw them off.

---◆---

GERMAN ONSLAUGHT.
HOW THE BRITISH KEPT THEM BACK.

---◆---

CAPTAIN H. C. REES,
2nd Battalion,
The Welch Regiment.

24 August. We dug trenches all day, starting at 4 a.m. and listened to the incessant cannonade. At dusk the South Wales Borderers took over and we were ordered to rejoin the battalion at Fourcaulx. There we had a splendid view of the Battle of Mons – an impressive sight with the flashes of the guns and the flames from the burning town. C Company was ordered to move on to the railway triangle. We took over the south face from Berkeley who had been trying to hold the whole of it with B Company. The Battalion was holding a frontage of about 3 miles and the situation was manifestly impossible. At the same time we had no orders of any description.

LIEUTENANT K. F. B.
TOWER,
4th Battalion,
The Royal Fusiliers.

Ashburn had been wounded in the head, and Steele took over command of the Company, which by now was seriously reduced in numbers and the dead and dying were lying all over the place. Colonel McMahon sent up about 100 men under Captain Bowden Smith and Lieutenant Mead to support us, but most of them were killed by shrapnel fire on the way up. Poor little Jo Mead reached where I was when he was immediately shot in the head and died instantly. Captain Bowden Smith was hit with shrapnel in the stomach and lay at my feet in fearful agony. One could do nothing for the wounded. The enemy had now got right round our right flank, driving in the Middlesex Regt. We were now being shot at from all sides and the position was hopeless. Dease and all his machine-gun crew and both guns had been knocked out.

We darted off under a hail of fire and I don't know how on earth we got away. I followed the embankment for a quarter of a mile and then got on top to see the way, and fortunately I saw Captain Carey commanding another Company, who shouted to me to turn left as there was a German battalion in between me and Mons. We eventually reached the rest of the Battalion about eight that night. I don't think I've ever had such a narrow escape, or even a more frightful day. I felt absolutely done and just lay down and slept for 4 hours, when I was woken up to continue the retreat.

◆

The British forces at Mons are reported to be gallantly holding their own, but may be compelled by the success of the German attack elsewhere to fall back on Maubeuge.

The Times, 25 August

◆

Our regiment and the Cheshires with a battery of Artillery were sent off to the left of our position in front of a village called Elouges. I got the men of my platoon on a hundred yards, and then – the shells began bursting like hail!

We lay in a potato crop like partridges. I think we were all too petrified to move. We lay just below the crest of a ridge waiting to crawl up to see if any German infantry came along. Before any came we had an order to retire, so that just where my platoon was we did not fire at all. This made it almost more trying, not being able to hit back. We lay under that shellfire for three hours, and I think that none of us will ever forget the feeling of thinking that the next moment we might be dead – perhaps blown to atoms. I kept wondering what it was going to feel like to be dead, and all sorts of little things that I had done, and places I had been to years ago and had quite forgotten, kept passing through my mind. I have often heard of this happening to a drowning man but have never experienced it before and don't want to again. I think you get so strung up that your nerves get into an abnormal condition. My brain seemed extraordinarily cool and collected, which I was proud of, but I

LIEUTENANT E.H.T.
BROADWOOD,
1st Battalion
The Norfolk Regiment.

looked at my hands and saw them moving and twisting in an extraordinary way, as if they didn't belong to me, and when I tried to use
my field glasses to spy at the Germans, it was as much as I could do
with the greatest effort to get them up to my eyes, and then I could
scarcely see. When the order came to retire, our company got it late.

I could not get some of the men along. They were too dead beat, as
it was a broiling day and all the time the sun had been beating on us,
but I and a last party of five, climbed up a pear tree and over a garden
wall and so, creeping along with the bullets now flying all around, we
got over another wall and up a path exposed for a short way. We ran
along, and I remember – as an instance of the stupid things one does in
moments of excitement – my little hairbrush jumped out suddenly from
my haversack and I ran back five or six yards to pick it up – and risked
a life for a hairbrush! I found, subsequently, two holes in my haversack
where a bullet had passed through, just grazing my clothes, and it may
have been then that it went through.

CAPTAIN H. C. REES,
2nd Battalion,
The Welch Regiment.

We got orders to retire and at the same moment a German cavalry patrol
appeared. When we had quite decided that they were really Germans,
a section opened fire and brought down the whole patrol, both men and
horses. We moved in extended order across the plain where we found
the Queen's Regiment in support. An officer I spoke to told me that
they had been very anxious about us, because from their vantage point
on the higher ground they could see a force of the estimated 10,000
German Cavalry, and at one time we and they were not more than a
thousand yards apart, hidden from each other by the folds of the ground.
We had a terrible march on a very hot afternoon. I remember thinking
that night that we had earned a good night's rest. It was a somewhat rude
awakening to the facts of the situation when the march was resumed at
2 a.m. after $3\frac{1}{2}$ hours sleep. In three days we had marched about 60 miles,
one day of the three being spent digging trenches, and had had only
about 4 hours sleep in snatches. In this condition the retreat really began.

◆

THE BRITISH AT MONS

It will be seen from the reports that our little Army was fighting at
Mons while unfortunate events were happening further east, and
that during Sunday and Sunday evening it held its ground firmly.
Our information is that it received the German attack absolutely
unmoved. What seems certain, however, is that our Army, doubtless
to its disgust and disappointment, must conform with the movements
of the French in retreat.

The Times, 25 August

It was wonderful how quickly the Reservists had got back into the swing of the Army again and how soon they were fit to march again after their years in civilian life, where most of their life they were wearing india-rubber shoes and never walking at all.

When trying to weed out the unfits, there was one most extraordinarily ugly little man in my company who could not march a bit and on each occasion had fallen out exhausted and sore footed. I told him that he would have to leave the battalion and go back to the base. He protested heavily and implored me to let him come along and fight with the battalion and told me in tones of great pride that he had won first prize for waltzing on a table in Hackney for thirteen hours! Eventually I gave way and let him come.

That man tried his hardest. He fell out exhausted day after day. He fell out really badly on the day we reached Mons, but struggled on and arrived in time to fight with the Company during those two days and gave a very fine account of himself. On the second day of the Retreat he collapsed at the side of the road and died in my arms. I have no record of his name, but as a feat of endurance and courage I cannot name his equal.

LIEUTENANT K. F. B.
TOWER,
4th Battalion
The Royal Fusiliers.

26 August. I met two officers of the 15th Hussars during the morning at different times. The first, Captain Nugent (who offered me £50 for a cigarette!) told me that if we couldn't march quicker we should not get away at all. The second, Captain Nelson, was equally convinced that we were only drawing the Germans into a trap. The main road was double-banked with troops and we heard that the heavy firing and shell-bursts we had seen was a great battle at Le Cateau.

CAPTAIN H. C. REES,
2nd Battalion,
The Welch Regiment.

◆

The British Army was engaged with a superior force on Wednesday, and it is cheering to learn that our troops 'fought splendidly', as their countrymen knew they would ... They are fighting again now, probably still against heavy odds, and we may be sure they are giving fresh proofs of British prowess.

The Times, 28 August.

◆

LIEUTENANT K. F. B.
TOWER,
4th Battalion,
The Royal Fusiliers.

The scene on the road baffles any description I can give of it. It was a veritable rout – men, horses, guns, refugees and wagons struggling along in disorder to get away at all costs. Progress was naturally slow and all roads seemed to be blocked in the same way.

Had the Germans only taken advantage of this, the Expeditionary Force must have surrendered. However, the enemy did nothing. He did not shell the roads and his cavalry did nothing. So, after continual blocks and fearful disorder, we managed to get away unmolested and unharmed.

And so the great retreat continued, all through the next two days and nights. No rest, no food and no excitement. We walked as if in a dream, seeing only the backs of the men in front and only longing for the end of it all. It was difficult to cheer up the men. We had obviously suffered two serious reverses and were in full retreat, our losses had been heavy and we were losing men daily on the road from exhaustion.

Nothing could have been finer than the bearing of the men through all this long tedious march, largely over cobblestones, over mile after mile of road, through endless flat country, past hundreds after hundreds of poplar trees acting as sentinels along our line of retreat.

We sang, we played mouth organs and penny whistles, we made endless fun of anybody we could, in fact anything to make us think of something else except the dull monotonous tramp of tired feet getting more and more sore as we went on.

25 August. Villages burning to the north of us and Germans advancing. 28 August. It is very sad to see the poor villagers flying south as we retire. Those who, as we came north a fortnight ago, looked on us as their deliverers, are now thinking we are broken reeds. They are crying and asking us to save them and their homes. They come swarming along, pushing prams and carrying babies in thousands. Houses, whole villages deserted, except for dogs, some cattle, fowls etc. A ghastly business. Poor creatures!

CAPTAIN C. J.
PATERSON,
1st Battalion,
S. Wales Borderers.

THE TRUTH FROM THE BRITISH ARMY
GERMAN 'TIDAL WAVE'

OUR SOLDIERS OVERWHELMED
BY NUMBERS

AMIENS AUG. 29

This is a pitiful story I have to write. Would to God it did not fall to me to write it, but the time for secrecy is past. Only by realising what has happened can we nerve ourselves for the effort we must make to retrieve it.

What you know in England may be something like the truth. But I write with the Germans advancing incessantly, while all the rest of France believes they are still held near the frontier...

The first inkling I had that the Germans had penetrated far into France was this morning. In a village where a banner inscribed with 'Honour to the British Army' (in English) hung across the road, I met a long Royal Engineers column... From some of the men I learned that orders had been received for the British base to be shifted with all possible speed. The Staff had left. The artillery had left...

'How is it going?' I inquired of a friendly sergeant. He shrugged his shoulders. At dusk the French were falling back. The tidal wave of German troops which has swept over North-Eastern France will spread still further unless a miracle happens. Our small British force could not stand before a volume so powerful, so immense. It has been scattered all over the country, so I learn from officers – staff officers among them – and men met here and there. The Headquarters staff moved hastily a long way back, and it cannot stay long where it is. As the Captain of the Dragoons said, 'They are everywhere'...

I hope I have not been guilty of exaggeration in anything I have written here. I have aimed at telling a plain tale of misfortune and defeat. It is a bitter tale to tell of British troops, but they were set an impossible task. Let us not try to hush up the facts. Let us face them and let them strengthen our resolve to see this war through whatever happens...

England should realise and should realise at once that she must send reinforcements, and still send them. Is an army of exhaustless valour to be borne down by the sheer weight of numbers, while young Englishmen at home play golf and cricket? We want men, and we want them now.

FALSE NEWS

TO THE EDITOR OF *THE TIMES.*

Sir,

Is it not possible for the Press of England to take a stand against the spread of false information calculated to play the game of Germany? The story about the annihilation of two well-known regiments a few days ago, and today the announcement that Mr Winston Churchill visited Lord Kitchener at 3 a.m., are only two cases of many. I will send one sum of £50 to be handed to the Prince of Wales's Fund to the first paper which discovers and denounces by name and address the author of the latter falsehood.

I am yours truly,
C. Hagberg Wright.

August 26th
Reform Club,
Pall-mall, S.W.

THE ATTACKS ON
THE TIMES
HISTORY OF THE AMIENS DISPATCH
A Statement of Fact

On Sunday last we published in a special edition a dispatch from a Special Correspondent at Amiens which has been the subject of much discussion and has exposed *The Times* to attacks in the newspaper Press and in Parliament. We desire, therefore, to make a plain statement of the facts...

The dispatch reached *The Times* office by special courier early on Saturday evening. The extreme gravity of its contents was at once apparent...A discussion took place, and it was agreed that, although it must be referred to the Censor at once, it was highly improbable, on the assumption that the news was true, that the authorities would allow it to be published except in the form of an official announcement.

The fact that the dispatch was retained by the Censor for two hours without comment seemed to confirm this view, and all preparations for issuing the edition without it were made. Between 11 and 12 o'clock at night, however, our messenger returned with the dispatch, and with a signed memorandum from the Head of the Press Bureau.

Certain passages from the dispatch had been cut out; other passages which we ourselves crossed out as undesirable for various reasons were marked *stet* over initials; and fresh sentences, summarising the effect of the news and pointing its moral, were inserted.

The memorandum accompanying it is marked 'Private' and we are therefore debarred from publishing it without the writer's consent. We are entitled, however, to say that in it the Head of the Press Bureau, over his signature, begged us to publish it in the form in which he returned it. With this document before us we could no longer hope that our Correspondent had been misled, *and we published it in accordance with the official request...*

A number of newspapers yesterday morning and evening commented severely on the publication of the dispatch. One paper, for example, informs its readers that the Censor 'merely excised names of regiments and places,' and proceeds to lecture *The Times* on the duty of journalists. Another paper refers to the dispatch as a 'disgraceful outburst', another convicted us of 'a grave error of judgement' in obeying the urgent request of the Bureau; and a third accuses us of deliberately inflicting 'needless agonies' on the public mind.

The subject was raised in both houses of Parliament yesterday by members who were unacquainted with the facts related above... Mr Asquith referred to the publication as 'a very regrettable exception' to the patriotic reticence of the Press. In reply to this we may observe that we should have been only too glad to withhold the message if we had not been urged to publish it by the official authorised by the Government to do so.

The Times, 1 September 1914

◆

Encouraged by F.C. Green, Head of the Press Bureau, The Times *had taken the unprecedented step of publishing The Amiens Dispatch in a special Sunday afternoon edition and on its front page – traditionally filled with advertisements. It was in stark contrast to stories of anodyne over-optimism which the censored communiqués had been feeding to the public, hungry for news. But it caused a scandal in high places and Green did not survive it. He was forced to resign. But he had achieved his object. The Army needed men, the first flood of enthusiastic volunteers had slowed to a trickle, and Green calculated that the grim truth that the Germans were in a fair way to winning the war would do more than a thousand exhortations on posters to bring in recruits. He was right. In the week that followed the publication of the Amiens Dispatch they flocked to join up.*

The whole idea was to get hold of a rifle, learn to shoot a bit, proceed to France at the earliest possible moment, kill vast quantities of Germans, possibly get wounded in some artistic place, win the war and march back with Colours flying and bands playing and the girls falling on your neck.

CAPTAIN ALAN GORING, MC

There was one frantic rush to join up and every unit quickly filled up. I thought of the London Scottish but the idea of seeing me walking round in a *kilt* on my home ground (Putney) put me right off. As it happened the wife of one of the partners of my firm came in to help out as most of the staff had joined up, or left to find other jobs. She had two cousins in the Honourable Artillery Company, so she gave me a letter of introduction. The qualifications to join the Honourable Artillery Company were having been to a Public School, two letters of recommendation, entrance fee of £3, and annual fee of £3. (Luckily they did not apply the Public School condition for me.) But when we eventually got out to France, if we happened to be marching through a village where others were resting, we would be greeted with, 'Look at the silly buggers who paid £3 to come out here. They'd pay thirty bloody pounds to go back!'

PRIVATE S. FRASER, MM.
Honourable Artillery Company.

RECRUITING OFFER.

Doctor's wife, middle-aged, will undertake to perform the work of any tramway conductor, coachman, shop assistant, or other married worker with children, provided that the worker will undertake to enlist and fight for his country in our hour of need. The wages earned will be paid to the wife and family. Apply to Mrs Lowry, Priory Terrace, Kew Green, London, S.W.

Daily Mail
28th August, 1914

I enlisted in the Queen's Own Cameron Highlanders on 9 September, 1914 at the Institute in Cambuslang. I really did not go up to the Institute with the intention of joining up. I just went up to see the fun of others joining up, because whenever a lad went in to join up, the crowd outside would give him a hearty cheer. So after standing around for a while I must have got carried away. So in went another recruit – me! I was duly sworn in and became a Soldier of the King in the Queen's Own Cameron Highlanders.

I was given a Railway Warrant to report to the Barracks at Inverness. Well do I remember arriving at the Barracks late at night about 14 September. In the morning I, along with the other new recruits, was paraded to give our particulars to an NCO: age, trade, place of birth etc. Then we were given a Regimental number. My number was 13013. Now, I ask you, with a number like that, what a start to my Army Career!

So many new lads were joining up that they could not cope with the rush, no uniform to be had. So we just had to parade in our civilian clothes that we had arrived in. The first day on Parade was a bit of a laugh, as the new boys were a very *mixed* lot, small ones, big ones, students 'tough guys' and some of the very Gentleman Type, and if you left anything down, then the 'Scruff Class' soon got their fingers on it, especially a watch or a good shaving outfit.

While I was in Inverness Hospital, the result of a kick playing football, I saw some queer tricks played by the soldiers, especially the old soldiers, the Regulars who had come home from abroad and who were acting the fly men. They used to swallow a bit of cordite taken from a bullet, so their heart would go pitter-patter when they were being examined by the doctor, and some of the cute boys rubbed their eyes with an onion to make them water and run. They were up to all the tricks. One lad was having a bad time by the injections he was having – the result of his going with dirty women. He used to faint when having the treatment. It made me scared to look at a girl.

Owing to the large number of new recruits arriving at Inverness, we were transferred to Invergordon, where we joined thousands of other Camerons of the 3rd Feeding Battalion. We had to sleep in bell tents in a huge field about fifteen men to each tent (too many). Then wet weather set in and our civilian clothes were in an awful mess. I looked a proper Charlie with my cap down over my eyes at times, as the skip was broken.

A problem at Invergordon was the sanitary arrangements. One had to go some distance to the end of the field to the WC, and sometimes the soldiers had a bet on – would he make it, or not? It was a big advantage when we got issued with *kilts*. It was a good laugh to watch the boys running to the WC.

The weather continued to be bad with food very poor. Under such conditions some of the boys volunteered for France, thinking the trenches could not be so bad, but they soon found out that the trenches

PRIVATE CARSON STEWART, 7th (S) Battalion, Queen's Own Cameron Highlanders.

5 Questions to patriotic Shopkeepers

1. HAVE you any fit men between 19 and 38 years of age serving behind your counter who at this moment ought to be serving their country?

2. Will you call your male employees together and explain to them that in order to end the War quickly we must have more men?

3. Will you tell them what you are prepared to do for them whilst they are fighting for the Empire?

4. Have you realised that we cannot have "business as usual" whilst the War continues?

   THE ARMY WANTS MORE MEN TO-DAY.

5. Could not Women or older men fill their places till the War is over?

YOUR COUNTRY WILL APPRECIATE THE HELP YOU GIVE

God Save the King.

4 Questions to the Women of England

1. YOU have read what the Germans have done in Belgium. Have you thought what they would do if they invaded England?

2. Do you realise that the Safety of your Home and Children depends on our getting more men now?

3. Do you realise that the one word "Go" from you may send another man to fight for our King and Country?

4. When the War is over and your husband or your son is asked, "What did you do in the great War?"—is he to hang his head because you would not let him go?

Women of England do your duty! Send your men to-day to join our glorious Army.

God Save the King.

were worse then Invergordon – a whole lot worse. Some of the young lads had only about two or three months training before being sent to France.

One of the first boys to go to France was Private Day. He was killed at Festubert on 9 May, 1915, in a grim battle that cost the Scots many lives. Another lad, Private Phillips, was wounded at Festubert. He was lucky to get home to Glasgow where I visited him in hospital. He told me to be sure to take my running shoes to France as you had to Get off your Mark at the Double. He scared the life out of me!

**ABLE SEAMAN
JOSEPH MURRAY,
Hood Battalion,
Royal Naval Division.**

I left on the midnight train from Newcastle for King's Cross and believe me there was more people outside the train than inside the train when the damned thing moved off. People saying 'Goodbye', some of the lassies hugging each other, Mums crying, it was dreadful. Anyhow, we got to King's Cross at six o'clock in the morning. We got off the train in a heap and the old Petty Officer, Charlie Sammes, he came out.

'Fall in here!' 'Come on, Straighten up!' 'What do you mean by "fall in?"' We knew nothing about training, no idea at all. 'Number!' 'What the Hell's that?' we wondered. 'One, two, three, four!' We had half a dozen go's at this numbering business. I thought to myself, 'Now, it's simple enough, I don't know what they want the numbers for, but it's simple enough.' I was Number 13, I was Number 12 the first time, but I thought, 'Well, sod that for a tale, I don't want to be Number 13 to start the War.' I started pushing back and we started numbering again and I'm back at twelve. The Petty Officer came along, 'Now, we'll do it again, shall we?'

He got us lined up and he said, 'Form Fours! What I want you to do is the outer numbers take a pace to the rear with the left foot and the others to the right and then stand still. All right, go on!' I didn't know whether I had to move or not. Some of them didn't know what to do, some of them moved off on the wrong foot. Really and truly, it was comical. Anyhow, he got us into four ranks eventually. 'Form Fours! Right, that's better, do it again! Form Fours! Fine! Now, when I say, "Move", get back in the train!' I thought to myself, 'Where the Hell are we going to now?' He said, 'Move,' and we all get back into the train again. 'Now,' he says, 'we'll have it done properly. Disembark!' So we all clambered out – perfect. I thought to myself, 'We're not going to get to the War, we're going to spend the rest of the War on Platform Six at King's Cross!'

4 Questions to Clerks and Shop Assistants.

1. If you are between 19 and 38 years of age, are you really satisfied with what you are doing to-day?

2. Do you feel happy as you walk along the streets and see brave men in khaki who are going to *fight* for the Empire while you stay at home in comfort?

3. Do you *realise* that our gallant soldiers are risking everything on the Continent to save you, your children, and your womenfolk?

4. Will you tell your employer *to-day* that you are going to *enlist*?

Ask him to keep your position open for you—tell him that you are going to fight for the Empire. He'll do the right thing by you— all patriotic employers are helping their men to join.

TELL HIM NOW AND ENLIST TO-DAY.

GOD SAVE THE KING.

**2ND LIEUTENANT
WILLIAM CUSHING,
9th (S) Battalion,
The Norfolk Regiment.**

I applied for a commission on the strength of three years in the Cambridge OTC, and in due course saw in an extract from the *London Gazette*, published in *The Times*, that I was a Temporary Second Lieutenant appointed to the Norfolk Regiment, and an order arrived telling me to join the 9th (Service) Battalion of the Norfolk Regiment at Brighton, as soon as possible.

During the train journey a patriotic young lady, evidently thinking that khaki was the only fashionable wear, conferred upon me the insignia of the white feather.

Then came the buying of my uniform, from a military tailor in Norwich who sold me not only a uniform, but also a long greatcoat which turned out to be quite useless. He also tried to unload on me a ceremonial sword! But he failed to persuade me that that was a necessary item of equipment for the trenches! I had been given a sum of money, and ten days leave of absence, to buy the uniform, and during that time I had a medical examination at Britannia Barracks, Norwich. I vividly remember a curious remark made by the MO. Observing that my feet were free of hammer toes, he said, 'Ah, yes, *we* do not suffer from such defects.' I stared at him in wonder and suddenly realised that I was an Officer and Gentleman (although only temporary) and that Officers and Gentlemen did not suffer from the same physical defects as Other Ranks. I have often wondered how we 'temporary gentlemen' escaped such blemishes!

We are Fred Karno's army
What bloody use are we?
We cannot fight, we cannot shoot
So send the infantry,
But when we get to Berlin
The Kaiser he will say
'Hoch, hoch, mein Gott
What a bloody fine lot
Are the boys of the Old Brigade'

PRIVATE A. V. SIMPSON,
2nd/6th Battalion, (T.F.),
The Duke of Wellington's
(West Riding Regiment).

I don't know who wrote the song *We are Fred Karno's Army* later in the war, but I am sure he would have been inspired by us had he seen us. England was so unprepared for war that it had to have an appeal for cast-off clothing for the troops. There was a catch in this, we discovered later. No khaki uniforms were available for us for some time, and regulations decreed that a man using his civilian overcoat was to be paid three-pence a day clothing allowance, and sixpence a day if he used his civilian suit. The nation's offering of old clothing was distributed among the newly enlisted volunteers, and as soon as you were fitted, your official clothing allowance was stopped irrespective of whether you preferred to wear your own civilian clothes or not. Worse still, if you had not got your 'jumble sale outfit' to hand in when you were eventually fitted out with khaki (if 'fitted' is the word), you were docked with the cost of the missing article as though it had been khaki issue. I was given an old 'Ulster', a sort of big cape-coat with wide kimono sleeves. I had seen a picture once of Edward the Seventh wearing one at a grouse shoot, so I suppose I ought not to have complained. I paraded with it, as did all the others with their temporary overcoats, rolled in bandolier fashion.

The whole battalion had only six rifles, and they were for drill purposes only. It's very doubtful whether any one of them would have fired, even if there had been any ammunition, but there was always a rush by men of the leading company of the day to fill the first four places and the two outside places of the next four, and so have the honour of bearing the precious arms when we went on our afternoon route march.

We were lodged in places like Radlyn School, and Beechwood Hotel etc., where we slept four to a room on palliasses on the floor. (The rooms had been cleared of all carpets and furniture.) Early in our training we used to assemble for tea at six a.m., and were then marched across Harrogate Strays. Eventually a whistle was blown, which was the signal for us to dash to our billets. We needed no second telling. The Army assumed that all recruits were in need of some purging, and so our early morning tea was 'jolloped'.

We saw fire on the tragic slopes
Where the flood-tide of France's early gain,
Big with wrecked promise and abandoned hopes,
Broke in a surf of blood along the Aisne.

Alan Seeger

The long retreat was over; the BEF had turned about and were advancing with the French pushing the Germans back across the River Marne, across the River Ourcq and finally to the River Aisne. But there on the heights above the river the Germans dug themselves into strong prepared positions. The BEF inched painfully across on the ruins of demolished bridges or on makeshift pontoons to gain a foothold on the heights beyond. And there they stayed. The great advance had petered out in stalemate. In the month since Mons, British, French and Germans had each paid a huge price in casualties – but, against the odds, the first round of the great fight had ended in a draw.

It is the morning of 9 September, 1914. The sun is shining again and we are continuing the advance which started on 6 September. It is more like summer than autumn today. We are marching in column of route along a road which is under the observation of the enemy on hills in front. There are two Divisions marching on one road, shelled by enemy artillery. What a target we are for them!

We begin to ascend a steep hill and our pace slackens and presently we halt for a rest. The sun is now overhead and it must be nearly midday. I have no watch to tell me the time and the days are all alike to me. The guns in front of us are still firing and must be captured – and the Lincolns have been informed to capture them at all costs. I hope the price will not be too heavy. *Fall in!* We feel like falling *out* with the person who gave the order! We grumble and grouse but we are regular soldiers and old soldiers (reservists) and we all know the first duty of a soldier is to obey. We sling arms and move on and up. Higher and higher. We sweat profusely. Slaves of the war machine are we!

Presently we halt and we are informed that two companies are to advance to capture the guns in a wood. A Company advanced in single file first and C Company followed a path in the centre of the wood which led in the enemy's direction. We knelt down close to the edge of the wood and to my left I saw the guns we had to capture. The German gunners were hard at work and we now opened rapid fire on them. Then

CORPORAL T. NORTH,
1st Battalion,
The Lincolnshire
    Regiment.

came the order 'Cease Fire'. Suddenly there was a shout as A Company charged with bayonets fixed towards the gunners and the guns. Sad to relate, as our men got near the guns, a shell dropped amongst them. We now got the order to retire and the Adjutant was leading us straight across the wood to get out quickly into the open.

A machine-gun was firing. Sergeant Jackson said, 'It's all right, it's one of ours,' but I had my doubts. A Maxim sounds *ta-ta-ta-ta*, but a Nordonfeldt sounds *tut-tut-tut-tut*. I warned the men to get off the path. I got off myself and I was just thinking I was getting away clear when I felt a jar like the kick of an elephant on my left leg, and I saw that my puttee was stained with blood. I stood up and started to walk, using my rifle as a staff, but I walked straight into two Germans! One of them grasped my rifle, raised it against a tree and planted his foot on the small of the butt and broke it. I pointed to my wounded leg, and they dressed my wound with my field dressing. I could have walked with the assistance of one of them, but they insisted on my leaning on them both. Soon we encountered a party of thirty or forty Germans. I saw Sergeant Jackson (after he left me he must have run into this party). He was not wounded. There were some others who weren't wounded and some who were.

Strange to relate, until now I had not been alarmed, because the Germans had been so kind and considerate to me. But now I had doubts about our safety. Here we were retiring, about fifty of us bunched together. What a target for the Lincolns if they came across us and opened rapid fire. We should share the fate of the German gunners. We kept moving in anything but military formation.

We were halted and Sergeant Jackson and the other unwounded Lincolns were marched off to the right, en route for Germany. Us wounded were taken to a village (I think it was called Montreuil). The two Germans who had captured me wanted to come with me to the dressing station, but the officers waved them away and five Germans with bayonets fixed escorted us to the dressing station at the top of the village street.

The medical officer who could speak English asked me all sorts of questions before dressing my wound. I was then put into a room along with the German wounded. I was exhausted and slept soundly for hours. The first intimation I had of our troops was when a sergeant of the Cheshires looked in on us, but he said he had not time to stop. I immediately got up and hobbled across to a German who had spoken English to me earlier and told him they were *our* prisoners now, and if they had any revolvers they'd better hand them over to me. So I went around collecting souvenirs. I got a lovely little revolver and about fifty rounds of ammunition.

The Germans had retired during the night, but their medical officers stayed behind with the wounded. Sir John French called during the day and had a look at the wounded, but I was not there – and I was sorry. I was examining shops in the main street, looking for a suitable cap to wear, and souvenirs as well. In other words I was looting. All the same I should like to have seen French.

I was several days at Montreuil before going on a hospital train to Rouen (where I write this). The German doctors worked like horses with our doctors to treat the wounded. They were busy day and night, and there were quite a number buried behind the village school.

In nine days we had regained a strip of France about fifty miles wide, the Cavalry having covered many times that distance. Strategists now announce that this engagement was *the* decisive battle of the war. We certainly didn't realise its importance at the time – it seemed but a succession of skirmishes – and we should have simply laughed at any suggestion that the disorganisation and discomfiture of the retiring Germans was anything like as great as our own after Mons and Le Cateau.

Yet that pursuit had been thrilling. Through the intermittent thunderstorms and heat and glare of the early September days we had pressed on; past Coulommiers and Chateau Thierry with their broken bridges, then across the Marne, toiling up the steep riversides in the broiling heat. Every hour a fresh situation developed, sharp actions, bursts of shrapnel, sudden pursuits. So past Oulchy and Braisne and Courcelles in driving rain to the Aisne.

CAPTAIN ARTHUR
OSBORN,
4th (Royal Irish) Dragoon
Guards.

LIEUTENANT L. A. STRANGE,
Royal Flying Corps.

My duties were rather to ascertain the positions of our own troops than to locate the enemy. I made nine landings in odd fields up and down the line and finished the day by taking Captain Furse on a reconnaissance. I noticed a few bullet holes in the plane, but did not think it had sustained any serious damage. We landed all right – but the king post collapsed and let down the extension on the top of the plane. That meant a night away from the other machines, which had meanwhile moved

An old French farmer came out from a farmhouse and from what I could gather he seemed to be as much concerned about the war of 1870 as the present one. His farm had been in German occupation a few days previously, neither his wife nor his daughter had been molested, but he was very much concerned for the safety of his two sons who were fighting somewhere in the Vosges. His greatest trouble, however, was that the Germans had commandeered his best farm horses and driven them somewhere across the Aisne, but he informed me that he hoped to fetch them back in a day or two. I thought him somewhat of an optimist!

The old fellow took me back to his farm, where he showed me with great pride about a hundred sacks of flour that he had annexed from some German lorries abandoned by the roadside. After giving me some hot coffee and bread and butter, he offered me a bed, but I declined, saying that I would have to camp out by my machine. I climbed on to a hay-rick, burrowed out a cosy hole and slept.

I was roused by the sound of voices and awoke to find a fierce argument going on between the farmer (who emphasised his remarks with a long single-bore sporting gun) and two Germans. He explained to me that he had caught them prowling round his farm – probably in search of food – and apologised to me for not having shot them at once, but he had no cartridges. My appearance was a great relief to all parties, because the Germans thought they were going to be shot, while the farmer imagined they would make off in my aeroplane. I'm afraid I disappointed the old chap by not shooting them! Eventually I handed them over to some British troops that happened to pass along the road.

CORPORAL JOHN LUCY,
2nd Battalion,
Princess Victoria's
(Royal Irish Fusiliers).

Our company had been forward in the attack which gained the plateau and was now called into reserve. We went underground into large caves a little distance in rear of the line. At the mouth of one cave the medical officer was busy attending to the wounded. Those he found to be dead he ordered to be taken out into the open.

We had hardly entered the caves when the Germans counterattacked and we were at once ordered to stand up and fall in ready to go. The sound of the battle heard from the caves was awe-inspiring. Clouds of smoke from bursting shells obscured the dim light which filtered through the cave mouth. Heavy shells crumped into the earth roof of our shelter and machine-guns rat-tat-tatted. The indistinct figures of stretcher-bearers collecting dead and wounded moved in the cloudy light of the cave mouth. We felt trapped and wished ourselves outside fighting instead of standing restless in the semi-darkness. We got nervy and fidgeted and avoided each other's eyes. One soldier at the cave mouth morbidly occupied himself by passing in the names of the latest dead and wounded. I did not want to hear them. Each fresh name bludgeoned my brain with a sense of misery and loss as the litany of familiar names continued and I moved over to my brother's platoon to be near him.

The German attack ceased. It had been beaten back, but the casualties seemed to be very numerous. Outside we saw some of our dead lying in grotesque positions. A few of these had previously cut their long trousers into shorts during the hot August weather, and now they looked like slain schoolboys. A hollow in the ground about ten yards from the caves was filled with bandaged wounded. I was looking at them, envying those with slight wounds who would go away back to England, or, with luck, to Ireland when there was a rising, tearing noise, nearer and nearer, then a shattering burst right on top of us. After a pause and a deep breath I raised my head and saw that the shell had exploded precisely over the hollow and killed every one of the wounded.

---◆---

General Headquarters,
15th September, 1914.

1. ... Our Army has successfully maintained its position and has repulsed numerous counter-attacks inflicting severe loss on the enemy ...

2. The Commander-in-Chief wishes the line now held by the Army to be strongly entrenched, and it is his intention to assume a general offensive at the first opportunity.

A. J. Murray, Lieut.-General,
Chief of the General Staff.

LIEUTENANT H. S. S.
   HENDERSON,
1st Battalion,
Prince of Wales' Own
   (West Yorkshire)
   Regiment.

20 September. We marched until 5.30 p.m., when we halted in a field and were searched by a German officer who told us some home truths about our own country which were weird and wonderful. This was done to try and insult me in front of my men. I was kicked several times and had mud and clods of earth thrown at me. We never halted again until we reached Laon at about 10 p.m.

I was taken into what seemed to be a big hotel and cross-examined by a Staff Officer. He asked me a lot of questions and I told him the answers – I don't think! I was then taken off by a guard and arrived after walking an hour at some barracks where I was taken into a filthy room amidst a lot of German wounded and given half a plate of soup. There was only one plate and it was passed round the room. Several of the German wounded here regarded me with expressions of hate and no one at home can realise how they hate us. A perfectly awful day.

About 9 a.m. we were marched off and met our men and a lot of French prisoners. We were insulted by epithets, swinehund, Englander, etc., etc., all the way.

We were put into a cattle truck with a few seats in it and reached Origny late at night and very cold.

We were marched off to a house which we entered through a cellar. The house inside was in a perfect chaotic condition, pictures torn to ribbons, empty fizz bottles all over the place, women's underclothing, men's clothes, children's toys all strewn about the floor; there must have been an orgy or two in the place at some time or other. We collected a mattress and a few odds and ends and dossed down.

Left about 7 a.m., and marched amid jeers and insults from the German soldiers in the streets. We left about fifty men here on a fatigue party for the Germans. When I say 'left', I mean they were just *taken* to unload stores from a train. We had a very long and trying march and were halted near Hirson where a German officer came up to the column and demanded us to give up any knives, scissors and forks as he said the wounded British soldiers had killed German doctors with their penknives! We complied and I reluctantly parted with an old penknife that couldn't cut butter. I had little left of my personal belongings by this time. We had another harangue from the German officer who said we should be shot if we were found with any knives etc., and most likely shot anyhow. By this time we didn't really care a hang if we were shot as we had had such a surfeit of insults etc. We went on the march again after this and Harry was made to run down the road for omitting to salute a German officer whom he had not seen. There was a soldier behind him with a bayonet! We reached Anor about 12.30 p.m., the German soldiers in the streets were aggressively hostile. We were all made to stand whilst the French were allowed to sit down.

A kind French officer however brought me some tobacco and smuggled it over to me. The eight of us, four French and ourselves, were taken over to the station, given a plate of soup, black bread and water.

Very soon we were surprised to see about twenty-five of our men all bandaged up about the head and bleeding badly, coming down the platform and being put into a truck with the wounded. We afterwards learned that the Guard and the loiterers outside the station had set about them with whips, sticks, and ropes with steel rings on them and butts of rifles while they were moving in small parties to get into the train.

The German officers had to draw their revolvers to stop their men, but I think it was a put-up job as the German officers were not there when the fracas started.

24 September. In train very cold at night, no food given us. Passed German troop trains going to the front covered with laurel leaves. Each train load would stare at us, jeer and cough up usual epithets. At the stations the German Red Cross women would give food to their wounded (we had one or two truck loads attached to the train) and would turn with disgust at any of our poor fellows who asked them for a cup of water. They gave them absolutely nothing... This seems a good example of how we were treated as Prisoners of War.

◆

Craonne, before thy cannon-swept plateau,
Where like sere leaves lay strewn September's dead,
I found for all things I forfeited
A recompense I would not forgo.

For that high fellowship was ours then
With those who, championing another's good,
More than dull Peace or its poor votaries could,
Taught us the dignity of being men.

There where we faced under those frowning heights
The blast that maims, the hurricane that kills;
There where the watch-lights on the winter hills
Flickered like balefire through inclement nights;

There where, firm links in the unyielding chain,
Where fell the long-planned blow and fell in vain –
Hearts worthy of the honour and the trial,
We helped to hold the lines along the Aisne.
                                        Alan Seeger.

◆ ◆

HORRIBLE STORIES OF GERMAN FIENDISHNESS

British war correspondents in Belgium have seen little murdered children with roasted feet. The tiny mites were hung over a fire before they were slain. This was done by German troops – men with children of their own at home, or with little brothers and sisters of the same age as the innocents they torture before killing.

At Tirlemont the Special Correspondent to *The Times* met a peasant woman who told him that her babes had been trampled to death under the hoofs of the horses of the Uhlans. As the Englishman was considering that he only had the woman's word for this atrocity, he saw a little girl come staggering along the road, as if she were blind. He found that her eye and cheek were laid open. This had been done, not by a chance bullet, but by a deliberate thrust of an Uhlan's lance, who charged upon the innocent child in sheer devilish sport.

The things done to Belgian girls and women, before their tortured, lifeless bodies with battered faces were thrown into a ditch, are so unspeakably dreadful that details cannot be printed.

The War Illustrated
5 September, 1914.

LEUTNANT FRITZ NAGEL,
Reserve Feldartillerie, Regiment Nr. 18.

Warfare in Belgium soon became a hideous experience because the population took part in the fight. Whenever they had the chance they shot down German soldiers. . . There was little defence against that sort of warfare because the streets were full of civilians and so were the houses. Unless they shot first, nobody knew where the enemy was. It was nerve-wracking in the extreme and resulted in savage and merciless slaughter at the slightest provocation. As we marched towards Louvain, most houses of the villages were burning and dead soldiers and civilians lay everywhere. . . Frightened civilians lined the streets, hands held high as a sign of surrender. Bedsheets hung out of windows for the same purpose. To see those frightened men, women and children was a really terrible sight. By now the German soldier was frightened, too, expecting to be shot at from all sides. I don't know whether these Belgians were ordered to resist or whether it was spontaneous, but it surely served no useful purpose. They could not kill enough Germans to influence events, though it was easy for them to shoot a German and then disappear in a crowd. The marching troops, the crackling of burning houses and the shouted orders made it impossible to hear even the crack of a single shot. . .

I noticed, sitting on the roadside, a solitary German prisoner with his escort, a solitary figure amongst numerous enemies. What were his thoughts, as we passed by with scorn written on most of our faces for an enemy who did not play cricket? We had been warned of treachery, of enemy white flag bogey, of numbers of Germans in front ranks holding their hands up in token of surrender, and then their front ranks suddenly falling flat while others behind opened fire on our surprised men. There were stories of poisoned water, tortured prisoners, and other things which filled us with disgust.

CORPORAL T. NORTH,
1st Battalion,
The Lincolnshire
 Regiment.

The Battalion I joined as *Offiziersstellvertreter* (deputy officer) was soon moved to the Western Front. Time and time again, particularly in the first half of August, the men's nervousness manifested itself in alarms about Belgian snipers. The sight of a windmill was enough to start a rumour that the Belgians were transmitting messages by code by means of the position of the sails. Catholic priests were favourite suspects as transmitters of such secret messages. During our entirely peaceful advance behind the front line I once saw a non-commissioned officer of my platoon training his rifle on a man running at some distance. I asked him why he was doing that, and his answer was: 'It's one of those Belgian snipers, he's thrown away his uniform and is trying to get away.' As evidence he showed me a tunic lying in a wet ditch where it had undoubtedly been for days.

HERR OTTO HAHN

   Coming to a house, we thought we would spend the night there. The peasant woman was quite beside herself, but I managed to allay her fears by telling her that we were not going to do her any harm and that we were not so wicked as she might think. All we wanted was some hay to sleep on. We had our own rations with us, so we should not deprive her of anything. The next morning she even offered me a glass with an old toothbrush in it. I thanked her warmly and we actually parted good friends.

I still remember having come across a French paper for the forces. One photograph covering a whole page, showed an awkward, plain girl, supposed to be a German, gazing enraptured at a slim hand, adorned with two rings, that was cut off at the wrist – allegedly the hand of a French woman. The caption read: *Le cadeau du fiancé*. That was a typical case of atrocity propaganda.

HERR OTTO HAHN.

'A PLACE IN THE SUN'
Superb Romance of the Great War

'Something in the cold sinister aspect of the cloaked figure, thrown into lurid relief by the flickering firelight; something in the imperious, arrogant tones of the voice suddenly caused Lucy Meadows to realise that she was in the presence of the Great Hun – The Kaiser William himself. But neither fear nor dismay was written in the proud, white face of the girl. The light of indomitable courage burned in her blue English eyes. Struggling in the cruel grip of the two Uhlan officers she looked the Kaiser full in the face. "Butcher of women and children – I defy you!" she exclaimed in an exaltation of scorn and contempt.'

An amazing incident in the superb War Serial by George Edgar, which begins in next week's 'Answers'.

A CALL TO ARMS

When a call to arms was answered by a hundred thousand men,
There were lots of chaps in Britain, 'twixt the age of four and ten,
Who'd have answered to their country's call and hurried off to war
If Kitchener had but reduced the fighting age to four.

Little Folk

In a side street off the Strand yesterday I met a jolly little dachshund –
the dachshund might be called the national dog of Germany –
walking cheerfully along well-bedecked in red, white and blue
ribbons. And round his neck he wore this label, 'I am a naturalised
British subject'. And he seemed mighty proud of the fact, too.

Daily Mirror, 18 August, 1914

GERMAN DASH FOR CALAIS STOPPED BY THE ALLIES
Daily Sketch
29 October, 1914

---

*Standing on the Aisne the British Expeditionary Force was now well south of its original
position, far from the coast and the life-lines of supply and communication stretching across
the Channel to the British Isles from Calais and Boulogne. Now those vital Channel ports
were in peril. Although the German advance had been stopped, fresh troops were on their way
from Germany and it was only a matter of time before they made a bid to capture the coast.
So the British began to inch north again and the Race to the Sea began. It ended at Ypres,
and in a few short weeks Ypres erupted from relative obscurity into a blazing battleground
at the forefront of the war.*

*Ypres was a jewel of ancient Flanders, rich in flamboyant architecture, with noble buildings,
towered, pinnacled, swirling with sculptures and carvings, built and embellished in the medieval
heyday of the rich Flemish wool trade. Ypres lay on the inland edge of the marshy coastal
plain of Flanders, almost at the tip of the tiny toehold of land that was unoccupied Belgium.
It was only a hop, skip and a jump from the coast. From Ypres, if they could capture it, a
mere hop would take the Germans to Dunkirk, a skip of fifteen miles to Calais, and a jump*

of twenty miles to Boulogne – and only Ypres stood in their path. By order of the King of the Belgians the sluice-gates at Nieuport had been opened, the tides swept in to fill canals and dykes and the River Yser swelled and flooded the low-lying land to the north of Ypres barring the way from that direction. But on the outskirts of the town the land rose in a semi-circle of gentle ridges and dropped eastwards to the plain beyond. Across this plain the German army marched, and the remnant of the British army, spread across the high ground with the towers of Ypres behind them, prepared to beat them back. At the end of a month of bitter fighting, when the Germans finally gave up, the British were literally at their last gasp, reduced by huge casualties, outgunned and outnumbered by more than ten to one. But the Germans did not know it. They did *give up and, for the moment, Ypres was saved – blackened by fire, battered by shelling, crumbling already into ruins, but still in Allied hands, and the weary survivors of the BEF dug in and stood fast on the ridges round its doorstep. This was the detested Ypres Salient, feared and loathed by every soldier of the line. Before long Ypres was reduced to a wasteland of rubble and, as the shelling and fighting raged on, the salient became a bog of mud and filth.*

It also became an emblem. Just as the cauldron of Verdun came to represent all the courage and the martyrdom of France, Ypres for the British became the leitmotiv *of the war, the focus of all suffering, the symbol of all endurance – and the First Battle of Ypres was only the start of the struggle.*

The green and grey purple day is barred with clouds of dun,
From Ypres city smouldering before the setting sun;
Another hour will see it flower, lamentable sight,
A bush of burning roses underneath the night.

Charles Scott-Moncrieff

Who's to fight for Flanders? Who's to set them free?
The war-torn lowlands by the English sea.

15 December, 1914

CAPTAIN MAURICE
MASCALL,
Royal Garrison Artillery,
(Mountain Regiment).

We have been shot into the 'Great War' very suddenly. We arrived yesterday morning at our destination (by train) at almost 8 a.m. It was rather extraordinary getting into war conditions so soon, but as we advanced we got the whole show brought home to us more and more – the motor-cycle despatch riders tearing about, two aeroplanes over our heads, some fresh graves by the roadside. Then we heard our first gun of the campaign and saw the flashes of one of our Batteries in action . . .

Eventually after numerous halts we got to the village where our billets are – a place with an impossible name and a nice old church.* We are in an old farmhouse, with the animals picketted in an adjoining field. The farm is built round a square, with a great double doorway opening into a courtyard – the middle of which consists of a manure heap, as I found to my cost when I tried to cross it! The drivers are in another farmhouse down the road, and we had some fun last night teaching them that *lukri* (wood) is *bois* and *parni* (water) is 'O'! They soon got to talk French quite well.

The Brigade is in trenches at the edge of a large wood, with the German trenches only about seventy yards distant. We were told to choose positions for our guns to support a future attack by our infantry, so we motored as far as the rear edge of the wood and were then guided by an Infantry Officer to the trenches.

It was quite an exciting walk after coming straight from home – bullets singing over our heads, and a more or less continuous fire from snipers on both sides.

The trenches themselves were quite different from anything I had imagined. They have been so often filled with water and rebuilt that nothing much was visible except seas of mud and holes full of water, and filthy but cheerful men standing about outside the bombproof shelters!

---

* Ploegsteert north of Armentières. The 'impossible' name soon became 'Plugstreet' to the troops.

**CAPTAIN BRYDEN
MCKINNEL,**
10th (Scottish) Battalion
King's Liverpool
Regiment.

21 December

Moon new and very bright. We get sniped all the way up and it's a much more horrible feeling than in the actual firing line. The field we advance to the trenches over is absolutely churned up by so many men walking over it. Great care has to be taken not to fall into Jack Johnson holes, which are very numerous. Meantime guns and company arrived and we were all kept very busy taking over the new trenches. It's a ticklish job at all times as the enemy 100 yards away can see us.

Open fields enclosed by hedges; the trenches are generally just behind the hedges. Our trench had small dugouts to crawl into, which one can only just sit up in, still they more or less protect one from rain.

This is a very dangerous trench to hold, being originally made by the Germans to face the other way. Also the communication trench which runs from the gateway to the trench for thirty yards was, as per usual, impassable on account of water.

So a few men at a time had to rush through the farm gate and make their way as best they could to their trench. Each time men showed themselves in the gateway they were met by a volley; luckily the shooting was very bad. As it was our casualties were very heavy.

**CAPTAIN MAURICE
MASCALL,**
Royal Garrison Artillery,
(Mountain Regiment).

18 December

The show started with an artillery bombardment – you never heard such a din. The enormous howitzer shells (our own) came over our heads, plainly visible in the sky, and burst with a deafening report just in front of us. Incidentally they wiped out dozens of our own men. One fell in one of our trenches and killed thirteen.

Then I opened fire on a house at 200 yards range and my second shot blew it to bits. About 30 Germans ran out of it and were, I believe, shot by our Infantry.

At 2.20 the bombardment abruptly ceased and the infantry advanced. When they arrived at the edge of the wood they were met by a perfect hail of bullets. I had an exciting run over to the officer commanding the front trenches. One man was shot through the head only a few yards off me and one or two of the others badly wounded. Meanwhile the stretcher bearers were bringing in the wounded. They came from the front, right over the parapet where I was sitting and they seemed quite oblivious of danger from the flying bullets. An officer was brought in shot through the lung and another officer was killed just in front of us. This went on till 4 p.m. and then it began to get dark, and the scene when darkness fell will live in my memory forever, I think.

There was a steady stream of wounded all through the night and it was a horrible sight seeing these poor fellows brought in covered from head to toe with mud. Some could walk with help and they all had to go down these horrible plank roads in the dark, tripping and stumbling and often falling into the mud.

At about 6 p.m. I found the Major and we left the dismal scene and went back to General Headquarters. What a very different aspect everything had, back there! The General and his Staff sitting round a table with maps and plans seemed infinitely far away from that horrible wood.

The Major and I were kept waiting for over an hour but eventually got our orders – which incidentally did not please us very much – and returned to the wood and started looking for the guns.

It was pitch dark and, after stumbling about in the sea of mud by the light of the Major's torch for an hour or so, we got absolutely lost.

We decided to separate then, and we wandered and wandered about in that infernal forest most of the night. I fell into trenches full of water and now and then came up against a barbed wire entanglement with a sentry on the other side telling me to put my 'hands up', fortunately he did not shoot. By 1 a.m. I was completely done, and if a Jack Johnson or other missile had come along and knocked me down I should have said Thank You.

I am glad to have seen war from the point of view of the Infantry. It was an experience that Gunners don't usually have. As I came back covered from head to foot in mud I passed the Artillery position. Some very smart RFA Officers had just done stables and looked wonderingly at me as if surprised that anyone with a gun badge in his cap should have the face to turn out so badly dressed, and so unwashed and unshaved. And I have seen the Artillery hit our own Infantry when I was in the Infantry position. It is awful. I heard one poor wretch say 'I have three wounds and two are by our own artillery', and it made me think a good deal.

'Little girls and little boys,
Never suck your German toys;
German soldiers licked will make
Darling Baby's tummy ache.

'Parents, you should always try
Only British toys to buy;
Though to pieces they be picked,
British soldiers can't be licked.'
Little Folks
Christmas 1914.

> The German newspapers deeply deplore the carrying on of hostilities during the Christmas festival, which they regard as a purely Germanic institution ... But they all profess satisfaction that the efforts made by the Pope and by American pacifists to call a truce of God for Christmas Day have come to naught, and that there will be no slackening – not even for this one sacred day – of the struggle to beat down the enemies of the Fatherland.
>
> *The Glasgow Herald*, December 23, 1914.

> It is thought possible that the enemy may be contemplating an attack during Xmas or New Year. Special vigilance will be maintained during these periods.
>
> GHQ St Omer: To all units
> 24 December 1914.

◆

LEUTNANT JOHANNES NIEMANN,
133rd Royal Saxon Regiment.

We came up to take over the trenches on the front between Frelinghien and Houplines, where our regiment and the Scottish Seaforth Highlanders were face to face. It was a cold starry night and the Scots were a hundred or so metres in front of us in their trenches where, as we discovered, like us they were up to their knees in mud. My Company Commander and I, savouring the unaccustomed calm, sat with our orderlies round a Christmas tree we had put up in our dugout.

Suddenly, for no apparent reason, our enemies began to fire on our lines. Our soldiers had hung little Christmas trees covered with candles above the trenches and our enemies, seeing the lights, thought we were about to launch a surprise attack. But, by midnight it was calm once more. Next morning the mist was slow to clear and suddenly my orderly threw himself into my dugout to say that both the German and Scottish soldiers had come out of their trenches and were fraternising along the front. I grabbed my binoculars and looking cautiously over the parapet saw the incredible sight of our soldiers exchanging cigarettes, schnapps and chocolate with the enemy. Later a Scottish soldier appeared with a football which seemed to come from nowhere and a few minutes later a real football match got underway. The Scots marked their goal mouth with their strange caps and we did the same with ours. It was far from easy to play on the frozen ground, but we continued, keeping rigorously to the rules, despite the fact that it only lasted an hour and that we had no referee. A great many of the passes went wide, but all the amateur footballers, although they must have been very tired, played with huge enthusiasm. Us Germans really roared when a gust of wind revealed that the Scots wore no drawers under their kilts – and hooted and whistled every time they caught an impudent glimpse of one posterior belonging to one of 'yesterday's enemies'. But after an hour's play, when our Commanding Officer heard about it, he sent an order that we must put a stop to it. A little later we drifted back to our trenches and the fraternisation ended.

The game finished with a score of three goals to two in favour of Fritz against Tommy.

On Christmas Eve there was a lull in the fighting, no firing going on at all after 6 p.m. The Germans had a Christmas tree in the trenches, and Chinese lanterns all along the top of a parapet. Eventually the Germans started shouting, 'Come over, I want to speak to you'. Our chaps hardly knew how to take this, but one of the 'nuts' belonging to the regiment got out of the trench and started to walk towards the German lines. One of the Germans met him about half-way across, and they shook hands and became quite friendly. In due time the 'nut' came back and told all the others about it. So more of them took it in turns to go and visit the Germans. The officer commanding would not allow more than three men at a time.

I went out myself on Christmas Day and exchanged some cigarettes for cigars, and this game has been going on from Christmas Eve till midnight on Boxing Day without a single round being fired. The German I met had been a waiter in London and could use our language a little. He says they didn't want to fight and I think he was telling the truth as we are not getting half so many bullets as usual. I know this statement will take a bit of believing but it is absolutely correct. Fancy a German shaking your flapper as though he were trying to smash your fingers, and then a few days later trying to plug you. I hardly know what to think about it, but I fancy they are working up a big scheme so that they can give us a doing, but our chaps are prepared, and I am under the impression they will get more than they bargained for.

GUNNER HERBERT
   SMITH,
5th Battery,
Royal Field Artillery.

On Boxing Day we walked up to the village of St Yvon where the observation post was. I soon discovered that places where we were usually shot at were quite safe. There were the two sets of front trenches only a few yards apart, and yet there were soldiers, both British and German, standing on top of them, digging or repairing the trench in some way, without ever shooting at each other. It was an extraordinary situation.

In the sunken road I met an officer I knew, and we walked along together so that we could look across to the German front line, which was only about seventy yards away. One of the Germans waved to us and said, 'Come over here.' We said, '*You* come over here if you want

2ND LIEUTENANT
   CYRIL DRUMMOND,
135th Battery,
Royal Field Artillery.

to talk.' So he climbed out of his trench and came over towards us. We met, and very gravely saluted each other. He was joined by more Germans, and some of the Dublin Fusiliers from our own trenches came out to join us. No German officer came out, it was only the ordinary soldiers. We talked, mainly in French, because my German was not very good and none of the Germans could speak English well. But we managed to get together all right. One of them said, 'We don't want to kill you, and you don't want to kill us, so why shoot?'

They gave me some German tobacco and German cigars – they seemed to have plenty of those, and very good ones too – and they asked whether we had any jam. One of the Dublin Fusiliers got a tin of jam which had been opened, but very little taken out, and he gave it to a German who gave him two cigars for it. I lined them all up and took a photograph.

CAPTAIN BRYDEN McKINNEL,
10 (Scottish) Battalion,
King's Liverpool Regiment.

Christmas Day opened with bright sunshine, and a good many went to Communion and the early morning service. 'Peace on earth and goodwill among men.'

How incongruous it sounds. Everybody was cheerful. The ground was white. A mist set in and made things feel colder. At 12.30 we were drawn up in a square to receive from the CO the presents sent by the wives and mothers of the officers and men in Liverpool. The CO said a few words and at the end asked: 'There's only one thing I want to know. Are we downhearted?' They simply roared 'NO!' The pipers then played. It was one of the most pathetic events of the day, and most of us had lumps in our throats. It's very nearly the first time they have played in France, it's not allowed. There they were, four of them (one of them was killed in the trenches the day before), uniforms tattered and torn, marching round playing regimental and other tunes better than they ever played them. What a reception they got, and they had to play over and over again.

Presents for the men consisted of a packet of the best chocolate, Oxo cubes, khaki handkerchiefs, peppermint drops, camp cocoa, writing paper and pencil. Nothing could have been more acceptable, and they were all frightfully pleased. Then we had three cheers for the battalion CO, Adjutant and other officers. Just then up at a gallop drove a pair of horses and transport wagon full of Princess Mary's Christmas Gifts. Off jumped the Quartermaster with beaming face and received another cheer.

They just arrived in time and couldn't have been staged better. The Princess Mary's present consisted of a good pipe and tobacco in a gift box, also a Christmas Card from the King and Queen. Lord Derby presented plum puddings to the whole battalion and a hamper consisting of bottles of green turtles, turkeys ready for eating, and cigars for the officers, and one cigar for each of the NCOs. Then we got our mail – a week's accumulation, 165 bags. What a crowd! Letters and parcels for everybody. The men had special rations of rum, bread and fresh meat. The officers had three messes and one turkey in each mess. We all subscribed some goods, so at night our menu was as follows:

Royau A Le Bordelaise.
Turtle Soup.
Pheasant Roti with Pommes Frites
and Sauce au Pain.
Turkey.
Plum Pudding au Rhum.
Pâté de Fois Gras.
Tangerines, Figs, Dates, Almonds et Raisons.
Café au Lait.
Cigars and Cigarettes.

WINES: One bottle of vin de Champagne of one kind and one bottle of another kind for the other end of the table, Cognac, and three bottles of Château Kemmel (otherwise Red Wine), (the Château was then our Headquarters) to say nothing of the preserved fruits and sweets.

Many of the men who are in very comfortable straw with wooden floor dugouts which hold about thirty, almost rivalled us as regards menus today.

Saturday, December 26th: Very cold, turned to snow and now thawing. Cleaning equipment and fatigue duties order of the day. If the people who send all the parcels only saw what tremendous enjoyment we have derived from them they would not for a moment regret having sent them. I think this Christmas will act as a good bucking-up tonic to us all. Several officers have gone to have a hot bath tonight at the Convent, and we are trying to arrange to get some for the men. Hope frost goes, for mud and ice-covered Jack Johnson holes to fall in would be too terrible.

Have written a lot – but Christmas comes but once a year!

◆

Our Soldiers' Half Guinea Box

CONTAINING–

1 tin H. & P. Oval Digestive Biscuits.	1 tin Matches, containing 12 boxes.
1 ,, C. & B. Jam.	1 ,, Potted Meat.
1 ,, Marmalade.	1 pkt. Candles.
1 ,, Sardines.	1 carton Muscatels and Almonds.
1 ,, Nestlé's Café au Lait.	2 tablets Soap.
1 ,, Bivouac Cocoa and Milk.	1 Christmas Pudding.
1 ,, B.F. Beef Cubes.	

Sent Post Free to the British Expeditionary Force.

HARRODS Ltd., London, S.W.

◆

ENTERTAINING THE TROOPS

By the kind thought and generosity of the members of the Wing Badminton Club, all the troops billeted in the village, were invited to a very substantial meat tea at the Hall on Boxing Day. After tea an entertainment was provided, tobacco and cigarettes were handed to all the men in the Hall and, after the concert, coffee and cake and other eatables were provided. The Boy Scouts made themselves very useful as waiters. The entertainment included Morris dances by Miss H. Tatham's class and songs by Mrs T. Gale who completely won the hearts of the soldiers with 'Tipperary'. Captain and Miss Daniels gave a club swinging exhibition and Miss Adams recited 'Play the Game'.

Bedfordshire Times & Independent

To the Editor of the Daily Mirror

Sir,

Your valuable and widely read paper may help the many wounded and dying soldiers here to bear their pain and die in peace, if you will print an appeal to the children of London.

They will doubtless be glad to help by trying not to scream and sing in the streets just now, and the boy workers will no longer awake the sufferers by constant whistling. Perhaps even the owners of dogs will try to quiet their barking in the small hours. The milkmen are a privileged class, and it is to be feared that milk will never be delivered without clamour. But if all classes could realise that unnecessary noise means torture to our men and lack of rest to our devoted night and day nurses! The English are the most humane people and will all help to suppress unnecessary noise.

Knightsbridge.

2ND LIEUTENANT J. D.
WYATT,
2nd Battalion,
The Yorkshire Regiment.

30 December
Same routine as before. Still no war! At about lunchtime however a message came down the line to say that Germans had sent across to say that their General was coming along in the afternoon, so we had better keep down, as they might have to do a little shooting to make things look right!!! And this is war!! This we did, and a few shots came over about 3.30 p.m.

2ND LIEUTENANT
CYRIL DRUMMOND,
135th Battery,
Royal Field Artillery.

On our part of the front the truce went on for a week. Troops of both sides worked on their trenches or did anything they wanted to do, quite uninterrupted by each other.

One of the Dublin Fusiliers was killed one day by a bullet which came from the front of Plugstreet Wood, and the Saxons immediately sent over and apologised, saying it hadn't been anything to do with them, but from those so-and-so Prussians on their left. That was the only casualty that occurred during that truce. But of course the war was becoming a farce and the high-ups decided that this truce must stop. Orders came through to our Brigade, and so to my own battery, that fire was to be opened the following morning on a certain farm which stood behind the German support line. Our battery was to put twelve rounds of high explosive shell into it at eleven o'clock. As luck would happen, I was the officer who would have to do this. We sent someone over to tell the Boches, and the next morning at eleven o'clock I put twelve rounds into the farmhouse, and of course there wasn't anybody there. But that broke the truce – on our front at least.

TROOPER G. HUGGINS,
Queen's Own
Oxfordshire Hussars.

I went on leave with Fred Rathbone and we got to Victoria about ten or eleven o'clock at night on the 31 December, and we were going through the gateway and there was two Redcaps there and they stopped us and said, 'Why haven't you cleaned your boots?' Rathbone gave them a filthy look and said, 'Where we've come from, Mate, they don't use bloody blacking!' And a grey-haired old gentleman standing by said, 'Where do you want to go to?' We said, 'Paddington.' 'Come along,' he said and he took us on a bus. It was just starting off and I'd got my rifle slung over my shoulder because we had to have all our pack with us, and it gave a lurch and it just caught a lady on the shoulder. 'Clumsy beast,' she said. The old chap said, 'Yes, Miss, he's out of practice, getting off and on buses.'

We caught the train at Paddington – the milk train that gets in about two in the morning, and I walked then from Banbury to Boscombe which was five miles and it would be about three o'clock in the morning when I got home. The house was dark. I knocked at the door and Dad put his head out of the upstairs window. 'Who's that?' I said, 'It's me. Aren't you coming down to let me in?' I can remember this quite clearly – he said, 'Good God, Mother, it's our Bill.' They came down, fussed all over me, Mother making tea and talk, talk, talk. I don't think we ever *did* get to bed! Then I wanted to have all my stuff washed so I got into my civvies and went in with Mother to Banbury the next day. We always put the pony and trap into the White Horse and as I was coming out from the White Horse stables, a girl gave me a white feather. I looked at her and put it in my pocket. Everybody in Banbury knew me except that one girl. Well, I went down the street and came back up after about an hour and I met this girl again. Oh, she did apologise, poor little thing! Somebody had put her wise.

> # To the Young Women of London.
>
> Is your "Best Boy" wearing Khaki? If not, don't **you think** he should be?
>
> If he does not think that you and your country are worth fighting for—do you think he is **worthy** of you?
>
> Don't pity the girl who is alone—her young man is probably a soldier—fighting for her and her country—and for **you**.
>
> If your young man neglects his duty to his King and Country, the time may come when he will **neglect you**.
>
> Think it over—then ask your young man to
>
> **JOIN THE ARMY TO-DAY.**

1914 closes with the hope that we shall soon be 'in it'. We have the usual Christmas dinners, leave, festivities and rejoicing. I go to London for ten days and become a civilian in mufti.

I find the ladies are very pressing in the metropolis, with white feathers for men unwilling to fight … I meet one in Coventry Street. She presents her feather and smiles. I do likewise.

'Why are you not in uniform?' she asks. 'Afraid to fight?' And so on. 'A visit to the recruiting officer?' she suggests. 'Certainly, if you wish,' I reply.

Off we toddle together to Trafalgar Square. The recruiting officer smiles at Miss Busybody and looks at me. 'A bit on the short side! However, times are hard!' he says condescendingly. Many questions are asked me. 'Well, I haven't actually served before, I *am* serving,' I state.

'What the hell are you doing here then?' asks the great man.

'I don't know, I'm sure. Better ask the lady.'

Both look blankly at each other and then at me.

'Who are you, what are you?' she asks.

'A major in the Royal Irish Rifles,' I reply.

I hope this well-meaning and patriotic lady will work as hard in the cause of Peace as she did in the cause of War.

MAJOR F. P. CROZIER,
Royal Irish Rifles.

1915

---◆---

Rugeley, Rugeley, We're all enjoying it hugely.
To and fro we gaily go – we're always on the tramp,
But if you think that Cannock Chase
Is a lively and attractive place,
You'll be Rugely awakened when you get to Rugeley Camp.

---◆---

By the end of 1914 the British Expeditionary Force of regular troops had suffered ninety per cent casualties. They had met the enemy at Mons, retreated fighting for 170 miles, turned and chased the enemy back across the Marne to the Aisne, raced them to the sea, and brought them to a standstill in front of Ypres. But they were almost spent. Now, while the men of the Territorial Force were flooding out to reinforce them and to help to hold the line, across the length and breadth of Britain Kitchener's Army of volunteers were training to be soldiers.

---◆---

RIFLEMAN W. WORRELL,
12th (S) Battalion,
The Rifle Brigade.

After weeks of wear in all weathers, our civvy clothes were beginning to look bedraggled. The natty straw boaters worn by the city types were curling at the brims. Many trousers had shrunk well up the calves and sleeves were showing a lot of wrist. We were getting the rudiments of soldiering knocked into us by a few old soldiers who were capable of instructing. C Company Sergeant-Major was a wonderful old chap, CSM Leslie. He must have been well over seventy, but was still spry. It was a life of dirt and discomfort, but there were few who grumbled. We still had that patriotic fervour that had driven us to enlist, and our only fear was that the war would end before we arrived at the front.

The battalion had a few old Lee-Metford rifles which were passed around the Companies for Drill and Musketry instruction. They had the long barrel and barleycorn foresight with V–backsight. We began as awkward squads but soon got the knack of things and learned to handle them like Riflemen.

Suits of khaki drill had been seen going into the Quartermaster's Store. Bales of khaki serge uniforms with black buttons were at Brookwood Station awaiting a fatigue party to collect, but nothing happened until one day clothing did arrive. It wasn't too soon either. No self-respecting tramp would have been seen in the clothes that most of us were wearing. The new uniform – Kitchener Blue. The model for it must have been a City Policeman. Dicky and I had about the same vital statistics, 32–22–28. We both finished with a modish 8–inch turn-up and double-breasted trousers. Having once done up the buttons of our tunics we never undid them again as we were able to pull them on like jerseys. The natty ensemble was crowned with a forage cap of the same material.

I had been at Winchester only one week, when the pair of shoes I had on wore out, and I had to report to the QM Stores, where I was issued with a brand new pair of boots. It only needed a morning's drilling on the barrack square and I was limping badly and suffering extreme pain. Corporal Lucas, in charge of our Section, called me aside and asked what was the matter. I told him that my new boots were just about killing me and he suggested that new boots sometimes required certain treatment before they became comfortable, and that the infallible method adopted by infantrymen was the sweet pea mixture. Officers, he said, sometimes used the sweet violet mixture, which consists of pouring half a bottle of whisky into each boot, but for other ranks, who could not afford such an expensive remedy, there was nothing to equal the sweet pea mixture. I was shocked and told him so very indignantly, but he firmly told me that if I could not march and drill, the MO would certainly mark me unfit for duty, which might mean my discharge.

The thought of being sent home, unfit for service, after such a brief spell in the forces, was too much for me. Corporal Lucas excused me from duty for the rest of the day and I went to the billet and reluctantly proceeded to put his remedy to the test. I gave each boot a good soaking and repeated the measure again at night (secretly and away from my pals) and the next morning, after emptying the contents of each boot, massaging the leather where it had hurt most, I reported back on parade. Oh! Joy, what a relief. I could march and drill without a twinge of pain. A quiet wink between Corporal Lucas and myself and none of my pals was any wiser. Army boots never bothered me after that – I had the cure!

RIFLEMAN J.
MCARTHUR,
13th (S) Battalion,
The Rifle Brigade.

RIFLEMAN STANLEY
HOPKINS,
2nd/18th Battalion,
The London Regiment,
(London Irish Rifles).

On the march at night sometimes the officer leading the battalion would lose us. This often meant we would 'About Turn' and it was the signal for us to start singing in a Cockney accent, 'Nar he's bin and lorst us' to the tune of 'Oh Come all ye Faithful' much to the discomfiture of the poor officer who would march down the length of the battalion to find out who was singing. As soon as he arrived at C Company, A or B would start up so he had no chance.

TAIL-LIGHTS FOR TROOPS

Sir,

Might I be allowed to point out the danger to which our troops are exposed whilst marching along roads at night – namely, that of being charged into from the rear by motorists, who, in all other respects, may happen to be complying with every police or military regulation? The prohibition of the use of headlights is, doubtless, a necessary one, but matters might further be improved by insisting on tail-lights for troops, as those motorists who are compelled to travel by night are not only prevented from seeing where they are going, but even what they are hitting. And we have no men to spare.

I remain, your obedient servant,

GEORGE BLAKE McGRATH.
3, East India-avenue, E.C.,
April 19
The Times, 21 April 1915.

Lecture given to officers of
3rd Battalion,
The London Regiment,
(Royal Fusiliers).

COMPANY TRAINING.

1. Up to the present we have been doing close order drill by Battalion, Company and Squad, to teach the men to act and move together on the word of command *almost without thinking*. We are now going to start Company Training.

Company Training is the work of teaching each man *individually* the real work of a soldier in the field. *To teach the man that he has now to think and act for himself.*

This does not by any means mean that a man is to be taught to act without orders. He should be taught that when given an order, say, to advance when in the firing line, he should be able to take advantage of the ground in his line of advance. Teach him what is cover and see that he understands the use and abuse of cover. Teach him to be observant of what is going on around him and to note it and draw his own deductions from his observations.

You will all get stupid men to deal with. As far as you can keep your own temper, and in dealing with a stupid man, don't bully or rag him – take extra pains with him. On no account be *sarcastic* and don't hold *any* man up to the ridicule of his comrades. It disheartens the man and often makes him sulky to be the butt of a parade of the whole Company. Take it step by step. Do not leave any exercise until you have got the whole Company to carry it out correctly and *intelligently*. The successful Company trainer is the one who brings his whole section, half-Company and Company up to a certain mark of proficiency – not the one who has twenty very sharp men and eighty dull half-trained men.

The training we had at Wendover was all right, up to a point. Colonel Prettor-Pinney always had designs on a monument on the top of the hill at Butler's Cross. It's something to do with the Bucks Regiment in the Boer War. It has a plaque on that monument up there telling you all about it. He used to fetch us up through Wendover Station, and as soon as we were over the railway bridge, he'd say we were under shell fire. We'd have to dive into the side of the road, then we crept in at the foot of the hill, got a little way up the ridge, and the whistle would go again – extended order under shell fire. One company would go on in front, one would go to the left, one go to the right and the other one would stand fast. We'd all spread out in four lines, to attack this monument.

Well, this particular day I was the right-hand man of 'C' Company, which was last. I had to creep all the way up alongside that road from Wendover down to Butler's Cross and when we got to the top of the hill, which is now a golf course, the whistle went and we had to stand

SERGEANT
JACK CROSS,
13th (S) Battalion,
The Rifle Brigade.

fast. They passed the word that in the barn below was a machine-gun nest. The two flanks had to pass round that and while we was waiting to sweep round this corner, getting into position to creep along, my mate says to me:

'Jack, there's pub here, look.'

I says, 'What about it then?'

He says, 'Come on!'

It was called The Crown, a dilapidated old place, one of those old thatched places, made of wood.

So we dived back, two more chaps followed us, and I said to the lady in the bar, 'Four pints, please'. She drawed these four pints and suddenly there was a shadow in the doorway.

'What the *hell* are you lot doing in here?'

I got a pint in my hand. I said, 'Here you are, Sir, drink that,' and I pushed it into the Company Sergeant-Major's hand. He picked it up and it went down like going down a sink.

'Don't be long in here.'

And off he went! We drank our beer pretty bloody quick and got out again.

We put a pincer movement on to the barn and attacked it from the rear.

Then the lads come down the hill, we formed up in the road below and the CO said, 'Now, we'll attack the monument on the way home. Creep up that slope!' And we'd already got the elbows out of our jackets and the knees out of our trousers because we hadn't got no uniform to wear. And he always used to do this operation on a Saturday morning when the boys were thinking about going on weekend pass.

COLONEL W. N.
NICHOLSON,
Suffolk Regiment,
Staff Officer attached,
Highland Division.

... I was challenged by a sentry. I knew the counter-sign was a Scottish Town; but I had forgotten which.

'Dundee,' I hazarded.

'You're wrong, man; it's Aberdeen ...'

◆

OUR MACHINE GUN'S DEADLY RATTLE.

Wooden dummies they may be,
Plain for any eye to see,
And they couldn't hurt a flea,
But they rattle.

They have been described as 'toys',
By some rifle-lugging boys,
But they do admit there's noise
    When they rattle.

They are minus fusee springs,
And heaps of other things;
They are patched with nails and strings
    But they rattle.

They've a wooden water jacket,
On the tripod there's no bracket,
But there isn't half a racket
    When they rattle.

Here's to the Inventor!
To him we owe a lot
For the idea that he got
From his baby in its cot
    With its rattle.

... Second Lieutenant Bobby Little, assisted by a sergeant and two unhandy privates, is engaged in propping a large and highly-coloured work of art, mounted on a rough wooden frame and supported on two unsteady legs, against the wall of the barrack square. A half-platoon of A Company, seated upon an adjacent bank, chewing grass and enjoying the mellow autumn sunshine, regard the swaying masterpiece with frank curiosity ... To be quite frank, they are getting just a little tired of musketry training. But the sight of Bobby Little's art gallery cheers them up. They contemplate the picture with childlike interest ...

'What for is the wee fella goin' tae show us pictures?'

A pundit in the rear rank answers, 'Yon's Gairmany.'

'Gairmany, ma auntie!' retorts Mucklewame. 'There's no chumney-stalks in Gairmany.'

'Maybe no; but there's wundmulls. See the wundmull there – on yon wee knowe!'

'There a pit-heid!' exclaims another voice.

This homely spectacle is received with an affectionate sigh. Until two months ago more than half the platoon had never been out of sight of at least half a dozen.

'See the kirk, in ablow the brae!' says someone else in a pleased voice. 'It has a nock in the steeple.'

Bobby Little, who has at length fixed his picture in position, whips round. 'Now,' he begins, 'what conspicuous objects do we notice on this target? In the foreground I can see a low knoll. To the left I see a windmill. In the distance is a tall chimney. Half-right is a church. How would that church be marked on a map?'

No reply.

'Well,' explains Bobby, anxious to parade a piece of knowledge which he only acquired himself a day or two ago, 'churches are denoted in maps by a cross, mounted on a square or circle, according as the church has a square tower or a steeple. What has this church got?'

'A nock!' bellow the platoon, with stunning enthusiasm.

'A clock, sir,' translates the sergeant *sotto voce*.

'A clock? All right: but what I wanted was a steeple. Then, further away, we can see a mine, a winding brook, and a house, with a wall in front of it. Who can see them?'

To judge by the collective expression of the audience, no one does.

Captain Wagstaffe has strolled up. He is second in command of A Company. Bobby explains to him modestly what he has been trying to do.

'Yes, I heard you,' says Wagstaffe. 'You take a breather, while I carry on for a bit. Lance-Corporal Ness, show me a pit-head.'

Lance-Corporal Ness steps briskly forward and lays a grubby forefinger on Bobby's 'mine'.

'Private Mucklewame, show me a burn.'

The brook is at once identified.

'Private M'Leary, shut your eyes and tell me what there is just to the right of the windmill.'

'A wee knowe, sir,' replies M'Leary at once. Bobby recognises his 'low knoll' – also the fact that it is no use endeavouring to instruct the unlettered until you have learned their language.

'Very good!' says Captain Wagstaffe. 'Now we will go on to what is known as Description and Recognition of Targets.

'Now, supposing I sent you out scouting, and you discovered that over there – somewhere in the middle of this field' – he lays a finger on the field in question – 'there was a fold in the ground where a machine-gun section was concealed: what would you do when you got back?'

'I would tell you, sir,' replied Private M'Micking politely.

'Tell me what?'

'That they was there, sir.'

'How would you indicate the position of the place?'

'I would point it oot with ma finger, sir.'

'Invisible objects half a mile away are not easily pointed out with the finger,' Captain Wagstaffe mentions. 'Thompson?'

'I would say, sir,' replies Thompson, puckering his brow, 'that it was in ablow they trees.'

'It would be hard to indicate the exact trees you meant. Trees are too common. Take some conspicuous and unmistakable object about the middle of that landscape – something which no one can mistake. The mansion-house will do – the near end. Now then – *mansion-house, near end!* Got that?'

There is a general chorus of assent.

'Very well. I want you to imagine that the base of the mansion-house is the centre of a great clock-face. Where would twelve o'clock be?'

The platoon are plainly tickled by this new round-game. They reply, 'Straight up!'

'Right. Where is nine o'clock?'

'Over tae the left.'

'Very good. And so on with all the other hours. Now for our fold in the ground. *End of mansion-house – eight o'clock – got that?*'

There is an interested murmur of assent.

'That gives you the direction from the house. Now for the distance! *End of mansion-house – eight o'clock – two finger-breadths* – what does that give you, Lance-Corporal Ness?'

'The corner of a field, sir.'

'Right. This is *our* field. We have picked it correctly out of about twenty fields, you see. *Corner of field. In the middle of the field, a fold in the ground. At nine hundred – at the fold in the ground – five rounds – fire!* You see the idea now?'

'Yes, sir.'

'Very good. Carry on, Mr Little.'

And leaving Bobby and his infant class to practise this new and amusing pastime, Captain Wagstaffe strolls away across the square to where Waddell is contending with another squad.

On his way to inspect a third platoon Captain Wagstaffe passes Bobby Little and his merry men. They are in pairs, indicating targets to one another.

Says Private Walker to his friend, Private M'Leary, 'At yon three Gairman spies, goin' up a close – fifty roonds – fire.'

To which Private M'Leary, not to be outdone, responds, 'Public hoose – in the bar – back o' seven o'clock – two drams – four fingers – rapid!'

Ian Hay, The First 100,000

National and Station Hotel,
Dingwall, N.B.

2ND LIEUTENANT
J. MACLEOD,
3rd (Reserve) Battalion,
Queen's Own Cameron
Highlanders.

24 January.

The 'fur cuirass' came safely, thanks. It will have to wait for wear until we get to France.

On Saturday Seaforth and Mrs Stuart-Mackenzie gave our men a bun-fight. There were some Seaforth Territorials too – about a hundred I should think, making a party of about two hundred and forty altogether.

Angry voice (to Bugler, after five attempts at Reveille) 'WHY DON'T YOU GO ROUND AND TELL 'EM?'

The Beano took place in the Masonic Hall. The Jocks had a fine spread, and sat at four long tables that ran the length of the Hall. But Pringle Pattison and I sat on the platform at one end, along with a Seaforth officer, Seaforth himself and Mrs Stuart-Mackenzie. We were on five chairs facing the main body of the Hall. The cakes oozed with cream. The agony of partaking delicately of drawing-room tea under difficulties was too much for us, and no one took more than one cup of tea and one cake. After tea Mrs Stuart-Mackenzie gave each of the men ten cigarettes, and each of the officers a hundred. After speeches – Seaforth's was interrupted by an aged aged man, upon whom tea, untasted for years, seems to have a most intoxicating effect – they all went to the Picture Palace. The men enjoyed themselves greatly.

... The Camerons, as you may have seen in the papers, have been very badly hit, only three officers have escaped. So we may be ordered out any day now....

THOMAS HENRY.
after PTE · N KIRBY.

GUNNER R. ELWIS,
Royal Garrison
   Artillery.

The last week in March we were considered fit for work and we were booked to go to Bristol to load up our new guns at Avonmouth for transhipment to Boulogne. My friend, Old Cowley, was in the cookhouse, and in my hut there were five youngsters like me. The jam (possy we called it) was issued in 14-pound stone jars, and as the older members of the room didn't bother about it, there was always a supply going spare. Friend Cowley used to collect a whole jar about twice a week and stole away over the shingle to Dungeness about two miles away, where jam was converted into beer at the only pub for miles.

When it was known we were moving, Cowley collected four empty jam jars, cleaned them nicely, filled them with shingle from outside the hut, covered them with a layer of jam and sealed the lot over good as new. Two men were seen stealing out the back of the camp with a jar under each arm, fifty-six pounds of first-class shingle. Two tipsy men crept into camp about midnight, and at 6 o'clock the following morning we boarded our train en route for Bristol via Ashford and London. We were laughing all the way!

The order has come today for a hundred of our fellows to go to the Front next week. Of course, I am not one, but I can see what we have to look forward to. As they are killed off at the Front we fill up their places. I haven't done my firing yet, but I shall go as soon as I possibly can afterwards. I didn't join to hang about England, and I'm afraid I shall swear terribly if I am kept here all the winter.

PRIVATE J. BOWLES,
2nd/16th (County of London) Battalion, Queen's Westminster Rifles.

---◆---

(Telegram) Dingwall. Received Cambridge 30th January 1915. Am for the front. No further orders yet. Starting tomorrow probably. Jock.

2ND LIEUTENANT J. MACLEOD,
3rd (Reserve) Battalion, Queen's Own Cameron Highlanders.

'Are we downhearted? No!' Canadian troops waiting to embark at Folkestone.

The War Office has sent us plans for the construction of pontoon bridges to 'cross the Rhine' for our remarks! I think they are somewhat optimistic and previous!

Diary of
GENERAL SIR JOHN FRENCH,
Commander in Chief.

Before the war was four weeks old some battalions of Territorials had been shipped off to take the place of troops who were garrisoning the Empire and release them for War Service. Among the first to arrive in the inhospitable fields of Flanders were troops from India. It was winter in Flanders; the war was young, supplies were short and times were hard.

◆

LIEUTENANT RORY MACLEOD,
V Battery,
Royal Horse Artillery,
2nd Indian Cavalry Division.

Early in March I was appointed to V Battery, Royal Horse Artillery, and joined them on 5 March in action at Croix Barbée, on the Neuve Chapelle front about 3,000 yards from the Germans. They belonged to the 2nd Indian Cavalry Division, and were part of the Meerut Cavalry Brigade. Only the guns of the Division were in action to support the coming attack at Neuve Chapelle; the cavalry were in reserve behind.

The Battery was in rather low spirits because of an accident just before coming into action. They had been detailed to demonstrate trench mortar firing. The Germans had trench mortars and we had not, so someone with a bright idea had invented one. The barrel looked like a bit of gas piping on a stand and it fired bombs consisting of jam tins filled with high explosive and nails. The Battery intended to practise first. They formed up in a hollow square round the mortar. The first three bombs were fired successfully, Wingate-Gray, a subaltern, being the demonstrator and lighting the fuse. The fourth bomb exploded in the bore and killed the Major, who was my old friend Mark Leigh Goldie, and thirteen men and wounded about forty others. In action at Croix Barbée the Battery was commanded by the Captain, Nicoll, and I was put in command of the centre section.

The country was flat and low-lying. Houses and farms were dotted about with clumps of trees round the farms, and the courses of streams were outlined by willow trees. But the Germans had a great advantage on the Aubers Ridge, half a mile to the east of Neuve Chapelle, which dominated the low ground to the west and provided them with excellent artillery observation.

Not far behind us was an 18 Pdr. Battery firing over our heads. They had one gun that 'prematured', that is to say, the shell burst near the muzzle of the gun and spattered us with bullets. We had to build an earthen bank behind each gun to protect the detachments.

There must have been something wrong with this gun because when we picked up the shell cases there were the marks of the gun rifling all down the case, indicating a choke in the bore.

The Battery indignantly denied that they were prematuring into us until we sent back some of the shell cases and showed them.

The units of the Indian Corps may justly claim that they had the good fortune to arrive at the very moment when their services were most required to relieve a very desperate situation. The British Army, consisting of battered, war-torn, and almost exhausted troops, was fighting against terrible odds, and was practically without reserves. The offensive towards Lille had been brought to an abrupt conclusion, and for some days the Germans had been attacking heavily along the whole line from La Bassée to Messines.

LIEUTENANT-
COLONEL D. H.
DRAKE-
BROCKMAN,
2nd Battalion,
39th Garhwal Rifles,
Garhwal Brigade,
Meerut Division.

The trenches we took over were very shallow, hardly deep enough to cover a man kneeling. I remember well, when going round with the Commanding Officer of the King's Own Yorkshire Light Infantry, that we had to go round over the ploughed fields, as there was no room to go round inside the trenches. It was a misty moonlit night, and the stacks of tobacco on stakes stuck in the ground looked like men advancing in extended order – so much so, that on more than one occasion later I was deceived by them swaying in the breeze. Shortly afterwards they were blown to smithereens by shell fire.

We had a long spell in the trenches for our first 'go' – twenty days without relief! It soon initiated us into the work. One thing struck us all, and that was the remarkable steadiness of our men under artillery fire. Considering that neither they, nor in fact any of us, had ever been under heavy artillery fire before, it was marvellous how well they stood it and how steady they were.

As a rule, the Germans did not waste much ammunition by shelling at night, so we were left in peace, though their snipers were hard at it day and night. In any attack, of course, they used plenty of ammunition and also had searchlights. We were far behind them in these early days of the war, and so could not effectively reply. If one telephoned up to the gunner officer for a little ammunition to be expended on some bomb gun or *minenwerfer* that was annoying us, the reply generally received was: 'Sorry, but I have used my allowance!' This was, at that time, eighteen rounds daily per battery. We had no bombs, consequently we had to grin and bear it.

CAPTAIN A. V. L. B.
AGIUS,
1st/3rd (City of London)
Battalion,
The London Regiment,
Royal Fusiliers, (TF).

We were attached to the Indians. There was one battalion of Gurkhas, the 1st/39th Garhwalis, the 2nd Leicesters and ourselves. It was very interesting because you would have expected that the Gurkhas and the Garhwalis, who are hillmen, wouldn't have taken to the flat Flanders country in all that mud. But they were very much better than what I'd call the more civilised troops, the Punjabis and the Sikhs. They were less frightened. I've only once seen a Gurkha really frightened and then he turned green which was a horrible sight. It was the time the Germans first used gas which was just north of us and everybody was afraid that we were going to be gassed, and this poor Gurkha, he was a Havaldar (that's a sergeant) turned literally green, but we got on marvellously, especially with the Gurkha. We used to call him 'Teak Johnnie', I don't know why. He was a little bit frightening at first. He used to be on sentry duty and you'd be passing along the road and out of the darkness would come this cry of ''*Alt!*'' and you'd find a little Gurkha about so high with his bayonet at your breast button. But they were extremely cheerful, the Gurkhas. They carried a *kukri*. One of my first recollections is a raid at Neuve Chapelle. I was supporting the attack with my machine-guns and I'll never forget seeing a Gurkha coming across in front from the German lines, holding something in his hands — and when I looked it was the face of a German! It wasn't his neck or his head, just his face cut vertically down. He was bringing it back as a trophy, and very pleased he was too!

3 April.

Many happy returns of the day! By this time next year, I hope to be a peaceful and irresponsible undergraduate again, and then I will be able to buy you a suitable present. As it is the best I can do is this small portion of German shell which exploded near the French trenches.

There are signs now that the war will soon be over. Could you arrange with Mr Spens to let me have my old rooms at College next October if all goes well?

Today is Easter and we are preparing to go into the new trenches tonight. They are much better than our old ones.

Talking about Easter, our Padre is of the Established Church of Scotland. He is a splendid fellow, and as he has never seen Cambridge, I asked him to come and stay with us after the war.

Thank you very much for the sweets, which arrived here where we are out at rest. They were most pleasant to the palate. This warfare makes the most promising young man (me) into a barefaced glutton. Where I am there are many cafés and my figure is getting more convex. The sweets were very choice, and the shortbread helped considerably to distend some of us. My false tooth struck from overwork the day before yesterday, and fell with a loud crash on to my dessert plate at dinner. Luckily this place has an Army dentist, and now we are again prepared to tackle any meal. I score in the matter of meals, for as Machine-Gun Officer I feed at Battalion Headquarters where we have a cook and can get warm food on coke fires. Thank you very much for the parcel containing the cake from Matthews', cream cheese, etc. The cake and cheese were both very good, and did not long grace the Mess, because they disappeared rapidly. Of course, home-made cakes are really the best of all! If the cheese was not too expensive, it would be worth sending another. Oh, and please do not send *Punch* any more, because nearly everyone else has copies, and my section to whom my copy goes do not appreciate it as much as they would *Answers* or the like.

The six shirts came today, and the Section were very pleased with them. They raffled them among themselves. They do not need any more shirts just now, but would like some more cigarettes – not tobacco as there are only two pipe smokers in the Section, and they get more than they can smoke from the remainder of the Section.

Our life is not too strenuous; we have a twelve-day tour of duty, two days in the trenches, and two out, two in, two out etc, and then six days rest in reserve. When out of the trenches we are billeted round, and can get quite comfortable. In the trenches we work at night and rest by day, so that the poem I learnt in infancy:

> Soldier, rest! Thy warfare o'er,
> Sleep the sleep that knows no waking
> Dream of battlefields no more,
> Days of toil and nights of aching

2ND LIEUTENANT
 J. MACLEOD,
3rd (Reserve) Battalion,
Queen's Own Cameron
 Highlanders.

should be:

Nights of toil and days of aching.

For, after all, we cannot expect a luxurious club room existence in the trenches! We have braziers with charcoal. Anyway I have never felt really freezing yet, though we had snow yesterday.

At present we are billeted in a pub ('*estaminet*'). We are three officers of A Company, Captain Ramsay, Collier, and myself. We have one quite large room, with a stone floor. We sleep in our valises, on straw, and I thank my stars that I bought a fleecy blanket at Havre! It is light and very warm. You have to walk carefully because the roads are pitted with shell holes. The nearer you get to the firing line the more desolate everything is. The only inhabitants of the deserted and shattered cottages are cats.

CAPTAIN W.G. BAGOT CHESTER,
3rd Queen Alexandra's Own Gurkha Rifles, (The Sirmoor Rifles).

2nd April, 1915 (Good Friday) Except for a short parade in the morning, I gave the men a holiday today. At 2 p.m. the Bishop of London held a service near Calonne in a field, to which I went. He stood in a wagon and gave us a good address, and we sang a few hymns. Afterwards Ryall and I were standing near the wagon. The Bishop came up behind us and put his hands on our shoulders. In the course of conversation he said that when he got home he was going to 'raise hell' about the shortage of ammunition. General French himself had told him that the war would be over in six months had we the requisite amount of ammunition. Shells, of course, he was referring to.

An offensive towards Lille failed to dislodge the Germans from the trenches and breastworks that snaked across the British sector, from Ypres in the north to La Bassée, fifty miles south. It was stalemate on the Western Front. But in Whitehall a new strategic plan was being mooted. If the Dardanelles could be forced, if Constantinople could be captured, Germany and her allies could be stabbed in the back. The Navy had tried – and failed – and the only result was that Turkey was put on the alert. With the help of Germany she prepared for invasion. The first of the Australian volunteers were now training in Egypt. A British contingent of Regulars, Territorials and Naval Reservists was quickly cobbled together and sent to the Mediterranean, to join them and towards the end of April they sailed in convoy for the island of Mudros, there to concentrate with the battleships.

The Isle of Imbros, set in turquoise blue,
Lies to the westward; on the eastern side
The purple hills of Asia fade from view,
And rolling battleships at anchor ride.

White flocks of cloud float by, the sunset glows,
And dipping gulls fleck a slow-waking sea,
Where dim steel-shadowed forms with foaming bows
Wind up the Narrows towards Gallipoli.
Geoffrey Dearmer.

MEMORANDUM

LORD HANKEY,
Secretary to the
War Council.

The remarkable deadlock which has occurred in the western theatre of war invites consideration of the question whether some other outlet can be found for the effective employment of the great forces of which we shall be able to dispose in a few months' time.

The experience of the offensive movements of the Allies in this theatre within the last few weeks seems to indicate that any advance must be both costly and slow. Days are required to capture a single line of trenches, the losses are very heavy, and as often as not the enemy recaptures his lost ground on the following day, or is able to render the captured ground untenable. When viewed on a map, the total gains are almost negligible, and apparently incommensurate with the effort and loss of life. Moreover, the advance is so slow that the enemy has time to prepare fresh lines of defence in rear of his many existing lines to compensate for the trenches lost...

There is no reason to suppose that the enemy's successive positions can be captured merely by weight of numbers... If, therefore, the new armies are thrown into France, all that can be done is to extend our lines and set free more French troops for an attack in some more promising quarter. But is it certain that a more promising quarter exists, or that the French want more troops?

Germany can perhaps be struck most effectively and with the most lasting results on the peace of the world through her allies, and particularly through Turkey...

It is presumed that in a few months' time we could, without endangering the position in France, devote three army corps, including one original first-line army corps, to a campaign in Turkey. This force, in conjunction with Greece and Bulgaria, ought to be sufficient to capture Constantinople...

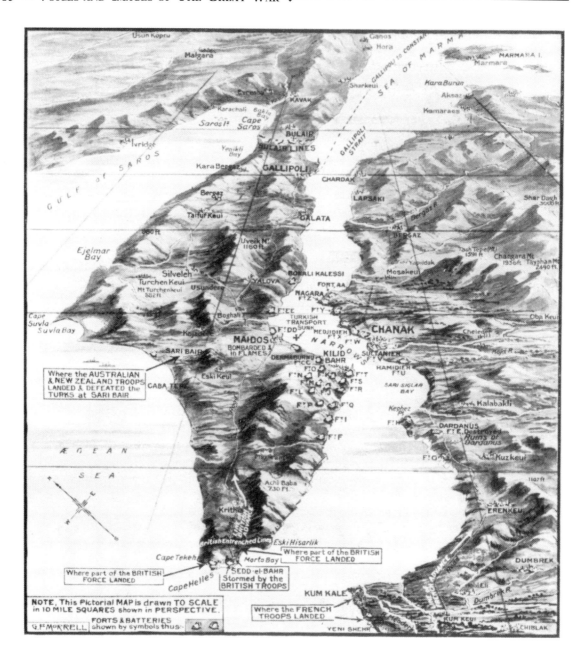

FATHER ERIC GREEN,
Roman Catholic Chaplain,
Army Chaplain's
Department.

The first few weeks of the expedition were to most of us a delightful time of cruising from one island in the Aegean to another – varied by a short stay in the brilliant sunshine of Egypt. One of these islands was Skyros. Roughly described, the whole island is of white marble, in great blocks and piled up to two or three thousand feet, and flashed all over with masses of lilac, sage, and purple thyme. It was here that we buried, one evening, in a small hollow under a low olive tree, quite near to the water, poor Rupert Brooke; he had only been ill a few days.

These laid the world away; poured out the red
Sweet wine of youth; gave up the years to be
Of work and joy, and that unhoped serene,
That men call age; and those who would have been,
Their sons, they gave, their immortality.

Rupert Brooke

I remember when Rupert Brooke was ill in his tent at Port Said. We got there at the beginning of April and we had tents there. It took us half a day to get these blinking tents up in rows. I was Arthur Asquith's runner and that meant often going to the other officers with messages and I was sent off to look for Rupert Brooke on these sands. Of course you can't knock on the door of a tent, so you've got to peep in. Well I eventually found him lying on a camp bed, and I said, 'Mr Asquith's looking for you, sir'. Just then Mr Asquith walked in himself and stood just inside the flap, so I couldn't get out and I stood there while they had this conversation, and I remember Brooke said, 'It's this blasted mosquito bite'. He was pointing to his lip and his face was all swollen up.

Later, when we got on the *Grantully Castle* he and Lieutenant Freyberg occupied the same cabin, so I saw him several times every day. He was up and about, and then he took poorly again. In the official record of his death it says he died of sunstroke, but when he was queer I heard him myself say that his trouble was the blasted mosquito bite on his lip. It killed him that mosquito bite, in my opinion.

ABLE SEAMAN JOSEPH
MURRAY,
Hood Battalion,
Royal Naval Division.

After the Last Post the little lamp-lit procession went once again down the narrow path to the sea. Freyberg, Asquith, I, Charles and Cleg stayed behind and covered the grave with great pieces of white marble which were lying everywhere about... The cross at his head was the

SUB LIEUTENANT
DENIS BROWNE,
Hood Battalion,
Royal Naval Division.

large one that headed the procession. On the back of it our Greek interpreter wrote in pencil (in Greek):

HERE LIES
THE SERVANT OF GOD
SUB-LIEUTENTANT IN THE
ENGLISH NAVY
WHO DIED FOR
DELIVERANCE OF CONSTANTINOPLE FROM
THE TURKS.

Fair broke the day this morning
Against the Dardanelles;
The breeze blew soft, the morn's cheeks
were cold as cold sea-shells

But other shells are waiting
Across the Aegean Sea,
Shrapnel and high explosive,
Shells and hells for me.

Lt. Cmdr. Patrick Shaw-Stewart
Royal Naval Division, Killed in action, 1917.

Three days later, an hour or two after nightfall, I landed at Gaba Tepe (Anzac), in the dark and in the rain. We were packed on a lighter, like sardines. As one drew nearer to the shore bullets and shrapnel were falling all around.

FATHER ERIC GREEN,
Roman Catholic Chaplain,
Army Chaplain's
   Department.

On land there was still a scene of indescribable confusion. On the narrow strip of sandy, stony beach, not more than about thirty to forty feet wide, at the foot of the cliffs, which rise range above range, men were moving in every direction. Troops landing, troops marching west, troops marching east, men laden with rations, mules and horses packed with stores and water barrels and bearers coming down the cliffs with wounded and dying on stretchers.

Hugging the foot of the cliff I found my first quarters. Two ambulance stations had been contrived here, one belonging to an Australian division, the other was to be ours, the RND ambulance. I say contrived, because it was a marvel how much had been squeezed in so small a space, when really there was no space at all.

Before half an hour was over my work began and it went on until 3 a.m. I had not one moment; one wounded and dying man following on after another. Just time, if the man was conscious, to hear his confession and a muttered act of contrition, to give absolution, and the anointing, before a new man claimed attention. Poor fellows, with wounds of every description, all disfigured and defiled with blood, and clay and dirt, in many cases unrecognisable, often features blown away. But being suddenly, as it were, plunged into this valley of suffering and death; in the very thick of it, I hardly realised the terror of things; there was no time to think, but only to do and act in what way I could to give the help that I was there to give. Sights that at ordinary times would have unmanned anyone, were passed over with a businesslike indifference, all save the case of one poor lad; a Haileybury boy, hardly nineteen, who looked as though he might be asleep, but was moaning for his mother; he was shot near the heart and died before an hour was over.

At 3 a.m., casualties, more or less, ceased coming in. I rolled myself up in my blanket and lay on the sand – next to a Protestant Padre.

The moon was brilliant, but I don't think I ever spent so cold a night before. It was not easy to get to sleep; the constant sound of the Turkish snipers came in waves from the cliffs overhead, now soft, now louder, and then firmly as though a whole Turkish horde were coming down from the slopes to overwhelm us. Just a few yards away a fire had been lighted, and the ambulance men, who were on duty all night, were making their tea; they were mostly Lancashire lads and how they talked and talked.

At 4.30 the din began again. I must have fallen asleep and I woke up in the greatest amazement I had ever felt. It was indescribable. The *Goeben* on the other side of the peninsula had sent morning greetings, and shell after shell rushed through the air over our heads and fell in the sea just in front of us. The mighty, rushing noise as though it was carrying everything before it, the enormous volumes of water that rose like huge geysers from the sea, when the shell met the water. The whole sea round about was literally riddled with bullets and shrapnel so that the water looked as though it were torn by a storm of wind and hail.

**MEMORABLE
SCENES AT
DARDANELLES**

**RACE TO LAND
BEFORE DAWN**

**AUSTRALASIANS'
GALLANTRY**

CAPTAIN T. A. WHITE,
13th Battalion,
Australian Imperial Force

Dawn, 25 April
Ominous and thrilling sounds in the distance. We all knew that our First Division mates were in it, and became impatient to join them. Passing Cape Helles we could see the battle and the shelling of the

village of Sedd–el–Bahr. At 4.30 p.m. we dropped anchor off Anzac Cove. On all sides battleships were bombarding the distant hills; nearer in towards the shore were transports discharging their troops into destroyers, which then darted towards the shore to discharge the men into rowing boats. Shells were bursting around and over the vessels and boats and we could hear the crackling of machine-guns and rifles.

At 9.30 p.m. destroyers came alongside. In the dark the laden men climbed down the gangways and unsteady ladders, feeling uncomfortable in spite of our practice, until we felt our legs gripped by the friendly hands of the sailors. As each destroyer received its complement it rushed towards the shore and soon came within range of the enemy bullets. Nearer the beach the men climbed into the boats and were towed by launches or rowed to the shore. Several were wounded and a few killed on the destroyers and in the boats.

The rendezvous of the Battalion was on the slope of Ari Burnu and from there at daybreak next morning, wet with dismal rain that had been falling since midnight, we moved in file on Monash Valley. Spreading out and lying down in the scrub we found bullets coming in all directions.

During the morning the swarms of Turks coming down were shelled by our warships and this caused them to break up into small parties of threes and fours and to advance these driblets down in short rushes to minimise losses. In this way, in spite of heavy casualties, they soon became overwhelming. All daylong we were losing cobbers and stretcher bearers were kept busy. At times the noise was deafening. Orders of a most contradictory nature came along from both flanks and worried us considerably. One officer of the First Brigade, utterly worn out and unnerved by thirty hours fighting, continually stood upon a conspicuous point and waving two revolvers shouted, 'Five rounds rapid, and charge!' For hours he led a charmed life.

Both sides were trying to entrench within forty yards of one another on the same narrow ridge and every now and again the digging was interrupted to 'Stand to' and our positions were so precarious that the enemy only needed to drive our thin line back a few yards in order to hurl us over into the valley. But our men were so solid that every Turkish attempt failed. All through the afternoon charge after charge was made. Sergeant Shapley (just promised his commission for splendid work) would jump on his parapet, followed by his platoon, charge into the scrub with fixed bayonets, yelling 'Imshi! Imshi! and, after each successful charge he would stand and cheer regardless of the enemy.

The Turks now quailed considerably, but further reinforcements and darkness increased their valour, and again they came on, determined to clear us off the Peninsula. After sounding *our* 'Cease Fire' they advanced to the weirdest accompaniment ever heard in battle. Bugles called eerily along the whole front, advancing and retiring, blaring suddenly close up and then in the dark distance, the echoes repeating in the gullies, while crashes of rifles and machine-guns occasionally drowned the efforts of the musicians. There was no tune about it – simply weird blasts, whistle-blowing and shouting – the blasts apparently being signals in Morse. If those signals were orders to drive us into the sea, they were of little avail. Our bullets mowed down line after line.

CAPTAIN THE HON.
AUBREY HERBERT,
Irish Guards,
(attached Anzacs).

Sunday, 25 April
We landed on a spit of land which in those days we called Shrapnel Point, to the left of what afterwards became Corps Headquarters, though later the other spit on the right usurped that name. I took cover under a bush with a New Zealand officer, Major Browne.

There were lines of men clinging like cockroaches under the cliffs or moving silently as the guns on the right and left enfiladed us. The only thing to be done was to dig in as soon as possible, but a good many men were shot while they were doing this. We remained on the beach.... We had no artillery to keep the enemy's fire down.

We spent a chilly night, sometimes lying down, sometimes walking, as the rain began to fall after dark, and we had not too much food.

We were very hard pressed; as every draft landed it was hurried off to that spot in the line where reinforcements were most needed. This naturally produced chaos amongst the units, and order was not re-established for some time. It was a terrible night for those in authority. I believe that, had it been possible, we should have re-embarked that night, but the sacrifices involved would have been too great. Preparations for the expedition had been totally inadequate. The chief RAMC officer had told me the ridiculously small number of casualties he had been ordered to make preparations for, and asked my opinion, which I gave him with some freedom. As it was, we had to put six hundred men on the ship from which we had disembarked in the morning, to go back to hospital in Egypt, a four days' journey, under the charge of one officer – who was a veterinary surgeon!

Monday, 26 April
We slept on a ledge a few feet above the beach. Firing went on all night. In the morning it was very cold, and we were all soaked. The Navy, it appeared, had landed us in the wrong place. This made the Army extremely angry, though as things turned out it was the one bright spot. Had we landed anywhere else, we should have been wiped out...

CAPTAIN T. A. WHITE,
13th Battalion,
Australian Imperial Force.

The Landing strength of the 13th was twenty-five officers and 934 other ranks; our strength on the evening of 3rd May was nine officers and 500 other ranks, and the 15th and 16th had suffered even more severely.

April 17th; shall we forget?
I rather think we'll not.
Our boys advanced with bayonets fixed
To face the shell and shot.

Mining and sapping began in a small way on the Western Front as early as January 1915. Manpower was still scarce. Many of the seasoned troops brought back from garrisons round the Empire had been sent to Gallipoli and it would be months before the first raw battalions of the Citizens' Army would be well enough trained and equipped to play their part as fighting soldiers. The line was thinly held, guns and ammunition were scarce and it was clear to the British and French holding the tiny salient round Ypres that, with the coming of the spring weather, the Germans would be likely to attack. Hill 60 was hardly more than a mound, but it was the hinge at the edge of the salient where the high ground swung south. It had changed hands several times. Now the mines had been laid, the charges were set and the infantry were poised to attack Hill 60 when it went up.

◆

We arrived in the trenches about 1 a.m. on the morning of 17 April and during the day we were told that Hill 60 was going to be blown up at 7 o'clock and that we were to be prepared for it.

At 7 p.m. exactly the hill was blown up and it was an awful sight to see, practically the whole hill blown up, for the miners or Sappers had undermined it like a spider's web, and there must have been a tremendous amount of explosive used.

As soon as the explosive had done its work the KOSB and West Kent regiments made a charge, followed by the KOYLI and the Duke of Wellington's Regiment. We men in reserve could see our comrades charging like flies on a ceiling and there were about 600 British guns shelling the Germans from behind the reserves, but I believe that the Germans had as many guns as we had for they responded so fast.

At night it was decided to make another attack so those men who had been in reserve were brought up and at 6 p.m., with bayonets fixed, we were away over the parapet, followed by the Queen Victoria's Rifles (a London Territorial battalion) who did good work all through the Hill 60 fighting. (One of their officers, 2nd Lieut. Woolley, ended by winning the Victoria Cross).

On the evening of 18 April the trenches, or rather the hill was strewn with the dead and wounded and it was an awful sight to have to both

PRIVATE CHARLES
BLANE,
2nd Battalion King's Own
Scottish Borderers.

run and walk over them. The Stretcher-Bearers did all that was possible to get them all away and all that were left helped, but it was a very slow and tedious job.

We were pelted with bombs and shells by the Germans, bombarded with high explosives and whizz-bangs, but we held the position through the whole of 18 April.

By noon the following day the Germans had recaptured the whole of the hill with the exception of a section of trench between the second and third craters which The Duke's still held.

I may add that this was the first time the Germans used the horrible gas. I mean on 17 April when the KOSB and West Kents made their charge. So Good Luck to the famous Hill 60 and up you go and the best of luck.

(Written at No. 22 General Hospital – Dannes Camiers, France – Ward C-3.)

TROOPER SYDNEY CHAPLIN,

1st Northamptonshire Yeomanry.

We were sent up to Hill 60. As usual we rode up as far as it was safe to leave the horses, then we carried on to the dump, where we picked up a shovel or pick. As we moved on to the hill we were halted to await a guide and we sheltered beside an old wall. Bullets rattled like hail on the wall for we were being fired on from three directions. As the guide did not show up we went on to the hill. What a ghastly sight. The dead lay everywhere. We were to dig a trench on the hill, but whilst waiting for instructions our officer decided we should take shelter in the front line, but when we got there the trench was packed full. Someone had blundered and two lots of reinforcements had been sent up. So we had to lay among the dead on the top. For over two hours we lay waiting among crossfire and an occasional shell. Then I turned over and looked up just as a shrapnel shell burst overhead. The flame was like an expanding star and then the bullets thrashed down. I heard them striking the dead bodies and at that moment a trooper near me gave a scream and kept on screaming. 'For God's sake, stop that man!' someone shouted.

I grabbed the man as he crawled by. 'I'm hit in the neck.' I tried to find the wound but it was not in his neck, but at the base of the spine. The stretcher-bearers took him away and after another wait we were ordered to move off. This time by a different way. I had the wounded man's rifle to carry as well as mine *and* a shovel.

We finally reached the outskirts of Boeschepe as the sun began to shine, all thankful that we only had one casualty. Then our Major came cantering up, called us to a halt and sections into line. Then he said, 'I am sorry, men, about the mess we have been in; I have been to see General Morland and explained the difficulty in trying to dig a trench on the hill. And he just dismissed me with the words that if he lost every man in the Northants Yeomanry he would have that trench dug!!!!'

Wounded horses en route to hospital

I had to guide six wagons of ammunition up to Hill 60. My own horse had not recovered from a wound he had received the week before so I had to take Sammy. Nothing much to look at, though he had a reputation for being a good jumper.

There was the usual congestion on the road, but we eventually got to Bedford House and dumped the ammunition and then took the GS wagon and water cart along the track route to the guns. This was no easy matter in the dark but we arrived safely. I had to report to the CO so I got a gunner to hold Sammy while I went to find him. Just then the Germans started shelling. I told the CO I had left my horse on the track, and he let me get away at once, and I found Sammy dancing about all over the place in fright. I tried to jump on his back, but at that moment a shell burst on top of me (or so I thought) and Sammy shot off like an arrow from a bow. I hadn't been able to get properly into the saddle, having lost my near-side stirrup and the rein, so I was lying across the saddle with my rear end pointing towards 'Germany' – and my head hanging down the other side. I managed to clutch the off-side stirrup leather and hung on. Sammy made a beeline for the road. Shells were bursting right along the track, but Sammy did not once even falter. He took those huge holes in his stride and I thanked God he could jump. I could see nothing but the ground below my face and the almost continuous flash of bursting shells.

BOMBARDIER ALEX DUNBAR,
Royal Field Artillery.

After what seemed an eternity, we reached the road. Sammy swerved down it, but fifty yards on he skidded to a halt in front of a convoy of motor lorries waiting for the barrage to stop. Directly Sammy stopped, he sank to the ground. My own feet were then touching the ground, so I stood up and waited for Sammy to rise. He didn't move. I looked at him closely. One of the side bars of the saddle had been shot away and there was a nasty wound in Sammy's rump, also several other small wounds in other parts of his body. I could see no sign, however, of a fatal wound anywhere, but he was undoubtedly dead.

The lorry drivers helped me pull his body to the ditch on the side of the road. I was in tears. Sammy had brought me safely through that terrific barrage without a scratch, but at the cost of his own life. And I had to leave him there in a ditch!

When I talked it over with our Vet. Officer, he thought that, although none of Sammy's wounds were fatal, he had probably broken a blood vessel owing to the tremendous effort.

I shall never forget him.

◆ ◆

SERGEANT S. V. BRITTEN
13th Battalion,
The Royal Highlanders of
Canada.

17 April
Rose at 8.30, went down to Ypres with Capt. Morrisey & Rae, & spent day there, saw over the ruins of the Cathedral & Cloth Hall etc. Stopped all the afternoon, bought a handkerchief of Flemish Lace (& sending it to Vera as a souvenir), brought back a quantity of stuff for ourselves, including two bottles of wine. Witnessed an exciting battle between a British & a German biplane. The latter was brought down about 7 p.m. Terrific artillery fire started about 6 p.m., & lasted all night.

22 April
Left at 6.30 p.m. for reserve trenches and reached our reserve dugouts via St Julien. Just rat holes! One hell of accommodation! Got to the trenches as a fatigue party with stake & sandbags, and thought they were reserve trenches, they were so rotten. No trenches at all in parts, just isolated mounds. Found German's feet sticking up through the ground. The Gurkhas had actually used human bodies instead of sandbags.

Right beside the stream where we were working were the bodies of two dead, since November last, one face downwards in full marching order, with his kit on his back. He died game! Stench something awful and dead all round. Water rats had made a home of their decomposed bodies. Visited the barbed wire with Rae – ordinary wire strung across. Quit about 1 a.m., came back to our dugouts and found them on fire. Had to march out to St Julien, & put up in a roofless house – not a roof left on anything in the whole place. Found our sack of food had been stolen and we were famished. Certainly a most unlucky day, for I lost my cherished pipe in the evening also. Bed at 4 a.m.

In the middle of January I received orders to go and see Geheimrat Haber, who was in Brussels on behalf of the Ministry of War. He explained to me that the Western fronts, which were all bogged down, could be got moving again only by means of new weapons. One of the weapons contemplated was poison gas, in particular chlorine, which was to be blown towards the enemy from the most advanced positions. When I objected that this was a mode of warfare violating the Hague Convention, he said that the French had already started it – though not to much effect – by using rifle-ammunition filled with gas. Besides, it was a way of saving countless lives, if it meant that the war could be brought to an end sooner.

Haber informed me that his job was to set up a special unit for gas-warfare, Pioneer Regiment No. 36. We received our first special training in Berlin, being instructed in the use of the poison gases and the relevant apparatus, including what was called the Drägersche Selbstretter, a protective device that had to be worn when discharging the gas. We also had to learn something about wind and weather, of course.

HERR OTTO HAHN

From that training-course I returned to Flanders and was attached to Infantry Regiment No. 126 as their gas pioneer. My first task was to be what was called a front-line observer, i.e., I had to evaluate positions from which gas might be used. Our position was in the vicinity of Gheluvelt, directly opposite the English lines, and so at times we could only talk in whispers. We were not yet very well entrenched and we were constantly under enemy fire, so the installation of the gas cylinders for the proposed attack was very difficult indeed.

The gas warning was given a number of times, but the attack had to be postponed again and again because of weather conditions. Every time the time of the attack had been fixed — which had to be twenty-four hours earlier — the wind changed and blew towards us, and the units brought up from the rear had to be taken back again. In the middle of April High Command decided to remove the gas cylinders again and take them to a sector of the front north-east of Ypres, where wind conditions were more favourable.

The reason why it was not entirely successful was probably that both the troops and the Command had become nervous as a result of the many abortive attempts, and also that by then there were no longer sufficient reserves available to consolidate the gains.

SERGEANT S. V. BRITTEN
13th Battalion,
The Royal Highlanders of Canada.

23 April

Up about noon and had no breakfast. Had a good view of the village of the dead, everything in a most heartbreaking state. We found a piano and had music. Furious shelling started about 4.30 p.m., and we took to the dugouts. Almost suffocated by the poisonous fumes! Got into marching order (without packs) & lined for action outside the village. Got to No. 7 station & found Captain Morrisey there, almost suffocated. Brought Lieutenant Molson out to St Jean, & we came to St Julien, getting a lift in an ambulance. Village a mess of dead horses, limbers and men. Went on ration fatigue & tried to get up to the trenches but failed. Scouted the road, waited under heavy shell fire for about two hours, then moved off, & made a circumference up to the trenches via 48th communication trench. Getting there at almost daybreak.

23 April

Terrible day, no food or water, dead & dying all around.

24 April

Dug ourselves in with entrenching tools on left flank approaching St Julien. Just got finished about 3 p.m. ($4\frac{1}{2}$ feet deep and a little later the artillery opened fire). At 7.30, trench blown to hell, and we were terribly cut up. Rae & I got separated from the rest, and I helped Gardiner (wounded) who got wounded again, and finally reaching reserve trench found Captain Ross and Sergeant-Major Jeffries there. At 8.10, took message with Rae to Colonel through artillery fire, entered St Julien, and found him transferred to a farmhouse outside. Brought him, and Sergeant Claridge, Colonel Batemare and four others up to trenches with all the ammunition we could. No casualties. Reached trenches, our left flank broke, and orders to fire on them. Captain Kenway killed on the road. Then went with the Colonel to relay message for him. Met Colonel Currie on way. Left Rae at farm, and went on to General Head Quarters (General Turner) with the Colonel, then back to local Head Quarters, and back again to General Head Quarters, with the Germans already in village of St Julien. Brought back General Retirement order from General Head Quarters, and gave same to Major Buchanan, and finally to the Colonel. Left the Colonel with Rae, to advise everyone in front of us. Then on the way back to General Head Quarters, met Irish Rifles extended, ready to attack village of St Julien. Shell fire most awful – never such known before. Knee gave way through a cut by shrapnel, so lay down and rested.

26 April
In canvas rest Camp Hospital at Etaples, in bed next to Fred. Many Canadians here. Division pretty nearly wiped out.

Word came down that the Germans had got through and they needed every man up the line, and we were sent up to St Julien to stand by the Canadians. We just put on everything and fell in and marched up the railway line. We met the refugees coming down the railway line towards Dickebusch, all sorts of people, old people, young people and kids and parrots and goats and all the lot, running away from Ypres and the shelling. We had a job to get past them, but eventually we got up to the line. When we first got there, I remember we were in a sunken road, lying against a bank, taking cover. A Canadian came down and he shouted to our Captain, 'The bastards have broken through; they've gassed us and they've broken through, so give them the bloody bayonet, Jock.' So then the order came, 'Fix Bayonets', right along the line. Of course, our hands were shaking, fixing the bayonets. That was our first counter-attack, but the strange thing was that when you'd got your bayonet fixed and you got your order to charge, all the sort of nervousness that you had, your fear and trembling, all seemed to go. You just – you were in action – your main concentration was to get there and not get killed yourself, so you lost these twitterings. Of course, the chaps were all gasping and couldn't breathe, and it was ghastly, especially for chaps that were wounded – terrible for a wounded man to lie there! The gasping, the gasping! And it caused a lot of mucus, phlegm, your eyes were stinging as well. You couldn't stop to help anybody, even if he was your brother, he'd still be lying there badly injured, and you mustn't

SERGEANT BILL HAY,
9th Battalion (TF),
The Royal Scots.

help, so you'd got to go on with the attack or there'd be nobody to contend with the attack, so you went on and the Jerries ran back, they fell back, they didn't wait for us to get close enough.

The ambulances took chaps away, and many chaps were jumping on the wagons and shooting off when they might have been able to stay a bit longer – not wounded – or not much – then, of course, there was all the chaps lying about wounded and crying. That was heart-rending, that was, all night long we could hear them. Before daybreak, we were told to dig in – we had no trenches – with an entrenching tool, and all we could do was dig funk holes – like a grave, more or less. We were digging these holes and I was sent in front, maybe about fifty yards, with a covering party – so many men went out in front to lie there and watch for the Jerries in case they made a sudden counter-attack – you were supposed to fire a few shots and warn the blokes behind. And all the time the shells are coming over.

I'll tell you this much, I might not have been wounded in body but I was wounded in my mind. I don't know if you can imagine it but obviously when there's shell fire, you get down to get cover, only an idiot wouldn't get down, so you get down and you can't get your nails into the ground and your head under the ground, you can't get down because you can't go any further. You're on the ground and your nails are dug into the ground and there you are and the shells are bursting round and there's screaming bits of shells and they're not just bits of metal, they're hot metal flying all over the place and there are machine guns going and pandemonium all round. How the devil did you get out of that unscathed? How did you get out? It's a miracle, if there's such a thing as a miracle.

LANCE-SERGEANT J. L. BOUCH, 1st Battalion, Coldstream Guards.

My brother was in the Canadians and they took a terrible pasting. We were carrying equipment up every night. Off you went to the Menin Gate and up to Hellfire Corner, and what a Hell of a job it was, because you never knew how many would get knocked down on the way. It was a shambles.

It was indescribable, all that area, after the fighting. It was a mass of dead bodies really. You sat on something, and it moved up and down. You knew perfectly well that underneath you was a dead body that had swelled up.

I tried to find out about my brother. We knew the Canadians were there and I had a word from Father that Wilfred was wounded and missing. Wilfred was a bit of a comedian. He sang and he wrote songs. He'd always fancied going to Canada. He'd been asked to go as a landscape gardener for three years to Canada, and he came back with them to the War. So I went up and then I met the Sergeant and said, 'Look, I'm trying to find out something about Private Wilfred Bouch'. He said, 'Was he the one who sang?' I said, 'Yes, he was.' He said, 'Oh, yes, we knew him. They were unprintable, his songs, plenty of effing and blinding.' I said, 'What happened to him?' He said, 'I couldn't tell you. The only thing I can tell you is we were over-run, as you know, and there were a lot of casualties. They were laid out waiting for the stretcher-bearers to come up and get them into the ambulances, and that's all I can tell you. That's the last I saw of him.'

Poor old Wilfred, he would be twenty-one. He was a year and three months older than I was. Never heard any more. The last letter he wrote me, he said, 'I shall send you another song in my next letter. It's a better version of "Tipperrary".' I got that letter, and that was the last I heard of him.

April 23rd, 1916.

Dear Jack,
I hope this letter will find you feeling pretty good. We are still resting but of course may move any old time. I told you that I'd send you my other song so I'll copy it out for you over the other side.

Well old boy I long to see you again and who knows but what we may before long.

I got a few cakes etc. from home today so I expect you won't be long before you get one.

Now I'll close before I get your goat, lots of love keep smiling.

From your affectionate Brother
Wilf Bouch.

IT'S A LONG WAY TO GET TO LONDON

Submarines beneath the sea and Zepplins in the air
Tons of Huns with great big guns, his soldiers everywhere
Said Bill, 'I'll first take Calais then for Dover, Oh Mein Gott!'
But Britain let her bulldog loose and fucked the Goddamn lot.

It's a long way to get to Calais, it's a long way to go
It's so damn far to get to Dover, that you'll never stand the blow.
Goodbye German Empire
Farewell Kaiser Bill
If you don't know the way to Hell, God help you
You Goddamn soon will.

Private Wilfred Bouch,
Canadian Expeditionary Force.

NEED FOR SHELLS.

**BRITISH ATTACKS
CHECKED.**

**LIMITED SUPPLY THE
CAUSE**

The Times, 14 May, 1915.

The Commander in Chief points out that the average number
of rounds per rifle on Lines of Communication has been:

January	216
February	191
March	138
On 19th April	134

From this it will be seen that the L. of C. reserve shows no
tendency to increase, but rather the reverse...

*Memorandum from Quartermaster General
25th April 1915.*

**IS THE BRITISH ARMY
SHORT OF SHELLS**

**Straight Answer Not Given To
Amazing Allegation.**

What is the truth about the alleged shortage of shells for the British Army in France?

The facts are as follows:
    The military correspondent of *The Times*, Colonel Repington, on May 14 said:
    The want of an unlimited supply of high explosive was a fatal bar to our success.

Speaking in the House of Commons on April 21, Mr Lloyd George said:
    The Secretary of State informs me that Lord Moulton has rendered invaluable services in the production of high explosives, and that by his energy he has now placed the production of high explosives in this country on a footing which relieves us of all anxiety, and which enables us, in addition to that, to supply our Allies.
                                                    Daily Sketch, 18 May, 1915.

◆

Owing to the heavy expenditure of ammunition which depleted our stocks and could not soon be replaced, we were cut down to a ration of sixty shells *per Battery* per week. The problem was whether to harass the Germans by firing ten rounds per day, or to save them up for a grand strafe on some important target.

LIEUTENANT RORY MACLEOD,
V Battery,
Royal Horse Artillery,
2nd Indian Cavalry Division.

He [Kitchener] is firmly convinced in his mind that we *waste* ammunition here. I told him quite plainly that neither he nor his advisers had any conception of what modern war was really like. This trench warfare was not brought about by any one army or nation, but was the inevitable outcome of the deadly nature of modern rifles and machine-guns. The old forms of attack and defence were of the past. Wherever he put the new armies he would find the same conditions prevail, and a free and stupendous expenditure of ammunition was the only way by which the infantry attack could be prepared. The enemy's trenches must be broken down, his wire entanglements torn up, and the machine-gun resistance reduced by artillery fire and an unlimited amount of ammunition.

Diary of
GENERAL SIR JOHN FRENCH,
Commander in Chief.

◆

To the Editor of *The Times*

Sir:

Will you allow me to point out one of the chief difficulties at the moment and its remedy? We have to deal not so much with shirkers, but with the very real temptation to enlist which constantly assails munition-makers to save them from the silly sneers of their ignorant neighbours or the well-meant persuasions of the Recruiting Sergeants. Many valuable men are leaving my own works to join the Colours from what is actually moral cowardice, though they were serving England infinitely better in the shop than they can ever hope to in the field. Put them in khaki and let them be amenable to a very simple code of military discipline. This would give them a status and a feeling of conscious pride and self-reliance. Human nature is just as strong in war as in peace, and who will deny that the young man in mufti does feel uncomfortable while the khaki-clad ones have a happy sense of *amour propre*, even though in some cases they are no whit more patriotic than their neighbour, who is being sneered at? And remember that sneers are painful to hear even when undeserved.

I am, Sir,
yours faithfully,
MUNITION-MAKER.
June 17th, 1915.

No 4.5 Howitzer Lyddite Ammunition left on Lines of Communication and only 24 rounds shrapnel aaa Hope you will dispatch at once at least 2,000 rounds to replace those sent to the Mediterranean aaa Please include as much Lyddite as possible.

Telegram from Commander-in-Chief to War Office
15th April, 1915.

Lady Gertrude Crawford and a number of other ladies are helping to make munitions at Erith. The work will come easy to Lady Gertrude, for she is highly skilled in the use of a lathe, and at Coxhill near Lymington, her charming country place on the borders of the New Forest, she fitted up a perfectly equipped workshop and has turned out work which has astounded her friends.

The Daily Mirror 26 July, 1915

At last has come the time for
which we always used to pine,
We're all aboard the **Viper** *and we*
lounge and smoke and dine,
And watch the wheeling seagulls
and the distant shores of France,
And the sunlight on the water and
the waves which gaily dance.
For we're all off together,
We're making for the War,
We don't need to worry
Or grumble any more.

2nd Lieutenant Jack Girling
(Killed on the Somme, October 1916.)

◆

We were all given ten days leave before going over to France on 25 July. I remember it was a Sunday evening that I had to return to Camp. I had to catch the 6 p.m. train from Tunbridge Wells. My father and both of my sisters came to see me off and when the train came in from Hastings it stopped right by where we were standing with a compartment full up with girls going back to Abbey Wood where they worked on munitions. They said, 'Come on Soldier, in with us.' I said, 'Not likely,' and got into an empty compartment next door. The train went off but it stopped at the next station and all ten of the girls got out and came in with me, so I had to keep one hand on my kit, the other on my halfpenny. Being only seventeen, I thought I might lose both! But they all made a fuss of me, gave me fags to smoke and told me lots of jokes, some of them pretty near the bone. However, I arrived in London in one piece, still a 'cock virgin'.

PRIVATE FRANK J.H.
DUNK,
7th (S) Battalion,
Royal West Kent
Regiment.

Well do I remember that early morning about one or two a.m. in August 1915, as we crossed the small bridge on the golf course at Tain on our way to the station, with the pipers at the front of us playing 'Happy we've been together'. Before we left for France we all had fourteen days special leave to go home and say cheerio to our folks. It was the Last Farewell for a lot of the boys.

In due time we got settled down in the troop train. Most of the boys were well prepared for the long journey as regards DRINK. I really seemed to be one of the few sober lads on the train. The drink made them happywise and I joined the lads in singing – mostly Scots songs, 'Dear Old Edinburgh Toon'. Also, 'We're no awa' tae bide awa'', also

PRIVATE CARSON
STEWART,
7th (S) Battalion,
The Queen's Own
Highlanders.

'Pack up your Troubles' and 'Tipperary'. Also others like 'There's an Old Mill by the Stream, Nellie Dean'.

So the train goes on, on its way to Edinburgh and as we enter the Edinburgh Station we all sing 'I can't forget Auld Reekie'. Most of the lads got down to sleep after we left Edinburgh – assisted by the drink, no doubt!

In due time we reached London and put up at Wellington Barracks for the night. It was late at night when we got into Wellington Barracks. We had not eaten a good meal for about twenty hours, so the Canteen boys at the Barracks said tea was ready. But the Canteen boys said we would have to *pay* for the tea. The Camerons were in no mood to be insulted after such a long journey! So we got stuck into the English boys and a Royal Donnybrook took place. The Camerons came out easy winners.

Next morning we got ready to leave for Shorncliffe near Folkestone, but, before we left London we gave it a real Scots set to. The officer in charge of us, who was also our guide, said he was never so pleased to get rid of such a lot of *wild men*.

On a beautiful Sunday afternoon we leave Folkestone to march down to the troop-ship, a perfect sunny day with the ladies strolling out in the Sunday Best Clothes.

Now the troop-ship leaves the harbour and someone starts to sing the old song 'The Anchor's Weighed, Farewell, Fare-ye-well, Remember me'. The whole body of troops joined in and made it a very impressive departure from the soldiers' point of view, also a bit sad, as we did not know then how many of us would return or what lay in store for us.

PRIVATE REG LAWRENCE,
3rd S. African Infantry Battalion, South African Brigade.

Cattle trucks are not the best means of travelling in France, as forty men with rifles and equipment go to a truck and when everybody is in and your legs tucked away safely, you discover that for the rest of that day or night you are unable to move them again, as there are at least half a dozen other pairs intertwined with yours and firmly held down by packs and rifles. You are usually quite glad to get out again and march twenty kilometres or so to billets.

2ND LIEUTENANT EWART RICHARDSON,
4th Battalion, **Princess of Wales' Own,** (Yorkshire Regiment).

I first saw the line from far way, looking over a country, apparently peaceful, from the crest of a hill. Somewhere behind a gun fired at intervals. The sound was not heavy – a gentle, dull explosion. Then away in front, after each explosion, a ball of smoke appeared from nowhere, a pretty conjuring trick.

The line is ugly and lovely by turns. By day it stretches as far as the eye can see on either side, gaunt, malignant, desolate. Broken, torn, and dying trees, rusted wire flinging tendrils upward like gigantic cobwebs. Stakes, stumpy, shattered, or miraculously intact emerge from the dank grass. Behind is a wilderness of brown torn earth, shattered and blown into the dustiest waste ground that ever made a city hideous; only this space is deserted, and its desolation is made sinister by death. Such is the line by day.

By night it is different.

It changes to a thing of delicate beauty. Flares, glowing and white, rise and fall continuously. Maybe a search-light stretches its penetrating ray through the night, and sweeps here and there across the country. A stranger might well believe he had come to some fête save that, for accompaniment, is a steady rattle of rifle fire, and now and then the rat-tat-tat of a machine-gun. Or maybe the guns are firing. There is a heavy boom far back, and a shell goes rushing invisibly overhead, to crash a mile beyond.

And beneath it all the working parties move silently, digging, sand-bagging, preparing in the darkness, for what may come. Casualties are surprisingly few; but here and there along the line, a bullet strikes home, and a man is carried to the rear wounded, or dead.

These are the quiet times. But sometimes the line wakes to fury. Guns flash and boom, the flares multiply in a madness of extravagance, and on the ear breaks the sound of a stupendous boiling. Sometimes the fury lasts for hours; sometimes it dies, as suddenly and inexplicably as it began, to the comparative quiet of the small arms again. But it leaves a hideous residue of maimed and slaughtered men, with their comrades appalled and shaken.

The Line alone, a moody giant, stretches his sinister length unmoved across the country.

I arrived at Boulogne on 9 June 1915 as a Lance-Corporal, part of a draft from the 4th Battalion, Durham Light Infantry. We stayed at St Martin's camp until 4 a.m. on the eleventh when we marched to Etaples.

SERGEANT W. F. LOW, 10th Battalion, Durham Light Infantry.

I was told off to see that none of our men were left behind and I formed the opinion that, in the first place, the training was wrong – the greatest complaint being the unusual pace and the unusual heaviness of the pack. In the second place, the stamina and physique of the men was low – much inferior to the type who marched further and carried more in hotter weather in the Boer War, in which I fought through three colonies. The older men, though good for a hard day's mining or quarrying, 'hadn't the legs and feet' as we would say of horses. Lastly, the spirit was lacking.

On 9 July I was promoted Corporal and went 'up the line' detraining at Poperinghe and marching out to the camp where I was posted to No. 12 Section B Company. I was employed mostly in making a plan and tracing of the trenches held by the 43rd Brigade at Zillebeke and saw much more of the closer fighting.

On the fourteenth I saw for myself the effect of rain in the trenches.

I had never really believed the descriptions of my friends but I found out that night to what depth you can sink and what a weight and quantity of mud you can transport – it exceeds the love of women and sticks closer than a brother! We had a long march on the fifteenth to HQ and for the first time in my life I suffered from sore feet. On reaching the camp I found my toes skinned. They were covered with fine sand and mud washed in by the paddling in the trenches. We camped till the eighteenth here in wet weather, wet fields, wet clothes, wet everything – save temper which on every side seemed dry and sharp, dulled in a few cases by hump. Even the sun which broke out on us in Ypres that afternoon in comfortable 'dugouts' got a fine crop of complaints. 'Ay! We'll be scorched now we're rainproof!'

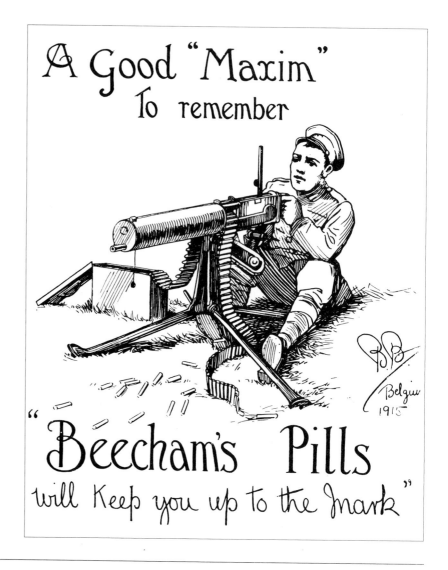

It was my first close view of Ypres. Though I have done all the real fighting I could get at in my time, I believe I am a kindly-natured man, yet that sight made me madder than anything I have seen or suffered in my life and gave me a real feeling of bloodthirstiness. I have seen ruined churches and wrecks of beautiful homes before and know well that tactical necessities or accidents often produce them, but no legitimate war practice even on this huge scale could produce the desolation of Ypres. It has produced a bent of mind I have not experienced before and makes me impatient of anything but real work against the Huns who have desecrated Ypres. Churchyards, altars, monuments, all that has been revered for countless ages even among savages, still receive their senseless spite and I think nothing of the man who after passing through Ypres could lay down his rifle before avenging it.

---◆---

You stand in a trench of vile stinking mud
And the bitter cold wind freezes your blood
Then the guns open up and flames light the sky
And, as you watch, rats go scuttling by.

The men in the dugouts are quiet for a time
Trying to sleep midst the stench and the slime
The moon is just showing from over the Hill
And the dead on the wire hang silent and still.

A sniper's bullet wings close to your head
As you wistfully think of a comfortable bed
But now a dirty blanket has to suffice
And more often than not it is crawling with lice.

Haig and his mob keep well in the Rear,
Living in luxury, safe in old St Omer,
Flashing Red Tabs, Brass and Ribbons Galore,
What the Hell do they know about fighting a War?

CSM Sidney Chaplin
4th Battalion, Gloucestershire Regiment.

In an old Australian homestead
With roses round the door
A girl received a letter
From a far and distant shore.
With her mother's arms around her
'Neath the blue Australian skies
She slowly read the letter
And the tears fell from her eyes.

'Why do I weep?
Why do I pray?
My love's asleep so far away
He played his part
That Autumn day
And left my heart
On Suvla Bay.'

2ND LIEUTENANT G. D. HORRIDGE,
1st/5th Battalion,
Lancashire Fusiliers (TF).

After the battles of 4 and 6 June the land in between the trenches was covered with dead. As the Turkish firing was almost incessant at night, and the dead were so numerous, it was impossible to bury a big proportion of them. It was a horrible job to do, because the very hot sun had caused very quick decomposition. The flies bred there until their number was tremendous. At night they lived on the dead and in the daytime they just buzzed around our trenches. They attacked our food remorselessly. In order to eat one had to wave one's hand about over the food and then bite suddenly, or a fly came with it. Any bit of food uncovered was blotted out of sight by flies in a couple of seconds. This was frightfully trying, and the contamination made everyone ill. Typhoid and dysentery were rife. Those that didn't get either had very unpleasant tummy trouble and were continually on the trot.

Our food now was something different. Bread was being baked, so the dog biscuits disappeared. Desiccated vegetables had been introduced and there was an alternative to bully beef in Maconachie's rations. However, the illness that the flies caused took away any appetite and I remember that eventually the smell of cooked desiccated vegetables as the meals were brought down the trenches was almost nauseating.

By July the troops had been fighting on Gallipoli for more than two months, clinging to the rough precipitous coastline, unable to penetrate the Turkish outposts and defences – often only yards away – unable to advance across the mountainous land that barred the way to the upper reaches of the Dardanelles. It was impossible fighting country and mere reinforcements were not enough to relieve the pressure. It was decided to mount a second expedition, to land troops further north at Suvla Bay where the terrain, at least initially, was easier, where defences were few and the Turks could be taken by surprise. The landing was planned to take place on 10 August, under the command of General Stopford, an officer of advanced years and vacillating disposition. There was little initial resistance, but Stopford failed to press the advance and the enterprise was doomed from the start.

SERGEANT WATSON,
8th (S) Battalion,
Northumberland Fusiliers.

We got our instructions before we left Lemnos that we hadn't to fire a shot; we had to take the Turks' positions and trenches at the point of the bayonet, and we were each given a white armlet to wear, pinned to one of our arms. The order was if we saw anybody without an armlet in the dark, we were to stick the bayonet into them. This was one of the biggest blunders we made as it was a fine target for the Turk in the dark.

Everything was quite peaceful until the Captain of the Destroyer shouted, 'Cast off the lighters'. As soon as the Captain had shouted, the Turks opened fire with their machine-guns and rifle fire – also artillery. There was a lot of poor fellows killed and wounded before we left the lighters. The lighters took us as near the shore as they dared, then we had to get into the small rowing boats rowed by the Naval Division. They rowed us until we were about fifteen or twenty yards from the shore, then we had to jump into the sea, up to the waist in water.

I always remember the first lighter going out with a load – about five minutes later it returned full of our lads badly wounded. We had to wade for the shore and I remember carrying the Vickers machine-gun on my shoulders when I got near the beach and fell over a tripwire which the Turks had put in the sea for that purpose and nearly all the rifles were useless after they had been in the water. The shore was thick with dead and wounded – there were dozens of chaps who never got out of the water.

It was bad enough in the dark, but ten times worse when it got daylight. Just at the break of day we had got safely landed and the Turks had retreated over the Salt Lake (a name given to a stretch of land which was white as snow with the salt left after the tides from the sea had been up). Our objective was a small hill to our left, which we called Hill Ten; we took it after very heavy losses. I always remember our old Colonel (Lieutenant-Colonel Fishburn) was hit in the shoulder and leg. I was close beside him when he fell to the ground wounded. When he was lying there he took off his cork helmet and waved it to encourage us fellows on, saying, 'Go on the same old "Fifth"'! [The Northumberland Fusiliers were the old 5th Regiment of Foot.] We kept the Turks on the run straight over the Salt Lake, then we rested for the night. The Turk made one or two counter-attacks on us through the night, but we repulsed him every time. The next day we tried to take another of his positions but we failed with heavy losses. It was too steep to get to his positions under such heavy machine-gun and rifle fire – also from his field guns.

We hadn't any field guns with us up to now. They landed a few days later – old-fashioned guns like they used in the African War. We got many a good laugh at them! When they fired a shot the explosion caused them to run backwards down the hillsides, and our gunners were running for their lives after them, and running them back into action again. At night times we were told off for Ration Parties to fetch the food and water from the beach. Water was very scarce out there. On these Ration Parties a good few of the party were killed or wounded with shell or rifle fire. The Turkish snipers claimed a good few. It was an awful sight on the beach with wounded lying about waiting to be taken on the hospital ships. I saw our poor old Colonel still lying there on the beach.

6 August.

After a few days' preparation during which bayonets were sharpened and encased with hessian, except for the points, and battle rations issued, on the evening of 6 August, the Brigade fell in to bid farewell to Monash Valley Area. At nine the head of the column marched out from Reserve Gully down towards the beach, and turned northwards to follow the beach for about two miles to the mouth of Aghyl Dere Valley, where it was intended to advance.

CAPTAIN T. A. WHITE
13th Battalion,
Australian Imperial Force.

Like a long, dark caterpillar the column moved through the intense darkness. The Aegean Sea could be dimly seen, rising up to the horizon as if to fall on us, and on it were the shapeless blotches of warships; overhead were stars in a cloudy sky, and on our right were cliffs illuminated by a searchlight from the *Colne* in order to blind the Turks who might be venturing to gaze beachwards in spite of the shells she was pouring into their lighted trenches. The gunboat had been playing this game on the Turks every night of late in order to get them used to the nightly stunt with the idea that they would retire to their dugouts until the strafe was over. Had those sailors accidentally slipped their lights onto us just a few feet lower than its beam, there would have been a different story to tell, but no one felt uncomfortable about that light. The attack had already commenced on our right and behind us, and we came in for a share of the 'overs', bullets caused several casualties in the column, and many shells screaming overhead into the sea. It was an eerie feeling to be marching in column over ground where by day no one could safely show his head.

This night became more intensely dark as the head of the column turned its back to the sea and our Scouts ran against an enemy post which was quickly rushed by them and the leading Platoon, giving us twenty prisoners. In the darkness we had turned up into Taylor's Gap instead of into Aghyl Dere, another 500 yards ahead. It was perhaps a fortunate mistake, for we cut off a Turkish outpost on Walden Point. The Turks fired heavily into and over us. The column halted while A Company went ahead to clear the way. No. 3 Platoon charged and soon had the Turks running, following them up the valley until they were fired on from another bank. Dozens of shadowy figures could be seen moving about in the dim starlight. Lee ordered two of his sections to cover the advance of the other two with rifle fire – the only possible way to advance here. The Turks were soon routed, but Lee and many of his gallant men had become casualties. No. 4 Platoon was doing similar work on the North of the Dere, so A Company were soon all engaged. B and C were also soon drawn into these outpost fights. Overton was shot dead at the head of the column at short range. The men nearest him rushed the enemy, a few more Turkish shots rang out above the crunching of the brushwood, a few agonised 'Allahs!' and silence until more crunching told that our men were again advancing. Still the Turks challenged from both sides of the narrow valley. Lieutenant H. Ford led his Platoon over ridge after ridge, climbing up by hanging on to prickly shrubs, charging the enemy flashes before chasing the runaways into other inky valleys. It would take a book to describe the work of the various Platoons that night, charging grimly up cliffs under the barrels of the enemy, and, without a word, cheer or shot, clearing the way at the point of the silent bayonet, that saved the march from being a disaster, but the 13th had lost eleven killed and fifty-nine wounded in and near Taylor's Gap, Aghyl Dere and Australia Valley.

PRIVATE LEONARD HART
1st Otago Infantry, Battalion, 5th New Zealand, Reinforcements.

We arrived at the outpost to which we had been directed with a loss of three or four men, wounded, and feeling pretty tired, for, besides our eighty pounds of gear we had had to carry boxes of ammunition (a box between two) as well. Sari Bahr, where we were ordered to reinforce our chaps, was about a mile from where we then were and the route which we were to take led up through a deep valley. We had advanced up this valley about half a mile, the Canterbury Company in advance, when the inevitable shrapnel began to burst over our heads. The valley was very narrow in this part, the hills rising almost perpendicularly on either side. A regiment of Tommies, who were making their way down the valley, met us at this point and with everyone trying to get out of the way of the shrapnel at the same time an indescribable mix-up occurred. The Turks made their fire hotter than ever and I do not know to this day how I escaped being hit. Men were falling all round me, and the Tommies, who were all Irishmen, got fairly mad with excitement. How we finally extricated ourselves from the mêlée I don't know but we did it somehow. A party was told off to look after the wounded, many of whom must have been badly trampled on. How the Turks knew that we were coming up I don't know. It is marvellous how they find out such things. We were now almost up to the firing line and the sight that presented itself is one which I shall never forget. There were dead and wounded lying everywhere. The wounded were so numerous that it had been impossible to cope with them all, and many had lain there since the Saturday. About thirty of our company were told off as stretcher-bearers and the remainder of us sent straight into the trenches. The events of the next few days I have not a very clear recollection of, except that it was little else but blazing away at the Turkish trenches to keep them quiet. We all learnt what real hunger and thirst are like. On Tuesday morning the remains of the Auckland and Wellington battalions were relieved from the trenches on Hill 971 (Chunuk Bair) by two regiments of Tommies (Hampshire Yeomanry and the Warwicks). These trenches were a little to the right of the position we were holding and it was this Tuesday night that Sari Bahr was lost. The Turks attacked in great force and after a short struggle drove the Tommies out of the trenches and occupied them. They then made a half-hearted attack on our position but were met with such a dose of rifle and machine-gun fire that they cleared back to their trenches at the double. In case you may have heard different, I may say that we never at any time held the whole of the great ridge known as Sari Bahr, but the most important part of it, known as Chunuk Bair, was in our hands and it was from our position here that, had we been able to hold it, we could have dominated practically the whole southern portion of the peninsula. Much blame and ill feeling has been created between the Colonials and Tommies over them not putting up a better fight when the Turks attacked, but I am inclined to think that, judging by the frightful losses sustained by the Wellington and Auckland battalions while holding the position, we would not have done much better. During these days our losses had been very heavy and a number of our men had been taken bad with dysentery and enteric fever. The smell of the bodies was becoming intolerable and the flies swarmed in millions. When a man was killed in the trenches all that could be done was to throw him up on the parapet and leave him until we could spare time at night to bury him. There we remained until relieved by the Australians a fortnight later. That fortnight was one of continual hard graft. Our numbers had been so much cut down by now that there were not enough men for the reserves, the result being that we had to do our twenty-four hours in the firing line, eight hours in the supports, and sixteen hours pick and shovel. This made only eight hours sleep out of forty-eight and the condition of the men after a fortnight of this can well be imagined. Many of them, especially those who remained of the main body and second, third and fourth reinforcements, broke down completely and had to be sent away. If we had not been relieved when we were there would have been hardly any men left to hold the place, for hardly a man amongst us was in any way fit to stand it.

We could plainly see the Tommies charging across the flat under a perfect mass of bursting shells and shrapnel. The scrub with which the flat was covered had caught fire and I afterwards heard that many of the wounded, unable to escape, were burnt to death in it. At one point I saw the Tommies charge right through the burning scrub with shrapnel bursting over them in clouds. The chaps who fell at this point would at least not have had to wait for the fire to creep up on them as some of the other poor beggars had to do.
Leonard Hart

'In August and September seventy-eight per cent of the troops were said to be suffering from dysentery and other intestinal complaints, sixty-four per cent had septic sores, and fifty per cent of the old troops who had been longest on the Peninsula showed symptoms of cardiac debility.'

Medical History of the War

*5 September. Today being a holiday, Company Commanders had to
go to St Omer to see how to kill our fellow creature with gas.*
                                  Captain W.G. Bagot Chester

◆

The firefly haunts were lighted yet,
    As we scaled the top of the parapet;
But the east grew pale to another fire,
    As our bayonets gleamed by the foeman's wire;
And the sky was tinged with gold and grey,
    And under our feet the dead men lay,
Stiff by the loop-holed barricade;
    Food of the bomb and the hand-grenade;
Still in the slushy pool and mud –
Ah, the path we came was a path of blood,
    When we went to Loos in the morning.

                Patrick MacGill, Loos, 1915.

◆

24 September. Left for trenches. A fine night with moon and clouds.
There are two extremes for the attack about to come off. If the wind is
favourable it will take place at 6 a.m., preceded by shell-gas, but if the
wind shows no signs of changing, there will be a night attack at 3 a.m.
We hope to do the day attack, as we have been induced to place great
confidence in the gas.

CAPTAIN W.G. BAGOT
CHESTER,
3rd Queen Alexandra's
Own Gurkha Rifles,
(The Sirmoor Rifles).

    At 12 midnight a message came through to say the 6 a.m. scheme
would be used, so we then went to sleep for a few hours, wondering
how many of us would be left to sleep tomorrow night. The attack
orders were:

5.00 a.m. Intensive Artillery bombardment.
5.30 a.m. Gas let loose. Assaulting infantry crowd into front trenches.
Smoke bombs thrown over parapet.
5.58 a.m. Gas cut off. Mine under German trenches blown up.

Diary of
SIR DOUGLAS HAIG.

Saturday, 25 September. I went out at 5 a.m. Almost a calm. Alan Fletcher lit a cigarette and the smoke drifted in puffs towards the NE. Staff Officers of Corps were ordered to stand by in case it were necessary to counter order to attack. At one time, owing to the calm, I feared the gas might simply hang about *our* trenches. However, at 5.15 a.m. I said 'carry on'. I went on top of our wooden look-out tower. The wind came gently from SW and by 5.40 had increased slightly. The leaves of the poplar trees gently rustled. This seemed satisfactory. But what a risk I must run of gas blowing back upon our own dense masses of troops!

MJR. H. F. BIDDER,
DSO,
Royal Sussex Regiment.

On the evening of 24 September I went across to the machine-gun position I intended to be with when the curtain rose. It consisted of a narrow, winding connecting trench, four good big dugouts, and six gun positions. It commanded a splendid view, the ground dropping in front, and then rising to the ridge on which Hulluch and Loos are – bare, open ground, seamed chalk parapets. The high road ran close by, into and through the German trenches. The panorama stretched from the Hohenzollern Redoubt to the Souchez hills. I hoped for a bit of sleep.

No such luck – I had to spend the entire night tinkering at old machine-guns and trying to make them work.

Dawn came on, misty and damp. We were to fire through the intensive bombardment just before the attack. At the given hour we started.

The light was growing; and then one noticed little wisps of white smoke at close intervals along our line. These grew longer and spread, joined and formed a wall, blotting out the other side of the valley (we had ceased firing now). The wall grew higher and higher, drifted in rolls very slowly towards the German lines, not as a blank mist, but as a mass of rolling curls of smoke, stretching away, mile after mile, till they merged in the dim clouds beyond Souchez.

It was like a Doré illustration to some scene in Hell.

The moment came when we knew our infantry had started. The noticeable thing was that there was hardly any answering artillery fire. At last the cloud moved far enough on for us to see the German parapet – and after a time I definitely saw the Highlanders on it. It was ours – but at no small cost, for Germans had been left, sniping and machine-gunning up to the last.

Our work was over, and the machine-guns went to join their battalions.

As I got back to HQ the horse guns were coming into action. They looked splendid: three batteries galloped down the slope over the grass – unlimbered – their teams galloped back, and the guns started firing. After all these months of sitting behind barbed wire it made a lump rise in one's throat.

CAPTAIN W.G. BAGOT CHESTER,
3rd Queen Alexandra's
Own Gurkha Rifles,
(The Sirmoor Rifles).

6 a.m. Assaulting infantry cross parapet. Towards morning the wind, which it was hoped would favour us, seemed to be blowing, what little there was of it, from the German trenches towards us. However, the order was to let loose the gas, but when those in charge of the cylinders turned on the taps, clouds of gas blew backwards. My throat became very sore. One of the gas men in the traverse in which I was standing, keeping an eye on my watch, became overcome and was lying at my feet groaning horribly. I was counting the seconds to 6 o'clock, and then I gave the signal to cross the parapet, I think we were all glad to get out of our trench full of gas. The distance to the front German trench was about 200 yards. For the first eighty the air was thick with smoke from the smoke bombs, but as we emerged into view of the Hun, they let drive at us. I found my men dropping all round me, and when I reached the German wire I was practically alone, and found myself with one or two others literally running along the outside cage of the German wire searching for a way through. Our Artillery had not, as we hoped, laid the wire entanglements flat, at any rate on my front. A moment later I felt a blow on my right shoulder, and over I went. Fortunately I fell close to a 'pip-squeak' hole. It was very shallow and small and already occupied by one of my wounded men.

Well! it didn't take a moment to realise the attack had failed hopelessly, and there was nothing to be done but to lie low as if dead for the rest of the day. There was only room in the hole to keep our heads and bodies below the level of the ground; our legs had to remain outside. Budhiman was my comrade in the shell hole. It was not long before I heard a squeal of pain. He got hit a second time. Next hit was my turn, and a piece of iron landed on my right groin. Now and then we would hear the thud of a bullet hitting the ground within a few inches of our heads. The Huns were doing their best to finish us off. The next thing to interest me was a piece of iron which hit me in my left foot, and yet another later on landed in my left leg, just below the knee.

PTE. W. H. NIXON, DCM,
2nd Battalion,
The Cheshire Regiment.

We went over. We'd got nothing to fight with. We'd got three machine-guns in our Battalion, that's all. I've got a bag of Mills bombs, that's all, twelve, we were rationed out, don't waste anything if you can help it, kind of thing. So when we went over at Loos I'd got twelve bombs, my rifle, 150 rounds of ammunition (plenty of ammunition) and we hadn't got half-way when Jerry started machine-gunning. He'd got a machine-gun every yard and there we were, three machine-guns, we'd got a few bombs. If a bullet had hit us, that was it, I'd have been blown to smithereens. I heard Tommy Winkler go 'Ah!' He was my mate – and he was gone – just like that.

We got to a big trench and I could hear them jabbering away. It was a vital trench. It was overlooking ours and it was our objective to try and get it, but every yard there was either a bomb thrower there or a machine-gun. We were outnumbered completely. I got under the wire and got to within twenty yards of the trench and I heard somebody shout, 'The Cheshires have retired,' and I looked round and there was nobody there! I just crawled on my hands and knees and got back in the trench. We got annihilated. There was nobody left. I was the only bomber left out of the whole Company.

---◆---

The turret towers that stood in the air,
    Sheltered a foeman sniper there –
They found, who fell to the sniper's aim,
    A field of death on the field of fame;
And stiff in khaki the boys were laid
    To the sniper's toll at the barricade,
But the quick went clattering through the town,
    Shot at the sniper and brought him down,
As we entered Loos in the morning.
                    Patrick Macgill,
                    Loos, 1915.

---◆---

We had five nights of marching down to Loos. Our Company Commander, Captain Powell, called together the Companies and addressed us and he told us that there was a battle raging, several Divisions had been in action and one Scottish Division had been on the outskirts of Lens. We were going up to relieve them. I can still remember the cheers. We never thought what was in front of us. A little later, we were issued with bread and cheese rations to last us for two days. We were told not to touch them until ordered. As we marched towards Loos the pace became a crawl owing to the shell holes, and the enemy was still shelling.

On the way up to the line, the Adjutant stopped me. He said, 'The CO's got a message for you to take up.' I can remember the words of

PRIVATE HARRY
    FELLOWES,
12 (S) Battalion,
Northumberland Fusiliers.

this message even to this day. It was written on an old signal pad. It wasn't dated or signed, it just said, 'The CO wishes the attack to be carried out with the bayonet in the true Northumbrian fashion'. It was the first I heard that we were going into action. When I got to the trenches all the lads were standing with fixed bayonets and as I walked through the back they started to climb out of the trench, running as fast as the equipment would ever allow. They were just a mob! I was looking for Captain Powell to give him the message, and then I realised he was up there with the lads, so I followed on. The leading men would be about 100 yards from the German wire and till then not a shot had been fired. Suddenly all hell was let loose. Some men began to stumble and fall, machine-guns were firing from the front of us and enfilading from the left-hand side from some Germans. A lad in front of me went down, shot in the head, and I tripped and fell over him. To this day I don't feel any shame – I stayed where I was.

I'll remember the sight until my dying day, the whole slope was full of prone figures. The Germans had suddenly stopped firing, just like they'd begun. Men started to rise to their feet, some stumbled and crawled any way to try and get back. Still the Germans never fired. Shortly afterwards I remember there was a report that the German General in charge of the area had said that his machine-gunners had refused to fire another shot. They were so filled with bitter remorse and guilt at the corpses at Loos that they refused to fire another shot. I do believe this.

When I got back in the trench I landed in the same place where I'd left. One of the lads handed me a water bottle. We lay there and it was awful listening to the cries of the men on that field, some were screaming. Terrible! I'm afraid a lot were dead before the night.

All this time I still had the message for Captain Powell. I didn't find him until afterwards. As a matter of fact, he was the only officer we had left in the Company, and I found him when we got back to Vermelles. I went up to him and I apologised and I told him I was sorry, I had a message for him. I gave him this message. He read it. He said, 'It doesn't matter, Sonny, now.' I could see tears running down his cheeks.

PRIVATE CARSON
STEWART,
7th (S) Battalion,
The Queen's Own
Cameron Highlanders.

When they took the Roll Call after Loos those not answering, their chums would answer, 'Over the Hill'. Also when the post and parcels that had arrived from Home were being dished out after Loos, we new arrivals got share of the parcels that were meant for the boys who got killed.

**THE BATTLE OF LOOS
CASUALTIES**

25 September to 16 October

**KILLED AND MISSING 15,800
WOUNDED 34,580**

FOR KING

HE BRAVELY AND NOBLY DIED IN THE CAUSE THAT HE KNEW WAS GOOD AND RIGHT

FOR COUNTRY

*Somewhere in France, beloved they have laid you,
In that sad land beyond the Channel blue,
Lonely, yet not alone, for all around you
Sleep your brave comrades, trusted, tried and true.*

*'Somewhere in France' – Oh surely my beloved,
Tho' sign and token all be swept away,
It is not in that land of desolation,
But in my heart that you will rest alway.*

*And though I know there's a hasty grave,
With a poor little cross at its head,
And the gold of his youth he so gladly gave,
Yet to me he'll never be dead.*

*And the sun in my Devon lane will be gay,
And my boy will be with me still,
So I'm finding the heart to smile and say,
Oh God, if it be Thy will.*

*For Peace must be bought with blood and tears,
And the boys of our hearts must pay.*

Composed in Loving Memory of Private R.B.
Lister, M.M., Late 1st Cambridgeshire Regiment,
killed in action in France, aged 23 years.

'Until the day dawns.'

OXFORD – Empty Colleges.
Oxford colleges have just begun their Christmas term. There will be
about 250 freshmen as compared with 571 last year. The average
number of freshmen between 1910 and 1913 was 934. Keble College
has the largest number of freshmen with 22.
Daily Mail (Overseas Edition), *23 October 1915*

◆

*The British Commanders had undertaken the Battle of Loos reluctantly on direct
instructions from the Secretary of State for War, Lord Kitchener, who wished for
political reasons to do everything possible to help the French in their offensive against
Vimy Ridge on the right of the newly extended British line. But they had strong
misgivings. The Regular troops at their disposal were mostly replacements, their
officers newly promoted and inexperienced and the few recently arrived Kitchener's
battalions were, at best, half-trained. The shell and gun shortage had eased but not
sufficiently to guarantee the success of a major offensive. The lines of communication
were bad and, in the event, the gains were infinitesimal. But the troops had at least
succeeded in breaking the German line for the first time in the war and despite the
huge casualties they were not despondent. Much was made of each small advance.
The battle dragged on in a weary pattern of attack and counter-attack, losses and
recaptures, until the serious fighting was quenched by the rains of late autumn. It had
been the blooding of Kitchener's Army and the first casualties among 'Our Boys' who
had sailed for France so cheerily a matter of weeks before.*

◆

We cannot but think of the large number, no less than 100,000
Britons alone, who have laid down their lives during the past 14
months of the War for their King and Country. May they rest in
peace. They are better off we trust but our loss is irreparable. 'The
souls of the righteous are in the hand of God and there shall no
torment touch them. In the sight of the unwise they seemed to die
and their departure was taken for misery. But they are at peace.'
Your sincere friend,
H. G. Bird
Newdigate Parish Magazine

RIFLEMAN BERT
BAILEY
11th Battalion,
Rifle Brigade

Wednesday, 27 October

My Darling Wife,

Another night has passed and another morning come and I am still in trenches and in good health. Although all day and night on Monday it rained steadily yet Tuesday (yesterday) morning broke fair and fine and we had a nice day except that underneath everything was mud and slosh. We were employed all the morning and afternoon in putting down boards along the trenches and have greatly improved it for walking. As I stopped to rest awhile I could not help being struck by the exceptional beauty of the moon as the clouds kept flitting past. The moon was nearly full, partially obscured by the thin fleecy clouds but these soon passed by and after a spell of clear shining the great black billows slowly closed in until it could only be seen shining dimly through a great rift in the clouds, then the whole closed up. The sky at that spot was absolutely black, but there was no rain, and although the great black ugly side was turned to me I knew the other side must be shimmering with the pure white light. Let us hope that this time of our lives is like that, a great dark cloud which passes away, so that afterwards the light is brighter than before. It has been raining in fitful showers all this morning up till now (ten o'clock) and we have not had to fall in for working yet.

Just a few words now about your last parcel. I don't often mention everything, but I do appreciate the rag you send me, it is so very useful. The piece this week is lovely and I make a very shrewd guess that, when I am using it as a tablecloth, it was not always used for that purpose but once formed part of my lady's – 'Oh dear, oh dear', what am I saying? – nevertheless it is grand to wrap my bread in and keep my food clean and nice. *Cigarettes – capital* but don't send any more until I ask you to. *Toffee, condensed milk, candles, rice and potted meat:* the toffee, milk, rice and one candle have all gone. Potted meat for tea today, candle tonight if necessary. The Oxo cubes will be very nice to augment my soup with no doubt. Don't send me any more Oxo or Bovril until I ask you to, Darling, will you. The little pat of butter is always welcome, and the bread dodge I think is an improvement on buying expensive cakes. Of course a little home-made cake is nice, but I was never a lover of cake. Good substitutes for things I have asked you not to send would be sardines, pickles or a bit of cheese. Please discontinue sending tea, sugar and salt for a bit, Darling, as I have plenty. Don't think I am trying to economise and stint myself because it is not that, and it all helps us, dear, doesn't it? And you never know I may want something ever so expensive one of these times, eh, what!

Now my little Darling you must be patient with me won't you and don't get cross because I have been having a lot to say about the parcels. You are a pet to send them and you know you asked me to guide you as to what I most required, didn't you?

That pastry of your own make was absolutely A1, and a perfect success – and she's the little girl who said, 'Oh, I can only cook a plain dinner'. One great thing is off my mind and that is that I need never fear for my life in the future when you send me or make me pastry!

The weather has remained fine all the afternoon and let's hope it will be fine tonight. A cold night's bad, but a wet cold night is worse. You must not worry about me, Darling, because I am just as able to look after myself as the other chaps. So, dearest little one, just keep cheerful and enjoy yourself all you can, and wrap up now the cold is here. If you require new clothes in the way of overcoat or mac or gloves or anything in fact for the winter, don't let yourself go short will you? Just take it from the cash and note it in the book as I told you, so that we can see how the cash is made up for the sake of keeping proper accounts. Now, love, I will answer the other letters later. I'm afraid I twaddle a lot but never mind.

                    I remain
                        ever your own devoted
                            Bert.

Rifleman Bert Bailey (11th Battalion, Rifle Brigade) was killed the same evening, a few hours after writing this letter to his young wife. Married 5 June 1915 on his embarkation leave.

                    60th Field Ambulance,
                    France.
                    October 30th, 1915.

Dear Mr Bailey,
It is with the deepest regret and sorrow that I write to sympathise with you upon the death of your son.

It was my painful duty to conduct the burial service yesterday. It was a sad blow to the whole of his Company when they heard that he had been killed for he was deservedly popular with everybody. His real Christian influence will be greatly missed.

I had come to know him as a real friend and it was always a pleasure to chat with him and to have him at our services.

Your sorrow will be very deep. But I pray that the heavy weight of sorrow may be eased by the knowledge that he was a true Christian and a true soldier and such sacrifice as his has made us all the nobler. You will meet him again when all tears shall be wiped away.

God bless you all.
                    I am,
                    Yours sincerely,
                    C. E. James (Wesleyan Chaplain).

'*Our Dear Bert was killed at 10 p.m. He was the leading one of a covering party mending the wire of the trenches. They were surprised by a German patrol and Bert was shot in the chest by machine-gun and bombed on his head – fire bombs.*

Captain James buried him on Friday 28th in a little cemetery at the "back of trenches".'

From the diary of Mrs Lucilla Bailey photographed at Bert's grave in Rue Bacquerat cemetery in 1924, just before the original cross was replaced by a War Graves headstone.

If your sleeping place is damp,
       Never mind!
If you wake up with a cramp,
       Never mind!
If your trench should fall in some
Fill your ears and make you dumb
While the sergeant drinks your rum,
       Never mind!

If you have to rise at four,
       Never mind!
If the morning's dark and raw,
       Never mind!
If a duck-board should elope,
And your container has no rope,
And you have to wade and grope,
       Never mind!

Keep a steady upper lip,
       And you'll find,
Every cloud you like to rip
       Silver lined.
Though the skies are looking grey,
It is ten to one there may
Be a parcel on the way,
       Never mind!

RQMSE Clark, 13th Battalion,
The Rifle Brigade.

TROOPER SYDNEY CHAPLIN,
1st Northamptonshire Yeomanry.

No one looking at this green and lovely country with the Somme flowing slowly along could ever imagine that it would be, before the war ended, the last resting place of thousands of poor mothers' sons.

At the end of September all the billets were taken over by French soldiers and we moved back towards Corbie. We took over a tract of land beside the river. We had no shelter so did our best to make bivouacs with ground sheets propped up with branches from trees. Three of us got together and with the three ground sheets over us, one blanket on the ground, and two to cover us at night, it wasn't too bad for a start – but when it rained we had to sit up all night. As Christmas drew near things got worse, the mist rising from the water soaked everything. The horses stood dejected and miserable on the lines. Sleep was impossible.

We would doze for a short while then the cold would wake us up. Our feet were like blocks of ice.

One morning I well remember, we turned out for morning stables. Horses all mud! Our feet and hands were numb and we could hardly hold the grooming brushes. Along comes the Orderly Officer from his civvy billet up the road. Riding boots, a lined overcoat, a large thick scarf round his neck – in other words, muffled up to the eyebrows – and, you can bet, a nice hot drink before he turned out! He looked at us all shivering in the cold damp air, then bellowed forth: 'Get them bloody tunics off and get stuck into the grooming. That's the way to get warm!' We could have cheerfully murdered him.

However, we moved back into our old billets before Christmas. The French had made them much more comfortable which suited the troops.

The 24th of December came. My turn to collect the mail from Mericourt Station. I arrived early, as an Expeditionary Force canteen had been set up in the station yard, the first we had seen, and I had been requested to get a few things. The mail was due in about 4.30 p.m., but the hours dragged on and nothing happened. The train arrived eventually about 1 a.m. on Christmas morning.

I soon had the Yeomanry mail on the limber and the horses did not waste any time getting back to Sailly. Here I found Bill Papworth, our Corporal, and the lads waiting. Bill decided to deliver the mail there and then, so we carried the mail bags to the farm.

'Mail Ho!' shouts Bill. What an uproar! Candles were lighted and all the lads gathered round us. Bill called out the names. Parcels were unpacked and letters opened. It was great to see the faces of the lads in the flickering light of the candles. Then the last bag was empty – with several who had not received anything looking wistfully on. However, with the usual comradeship of C Squadron, first one then the other shared their parcels with them, and off we went back to our billet leaving everyone happy. Was it worth while? I'll say it was!

A few days later all the Squadron sat down to a meal in the café. The cooks had done a fine job in providing a first-class meal from rations saved and some birds and pork purchased locally. Each man also received a generous tot of rum, and beer could be obtained. As it happened, I had to go to Mericourt and was late getting back, so when I arrived at the café dinner had started, and as far as I could see there was no place for me to sit.

As I stood looking round, a shout came from Captain Litchfield. 'Over here, Chaplin,' and he had a spare seat next to him. So I was soon supplied. My rum also came, and as the Scotch was handed to the officers the Captain handed me a snorter as well. Yes, I enjoyed that dinner!

You love us when we're heroes, home on leave,
Or wounded in a mentionable place.
You worship decorations; You believe
That chivalry redeems the war's disgrace.
You make us shells. You listen with delight,
By tales of dirt and danger fondly thrilled.
You crown our distant ardours while we fight,
And mourn our laurelled memories when we're killed.
You can't believe that British troops "retire"
When hell's last horror breaks them, and they run,
Trampling the terrible corpses – blind with blood.

O German mother dreaming by the fire,
While you are knitting socks to send your son
His face is trodden deeper in the mud.

Siegfried Sassoon

COMFORTS FOR OUR BATTALION

We hear from the Front that in addition to socks, mufflers and mittens (with thumb only) will be greatly appreciated. We hope that committees of ladies will be formed in different Companies and districts and forward *quickly* to the Headquarters' Chaplain both mittens and mufflers. The Battalion wants 1,200 of each before the end of the month. If kind friends cannot get to work, will they please send him a donation to buy mufflers and mittens.

Church Lads Brigade Gazette, December 1915

CONFIDENTIAL
140th Infantry Brigade

The GOC directs me to remind you of the unauthorised truce which occurred on Christmas Day at one or two places in the line last year, and to impress upon you that nothing of the kind is to be allowed on the Divisional Front this year.

The Artillery will maintain a slow gun fire on the enemy's trenches commencing at dawn, and every opportunity will as usual be taken to inflict casualties upon any of the enemy exposing themselves.
19th Decr. 1915.

(Sd.) B. BURNETT HITCHCOCK,
Lt. Colonel, General Staff, 47th (London) Division

THE HISTORY OF A
PAIR OF MITTENS

GEMEINER
ERNST BERGNER,
143rd Infantie Regiment.

Already a year since the 143rd Regiment arrived in the Ypres area. The worst time was the winter of 1914 till spring 1915.

As far as the knees we were in the ice-cold water. We didn't know what a dugout was. A lot of the time we huddled together when it was snowing, during the long winter nights. Now we are in front of Hill 60 and it's Christmas Evening 1915, our company is in the second line in the concrete bunkers. We worked ourselves into a sweat making this. Every sack of cement and sand must be dragged along 'Knuppeldamm'. We lost a lot of comrades by enemy shrapnel.

In the cemetery near 'Drei Hauser' and in 'Ten Brielen' we buried a lot of good comrades in the cold earth; 'They rest in peace'. Now we are sitting in the bunker, our work has not been in vain. Snow is covering the earth, we are homesick for wife, children and sister. Now it's Christmas for the second time in this war. Along the front line all is quiet, only some rifle-bullets are crossing the air like lashes. It's three o'clock in the afternoon. I have to look for a Christmas tree, without a tree there is no Christmas. I fill my pipe, take my trench stick and pick-axe and go to the exit of the trench. I jump over the parapet, I look for the most beautiful tree and after three hews of the axe, I take the tree under my arm and go up to Hill 60.

It's a wonderful winter day, there is a rare silence over the Front.

What would be the life at home in a little town on Christmas Eve? Everybody would be in a hurry, going home with presents under the arm. And here I am alone with my tree in the small trench. Only the crosses of the fallen comrades in the autumn battles are covering our trenches.

I am received with joy by the comrades in our bunker. The tree is placed in the middle of the room. Some candles are fixed on the branches and an old steel helmet. The festival can start. Night is coming over.

CORPORAL C. COLES,
1st Battalion
Coldstream Guards.

I was in my dugout having a bit of a fry-up for breakfast, and my sentry called out, 'Corp, Corp, they're over the top.' I rushed out and stood on the firing platform and the Germans had no arms of any kind. They were waving. First one German walked over in No Man's Land and one or two of our boys did the same. And in the middle of No Man's Land they were shaking hands and one or two could speak English. I didn't see all that was going on, that was reported to me by my boys and they was exchanging souvenirs and I got one souvenir, it was a full-sized photo of a German-Prussian Guard with his helmet and coat on. They said, 'We have to fire, but we'll fire high' and you could hear the *ping ping* going above your head.

It lasted all day Christmas, after the first hour. What stopped the troops was our officers, except one. He was a Lieutenant and he went over the top and he got sent home in disgrace. But the likes of Captain Dickie and Humphrey de Trafford, they wasn't having that. They sent through to the Artillery. The Artillery fired 18-pounders on No Man's

Land where we were, stopping the thing altogether. The Germans retired and we went back in our trench. Well, the Germans wasn't going to be done! It was Christmas Day to their idea, and in the evening, well, we had in our dugouts braziers like oil drums with holes in and coke and suddenly we looked across the trenches and they was placing their braziers all along the parapet. So we did the same, and it was just like Fleet Street on Christmas Night. It was a wonderful sight. I shall never forget it.

We had an order from GHQ saying that it was hoped that there would be no repetition of the regrettable recurrences of last Christmas Day, and that any German who ventured to show himself was to be shot at once. We subsequently heard that the Huns had a similar order. Opposite us there was no attempt at a truce, and no insulting messages were shouted across. On our right the French, after singing carols most of the night, and the Huns replying, did go out for about three minutes, and as soon as they got back put over covey upon covey of rifle grenades. A true conception of the Christian spirit!

Day carried on as usual, except that we did have plum pudding, flaming with rum, for our dinner.

LIEUTENANT GORDON
   BARBER,
1st Battalion,
The Queen's Own
   Cameron Highlanders,
1st Brigade,
1st Division.

◆

Confidential
XI CORPS
I much regret to report that in spite of special orders there was some communication held between the lines occupied by the Guards Division and the 13th Bavarian Reserve Regt. this morning.

I have seen the Brigadiers concerned who were on the spot within twenty minutes of hearing of the episode, and our men were back in the trenches within thirty to forty minutes after first going out.

I have ordered a full and searching enquiry to be made tomorrow as to how my implicit orders came to be disobeyed, which I will forward in due course.

Large parties of unarmed Germans were the first to appear but this is no excuse, and I regret the incident more than I can say.

Our Artillery fired throughout the day as ordered.
25.12.15.   (Signed) Cavan Maj. Gen.

Report by MAJOR-
   GENERAL CAVAN,
Commanding Guards
   Division.

◆

17 December.
(Buckingham Palace),
King George V to Sir
Douglas Haig.

My Dear Haig,

I take the earliest opportunity of expressing the great satisfaction with which I approved of your succeeding Sir John French as Commander in Chief of my Army in France.

I know you will have the confidence of the troops serving under you, and it is almost needless to assure you with what implicit trust I look forward to the successful conduct of the war on the Western Front under your able direction.

Remember that it will always be a pleasure to me to help you in any way I can, to carry out your heavy task and important responsibilities.

I hope you will from time to time write to me quite freely and tell me how matters are progressing. Naturally I shall consider your letters in the strictest confidence.

I saw Lady Haig yesterday evening and am glad to tell you she is extremely well and very pleased. Believe me, very sincerely yours,

GEORGE R.I.

COLONEL W. N.
NICHOLSON,
Suffolk Regiment,
Staff Officer attached,
Highland Division.

We spent our second Christmas of the war in Senlis. Strict orders had been issued against any form of truce on the trench line. The Germans caught one of our men on patrol and we shelled them when they started singing carols.

But it is a commentary on modern war that commanders should fear lest the soldiers on each side become friendly. Our soldiers have no quarrel with 'Fritz', save during the heat of battle, or in retaliation for some blow below the belt. If whole armies fraternised politicians on both sides would be sore set to solve their problems. Yet it is possible that if there had been a truce for a fortnight on the whole trench line at any time after the Battle of the Somme the war might have ended – and what would mother have said then?

◆ ◆

1916

Having regard to the opinions expressed by Lord Kitchener in his telegram dated November 22nd, 1915, and by the General Staff in their memorandum dated November 22nd, 1915, the War Committee feel bound to advise the evacuation of the Gallipoli Peninsula on military grounds, notwithstanding the grave political disadvantages which may result from the decision.

Conclusions of War Committee, 23 November.

No colour breaks this tongue of barren land
Save where a group of huddled tents gleams white;
Before me ugly shapes like spectres stand,
And wooden crosses cleave the waning light.

Geoffrey Dearmer

The Gallipoli campaign, ill-conceived and ill-planned from the start, had been the cause of much controversy and much heart-searching between those who believed that it could still succeed and those who wished to concentrate men and resources to beat the Germans on the Western Front. Neither party, deliberating at a distance of more than a thousand miles, had any idea of the difficulties of the terrain and the climate, scorching in the arid disease-ridden summer, freezing in the stormy exposure of winter. The sick far outnumbered the wounded. The Peninsula itself was the enemy. In October Lord Kitchener sailed for Gallipoli to judge for himself. Within a short time of his arrival he ordered the Army to evacuate.

The last of the troops were taken off on 8 January and people reflected ruefully that the Evacuation of Gallipoli was by far the most successful episode of the whole campaign.

SECRET   Headquarters,
0/424   8th Army Corps.
                                     30th December, 1915.

                    MEMORANDUM

General Principles.
1. The evacuation of the position at CAPE HELLES will take
place at a very early date which will be notified to all concerned
as soon as it is settled . . .
    During the first period, which will commence at once, all
sick and weakly men and all superfluous material, transport,
stores, supplies and ammunition will be removed, leaving only
sufficient to maintain a minimum garrison in our present positions for a period of one week . . .
    The final period will last 48 hours during the first night of
which all personnel and material will be removed except such
numbers as can be taken off in one night by the Navy . . .
    The 15 pr. guns of each group will continue to fire at a normal
rate till the hour notified for their destruction.

Destruction of Material.
Arrangements must be made beforehand to:

    (a). Destroy all guns both at their present positions, and at
          the Beach. Each gun must, if orders for destruction are
          issued, be so completely blown to bits as to prevent its
          use to the enemy even as a trophy . . .

A method which is suggested and which can be carried out
with little preparation is to ram a partially filled sandbag into
the muzzle, load with an H.E. Shell and fire the gun by means
of a length of telephone cable, the man firing to be under cover,
to run the muzzle of the gun into the parapet would probably
help. For this purpose one 12 pdr. H.E. Shell for every 15 pdr.
gun should be retained and thrown into the sea on embarkation
if not required.

Stragglers.
Every precaution must be taken to avoid straggling, or men
being left behind, every detachment and other party must be
checked before embarkation . . .
                                        H.R.S. MASSY,
                    Captain, RA, Staff Officer, 8th Corps, RA.

The idea that so great and bold an enterprise, upon which such splendid courage and so many invaluable lives have been spent, should be abandoned at the first opportunity as impossible from the outset is enough to make the men who were killed in the Anzac landing turn in their graves.

At the same time the fact remains that they would be the first to take a common-sense view which all of us must take – that if the Allies' military leaders come to the decision that the Gallipoli Peninsula should be abandoned, then abandoned it must be.

Such a decision would be evidence of gross incompetence somewhere, for which hardly any punishment would be too great.

Sydney Daily Telegraph, 19 October 1915

GENERAL SIR WILLIAM BIRDWOOD

An ingenious assortment of ruses was devised to hoodwink the Turks as to our intentions, apparently with entire success. One factor which may have helped towards the deception was that we had pitched, and purposely left standing, large hospital camps at Suvla and Anzac. These, manned by a few doctors, were for the reception of any men wounded at the last moment; and though they may well have appeared to the Turks to be occupied, they were in fact never required. Another artifice used to puzzle the enemy was our practice of not allowing a single gun or rifle to be fired for two or three days at a time, except in cases of real emergency; and then this period of uneasy silence would be succeeded by some days of constant firing, so that the Turks began to fear that we were on the point of launching the big attack which, to the last, they continued to expect. In the final stages of the withdrawal other devices were used, such as leaving rifles that would go off by themselves when a burning candle had destroyed a string, well after the last troops had left. It was all very exciting – but very sad as well. On the very last day I was passing one of our cemeteries and talked with a 'Digger' who was giving a final touch to the grave of an old friend. He said, 'I hope *they* won't hear us marching to the beach tonight.' It made one think back a lot. . . .

CAPTAIN T. A. WHITE,
13th Battalion,
Australian Imperial Force.

The enemy was exceptionally quiet, a fact that aroused suspicions. Each of the 170 'Die-hards' was given a card showing the exact timetable and map for his departure and route. Heavy weather began to threaten and a strong wind to blow. The night air had become freezing, and the small band of watchers had neither overcoats nor blankets left to hamper, or to warm them. It seemed incredible to them that the evacuation was actually in progress behind them, so silent were all movements. During the last few days many had visited the graves of comrades for the last long look, a tear or a prayer.

Our four 'Die-hard' officers had found great difficulty in selecting their men. Practically every man volunteered. Several pleaded hard over and over again. 'I've been with you all along and I want to see the finish.' Charlie Kaler fairly broke down when refusal met his repeated requests.

On the night of the eighteenth 125 men of the battalion left, and the remainder spread out. From eight that evening until eight the next, all watches were synchronised every hour. All day Sunday the few paraded the Deres. At 5 p.m. on Sunday, 170 men, under Lieutenant Barton, left. At nine the Turks were wiring. At 9.15 Marks took another 100 away, including the MO. These parties moved off after quiet hand-clasps and whispered 'Cheeros' and 'Good Lucks'. There were now less than 4,000 men on the whole of Anzac against 170,000 Turks. Still they could be heard wiring – joyful sounds – against us. The night was clear, bright and icy.

Now commenced the most anxious time. For over four long hours about fifty men of the 13th and 16th held a front that should have been held by more than a brigade. The stillness could be felt. On other nights they had been able to walk through the trenches and yarn and smoke with mates, but now long stretches were deserted. To pass the time the few not actually watching destroyed what little material was left in the shape of rifles, dixies, bully and spades, and burying bombs. Private Butler remained in lonely charge of a signal lamp on Little Tabletop until midnight.

At 1.50 a.m. on the twentieth Twynam left with ten men. There was now no connection between the three small parties out there and the beach. At two, Gardiner, with ten, left his lonely post out on our extreme left; at 2.05 Murray with his two heavy machine-guns and their crews. Ford and his four men climbed out over the parapet and occupied a hole commanding a wider view; each with two rifles and a heap of bombs, determined to go out dearly if attacked. Still the Turks could be heard strengthening their wire in the distance.

All the party had labels on, orders having been given to write on them, in case of casualties, the nature of the wounds. Two tablets of morphia were to be placed under the tongue of a casualty before leaving him, but things would have been serious indeed for anyone to have left a wounded mate behind.

The last ten minutes seemed even longer. They listened to hear if their watches were ticking. Five men where a Brigade should have been.

At last – 2.15. They crawled back to the trench. A last seemingly long look into the darkness of No Man's Land. A Turk was hammering a stake into the ground, driving it home to make his wire a greater obstacle to the Anzacs. A few shots were crackling on their right in the distance. Stunted shrubs looked like enemies creeping towards them. They dropped down into the trench. Round the bays in the deep trenches they filed, and across narrow gullies with even steady tramp. The lonely trenches and gullies were soon left behind and the ocean gleaming and rising up in front. Ford reported to the Senior Officer: 'Last of the 4th Brigade' and they were taken to a transport which took them, just before dawn, towards Lemnos.

Many weeks before, with a view to making another big assault across the Nek on Sari Bair, Legge had been busy digging a tunnel which went right through the Nek and under the Turkish trenches, and which was now loaded with $3\frac{1}{2}$ tons of ammonal. At the last moment, after the last man had left the trenches, Lieutenant Caddy, RE, fired the mine. There was a gigantic explosion. From the deck of the cruiser below I saw an eruption that seemed to rival Vesuvius; the whole area was lit up, and against the glare could be seen the dark figures of men flung high into the air. At the same moment a great fusillade broke out along the line of Turkish trenches, evidently in expectation that the long-awaited attack was now at hand. Rifles and guns kept up their feverish fire for

GENERAL SIR WILLIAM BIRDWOOD

hours, though there remained not a single man in our own positions. The enemy's nerves were badly frayed, and it was some consolation to watch them wasting millions of rounds of ammunition against our empty trenches . . .

◆

Although Suvla and Anzac have cost us much in blood, it would be a mistake to regard this withdrawal as a confession of entire failure there.

The evacuation is, rather, a pulling of ourselves together, a step towards that concentration of strength upon sure ground which is of such importance to our fortunes here at the crossroads of the Empire.

By cutting our losses here we do something towards acting with greater deliberation and in better organized strength elsewhere.

The Times
1 January 1916

◆ ◆

SIXTEEN ARMY CORPS OF SLACKERS WAIT TO BE FETCHED

If the 650,000 unstarred and unattested single men had enlisted and been trained and equipped, it cannot be questioned that such a force could have:–

Saved Belgium,
Prevented the retreat from Mons,
Made it impossible for the Germans to undertake the invasion of Russia,
Preserved the freedom of Serbia,
Triumphantly stormed the Gallipoli Peninsula and advanced on Constantinople from other points.

If such a force were now available it would make an immediate offensive possible in the West. At any time during the campaign it could have acted with decisive effect; and in the critical year of 1916 it will be able, if ready, to decide the war.

But the 650,000 men will be too late again *unless they are fetched at once.*

Daily Sketch 5 January 1916

I'm back again in the depot, with a pot of beer in me hand.
Hark at them cheering the draft off. Hark at the strains of the band.
As I watches a crowd of chaps there, standing around to shout,
Somehow the thought comes to me – 'It's the same old crowd goes
out'.

Out to the slush and muck, son, out to the stink and blood,
Where the streams of jolting lorries splash through the greasy mud.
Where the lights go up on the skyline and the gas-shells plop and spout
'Hurry, blokes, get your masks on!' – and the same old crowd goes out.

You'll know its the Push when you see them coming along the road,
Wearing the old blue chevrons, humping a nice new load,
To pick up another wound stripe where the rats all scuttle about,
Or lie on the wire forever. Still, the same old crowd goes out.

Yes, pick up another Blighty (under the knee-cap for me)
Or loaf about in the billet, chaffing of Gay Paree.
Look at that blooming officer finding his way about –
Know him? I think we ought to! He's the same old crowd come out.

We've all of us had the wind up, most of us fed to the teeth,
And the things we've done and the risks we've run go far beyond belief.
But *après la Guerre est fini*, and things is nice and slack,
I'll be sorry for them lead-swingers when the same old crowd comes
back.

> *Private E. Lowe,*
> *13th Royal Fusiliers.*

I found on arrival at the Remount Section at Welling that I was 'spare', that is, I hadn't got a sub-section to look after unless anybody went sick or on leave. Practically all the staff (Sergeant-Major, QMS, and Sergeants) were Regulars, and several of them had been there since 1914. They were all perfectly happy and what was more fighting fit. Why they hung back I don't know. Others drifted in for a few weeks and soon went, when they realised what company they were in. I was thoroughly disgusted with the skulkers here.

There were two spare Sergeants beside myself, one named Phear and the other Nuent. Both were recently recovered from wounds, and hadn't been away from France very long. If anyone should have been on the permanent staff it should have been these two. I know they dreaded going back. Phear had the Military Medal and was so youthful in appearance that we called him 'Baby'.

If an inspection was held by the GOC of the Woolwich area, the rabbits were always in their holes, and Phear, Nuent and I were on

SERGEANT HARRY BARTLETT,
293 (Army) Brigade,
Royal Field Artillery.

parade, with the last joined officers, usually recently home from one of the fronts. Slackers outside were bad enough, but slackers *inside* the Army I couldn't understand.

SIDNEY SAVAGE,
Oundle School,
Officers' Training
Corps.

At Oundle School, at the age of fourteen, I was in the OTC. We used to have a lot of field days and drills on the parade ground – firing at the ranges with full service rifles – bayonet practice with sacks representing 'Germans'. Many of the sacks were held up on ropes and we used to 'charge' at them but it was difficult to withdraw the bayonet when the sacks were on the ground – we had to hold the 'German' with our left boot as we withdrew the blade.

Old Boys used to visit the school in Army uniform – and often a few weeks later it was announced at Morning Prayers that they had been wounded or killed on the Western Front.

On one particular day, four schools – two on each side – were taking part in an exercise. After about half an hour the train stopped at a small wayside station and we quickly got out and formed up into sections for a march of several miles.

I saw several men on horses in very superior uniforms. 'Who are they?' I said. 'They are the Umpires who decide whether we win or lose.'

We were soon approaching a village and were spread out in open formation, running forward when ordered and at times lying in the long grass which was damp and very disagreeable. The noise was terrific as we all had several 'clips' of blank cartridges and they seemed to be going off all round me.

Suddenly one of the Umpires came over on his horse and announced, 'The village ahead has fallen'. We were ordered to move in and flush out pockets of resistance.

We gathered in small groups of a dozen or so and proceeded into the village (what the inhabitants made of it I can't think). We were running along with a wall on the left of us when suddenly the muzzles of several service rifles appeared on top of the wall and were fired. The next thing I knew I was on a stretcher some distance away with blood rushing from my head. (A wad of compressed cotton wool will go through a piece of steel if driven fast enough at point blank range and I was lucky that it didn't hit my eye or ear.)

I was soon lifted and put in a motor car and taken to Oakham Hospital where I was put in a ward with *real* casualties – poor devils moaning and groaning. Later I was taken to the operating theatre where the wad was removed.

Next day the Headmaster's chauffeur-driven car was sent over to fetch me. The next issue of the school magazine carried a headline – *How to Get Shot without Going to the Front.*'

My father said, 'When do you do any school work!?' But none of the boys worried. Nobody seemed to doubt what they were going to do in life – we were all going to the Western Front! I was booked as a Machine Gunner when I was seventeen and allowed to stay at school until I was eighteen and a half – so as to be a really efficient Second Lieutenant 'commanding his men' in the battle line!

LORD DERBY'S SCHEME
LAST **2** DAYS.
Come in Now
and Train with Us.

MILITARY SERVICE ACT
1916
EVERY UNMARRIED MAN
of
MILITARY AGE
Not excepted or exempted under this Act
CAN CHOOSE
ONE OF TWO COURSES:
⑴ He can **ENLIST AT ONCE** and
join the Colours without delay:
⑵ He can **ATTEST AT ONCE UNDER
THE GROUP SYSTEM** and be
called up in due course with his
Group.
If he does neither, a third course awaits him:
**HE WILL BE DEEMED TO HAVE
ENLISTED**
under the Military Service Act
ON THURSDAY. MARCH 2ⁿᵈ 1916.
HE WILL BE PLACED IN THE RESERVE.
AND BE CALLED UP IN HIS CLASS.
as the Military Authorities may determine.

Excellent as the recent recruiting returns are, the need is vital and immediate for more and more men. There has been great difficulty in making many eligible men understand that their services are urgently required, and there have never been wanting pestilential persons who insidiously hinder recruiting. They are to be found in many bars and working men's clubs, and one hears stories of their being occasionally roughly handled. Generally speaking they base their arguments on the doctrine of universal brotherhood, and if these be backed up by a readiness to stand drinks they run very little risk of maltreatment. The authorities are perfectly aware of what is going on, but it would appear that there are legal difficulties in the way of checking the enemy's best friends or agents. Strange to say it is the younger men who are the more inclined to listen to the seditious poison, and it is not pleasant hearing that a greater proportion of married men than bachelors have answered the call to arms since the war was declared.

The Times

It ain't *our* fault we're 'ere, missus.
I'm sick of digging, but it's gotter be done.
Poor old Bill's done in.
I'm on'y gettin' a bob a day an' Jim's gettin' six, and he ain't shot at, but –
I'm sorry, but I 'ad to use the door to cook the dinner as I 'adn't got no fuel – } Say La Gaire.

I have none
You have none
There are none
Finish
No good   } Napoo.
There are no more
There never were any
I am no more

I want someone to help me billet . . . men
Donnez-moi quelqu'un pour m'aider à loger . . . hommes
(*don-nay mwah kel-kun poor may-day ah luzhay . . . ohm*)

Put as much clean straw in their billets as you can
Mettez autant que vous pourrez de paille fraiche
(*May-tay oh-tong ker voo pooray de pahl'ye fresh*)

The men only want accommodation to sleep on the floor
Les hommes peuvent dormir sur le plancher
(*Lay zohm peuve dor-meer seur ler plongshay*)

What You Want To Say in French and How to Say It.
War Edition.

---◆---

How do you like this for a bit of international language? I heard one of our men trying to explain to a French landlady that the Boche had been nearly wiped out in the fighting. His words were 'Kamerad napoo'!

MAJOR H.F. BIDDER, DSO, Royal Sussex Regiment.

---◆ ◆---

'Keep your head down, Alleyman, keep your head down, Alley-
man,
Last night in the pale moonlight, I saw you, I saw you,
You were trying to cut the wire when we opened rapid fire,
If yer want to see your dear Fatherland,
Keep your head down, Alleyman.'

CORPORAL C.R.
RUSSELL,
1st/14th (County of
London) Battalion,
(London Scottish).

When you were up holding the line the battalion usually would come up and there'd be a support trench, perhaps one Company, A Company, might occupy that and B Company might occupy the front line and C and D Company would be in support as well, and after about three or four days you'd swap over and another company would come in the front line. And all along the winding trench you used to have three men in a little bay. One was on guard, one was cleaning up the trench and trying to improve it, and the other one would be having a sleep and you'd swap round, so you got an hour's sleep out of three unless someone got the wind up, then you'd jump up and get on the fire-step. That's how you passed the night. In the day it was much the same, but you got the periscope out now and again, so you could see, but we didn't bother much because if Jerry was coming across he'd be spotted in daylight. So the day was really a quiet time. Now and again they'd send over Minniewerfers just for about five or ten minutes, then we'd reply, so it didn't take long for us and the Jerry troops to say, 'You keep quiet and I'll keep quiet'. Just an unspoken understanding.

I remember once being on guard, being on the fire-step, and it was damned hard to keep awake, because you're standing there and it's quiet. Perhaps you'd hear a bang or see a flare now and again, but you're doing nothing and you think, 'If I could only put my head down and go to sleep'. So I was on this fire-step dozing off, and all of a sudden I heard a quiet voice say, 'And what can you see, Corporal?' I said, 'Nothing at all, really, Sir; there's nothing we can do.' I cottoned on quick, thank God, it was our blooming Commanding Officer doing a walk round. If he'd found I was asleep I don't know what he'd have done, he was a very conscientious chap. It wouldn't have been at all pleasant. Mind you, he had a half idea I was half-asleep, so he said, 'What you want to do is to get your rifle and now and again loose off two or three shots. Imagine there's somebody coming along.'

If you're an Infantryman that's the last thing you want to do, because it takes days to get it clean again. You get fouling up in the barrel and you have to keep on with the oily rag, pulling it through with a pull-through, until at last it would be a dull glow. So we used to try and find an old rifle to let off shots in the trench. You don't use your own rifle unless you want to keep cleaning it for the rest of your life!

As far as work is concerned the front line is by far the easiest.

In the morning we work on the trenches, in the afternoon generally rest and every other night take turns at sentry-go, either in the bay or on an advanced post. The advanced posts are in saps that run out towards the German lines within twenty or thirty yards. One night I was in one of these posts, and it was most exciting. At night you stand with your head above the parapet with a bag of bombs by your side. While I was on, a terrible strafing took place a couple of hundred yards to my right. It was splendid to watch, but as shrapnel fell within a yard or two, it was quite close enough to be unpleasant. The trench mortars are the things we most dread. They drop right into the trench, and if you are near you don't stand an earthly. I am getting familiar with the different shells used, but have no wish to become closer acquainted with them. Whizz-bangs are small shells, that don't give you time to say Jack Robinson. All you hear is a whizz and a bang. You automatically duck, but if it is near you it is of no avail. Oil cans are really old oil drums filled with High Explosive and any rubbish they can put in of a killing nature such as small pieces of iron, steel and broken bottles. You can see these coming in the daytime, and, depend on it, we give them a wide berth! Sling bombs, hand and rifle grenades are very similar to our own, and don't do a great deal of damage unless one drops at your feet. The trench mortar shell is like a football on a stick. You can see them coming in the daytime, and at night they are followed by a trail of sparks, so if you keep your eyes open, you have some chance of getting clear.

Every morning for breakfast we had about an ounce of cold ham and about three parts of a mug of tea. On some days we had from a half to one-sixth of a loaf of bread to last the day. Occasionally we had no bread at all. Butter we generally had every other day. Jam is a daily issue. Once we had a pound between eight per day. When there was no bread we had three biscuits and a piece of cheese. I am obliged to say that when we left the trenches we were practically starving, and since being out (five days) I have spent twenty francs on food alone.

The 'rest' we had all looked forward to consists of fatigues, parades of all kinds, and guards. Last Saturday I was sent to Maroeuil on guard, and I am writing this in the sentry box.

We expect to be relieved tonight but I don't care if we are not for this isn't a bad 'stunt' and I must say I have enjoyed myself immensely. I was off duty at 6 p.m., and as the estaminets were open from six to eight everything was OK. We cooked our own grub and lived like lords. Eggs and bacon for breakfast, Welsh Rarebit and tea for supper, tinned fruit and cream for tea. But such things ended on the twenty-eighth when we returned to the firing line.

PRIVATE J. BOWLES, 2nd/16th (County of London) Battalion, (Queen's Westminster Rifles).

RAGOUT MACONACHIE

Open one tin of Maconachie Ration. Warm gently until the greasy oil floats on the top. Remove this by blotting up with a piece of 4 by 2 flannelette. Place this on one side for later use. Remove the black lumps in the ration Mc. These are potatoes. Squeeze out the greasy oil from 4 by 2 into a frying pan and gently fry the potatoes. Take two handfuls of dried vegetables. (They look very much like any other dried leaves.) Mix with a little water flavoured with chloride of lime and pat into croutons. These should be gently fried after the potatoes are cooked. Re-heat the Mc Ration and serve the whole on cold enamel plates.

TRENCH PUDDING

Take 4 hardtack biscuits. Place in dishcloth and bang with entrenching tool handle until pulverised. Soak in water for two to three hours until it is a pulpy mess. Add one tin of Tommy Ticklers Plum and Apple Jam. Stir well. Heat over a brisk fire and when the bottom burns serve with a teaspoon per person of condensed milk.

This should be more than enough for four persons.

Bully Beef and biscuit,
Tea and grease combined
Make a British soldier
Think that he's just dined.

You just existed. We used to have a loaf of bread sometimes and, according to who was in the platoon, we used to cut it in half first and then in quarters again ... we've had as many as sixteen or twenty out of one loaf of bread. And the butter was in tins, the tea and sugar were mixed together in a bit of paper and that all came up in a sandbag. Course then we had the usual rum issue. The sergeant used to come round ... 'Had your rum issue?' 'No' – he had a dessertspoon – 'Here you are. And I'll have mine now.' When he got round the next shell-hole, same thing happened. 'Had your rum issue?' 'No.' 'Right! I think I'll have mine now.' And by the time he got to the last one, he only got a drop and the sergeant was staggering! But what annoyed me was when, say you were coming out of the line at night, being relieved, when you got back to the billets or the transport lines, there was tea and that ready, but they put the rum in the tea. To me, that spoilt two good things ... that spoilt a good drop of rum and a good cup of tea.

CORPORAL P. J.
CLARKE,
13th Battalion,
The Rifle Brigade.

The telephone is another curse of modern war. It rings all hours of the night and day:

Specimen:

10.15 p.m. 'Tonight you will fire ten bursts on (target given).'

This has to be worked out.

After this to bed.

12. midnight. Telephone rings and wakes me up. 'How many size 6.4 boots were you issued with last Wednesday?' Send for QMS and his ledger.

1 a.m. A report is immediately required on what is visible from your OP.

2 a.m. 'How many men have you in the battery who have had no leave for 12 months?'

3 a.m. 'How many horses in your battery have died of colic in the last year?'

4 a.m. 'What is the average number of children per man in your battery?'

5 a.m. 'A company of enemy is reported moving through ——— Turn on to them at once.'

6 a.m. 'How many miles of cable have you used in the last fortnight, and on what has it been expended?'

7 a.m. 'At what ranges do you clear the crest all round the compass?'

In the above game the number of questions that can be asked is practically limitless. The winner is the one who guesses most of the answers right.

CAPTAIN R. A.
MACLEOD, DSO, MC,
C.241 Battery,
Royal Field Artillery.

GUNNER N. TENNANT,
D. 245 Battery,
Royal Field Artillery.

The Observation Post was a wooden shed standing in the corner of a field bordering the road from Ypres to the village of Boesinghe lying just on our left. Beyond the drained bed of the Yser canal which lay just across the road in front of us was the tumbled area of trenches on an almost imperceptible slope up to Langemarck, held by the Germans whose defensive positions always seemed to overlook ours.

To the right of the OP a number of cottages lined the road and it was interesting to explore these; this could only be done on a misty day as they were visible by the enemy and all movement near the OP was forbidden.

Billets for three officers

Billets for 120 men

Drawings by Gnr. Norman Tennant

The buildings were badly damaged by shell fire and in the upper rooms the windows commanding a view of the canal had been hurriedly barricaded. Everywhere were ample signs of retreat in the early days of the war. It was a sad sight to see the contents of drawers tumbled out on the floor and one turned over these pathetic fragments in search of some small souvenir with a feeling of guilt and sorrow for the inhabitants who had been forced to leave their home in hurried flight. I picked up a small photograph of a charming old lady in a lace cap trimmed with black ribbon which had been taken by a photographer in the rue au Beurre, Ypres.

At dusk the silence became even more haunting and menacing. As daylight faded countless frogs in the ponds and ditches set up their melancholy croaking. The rise and fall of Verey lights caused the shadows of broken buildings to move silently across the brightly illuminated ground and occasional rifle shots gave evidence of watchful life in the seemingly deserted landscape.

The next building was a rather longer one with a range of outhouses behind separated by a paved yard and this had belonged to somebody who had repaired bicycles. Scattered about one of the rooms were hundreds of cycle parts but, much to our disappointment, there was nothing like a whole machine.

One evening I started out for a mooch around, in the haunted silence. I passed the first cottage and had just reached the centre of the paved yard when I heard stealthy footsteps that seemed to come through the open door of one of the outhouses.

We never carried arms on our visits to the OPs or even to the front line and I stood there with prickling scalp expecting to see a concealed sniper emerge to start his nightly work.

Nearer and nearer to the door crept the footsteps and then, a complete anticlimax, there staggered out a weak and emaciated calf which tottered off round the corner. My relief was so great that I never thought of trying to do something for the poor thing as I made my way back to the OP.

Living in billets in France we never stayed in the homes. We were always billeted amongst the animals. The layout of the French farmhouses, the home and the stables are in the form of a hollow square and the cows and the sheep and the pigs and stable horses and the wagon are all in buildings on three sides and the house is in the middle. Now, all the refuse from that house, animal and human, was shoved into a pit in the middle of that square. Over twelve months it would be there! It stank to high heaven. Of course it would! That was the only source of manuring for their land and at the time when the sowing came round they would very laboriously drag it out with scoops and rakes and take it round the fields and put it out.

We were told when we got to France, 'Now you've got to be most careful how you behave to the women folk of France. It's most essential.'

CAPTAIN F. C. RUSSELL, 22nd Battalion, Australian Imperial Forces.

Well, there was never any breaking of that rule. We accepted it. We got there and we got into the first farm billet about two or three o'clock in the morning. There was nobody to receive us of course. 'Righto. Twenty men in there, forty men in here.' All we got was a flagstone floor so we dossed down on these bluestone flags for the rest of the night. Then daylight come on the scene and the girl from the household came out. The girl came out and she started to rave in French at us. 'What's up with her?' We found out. Ah! We were in the wrong place. We should have been in where the cows were, which was a good bed of 3 or 4 feet of straw. So we thanked her very much!

Everywhere we went later on we were out amongst the animals. In a place called Hailley-sur-Somme. It was a very wet sort of a night, late evening, when we got into a farm. The place had been well and truly under shell fire and the walls were full of holes, and half the roof was gone. Anyhow, we got in there and found some straw, got down into it, draped some over you and got off to sleep. One sergeant wasn't too happy with his place. He found a pig in a pigsty that was dry and had a roof, so he got in there and kicked the old pig out – booted him out of the sty and got in there where the pig had been. He said the pig didn't like it at all! He grunted and was very upset. That was the way we were forced to live. There was no other way for it. In the whole of France and Belgium the same applied. Sometimes you'd get a very decent billet. You'd get very fine straw. If we got a place and found there was not enough straw or there was none at all we'd scramble and find some.

In one place about two or three doors away we found that there was a barn full of straw so we hopped in and the whole lot of us got an armful of straw each and back we went. We left a trail of broken straw from where we got it to where we took it. Out come the old Froggie and he started to rave and wave his arms about and shouting, *'Gendarme.'* He rushed off and got the gendarme. The gendarme got the town major who was an Englishman, an officer who was stationed in every village where there was billeting and he was supposed to keep the civil order. That was his job. When the Frenchman goes to him he gets hold of the gendarme then he goes round to where the cause of the trouble is. 'Nobody's pinched any straw,' we said. And here was this trail of straw – like a gangway to heaven! So we finished up by taking it all back again. By nightfall we'd pinched it again but that doesn't matter.

◆ ◆

I'm thinking, Mrs Atkins, now that Tommy's gone away,
You'll be sending a letter from Home.
Don't tell him all your troubles, though for instance yesterday
The children's boots you bought took half your separation pay.
The eldest boy wants trousers and the rent is overdue,
You're planning and you're scheming for of debts you've got a
few!
But don't you write and tell him, for here's my advice to you
When you send him a letter from Home.

Send him a cheerful letter.
Say that it's all OK.
Tell him you've ne'er felt better,
Though it's all the other way.
Don't send a word of sorrow,
Send him a page of joy,
And don't let your teardrops
Fall upon the kisses
When you write to your Soldier Boy.

Popular song on the Home Front 1916.

France.
24 June, 1916.

PRIVATE W. PARKER,
12th (S) Battalion,
(Sheffield Pals),
The York and Lancaster
    Regiment.

Dear Blanche,
Just a line to say Reg and myself are all right. I am a little over a mile away from our Reg in a barn, so you see I have a soft bed to sleep on, but everything has some drawback and this billet has, every night as soon as the light goes out, the rats start their nightly manoeuvres, they are just like young cats running over you, the other night we were awakened by one of the fellows swearing as hard as he could. A rat had knocked a tin of bully beef down and it caught him just under the eye, it made a nice eye for him. I think I would rather have the bugle to wake me up than a tin of bully. Our Spot would have a birthday if he was here. I often think about him. There is a little terrier on the farm but he doesn't understand good English.

Some chaps came in the billet last night out of the trenches and brought a dog with them. It came over from the German trenches into ours. The men have christened it 'Boche'.

Will you send me ten shillings as I have only drawn five francs since I came to France. Our Reg and myself went in a café (just a cottage), he ordered two coffees and four buns. He gave her a five franc note and she charged ninepence. (1d. under one franc), then I ordered the same and offered her a five franc note. She reckoned she hadn't change – she knew our Reg has some small change. So I put the note in my pocket. We finished our coffees and was walking down the yard innocent like and the old girl came rushing out screaming '*Café, café*'. I asked our Reg what was the matter. He said she wants paying so I gave our Reg my five franc note to pay her and she snatched it out of his hand. So we started having our money's worth. We had two bottles of wine, box of buns and chocolate. She gave us the note back when we got as far as this. All the French people think about is getting as much as they can out of the English soldier.

Remember me to Harry and all at home.

I remain
Your affectionate brother
Willie.

My dear little Katherine

MAJOR T. D. H. STUBBS,
Royal Artillery
from Ypres Salient.

Many thanks for your nice letter which I received yesterday. It was good of you to write such a nice letter & in such good writing. I gave your love to Capt. Hedley & Mr. Burnley, but Mr. Ingham & Mr. Harris were both jealous. We live here more like rabbits than anything else & we have a lookout rabbit with glasses & a whistle who blows 3 blasts when he sees a German aeroplane then we all dive below & remain there until our lookout blows one blast. The German aeroplanes have a horrid habit of coming out just as our dinner & tea is being brought up to the Battery with the result that the men carrying the meals have to squat down perhaps 100 yards away. We sit in our rabbit holes & peep out at our dinners while the dinners get cold. It is very annoying of them & is altogether a bad habit but three days ago our airmen went up after one of the Germans & shot him down, he also did the same thing with another the day before yesterday so that is two less anyway to bother us.

I am very well indeed & really am liking the life, if only we don't get too many shells at us. I am sending you a small piece of a shell which came to call yesterday. We were sitting having tea when we heard him & two friends coming, they whistle as they come to show how cheerful they are, this particular one sailed over just beyond the end of the Battery & burst right in the middle of the road 200 yards or so behind. There was a French ambulance coming along the road at the time, the shell must have missed it by inches as it burst only 10 yards behind it, the horse took no notice at all, a Frenchman had the top of his finger blown off & the French surgeon some distance away got it in the leg. One of the other shells burst quite close to another battery but hurt no one.

I went out afterwards & found this piece of shell which you should keep as a souvenir. Some day I will tell you the name of the place. The only other damage done was a blackbird killed which one of our men found & the road with a big hole in it, which we repaired as our wagons use it. We are ordering things for the men to be sent out weekly from Fortnum & Mason so except for a slab or two of chocolate & occasionally a cake I really don't want anything at present. I could do with another dozen drawing pins. We are now getting enough to eat if only the horrid German aeroplanes will leave us alone to eat it. You see it is very important that the German aeroplanes should not be able to see where we are as if they do they will quickly begin to shell us out & we would then have the bother of finding another position & digging our rabbit holes again & of planting a new plantation round the grass, so we are very careful. I have to preside at a Court Martial tomorrow which I am not looking forward to at all. Give my best love to Mummy & heaps to yourself. I know you will be good & will make Mummy happy.

Your own
Daddy

◆

> Letter writing had become practically a lost art until the yearning of the men in the trenches for the precious letters from home revived it; and the duty of having to write a weekly or even more frequent letter to menfolk at the Front has developed latent literary talents till lately undreamed of in many people. There is perhaps no more delicate or delightful art. It is capable of giving the most exquisite intellectual pleasure, both to the writer and the recipient of the letter, of conveying subtle atmosphere, sympathy, and the intimate interchange of ideals that belongs to no other mode of human communication. It is one of the most priceless and humanising of gifts, and one that is worthy of diligent cultivation. The letter-writers of all ages give us a far truer and more vivid picture of the times in which they lived than their historians. It is the human document that has the power to make history really live for us. In all probability some of the letters that are now passing to and from the trenches will make the poignant history of these – our own times – live far more thrillingly and truly than all the memoirs of the Joffres, and the Hindenburgs, and the Grand Dukes that will come out after the titanic struggle is ended.
>
> *The Sphere*
> *20 November, 1915.*

RIFLEMAN STANLEY
HOPKINS,
2nd/18th Battalion,
The London Regiment,
(London Irish Rifles).

Amongst the parcels arriving in the front line was one for a titled Rifleman which included a tin of caviar. It was the custom to share parcels and we were just enjoying the food when the Orderly Officer of the day arrived and, as usual, asked if there were any complaints. There was! One Rifleman who had been given some caviar to spread on his biscuits complained that his 'pozzy' tasted of fish.

Quite often the Huns would bombard the only road to our sector – many food parcels and letters were lost this way. This frequent loss of parcels (mine always included a seed cake) gave me an idea. I wrote to Huntley and Palmers from the front line – hoping they would get my field letter safely in spite of the gunfire aimed at the road – explaining how a lot of our food parcels were not reaching us. Could they possibly send us some biscuits? Twelve four-pound tins of fancy biscuits duly arrived. As this worked so well I wrote to the Ingersoll Watch Company explaining that we had only one watch in our platoon and that was not always reliable. They sent us six! I had one of them in civilian life for years.

It fell to me as an officer to censor the men's letters. Sometimes they were really funny. One Jock wrote home very briefly and to the point:

Dear Jeannie,
I am expecting leave soon. Take a good look at the floor. You'll see nothing but the ceiling when I get home.

CAPTAIN R. MCDONALD, 7th Battalion, Queen's Own Cameron Highlanders.

Dear Father,
Thank you for your letter. The weather has now turned slightly warmer. We appreciated the change this morning, for we had Reveille at 3.30, breakfast at 4 and started off on a 10 mile march at 5 o'clock.

I am now using a new pony.
*N*othing seems to do any good
*T*o my old pony, which still
*R*emains lame in spite of
*A*ll bandages. The pony that
I now have belonged to our origi-
*N*al padre, who has left us
*F*or the Base Camp at Havre.
*O*n the completion of his year he
*R*eturns to his parish. He had
*M*erely six weeks to do until then,
*A*nd so the authorities decided to
*R*etain him in France. It did not
*S*eem worthwhile to
*E*mploy him with us, and then
*I*mmediately send him back.
*L*ast night we had a
*L*ong rumour that a Bulgarian gen-
*E*ral had been assassinated.
*S*orry that I have no news!
　　　　　Yours Aye,
　　　　　　Jock.

[This coded letter contains the message: 'In train for Marseilles'.]

2ND LIEUTENANT J. MACLEOD 3rd Reserve Battalion, The Queen's Own Cameron Highlanders

This Great Store, which covers seven acres of ground, is designed to hold a stock of 500,000 shells. Working at full pressure the operatives in this store can unload from railway wagons, clean, paint, examine and reload in wagons for despatch to the Filling Departments up to 40,000 shells in 24 hours ...

Chilwell.
Factory Inspector's report

In April 1916 Polly, a workmate of mine, and myself decided we would get a job on munitions. After some controversy about my age, I was only seventeen just, and the authorised age was eighteen, I was taken on as an overhead-crane driver.

Along with about eight other girls we were taken over to the building later to be known as the Filled Shell Store and to our consternation we were told we were to be trained to drive the overhead-cranes which were suspended on rails in the roof of the building.

We could hardly believe our eyes, we had to ascend a ladder to man the crane and descend by way of a rope. I was never very brave but this procedure fairly took the cake. If I failed to mount the ladder I would be out of work, so up I went, but it was some time before I mastered the rope.

My first impression of that store was sheer fright, rows and rows of 8-inch, 6-inch and 9-inch shells not forgetting the 12-inch which reached to my waist and higher. I hardly dared walk near them but had to overcome this feeling. As I remember it there were fifteen bays in the store and four cranes in each. On the lower side of the building there were two cranes to each bay and six large wall cranes, these only travelled the length of the wall but the smaller ones went the whole length and were responsible for loading all the filled shells sent out from the factory to France.

We were on eight-hour shifts at first but this was changed to twelve hours, this meant two shifts instead of three. Twelve hours Monday to Saturday then we changed to eighteen hours going on duty at 6 o'clock Saturday evening and working to 2 o'clock Sunday afternoon when the opposite shift would take over and work through until Monday at 6.00 a.m., when we would resume normal twelve-hour shifts. No one would work those long hours today, the Unions would step in. Of course this was war and everyone was out to get results. Soon the weekly output of filled shells reached 130,000 which required 900 tons of Amatol. Practically every big shell fired by the British during the Battle of the Somme was filled at Chilwell.

LOTTIE WIGGINS

At this factory it was found that a certain percentage of the women, not a large one, spent a very considerable amount of their working time in the latrines gossiping, instead of remaining in the far better atmosphere of properly ventilated workshops. That this was most undesirable from a health point of view would be obvious to anybody who chose to consider the question.

In addition to the above, it was obvious that a very considerable amount of working time was lost by the practice. With a view therefore to killing two or three birds with one stone, I tried the system of lavatory cards in one Department of this Factory, among the women, under which such operatives as adopted regular habits, and thereby did not

(From a letter written by Lord Chetwynd.)

waste their time gossiping, would benefit to the extent of a small sum weekly. Having tried it in one Department of the Factory for a few weeks with admirable results, I decided to extend it, and have done so.

The large bulk of the operatives to whom the tickets have been applied like the system and are thoroughly happy and contented, and I have not the slightest intention of modifying the system in any way.

ALL TICKETS PLEASE!

HURRAH, for old England, the land of the free,
We have tickets for butter, for sugar, for tea;
Also tickets for breakfast, for pudding and dinner,
You can take it for granted – the word of a sinner.
We have now reached the limit, I'm sure you'll agree
When I tell you we've got to have tickets to P.

When the war's at an end, and they've done making shells,
And our Tommies return from the trenches like swells,
And the Kaiser is hanged on a sour apple tree
With his lunatic son, we shall go on the spree;
But Tommy will swear and I think you'll agree –
Should he find we've been forced to have tickets to P.

Dear friends, to a close I must now bring this rhyme,
As I've wasted enough of your valuable time;
We shall stick to our work till this blooming war's o'er,
And then I expect you will want us no more,
But while we remain we shall never agree
To the order that WE MUST have tickets to P.

This was written by an employee. I got hold of it and had it printed in our own printing works. I sold thousands at a few pence each and all the funds went to the Red Cross. The author was furious.

                                                    CHETWYND.

I was sent to the convalescent depot at Sutton Coldfield where they rehabilitated wounded soldiers to get them fit again for the Front. Birmingham City I liked, but I regret I was not at all impressed with the men folk. The munitions lassies – the girls in overalls and clogs – were always good company, or so I found them. The moment they found out a soldier was from the convalescent depot, then that soldier was point blank refused to be allowed to buy a round of drinks. I felt damned embarrassed when I walked into a pub with 'Tich' one night and called for two drinks. Some factory girls were also present and when I put my hand into my pocket for cash to pay for my order one girl forestalled me saying, 'You keep your money, Corporal. This is on us,' and with no more ado she pulled up her frock, turned back her stocking from under the flashy garter and produced a roll of notes big enough to choke a cow. Many of the girls earned ten times my pay as a full Corporal, and they said so, and they were generously big-hearted where we were concerned.

One evening three of us NCOs from the camp, myself, 'Tich', and a DCM Sergeant of the Hampshire Regiment, entered the pub at the invitation of some munition lassies. Between the three of us we had seven gold wound bars. The six of us occupied a little alcove in a corner of the bar. Up at the far end of the bar a small group of soldiers were deep in discussion with some male munition workers. There was definitely no reason to anticipate any trouble – till one of the civvies uttered the fatal word 'strike'. That one word had the same effect on the military as would a red rag to a bull. Most of these soldiers had shed their blood and were badly scarred. Some had been in those tight spots where cold food and hard biscuits was all they could get, and little of that. And here were over-paid, over-fed civvies talking about striking!

A little stockily-built, bandy-legged soldier, a Private of the Cornwall Light Infantry, faced up to the much bigger munition worker who used the word 'strike' and called him everything that was vile. I could smell trouble coming. I gave the DCM Sergeant a nudge and said it was time to get the girls out of it. He didn't stand on ceremony. He put his arms around the waists of two of them – left and right – and pushed them towards the door, their clogs thumping the bare floor-boards. 'Tich' and I pushed the third girl towards the exit. Just as we got to the door the fun started. I lingered just long enough at the door to take a backward look at the rough house and saw the little man from Cornwall seize his opponent in a wrestling hold and then throw him against the wall. He didn't get up again, at least for a while. 'Tich' was yelling to me to 'beat it', which I did just in time, as Red Caps came running along the street.

RIFLEMAN H. V. SHAWYER,
13th (S) Battalion,
The Rifle Brigade.

The Gunner rides on horseback, he lives in luxury,
The Sapper has his dugout as 'cushy' as can be.
The Flying man's a sportsman, but he lives a long way back,
In painted tent, or strawspread barn, or cosy little shack.
Sapper and Gunner and Flying man, each to his job say I,
Have tickled the Hun with mine or gun, or bombed him from
on high,
But the quiet work – and the dirty work – since ever the War
began,
Is the work that never shows at all – the work of the Infan-
tryman.

PRIVATE W. LUFF,
1st Battalion,
The Queen's (Royal West
Surrey Regiment).

When I joined, in 1916, being under age, there was an outcry about youngsters going to the Front, so they put me on what they called A3, which was training the officers. Two men with toggles and ropes represented platoons and battalions, and our old Regimental Sergeant-Major, Chokey Sullivan, used to stand there with about half a dozen Subalterns and he'd say, 'Mr So-and-So!' And Mr So-and-So would come out and Chokey would say, 'Back! Step off your left foot with your cane in your right arm, bring your cane up and slap it on your left arm and walk smartly'. And the officer would have to go back and do it again.

'Now,' he said, 'you've got your Battalion facing south in routing order,' he said, 'now get them facing east in open order.' Of course, we had to do just as the officer ordered, and, of course, some of those young Subalterns tied us up in all sorts of knots. And he'd say, 'Now, Mr So-and-So,' (he always addressed them as Mr So-and-So) 'NOW what have you done?'

It was the 3rd Training Battalion, and it included we recruits and two Companies of Old Sweats who had been wounded and they were there training before they were sent back again. Chokey used to drill in front of them with a pace stick, and he used to stand there and he'd slap the old stick, like that, you know? And one of these Old Sweats said, 'You can do that with that stick,' he said. 'Can you do it with this rifle?' Chokey said, 'Stand at Ease! Now, that man. Six paces forward, March! Give me the rifle!' He gave Chokey his rifle and he went through all of it. All the blasted drill there was! Slope Arms, Present Arms, the lot! 'Now,' he said, 'Let's see if YOU can do it.' And he put that poor blighter through it for about half an hour! Up and down, up and down that parade ground. Oh, he was a tough old So-and-So.

Please Mr Officer tell me do,
are we getting relieved tonight?
Because I've found a dugout, very nice too,
and I've fixed it up all right.
With corrugated iron and a sandbag roof
it's as cosy as can be.
And I'll be pleased to show it to you
If you'll come along with me

Way down the communication trench
In the middle of Whizz Bang Lane,
I've got a real little sandbag villa
Where the Krupps and Johnsons rain.
Very, very close to a sniper's post
Where the Hunnish bullets visit us most.
If they charge we'll give 'em some machine-gun toast,
Way down Whizz Bang Lane.

Private F. Longbottom.
2nd Battalion, Duke of Wellington's West Riding Regiment.

SERGEANT JACK
CROSS,
13th (S) Battalion,
The Rifle Brigade.

We were at Auxi le Château at the time when the Irish people cut up rough in Dublin and the Irish Division were in the line. We got the order one morning about half past four, 'Stand to, Harness up, Fall In,' we fell in in the street. I said to my platoon officer, Mr Cox, I said, 'What's going on, Sir?' He said, 'We've got a forced march up the line today, Sergeant. They're afraid the Irish are going to cut up rough and go over to the Germans. We've got to go up and relieve them.' So we done a forced march that day and was it a hot day!

We got through Doullens, up that main road, and it got to the middle of the afternoon and we pulled into an old apple orchard. Had a rest and a meal, then on again, and we went straight up into the line and relieved these Irishmen and took over that night at a place called le Gastineau.

It *was* a long march, I know we didn't get in there until about eight or nine o'clock at night and was we tired!

They brought soup up the line to us and we had that and of course felt a good deal better.

We were stretched to our full extent. There might have been two Irish Battalions in there; we'd got to go in with one battalion and fill up that gap. We hadn't got two men to put on a post and Bob Phillips, he was a man of my Platoon, he was at this Listening Post, and the Marquis of Winchester was our Second in Command, and during the night he went up to this Listening Post and found Bob Phillips stood there, sound asleep. So he come along and found me in the trenches and he said, 'Have you got a man up at that Listening Post, Sergeant?' I said, 'Yes, Sir.' 'Come with me,' he said – and Bob was sound asleep! So he said, 'Wake him up.' I shook him, I said, 'Bob, Bob, wake up! What are you doing?' He said, 'Oh, I just dropped off, oh, I am tired.' He couldn't see the Marquis, because it was dark, he stood behind me. I said, 'You know, you've done a wrong thing, it's a terrible thing to be asleep at your post.' And he wasn't the only one I found that night in the Battalion! We were stretched to full extent, even in the trenches where we should have had three men in the fire bay we could have only one, and the next chap was perhaps four or five bays further away. You could hardly shout to one another even.

'Well,' said the Marquis of Winchester, 'you've got to see the Company Officer in the morning.' So I found Captain Lezard. I said, 'We've got a terrible thing happening in our Company tonight, Major, the Marquis of Winchester has been along and found one of our sentries asleep.' 'Oh, God!' he said, 'What the Hell do they expect, marching us all that way and those poor devils stretched out as far as we can stretch them? And only one man on a post!' Anyway, he come up next morning in the Company dugout, and, of course, Bob admitted, he said, 'Yes, I did drop off to sleep, I must admit I lost myself.' How long he'd been like it, I don't know. That was nearly a quarter of an hour from the time the Marquis of Winchester found him, found me and the time we got back because we were so far away. Captain Lezard said, 'We shall have to sort this lot out at Battalion Headquarters.' So, anyway, it was held over until they'd had a talk at Battalion HQ. And Bob was admonished. He was lucky. You got shot for being asleep at your post, but during the course of the night they found three or four more asleep in different Companies, so they made an appeal to the Brigade for more troops, said how thin we were in the line, and eventually we had a lot come up and we squeezed up a bit, and they took part of the line between two Companies of ours. And that made us so we could get more than one man on a post. It was all thrashed out at Brigade Headquarters, I suppose they realised that this was a very trying time.

I had leave again in April and spent it with my wife visiting relations. England was wonderfully peaceful, quiet and beautiful after France. There were few shortages of anything, but nearly everyone was doing war work of some sort. On my returning to France we again had Cavalry manoeuvres, this time directed by General Gough. Apparently GHQ was not satisfied with many of the older officers in command of the Indian brigades and regiments, for soon afterwards he took them on tactical exercises and set them small problems. Major Walker attended most of them and told us what happened.

CAPTAIN R. MACLEOD,
DSO, MC,
C. 241 Battery,
Royal Field Artillery.

General Gough to a Lieutenant-Colonel:

'How would you move across this country?' (It was a wide open, rolling country with few obstacles.)

Lieutenant-Colonel:'I should move by bounds, Sir.' (This appeared a correct solution in such country.)

General Gough: 'What? Like a ballet girl jumping on to a stage?'

General Gough to another Lieutenant-Colonel: 'I am Corporal Gough in charge of a section, and you are my troop commander. What orders would you give me to move through that wood?'

Lieutenant-Colonel, after thinking a bit: 'I should tell you to keep close together.'

General Gough: 'Keep close together? There is no word of command in the book "Keep close together".'

General Gough gives a tactical situation to a Brigadier and tells him and his Brigade-Major to write their orders. He takes out his watch and after five minutes says: 'Time is up. Your orders are too late, and the enemy will be on you.'

In this way nearly all the senior officers of the Indian Cavalry Corps were 'ungummed'. Most of them had had long service, but were now old, and out of touch with modern European war. I think it would have been kinder if a less brusque way of dispensing with their services had been used. They were replaced mostly by younger officers of the British service.

We continued our training for the big battle which we knew was coming soon, and had more manoeuvres with the new senior officers.

CAPTAIN ALAN
GORING,

6th Battalion,

The Yorkshire Regiment.

I liked Gough. I think he had a very raw deal later, over the 5th Army retreating. They made him a scapegoat. I don't think he was the world's greatest general, but we hadn't any great generals. There was no scope for the great general. There were no real strategic movements to carry out. It was a case of 'Over the top and barge ahead'. It was stalemate. The idea was to break the line and then we would follow the cavalry through, first stop Berlin. Of course that didn't happen until the end of the war. Then they produced a few ideas, but for all the rest of the time it was just a case of slog, slog, slog. And yet we put up with it. Of course we cursed about the weather and groused about this, that and the other but, by and large, there was very little loss of morale. When we went into an attack we always left so many men and so many officers behind and the rest of us went into the line so that there would be someone left in case of disaster. Theoretically, if you survived, you switched over next time. It was a good idea because then you always had *some* left, otherwise you might have had the whole expertise wiped out in one go. But the morale *always* comes from the top. You show me a good battalion and I'll show you a good command; show me a bad one and nine times out of ten it was the officers at fault.

On one occasion I remember the five or six officers who were picked to be left behind nearly mutinied. My best pal was one and he nearly quarrelled with me. 'Why are you in this show and I'm not?' They marched in a body to HQ and protested. If it hadn't been that their hearts were in the right place they'd have been charged with mutiny I should think. But they were that loyal. That was just before the 1st July. Of course we hadn't been blooded then.

TRAGIC DEATH OF LORD KITCHENER.

WAR MINISTER AND HIS STAFF LOST BY SINKING OF BRITISH CRUISER: NOT A SOUL SAVED.

EMPIRE STRICKEN WITH SORROW.

Douglas had to come to London again on the 6 June for an important meeting at the War Office. General Joffre and the French Premier were also present. Immediately on landing at Dover Douglas was shown a telegram by the Military Landing Officer which reported that Lord Kitchener and his staff on HMS *Hampshire* had been drowned.

Douglas's arrival was very unexpected and I had only been advised by telegram of his coming. My children had just arrived the previous evening from Wales and I had arranged to take them to Deal a day or two later. Meanwhile they were to have stayed in my flat, which was so tiny that I had to make arrangements for them to sleep in the dining-room. Everything, therefore, was in rather a chaotic state when I heard that Douglas was coming. To get over the difficulty I decided to rent an adjoining flat which happened to be vacant, and was just moving in his clothes, prior to walking to the station with the children to meet Douglas, when I heard the excited voice of a lady asking to see me at once. Alan Fletcher's wife then rushed into the room and informed me that our husbands had been drowned. I simply cannot describe my horror at hearing this news. Without waiting to ascertain where Lady Theresa had obtained her information, I telephoned direct to the War Office and was informed by Sir George Arthur of the tragic news about Lord Kitchener. I am afraid that my relief was so great I could only exclaim 'Thank God'. I learned afterwards that Lady Theresa had simply read the newspaper bills, and knowing that Douglas and her husband were crossing from France, jumped to the wrong conclusion and came straight to me. This delay made us late for Douglas's arrival, and he was almost leaving the station when the children and I met him. Douglas fully realised how much Lord Kitchener's death would mean to him personally, and he knew he would miss his help in directing the councils of war at home.

For the next three days Douglas's time was almost entirely occupied with conferences at the War Office and Cabinet meetings. He was also sent for by the King, who had a long talk with him. His Majesty was evidently very upset by Kitchener's death.

On the ninth, however, we left London for a short stay at Deal, where we managed to have a few games of golf. A very funny incident concerning our two daughters occurred while we were there. We had taken them for a walk and were resting by the sea, leaning against some rocks while the children played near by. We suddenly became aware that as people passed they stared at Douglas with more than ordinary interest, and we were rather surprised because usually he was passed almost unnoticed. Happening to look up, I noticed chalked in large letters on the rocks above our heads 'THIS IS SIR DOUGLAS HAIG.' This, of course, was the work of our little monkeys.

I accompanied Douglas on 12 June to Dover, where he met Admiral Bacon and his staff. After lunching with the Admiral and Lady Bacon, Douglas left for Folkestone, whence he returned to France.

**GUNNER NORMAN
TENNANT,**
D. 245 Battery,
Royal Field Artillery.

June 11
Reveille at 3.30 and we left Pernois for Senlis which is packed with
troops, mostly Scottish, who are wearing the new steel helmets. We
thought they looked rather silly, the helmets not the troops.

June 14–18
Went up to the gun position with four other signallers in the mess cart,
wearing the tin hats with which we too had been issued.

The whole area is alive with men working on gun pits, dugouts and
trenches without any apparent attempt at concealment from aerial
observation. The space allotted to us lies between the road from Aveluy
to Authuille and the river Ancre just behind us. In front the ground
rises gently towards Authuille Wood and the valley beyond where the
front line is overlooked by the strong German defences round Thiepval.

The gun pits and dugouts had already been constructed by fatigue
parties.

The guns arrived between 4 and 5 p.m. on the 15th and were pushed
into their emplacements. RE signals turned up with some large drums
of armoured cable (so called) which had to be buried in 6-foot trenches.

It was while digging one of these that the value of our new steel
helmets was very clearly demonstrated. Just as Jim was bringing his
pick-axe down Arthur suddenly bent forward in the trench and there
was a nasty clang as it hit Arthur's tin hat. It could easily have been
curtains for Arthur!

We moved up to Bertrancourt on June 11th. The whole battalion concentrating round HQ and were accommodated in huts in an orchard. Found the floor extraordinarily hard I remember, but only had to endure it for one night as, on the Monday, my presence was requested at the Brigade office, which I found meant remaining there for an unknown period to understudy the BM Major – d'Esterre. This was apparently the result of having volunteered a few days previously to paint some spots on maps, for Findy.

I was chiefly employed in making fair copies of d'Esterre's draft orders for the attack. These orders were very lengthy and detailed, and the instructions concerning dress, equipment, rations, etc, etc, were colossal. The number of encumbrances which every man was made to carry in this battle was far too great and resulted in a gigantic wastage of material, as everything was thrown away wholesale immediately after Zero Hour. Besides the ordinary equipment, rifle, and SAA, the following (among other articles) were loaded on to the unfortunate Infantryman – two days rations, bomb, pick or shovel, Ayston fans (for clearing gas out of dugouts), flags for showing our position to Artillery, Verey lights, and on each man's back was fitted a triangular piece of tin in order to show the position of our advanced line to aeroplanes when the men lay down.

If the success of any operation were entirely dependent on the preparations made before Zero Hour, then the Somme battle should have been a complete success.

CAPTAIN R. J. TROUSDELL,
1st Battalion,
Princess Victoria's,
(Royal Irish Fusiliers).

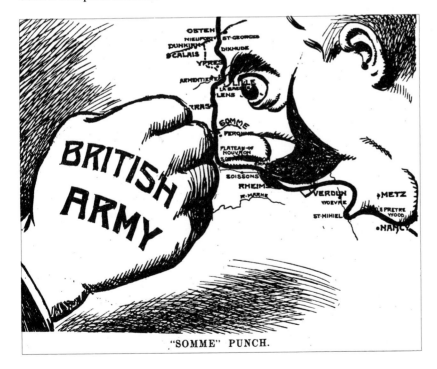

"SOMME" PUNCH.

The role which each unit was to play on the opening day had been allotted well in advance: training grounds in the back areas were marked out to represent the sectors over which one was to operate, and the attack was rehearsed till everyone knew his part. The actual ground was studied, units being put into the line some days beforehand, and clay models were also made by some units in order to get an idea of the terrain from the enemy's point of view. Aeroplane photographs more or less disorganised. I confess to having felt no desire to penetrate further than was necessary, having no certain knowledge whether any Boches were in our trenches or whether we held theirs.

———————◆———————

ZERO HOUR

How do you feel as you stand in a trench
Awaiting the whistle to blow?
Are you frightened, anxious, shaking with fear
Or are you ready to go?
No one is anxious to go, my friend
It's a job which must be done
Discipline ensures we obey the rules
Though for many their last day has come.

Me! I'm scared! Though I try not to show it
It's my third time over the top
I'm a lover of peace but a bullet don't know it
I could be getting the chop!
May the Good Lord grant me a nice Blighty wound
One which allows me to run
Out of this shambles, I've had quite enough
Let 'The Butcher' keep his fun.

That's how we feel as we stand in a trench
Awaiting the whistle to blow
Those are the thoughts which pass through our heads
Emotions we are not keen to show
All men react in different ways
Few to heroics aspire
But should a man boast that he never knew fear
Then, in my book, that man is a liar!

Sergeant H. Fellowes

———————◆———————

Word came round that the start was to be at 7.30 a.m. Soon after five I was out, looking round. The sky was clear, and so was our ridge, but the lower ground where the British and German trenches were was hidden in a sea of white mist. The sun was just topping the mist and catching the dewdrops on the grass and thistles round us. The stakes of the barbed wire round our work threw long shadows towards us. The guns were blazing away; and great black mushrooms were shooting up out of the surface of the white sea in front as the big shells burst in the German trenches. It was a strange scene – we stood about on the grass round our positions, apparently alone in the world on this brilliant morning, only disturbed by the crashing of the guns behind and the weird upheavals in the mist surface.

We stood about a little too long, a chance German bullet getting two of my men – one very slightly.

At seven the intense bombardment began, and our machine-guns opened again on the German communication trenches. The mist was clearing off, and I went forward to the HQ of the supporting battalion, which was to be my HQ also.

There was a wonderful air of cheery expectancy over the troops. They were in the highest spirits, and full of confidence. I have never known quite the same universal feeling of cheerful eagerness.

The moment came, and they were all walking over the top, as steadily as on parade, the tin discs on their backs (to show the guns where they were) glittering in the sun.

MJR. H. F. BIDDER, DSO.,
Royal Sussex Regiment.

We were moved up and we were herded into this field behind the reserve line, and when we looked back it appeared as if we were sitting on the lea of a hill, it would be like a big mound. Well, the next thing we knew, we were being given this cotton wool and told to put it in our ears. Well, there was no guns firing, but we had to do as we were told and put this cotton wool in our ears. The next thing is, this mound, what we thought was a mound, well camouflaged, is two big twelve-inch Naval guns, came out on a track, just the muzzle of the gun showing and manned by Royal Marines. Well, without any warning (and from where I was sitting, it couldn't have been thirty yards), these two guns blasted off. Well, we shot up in the air! We were lying in front of them and the blast from those twelve-inch guns! My God! It shook us!

Our artillery had been bombing that line for six days and nights, trying to smash the German barbed-wire entanglements, but they hadn't made any impact on those barbed-wire entanglements. The result was we never got anywhere near the Germans. Never got anywhere near them. Our lads was mown down. They were just simply slaughtered. It was just one continuous go forward, come back, go forward, come back, losing men all the time and there we were, wondering when it was going to end. You couldn't do anything. You were either tied down by the

CORPORAL W. H. SHAW,
9th (S) Battalion,
Royal Welch Fusiliers.

shelling or the machine-guns and yet we kept at it, kept on going all along the line, making no impact on the Germans at all. We didn't get anywhere, we never moved from the line, hardly. The machine-guns were levelled and they were mowing the top of the trenches. You daren't put your finger up. The men were just falling back in the trenches.

Now there was a saying in the Royal Welch Fusiliers, 'Follow the flash.' Now, I don't know whether you've ever seen a Royal Welch Fusiliers officer, but there's a flash on the back of his collar. The officers were urging us on, saying, 'Come on, lads, follow the flash!' But you just couldn't. It was hopeless. And those young officers, going ahead, that flash flying in the breeze, they were picked off like flies. We tried to go over and it was just impossible. We were mown down, and that went on and if some of the Battalions did manage to break through, it was very rare and it was only on a small scale. If they did, the Germans would counter-attack and that's what was going on. You'd attack, fall back, the Germans would counter-attack, they'd fall back, and that's how it was, cat and mouse all the time.

When they were counter-attacking, well, they were mown down, just the same as what we were, and yet they were urged on by their officers just the same as our officers were urging us on. They were coming over just like cattle, whole Battalions of them. You just felt, 'You've given it to us, now we're going to give it to you,' and you were taking delight in mowing them down. Our machine-gunners had a whale of a time with those Lewis machine-guns. You just couldn't miss them.

Almost imperceptibly the first day merged into the second, when we held grimly to a battered trench and watched each other grow old under the day-long storm of shelling. Big shells landed in the crowded trench. For hours, sweating, praying, swearing, we worked on the heaps of chalk and mangled bodies. Men did astonishing things at which one did not wonder till after. Here is an instance of fortitude.

SERGEANT J. E. YATES,
1st/6th Battalion,
The Prince of Wales' Own,
(West Yorkshire Regiment)
(TF)

A man had his right arm and leg torn off clean. His mind was quite clear as I laid him on the fire-step. His left hand wandered over his chest to the pulp where his right shoulder had been. 'My God,' he said, 'I've lost my arm.' The hand crept down to the stump of the right thigh. 'Is that off too?' I nodded. It was impossible to move him at the time. For five hours he lay there fully conscious and smoking cigarettes. When at last we tried to carry him out the stretcher stuck in the first traverse. We put him on a groundsheet and struggled on. But our strength was gone: we could not hold his weight. 'Drag me,' he suggested then, and we dragged him along the floor of the trench to the medical dugout.

At dawn next morning we were back in a green wood. I found myself leaning on a rifle, and staring stupidly at the filthy exhausted men who slept round me. It did not occur to me to lie down until someone pushed me into a bed of ferns. There were flowers among the ferns, and my last thought was a dull wonder that there could still be flowers in the world.

One meets nowadays on the roads many wagons returning from the direction of the line, loaded with 'swab' equipment. The troops of the new army wear pieces of cloth of different colours to distinguish their Divisions and Brigades. A Battalion – I think of Royal Fusiliers – which I saw marching up, fresh and clean and full of life and vigour, a day or two before July 1st, had pieces of pink flannel over their haversacks, displayed in such a way as to be recognisable in battle by our aeroplanes.

COLONEL ROWLAND
FEILDING,
6th (S) Battalion,
Connaught Rangers.

A few days later I passed a wagon-load of salved equipment returning from the line. It was interleaved with the same pink flannel, now no longer fluttering gaily, but sodden and bedraggled, and caked with sticky clay.

**CAPTAIN GUY
CHAPMAN,**
13th (S) Battalion,
The Royal Fusiliers.

*The whole battalion,
except the cooks and the
half-dozen officers who
had been left out of the
attack, was asleep. They
lay stretched on the
hillside, their uniforms
daubed with chalk, their
faces and hands brown
with mud, their hair
tangled and their
unshaved cheeks
bloodless, the colour of
dirty parchment, just as
they had fallen in
attitudes of exhaustion.*

*There was a sudden stir.
A few men rose, others
woke and joined them,
collecting in a mob round
a khaki figure with a
camera. Pickelhaubes,
German helmets,
Teutonic forage caps,
leaf-shaped bayonets,
automatics, were
produced from
haversacks. The faces
which ten minutes earlier
had seemed those of dying
men were now alight with
excited amusement.
'Come on, come an' have
your picture took,' echoed
from man to man; and
amid much cheering, the
official press was obliged
with a sitting.*

6 July, 1916.

To James W. Murray, Esq.,
President of the Glasgow
Chamber of Commerce.

My Dear Murray,

I suppose you will have heard of the very severe losses sustained by the 17th HLI on the 1st of July.

Up till now, I have made it a rule to write to the next of kin of any of our men who have fallen out here, but in the present circumstances it is beyond me to continue this practice. I have, therefore, no course open to me but to ask you to send this letter to the Glasgow papers for publication.

I should like to express to all the relatives of those who have died, my sincerest sympathy with them in their present great sorrow, and to assure them that all the remaining Officers, NCOs and men share their grief with them.

It may be some consolation to them to know that the battalion walked into action as steadily as if it had been on the Parade Ground, and I cannot adequately express my feeling of admiration for the spirit, gallantry, and daring with which all faced their terrible task.

Those who have, in this battle, given their all for their country, did so in a spirit worthy of Scotland's best traditions.

It may be a comfort to the relatives of the wounded to hear that all who came in contact with them testify enthusiastically to the patience and fortitude with which they bore their sufferings, and to know that the spirit they displayed very greatly increases their chances of rapid recovery.

I have always been very proud of my Battalion, but in the action of July 1st, Officers, NCOs and men, one and all, displayed so much coolness, courage, and resource, that my pride has been more than justified.

> I am,
> Dear Murray,
> Yours very truly,
> (Sgd.) David S. Morton, Lt.-Col.,
> Cmdg. 17th HLI.
> (Glasgow Chamber of Commerce Battalion)

On 1st July the great offensive opened up. The rumbling of gunfire was incessant. The Adjutant called a parade about 9 a.m., and read the wonderful news: '2nd Corps all objectives taken; 8th Corps slight hold-up on left flank; 3rd and 5th Corps no report yet; 13th Corps striking advance etc.' Somebody miles behind must have dreamt it all. An hour later the walking wounded came struggling back with a luggage label tied on their tunics with details of wound and treatment. They were mainly the 36th Division. They came on day and night for days. We did not go into action until the 10th July 1916. Then we had to cram our belongings into our pack, retaining only our haversack and ground

CORPORAL H. DIFFEY,
15th Battalion,
Royal Welch Fusiliers.

sheet so that we would not be hampered in 'chasing' the enemy. Meanwhile the First Aid Post had run out of luggage labels, but each casualty had the same treatment, viz their first aid pack was slapped on with iodine and they lumped it.

As we approached the village of Mametz there were scores and scores of 18-pounders, wheel to wheel, firing away without any camouflage whatever, and half a mile behind scores of horses waiting to be coupled up to the guns to chase the enemy back to Berlin; but it didn't happen. Months later the guns had hardly moved and the horses had gone to greener pastures! We moved in at dusk, relieving some battle-weary troops. The RAMC were much in evidence, we had never seen them before, but casualties were so heavy it was impossible for Company stretcher-bearers to cope.

I and a dozen others were detailed to meet a couple of mule-drawn GS wagons containing 303 ammunition outside Mametz village. The boxes were damnably heavy to carry along with one's own equipment, but we soldiered on down the road to the wood with fountains of earth spouting up each side of the road from enemy shells. Stopping for a rest I and another chap tumbled into a trench and a second later a terrific bang and asphyxiating cordite filled the air. A 5.9 had made an impact! I heard a faint cry of 'stretcher-bearers' and returning to the road came across a scene of complete devastation. There were six bodies and ammunition thrown everywhere as if a giant had smashed the boxes. I was in a daze, a couple of stretcher-bearers appeared and did what they could for the poor devils.

Then came an order that you must not stop to help a wounded comrade during an attack. Those that did were sitting targets for enemy machine-gunners and consequently nobody reached the objective. Nobody knew what was happening or supposed to happen.

And newspapers in the UK wrote of tremendous victories and killing Germans as a sport similar to ratting. We could laugh aloud at these reports, plagued by lice and living amongst the debris of war and the legends that sustained our armchair patriots at home.

PRIVATE W. HAY,
The Royal Scots
1st/9th Battalion, (TF).

You were between the devil and the deep blue sea. If you go forward, you'll likely be shot, if you go back you'll be court-martialled and shot, so what the hell do you do? What can you do? You just go forward because that's the only bloke you can take your knife in, that's the bloke you're facing.

We were sent in to High Wood in broad daylight in the face of heavy machine-gun fire and shell fire, and everywhere there was dead bodies all over the place where previous battalions and regiments had taken part in their previous attacks. We went in there and C Company got a terrible bashing there. It was criminal to send men in broad daylight, into machine-gun fire, without any cover of any sort whatsoever. There was no need for it; they could have hung on and made an attack on the flanks somewhere or other, but we had to carry out our orders.

But there was one particular place just before we got to High Wood which was a crossroads, and it was really hell there, they shelled it like anything, you couldn't get past it, it was almost impossible. There were men everywhere, heaps of men, not one or two men, but heaps of men everywhere, all dead. Then afterwards, when our battle was all over, after our attack on High Wood, there was other battalions went up and they got the same! They went on and on. They just seemed to be pushing men in to be killed and no reason. There didn't seem to be any reason. They couldn't possibly take the position, not on a frontal attack. Not at High Wood.

Most of the chaps, actually, they were afraid to go in because they knew it was death. Before we went in, we knew what would happen, some of the blokes that had survived from previous attacks knew what they'd been through. It was hell, it was impossible, utterly impossible. The only possible way to take High Wood was if the Germans ran short of ammunition, they might be able to take it then. They couldn't take it against machine-guns, just ridiculous. It was absolute slaughter. We always blamed the people up above. We had a saying in the Army, 'The higher, the fewer'. They meant the higher the rank, the fewer the brains.

10 July. After being relieved in the morning we returned to the dugout in the wood (High Wood). The artillery fire there was absolutely frantic. Nearly every shell landed in the trench. Some men were buried alive while others were blown into the air. Unteroffizier Wahlen's squad had dug the deepest hole into the side of the trench for protection. It was too deep, for two shells landed directly on top of them and six men were entombed inside. We immediately began tearing away at the earth and could hear someone shouting, but our rescue efforts did not save everyone.

11 July. At 4 a.m. I left with three men and took up residence in the field of craters between the company's forward trench and Mametz Wood. We immediately set to work deepening our holes, digging for two hours. Around eight o'clock the English began to systematically strafe the company sector with heavy-calibre shells. Geysers of earth a hundred feet high shot from the ground. With my field glasses I could see past Mametz Wood all the way to the village of Mametz. The entire area was swarming with the activity of English troops, wagons and ambulances moving forward, and prisoners going to the rear. It was a shame we did not have contact with our artillery. We sat watching this panorama until midday. No relief came. The shell fire increased in our vicinity and every fifteen minutes we had to shovel clods of earth from

SERGEANT GOTTFRIED
  KREIBOHM,
10th Company,
Lehr Infantry Regiment,
3rd Guard Division.

our holes. Pieces of equipment were sent flying out of the Company's trench while the barbed-wire stakes tumbled crazily in the air. The ground rumbled and heaved with each explosion. Suddenly, a noise like a roaring freight train rushed down upon me and I instinctively covered my head with my hands. I waited one, two, five agonising seconds – for the explosion. When nothing happened I opened my eyes and saw, to my immense relief, a large shell half buried in the earth only one and a half metres away from me. It was a dud. Thus we waited in our holes for ten hours – the most fearful ten hours I had ever experienced in my life.

GUNNER FRANK SPENCER,
C Battery,
152nd Brigade,
Royal Field Artillery.

14 July

Out of range on our own front, very quiet all day. We enjoy a nice game of cricket with an improvised bat. During the evening the Regimental Section Officer asks for ten volunteers to go over to the German lines to fetch one of six guns from beyond Contalmaison that have been disabled. He has very little difficulty in getting these few men for all of them jumped at the chance of a real adventure, and what an adventure it was, and what a chance to get souvenirs, beside the great souvenir which our General had promised to send to Nottingham, when our Brigade was raised. Well, we started off at 8 p.m., as it was a long way, and as it led right over the battlefields of July 1st and on to date. They presented a most wonderful sight, equipment, rifles, shells, unexploded fuses in thousands and innumerable material; over ours as well as the Germans we kept falling, as many bodies had been removed, and many had not, these having been fallen so long the odour was quite sickening. Here and there, the ground was a mass of upturned earth every yard dotted with shell holes, but on we went, giving hasty glances at numerous things of very special interest. In one place a huge unexploded projectile of 12-inch shell lay as it had flopped on the surface as though it had ricocheted to the left along a byroad leading on to Pozières. A little further on and we could get no further, as the road was all barricaded against the enemy. We halt here while our officer consults an Infantry Officer. We are now over the crest and the enemy is not many yards away, and to reach the guns now means to leave the trench and go about sixty yards and, the ground being shelled but not directly in front, a little to our right. The Infantry Officer cautions our leader, trying very hard to persuade him to give up the venture, but not one would hear of it now, as we was so close to our objective. A word from our leader and over the parapet we went and doubled up to the dark objects in the distance which were quickly reached. There was a new difficulty; the guns were covered with ammunition and debris, and the German gunners all lay dead around their gun pits. Drag ropes were soon fixed and a stout pull moved the gun out, but the noise of the disturbed debris awed us all, and we stood still. Up went a crowd of rockets. We thought we were spotted, but anyway the lights died out, and on we went. It was a most awful deed, over shell holes and corpses. We could not miss them. The shells were falling quite close to us now, but no one heeded them. We had started out not knowing what an undertaking it meant, but having got there so far, we could not give in now. We could not return with the gun by the trench, so we made half-left towards the junction with the Contalmaison road, a distance of several hundred yards, and having reached the road, how are we to get the gun down, for the Infantry had built a parapet eight feet high protected by barbed wire entanglements. After much delay we were all over-done and wearied out, so we got the gun down the parapet on two planks. No shells were falling now, but the parapet afforded us good shelter from the bullets. The parapet unfortunately ended a little further down the road. All along the road the enemy was close on our right, and the gun was frightfully noisy, the trail dragging on the road being too heavy to lift. The crest now hid us from view although Fritz sent up many lights, no doubt in hopes of seeing what all the noise was about. All of us was completely done up and the situation was most dangerous. We had now got the enemy on three fronts, 'Right', 'Front', 'Rear', and from the front we could be seen, although we was a long way off in that direction, so our leader rested us here whilst he went to bring up our team of six horses and limber we had left under cover of a wood.

Now came the worst moments, while resting in shell craters one of our party touched the electric torch (By accident or not, I cannot say), but only a few seconds elapses and we are in a hail of shells from the right and machine-gun fire front. We crouched low down in the craters, but were all covered with fallen earth and shrapnel. One by one we crept from hole to hole down the road and eventually land in a good trench here and find a machine-gun and decide to add it to our trophy. All of a sudden we are stopped by an Infantryman who emerged from a dug-out. This was the first intimation that the trenches were occupied. They had sought shelter in their dugouts from the shells and hearing our voices came out fully expecting a counter-attack was in progress and the enemy had entered their trenches. They were much surprised to find us all unhurt. On the way down to that friendly trench myself, a Corporal and a Gunner hear a shell coming, on our left is a row of enemy dug-outs into which we dived for shelter from the shells directed at us, so off we went in these dugouts, the Corporal and Gunner in one and I in the other, but, Oh, the ghastly sight that met me. (I often see it in the dark now) for just inside the entrance, which, in the dark, was only a black hole, was a corpse, almost in a standing position against the wall, and it seemed to meet me as I entered. No second thought was needed to make sure it was a corpse – that ghastly face and glassy eyes against the inky blackness of the interior was sufficient. It was as if death himself and I had met, although the air was full of bursting shells, the open was most preferable to me to this awful place, so I turned and fled into the open, faster than if a brigade of Prussian Guards were after me. All at once, the shells quietened down. We ventured back very cautiously to the gun, encouraged by the sight of a dark moving shape not many hundreds of yards from us which we knew was our team of horses and limber and once we reached them our labours at least would cease if not the dangers.

We reach the gun and start off with it at right angles to the road on our left. Down the slope here we are exposed to view from Ovillers and exercise great strength and care when lights go up, but without avail. We are seen again and he measures with both artillery and machine-guns, but owing to the crest of the hill which his machine-guns have to clear, the bullets fly high over our heads and his artillery is less accurate than before, thus encouraging our party to push on.

We were close to the team now, but one more difficulty arose – an elaborate enemy trench with barbed-wire entanglement intact at this point, and to cross it elsewhere, meant much labour and going up the hill into view of the enemy. Long labour and many small scratches and a lavish use of the new revised and enlarged edition of the English Language and the wire was passable. The only way of crossing this trench was where a big shell had lowered the parapet and strewn debris into the trench bottom, presenting a sort of a ford across. We decide to try it and we met with better success than expected, due no doubt to the relieving team of horses just the other side, inspiring the party to inflated effort in dragging her over. The trophy was roped to the limber with a feeling of triumph, which but for the close vicinity of the enemy, would no doubt have found expression in a hearty good cheer. The horses were set going, the weary party trailing far in the rear. Coming along the valley, the smell of lachrymatory gas causes much comment, and before going much further it became necessary to put our helmets on as the valley was clouded with gas and fumes from shells. Once across the valley (of the shadow of death might well be added as it was the scene of the first blow in the great battle) the atmosphere became clearer and it was decided to risk it in preference to the dreadfully smothered feeling of the British helmet on, so we removed them. Down the hill across the right and we are back to our position with the gun. Officers came to view the gun with interest and warmly congratulated the party, so after a real good issue of rum we turn in about 4 a.m., and I for one slept a dreamless sleep.

◆ ◆

QUESTIONS FOR YOU!

In this the greatest War of any time
THE GAPS IN THE RANKS NEED FILLING.
Have you a friend who has fallen?
Can you, will you fill his place?
On Land and Sea ALL HAVE BEEN HEROES:
Each one we lose IS A LOST HERO!
EVERY ONE WHO STEPS INTO THE BREACH
TO FILL THE GAP BECOMES A HERO TOO!

Memorial Service,
Bermondsey Parish
  Church.
(From the printed Order of
  Service.)

---◆---

4th August 1916. Second Anniversary of the War. Patriotic shrine in East London.

And still we laughed in Amiens,
As dead men laughed a week ago.
What cared we if in Delville Wood
The splintered shells saw hell below?
We cared ... We cared ... but laughter runs
The cleanest stream a man may know
To rinse him from the taint of guns.

T. P. C. Wilson

2ND LIEUTENANT
EWART
RICHARDSON,
4th Battalion,
Princess of Wales' Own,
(Yorkshire Regiment).

Last night a strange thought came to me. I was with a working party in the trenches. We had come up the communication trench, zig-zagged our way thither for a mile and a half or more. Now this time of year the communication trench is a thing of beauty. On either side the piled earth has covered itself with vegetation, fresh thick grass, heavy growths of bunched white daisies interspersed with blood-red poppies.

The daisies are, in fact, camomile, so I am assured by one who is by way of a botanical expert. And through the camomile and poppies we make our way to the line. Through camomile and poppies we make our way back to rest and peace for a brief spell. Through camomile and poppies are borne the wounded, their bandages of white splashed with scarlet, like the flowers themselves, and through camomile and poppies passes the last sad procession when, over the line, death has suddenly shaken his dread spear.

Our objective lay some 500 to 600 meters in front of us – Delville Wood. The ground to be covered in the attack sloped gently toward the shattered wood and could be seen from all parts of the wood's eastern edge. The first wave, to which I belonged, went over at exactly 2.15 and began to run down the slope toward the wood. Until this moment the enemy had held his fire, but now he let loose. The entire length of the wood's edge was one giant machine-gun nest. After running about 150 metres I laid down in order to catch my breath.

Again I ran forward a short distance and leaped into a very large, deep shell hole already occupied by two pioneers who were seeking refuge from the murderous fire. They had gone over with us in the first wave. We could see how the entire line of attack was stopped cold by the enemy's fire. Here and there a few small groups tried to push forward, but the men were either driven to the ground or shot down. Every attempt to move forward meant certain death and useless sacrifice, while No Man's Land and our trenches behind us were plastered by the enemy's artillery. Caught between the enemy and exploding shells, the next seven hours were the most difficult time of my life at the Front. If someone was wounded he was better off dead since no help was possible during the day. And who would find him at night? In the meantime, the August sun burned down through the cloudless sky.

GEFREITER HEINRICH RENZING,
7th Company,
88th Infanterie Regiment.

In 1915 the War Office decided to form a corps of highly mobile machine gunners to be carried on motor-cycles.

Mr Geoffrey Smith, the Editor of *The Motor Cycle* was invited to organise the supply of recruits, able to drive, and with a sound knowledge of the internal combustion engine for this new unit, to be called the Motor Machine Section of the Machine Gun Corps.

We were all very young and very raw, with practically no officers or NCOs. I was given a stripe as Acting Lance-Corporal (Unpaid) after only ten days' service because I knew the rudiments of drill through a year in my school cadet force.

Unfortunately, before we could be trained in gunnery and equipped with machines and weapons, the armies in France had settled down to trench warfare and the sidecar guns were immediately rendered obsolete. Then early in 1916 while we were all wondering what our future was going to be, the name of the unit was changed to the Armoured Car Section of the MGS, and rumours of a heavy fighting vehicle began to circulate in the 'latrine news'.

A secret area for training was required, and this was found in a sparsely populated part of Norfolk, on Lord Iveagh's estate between Thetford and Bury St Edmunds. A large part of the estate was cleared of all inhabitants and cordoned off. All roads passing through were closed, and notices stating '*Explosives Area – No Admittance*' were put up.

CORPORAL A. E. LEE,
MM.,
A Battalion,
Tank Corps.

We received our tanks and spent the long summer days of June and July practising driving and maintenance. On the very few occasions that we were able to obtain a pass to visit Thetford or Bury St Edmunds we found the local people very curious as to what was happening in the 'Explosives Area', and many tall stories were told; but nothing approaching the truth, and the tanks, or 'Willies' as they were called at that time, remained one of the best kept secrets of the war.

We had no books of instructions to learn from and had to find out for ourselves how to operate the tanks. We learnt by a system of trial and error and somehow, by sharing our knowledge, we got results and soon every man in the crew became a competent driver, working on the principle that every man must be able to do the job of everyone else in an emergency. (We had already been trained on guns.) Training was finally completed except for actual practice in battle, and we entrained for Southampton – and from there by ship to Le Havre.

We joined up with our tanks at Yvrench, a small village near Abbeville. Then we had a great disappointment. C and D Companies had left England a fortnight before us and it had been understood that we should all go into our first action together and so open up a fairly wide front; but for some reason the General Staff insisted that we should be used piecemeal instead of in one large attack, and the great advantage of surprise was thrown away.

PRIVATE CHARLES
COLE,
1st Battalion
Coldstream Guards.

Something was brought near to the reserve trench, camouflaged with a big sheet. We didn't know what it was and were very curious and the Captain got us all out on parade. He said, 'You're wondering what this is. Well, it's a tank,' and he took the covers off and that was the very first tank. He explained what the capabilities were. We was due to make an attack on the Germans in forty-eight hours from the time he showed us, and what we had to do when we made the attack at Zero Hour was just to wait for the tank to go by us and all we had to do was mop up, consolidate our trench.

Well, we were at the parapets, waiting to go over and waiting for the tank. We heard the *chunk, chunk, chunk, chunk*, then silence! The tank never came. It was split-second timing, we couldn't wait for it, we had to go over the top. Well, we went over the top and we got cut to pieces because the plan had failed. Eventually, the tank got going and went past us. The Germans ran for their lives – couldn't make out what was firing at them. We didn't know anything at all about tanks, *they* didn't know anything at all about tanks, so the tank went on, knocked brick walls, houses down, did what it was supposed to have done – but too late! We lost thousands and thousands and what was left of us Coldstreams, we didn't know what to do, so we got into shell holes and bits of wall where there was cover.

Colonel Campbell of the 1st Battalion, Coldstreams, got up on the trench and he got a hunting horn and he blew the hunting horn and got us together and he stood on top of the trench. They say God was in the trenches. There was a book came out, *God in the Trenches*, and if God was ever in the trenches, He was there looking after Colonel Campbell. He won the Victoria Cross. He was just over there from me and I saw that VC won. If ever a man deserved it, it was Colonel Campbell. He got us together and we dug ourselves in and consolidated our position.

The sunken road running from Flers to Eaucourt l'Abbaye was being enfiladed with rifle and machine-gun fire coming from Goose Alley which was still in German hands and was on somewhat higher ground. In places the road was covered with New Zealand dead. We paused under a bank for a moment. It is strange what tiny things can capture the attention when danger looms. An officer in front of me had kneeled in the soft soil and the imprint of the knee of his corduroy riding-trousers took my interested attention for a few seconds. We then left the road and ran over open ground towards our objective, Grove Alley.

At that moment, a sledge-hammer hit me just above the left knee. I crashed on to my face and my military career came to an abrupt and

PRIVATE H. BAVERSTOCK, 1st Canterbury Battalion, New Zealand Division.

painful end. My thigh-bone was shattered and my chief concern was whether the femoral artery had been cut. If so, it was the end of me, for I was in no state to apply a tourniquet. Any movement was agony, and I had to lie there trying to endure it.

I suppose the time was about 2 o'clock on the Saturday afternoon. After a few hours, two stretcher-bearers of the Hauraki Regiment found me and dragged me quite a distance to the sunken road. The pain was unbearable; it felt as if my leg were coming off. Having put me in a shallow funk-hole, they turned me on to my back, ripped out the field dressings from inside my tunic, cut open my trouser leg and bound the bandages round the wound, a gaping hole with a terrific bulge on the opposite side. All the while, they were being sniped at, for we were pretty well exposed. Having done all they possibly could for me, they told me they would have to return to Flers to get their stretcher.

Whether those two brave Medical Corps chaps were killed I could not say, for I never saw them again. The chances of their reaching Flers were poor, for the sunken road was a complete death-trap. There I lay for about two days. To the best of my judgement, a slight retirement took place that night, so I assumed that I was lying in No Man's Land. Before long, the pain increased and the slightest movement was unbearable, but I managed to fling my two Mills bombs out into the field, wriggled painfully out of my web equipment and took the bandoliers of cartridges from around my neck. The back of my clothes was soaked in blood. I spent the time that Saturday night smoking some 'Tweenies' that I had got in a parcel from home and taking small sips of water flavoured with petrol from my bottle and listening to the sounds about me – the chattering of our machine-guns nearby, the sighing of big shells lolloping over, the shriek of stray pieces of metal hurtling through space and shell-bursts. One shell that burst fairly close must have sent up a lot of earth for one big clod came smack down right on my wound. The hardest sound I had to try to bear was the shrieking and groaning of some poor chap a few yards away. That went on for an hour or two and then suddenly stopped. During the afternoon of the Sunday the weather broke and heavy rain came down. I managed to put my greatcoat over me and put on a thick woollen cap I had received in a parcel and put in my haversack.

At long last, early on the Monday morning, two other stretcher-bearers found me and lifted me on to their stretcher. They took me to Bogle's Post, an advanced aid-post somewhere near Flers. It was merely a shallow depression in the ground, very exposed, and was being heavily shelled. Near my stretcher lay a captain of the Field Ambulance, on his face. I was told it was Captain Bogle himself who had been killed by a shell-burst just behind him while doing his dangerous duty. A German gun had his post properly marked for every five minutes a shell came over to burst on or very near it.

We passed along the fringe of Switch Trench where the stench was nauseating. The odour of death permeated everything. We crossed over that terrible battleground between the two woods, so honeycombed with trenches that many deep dugouts must still lie buried intact beneath that ground. Arriving at Thistle Dump, I gave the stretcher-bearers a tin of pipe tobacco by way of thanks. I saw some poor fellows who had died on the stretchers on the way from Flers being lowered into graves already dug and waiting for them. The whole battlefield was strewn with the bodies of New Zealanders killed on the fifteenth and sixteenth and not yet buried.

Mouquet Farm, 26 September, 1916
Suddenly, at half past two, the enemy let loose with devastating drumfire on the position lying in front of us. It was clear the English were preparing to attack. Another man and I ran left and right in order to see whether we had any neighbouring troops on our flanks. We found no one. We quickly prepared for the worst. The situation was not very favourable for we only had our rifles – and no machine-guns or hand grenades. Then came the anxious shouts, 'They're coming!' As far as we could see the Tommies were moving forward at a trot. Our front line must have been completely torn up by the frightful shelling for we had not heard any rifle or machine-gun fire. Facing the oncoming wave, we could not think of getting up to run to the rear. We would have been shot down like rabbits. And staying to defend the place was as good as committing suicide.

GEFREITER FRITZ HEINEMANN,
2nd Company,
165th Infanterie Regiment.

The Tommies soon bypassed our position on both flanks and it wasn't long before we received fire from behind, wounding one man. The English were close enough to throw hand grenades now. After several of them exploded nearby we jumped from our holes and headed for the two dugouts. We quickly scrounged some wood and two overcoats, hanging them in the dugout's entrance to help protect against the flying splinters. I peeked out through the overcoats to observe enemy troops carrying machine-guns and ammunition forward. Two Englishmen walked past within a few feet of the dugout's doorway but did not attempt to enter.

Hours slowly passed in absolute uncertainty. Were we to die, or be taken prisoner? Still, all of us held on to the faint hope that we might be rescued if our own infantry counter-attacked. We had no water and the thirst was unbearable.

Suddenly a tremendous crash shook the dugout, knocking us down and extinguishing the few candles that served as light. A large-calibre shell had fallen directly outside the entrance. We were buried alive! My head ached terribly from the shell's concussion. The air was thick with fumes and difficult to breathe. Since we could no longer hope to escape, one man started yelling and pounding to attract attention. Leutnant Liebau stopped him, explaining that the racket would only start the English shooting.

The man who was wounded twice was the only one among us who could speak English well. He had not lost consciousness so we moved him to the dugout's blocked entrance. Then we began banging on the steps, hoping someone would hear the noise and investigate. Suddenly we heard faint English voices. It was difficult at first for him to shout and hear through the earthen barrier, but he made those on the other side understand that we were completely exhausted and could not dig out by ourselves. With that we heard the sound of shovels hacking away at the ground. Thinking of the fresh air outside, I was flushed with new-found strength and tore at the earth with my hands. In the meantime, Leutnant Liebau collected letters and other papers from the men and ripped them into small pieces. At last, a plate-sized hole was punched through the entrance, letting in light and flooding the dugout with air. Soon the hole was enlarged sufficiently for each of us to crawl out, one after the other. Two soldiers wearing khaki stood waiting with their rifles levelled. Several of our men ignored the weapons upon seeing some grass growing from the wall of the trench. They ripped clumps out and immediately stuffed as much as possible into their mouths. Watching this, one of the enemy soldiers removed his water bottle and passed it around. I will never forget this gesture as long as I live.

Those troops now occupying our position turned out to be Canadians. After being searched for weapons and documents we were led away. Passing through the enemy's lines we saw an enormous number of artillery pieces, collected and lined up in unending rows. But at the same time we saw evidence of the work of our own guns – dead Englishmen were lying everywhere.

So marched into captivity all that was left of the 2nd Company of the 165th Infanterie Regiment: two officers and twelve men.

We stayed for a week at Daours and practised a Brigade attack over a flagged course, representing the ground between Lesboeufs and le Transloy. On Friday the 6th I went to the forward area for a preliminary reconnaisance.

I have forgotten nothing of that first visit to the Somme battle area. In the open, no sign of vegetation was visible: shell craters literally overlapped over square miles – gashes in the torn surface, more or less continuous and deeper than the rest – indicated trenches, and in these our troops managed to exist, shelled day and night until they went forward to the attack or were replaced by other troops – only less muddy and tired than themselves after a few days so-called 'rest'. Thickly timbered woods were reduced to a few gaunt and splintered trunks. Stripped of every leaf and twig – without undergrowth – almost without roots. Villages disappeared as though they had never been; what the bombardment left the Army removed – wood was taken for fuel or for making trench shelters; bricks and stones for repairing roads. As a result one could stand in the centre of what had been Mametz or Fricourt, or many another village of perhaps three to four hundred inhabitants and the only intimation of one's position was a noticeboard bearing the name of what had been.

From far to the west of Montauban to Bernafay Corner was an endless line of transport – motor lorries, ammuniton wagons, ration carts, RE material and ambulances. The congestion of traffic on the few bad roads of this district was appalling. Ration limbers took anything up to sixteen hours to do a single trip from their lines to their unit's HQ and back. The roads were awful, a column might be halted a full hour without making a yard of progress, liable to be shelled at any moment, and when they got back their billet was a muddy field, a wagon sheet the only cover for men and harness – horses standing in mud to their hocks – never dry, never clean – yet they never failed us.

CAPTAIN R. J. TROUSDELL, 1st Battalion, Princess Victoria's, (Royal Irish Fusiliers).

Le Transloy, 2–8 November, 1916
We are in a chalk tunnel. It is full of men – sleeping comrades lying everywhere. The air is horribly foul since most of the ventilation shafts are plugged. Night falls, and I make preparations for the move forward. The sunken road behind the cemetery along the main road to Lesboeufs is full of men and material.

There is not a single tree stump on the way to use as a guide in finding the forwardmost line. Only craters. The line is where a helmeted head

UNTEROFFIZIER PAUL MELBER, 1st Machine-gun Company, 28th Ersatz Infanterie Regiment, Bavarian Ersatz Division.

sticks up out of the ground. If one has bad luck and strays too far he ends up a guest of the English. Searching for the position I call out softly and finally am answered by a 'crater dweller' in a hole next to the machine-gun. The crater is at least five metres across and full of slime and water at the bottom. The gun stands ready to shoot at the edge of the crater. A few feet away a hole has been dug into the side of the crater and is covered with a groundsheet. Here is where one sleeps. If Tommy does not bother us, this will be our home for four days.

Our 'friends' in their own craters across the way remain strangely silent. That is always suspicious. Around 10 p.m. a man of my post yells, 'Corporal! The yellow flares!' In an instant I am out of our sleeping hole and fire the flare pistol skyward. In another instant, even before the flare's light burns out, Satan's howling fury comes crashing down in the form of a German barrage, laid out only thirty to fifty metres in front of us. The English attack or scouting patrol dissolves. Rifle shots and exploding hand grenades continue for a time, but we do not fire the machine-gun for fear of betraying its position to the English.

At 10 p.m. the following night the English resume their bombardment of our rear areas. White flares shoot to and fro through the blackness. Then, *pfff* ... yellow rockets, immediately to the left of us, freezing the blood in one's veins. They're coming! Instantly, our own barrage rips through the air and into the ground. The shells' explosions silhouette the Tommies. Screams ... The earth heaves from the furious fire of the guns. Everyone is shooting, throwing grenades. All hell has been let loose. We have already fired 500 rounds with the machine-gun. My loader fumbles with a new box of ammunition, finally shoving the belt into the gun's feed block. It is firing again ... *tack-tack-tack* ... *rrack!* God in heaven, a jam! The gun is yanked down into the crater and carried quickly to our covered sleeping hole. In feverish haste the block and belt are examined. The belt is wet. Rip it out! Pushing in a new one, I notice that everyone's face is covered with sweat. The machine-gun is thrown back up on the crater's edge. Thank God, the new belt runs through freely.

The muddy earth out front spits fire. We must duck continuously as the shells from our artillery scream overhead and slam into the rows of Englishmen. Eventually the shooting stops. White flares still illuminate the shattered landscape, but no one can be seen. The attack is broken. We lay exhausted on the crater's edge – hearts pounding, eyes burning and throats parched with thirst. But our bones are still sound.

Steady rain had settled in for some hours, and the trenches were in a bad state. I scrambled and slid along and I tried to be cheery with the men as I passed; but it was perfectly obvious they were out of heart, after their long exposure to shelling and with the atrocious weather conditions. Their rifles were nearly all unworkable with clay, and they knew it; and that took the heart out of them too. One said, 'The truth is we aren't hardly fit for it, sir.' Well, it was the truth. Another said, 'We'll do our best for you.'

MAJOR H. F. BIDDER, DSO,
Royal Sussex Regiment.

I then went out with the bombing officer, to see that his preparations were complete.

Back again to the dugout, to sit down and await events.

There were there besides myself, the adjutant, the Lewis gun officer, and the signalling officer – all three aged from nineteen to twenty-two.

The minutes went by. Then at last there was a crash and a roar, and the bombardment had broken out. Soon I went up to see what I could see.

It was hell out there – shrapnel bursting, bombs exploding, our own barrage further on – it was one long crash and roar. And the Verey lights were going up in large numbers from Rifle Trench; and then I clearly saw, silhouetted against the Verey lights, some little black figures running – back. The attack had failed. Presently the Brigade HQ rang up to ask for news, and I told them what I believed had happened.

A message came from Brigade to say a tank was coming up, and on its arrival the attack was to be renewed. I pointed out that this could not affect my right, that if the men could be got out of the trenches again it would only be to be mopped up by machine-gun fire.

Presently it was rumoured that the tank was around. In spite of all the gloom of failure and loss, nothing could make that tank anything but comic. We stood along the trench to watch it. First a humming sound, then the squat longish animal lurching along the Boche front line, every now and then firing a six-pounder gun that stuck out from the side. On it came, nosing along the trench; then, as if struck by a new idea, it turned off and went across to the Boche support line; and then went away, nosing along that. It produced for a time quite an air of cheeriness in our part of the world.

The Brigade wanted to know how our bomb attack had got on; but it hadn't got on at all. The tank had not been near it, such as it was. They then said that a second tank was on its way, and we must then advance. I knew, and the bombing officer knew, that the men were totally unfit to attack at all, but thank goodness the second tank stuck and remained behind our lines all the afternoon.

The day wore on, and in the early afternoon I was sitting on the floor of the dugout. Further in were the bombing and signalling officers; on the steps was the Lewis gun officer; the adjutant was standing at the entrance, and near him were the machine-gun officer and the trench mortar officer. Suddenly there was a very tremendous noise, quite unlike anything else I have experienced. For the moment all was darkness and the earth dropping. The first thing one did was to take stock of oneself – no, unhurt. Then to look up and see if we were buried. No – through the cloud of smoke that filled the opening a small light hole was visible.

Someone outside enlarged the hole, and out we came. The Lewis gun officer, sitting on the stairs, had been hit in the neck; he went straight off, and we saw him no more. The signaller, poor boy, was badly shell-shocked. It came on worse after the first half-hour, and he was practically unable to speak or move till next day. The bomber, with this on top of the fight, was pretty badly shaken for the moment. It was obvious he could no longer lead an attack. When I crawled through the opening, helped by the people outside, I stepped over two men lying just outside and climbed through the debris, finding the trench mortar officer lying there dead. They were working to get out the adjutant and machine gunner – both just alive, lying among earth and beams. As they pulled the adjutant clear he gave a little quiver, and died.

The gunner was very badly injured in the legs. He was alive, and was carried down the trench to the dressing station; but died soon after.

I felt that I must make it quite clear to the General that any renewal of the attack now by us was absolutely out of the question; so I went down to Brigade HQ. I explained matters, and the General was quite sensible and nice. I also asked for some reinforcements, as I was holding something like three-quarters of a mile of front with something like three hundred shaken men. Next afternoon we were relieved.

◆

No more we'll share the same old barn,
The same old dugout, same old yarn,
No more a tin of bully share,
Nor split our rum by a star-shell's flare,
                    So long old lad.

Just one more cross by a strafed roadside,
With its GRC*, and a name for guide,
But it's only myself who has lost a friend,
And though I may fight through to the end,
No dugout or billet will be the same,
All pals can only be pals in name,
But we'll all carry on till the end of the game
                    Because you lie there.

                    * Graves Registration Cross

CSM W. J. COGGINS,
DCM.,
1st/4th Battalion,
Oxfordshire and
Buckinghamshire
Light Infantry (TF).

The Somme was the worst. That's all I dream about, mostly, now. I never saw so many dead.

They sent me and my section back for a week's rest to a clearing station for the wounded. A week's rest! My God! We were carrying the wounded. We were at it day and night! We met all the ambulances coming down from the front line, and some were dead when they arrived back there in the ambulance. It was in marquees then. There was a big marquee – that was kept for men that weren't expected to live – and the doctors examined each one as we carried them out on a stretcher and carried them into the reception tent. If they put a red tab on them they were the ones that had got to go into the big tent, they weren't expected to get through it, and I used to hear them poor sods at nighttime, moaning and crying for water. Nobody went to them, you know, nobody went anywhere near them. First thing in the morning, we had to go into that marquee, take blankets in with us, sew these bodies up in blankets, carry them from that marquee into GS wagons, then go with them to the burial ground. Some old Frenchmen were there, digging long trenches for the burying. We used to lay them side by side in the grave and wait until they'd read the burial service over them and then back again for the next lot of ambulances. And this was a week's rest! *What a bloomin' rest!*

MRS LILY HENRY

We were married less than a year. I got a telegram on the Saturday saying George was slightly wounded. Then the *same day* I got one, 'Seriously Ill'. Then one came, 'Dangerously Ill. Visit possible'. Well, I'd never dreamed of going!

He was in the 8th General Hospital, Rouen. When we'd had several telegrams like this a policeman came late at night when I was in bed and said that the specialists at the Rouen Hospital would like his wife to go because they thought it might just be the turning point and that gangrene had set in. Mother didn't tell me about this until morning. She came in about six o'clock with a cup of tea and said, 'I'm afraid we've had more news. They want you to go to see George because he's not improving. But,' she said, 'you'll not go, will you? You'll let your father go?' 'Oh,' I said, 'but I must!' This was about six o'clock, and by eight we were off, me and my father.

We went to the War Office. We got all information from there. Everywhere I went we would be met so I had nothing to worry about. But my father was worried, so he said, 'Can I go with her? I'll pay my own expenses'. And in the end they decided, yes, he could go with me. We went from Southampton to Le Havre. They took us up to the hospital. There were huge iron gates – beautiful gates – and a very wide drive. Coming down the drive was the Matron with her cap flowing and she said – she knew who we were – they knew who we were all the way, everywhere – she said, 'Your husband has now had his left leg amputated – but he seems to be all right.' Then she took us in. My father couldn't stay. He stayed one night but he was quite disturbed about going because he didn't expect George would recover and he thought he was leaving me there with a dying man. I can remember seeing him walk down the ward and turn round and just put his hand up and then I don't remember any more except that each day I came to the hospital. They usually took George out to have his leg dressed. They gave him gas every day. He never spoke.

I asked the specialist if I could go at the end of a fortnight. I said, 'Do you think I could go now because I have a job?' 'Well,' he said, 'if he has a haemorrhage again I can't answer for him. So I advise you to stay another week and I'll let you know what I think.' So I stayed another week in the Red Cross Hostel for relatives.

We saw one old couple. They'd come from Newcastle and they were sitting on their cases in the hallway. They were both seventy and their son had been buried that day. They were too late!

By the time I went back, George was on the mend and soon after he was sent over to England. Of course, with just one leg, he was out of it then.

Our custom at all funerals behind the line was to bring a party of buglers to the grave to sound the Last Post. I buried the men with the following order of service. I said the first introductory verse; *I am the Resurrection* ..., the psalm *De Profundis*, the committal words, a prayer for the dead *We commend into thy hands, O merciful Father, the soul* ..., sometimes a prayer for the mourners: the grace. Later I added the Psalm *Eternal Rest*, having heard it at a Roman Catholic funeral and being impressed with the beauty and aptness of it.

THE REVEREND J. A. HERBERT BELL,
4th class Chaplain,
Prince of Wales' Own
(West Yorks.) Regiment.

CORPORAL W. HOLBROOK,
4th Battalion,
The Royal Fusiliers.

I was taken down to Etaples on the coast and I went from there to Le Touquet convalescent. While there the first morning, you had to go on parade, the Colonel doctor inspected us. Some fellows had been there three or four months in this camp and some of them said to me, 'If you tell a tale, you can stay on for month after month. Make out you're queer and all that, then you've a chance of staying for ages.' I said, 'Yes, all right. Lovely!' So the first morning, this Colonel, nice sort of man said, 'How are you?' I said, 'Well, I've got rather bad pains in the back, Sir.' Nothing wrong with me really. So he says, 'Oh, well, a few weeks here and we'll soon put you right. Don't worry.' So I thought, that's all right, went back to the hut. In the afternoon Sergeant come and he says, 'Brown, Smith, Holbrook. Parade tomorrow morning to go up the line.' 'God', I thought, 'I shall only be here two nights.' So I had to go, back to Rouen into camp. It was cold in that camp at Rouen. Next morning I had to parade and go in front of a General. Lined up with some others in front of this hut. When I got inside this hut this General's got a damn great coal fire behind him – and it's all cold outside and wet and mucky in the cold icy weather – and a damn great fire he's got, this red-faced General sitting there. And there's a big coloured picture on the wall, a text, 'Oh, death, where is thy sting! Oh grave, where is thy victory?' I thought, 'There's a damn fine thing for a fellow to walk in and see in big letters.' He said to me, 'Name?' I said my name. 'You been up the line before?' I said, 'Yes, Sir.' 'Just the man we want!' And out I went. He didn't ask me a damn thing! 'Just the man they want,' he said, 'so out you go.' When I got back to the tent and told them they said, 'He only asks one question. If you say "yes" he says, "just the man they want" if you say "no" he says, "Damn high time you did go!"' I was only there a night. And he was sitting there, that damn red-faced General, in front if this damn great fire!

SAPPER E. DAVIDSON,
Royal Engineers.

I got wounded during the Somme. We went down to St Valéry, near the coast and that was absolutely wonderful down there. We were at a Convalescent Camp where there would be about a thousand soldiers recovering from slight wounds and they put up very, very good meals for us. They tried to nurse us back to good health, those of us who weren't wounded badly enough to go to England. They marched us down every day down to the beach with a smashing band, and a chap there who knew how to arrange us, and we had to do country dancing to try to take our minds off the war. We had to do dances like 'Sir Roger de Coverley', and my partner was a bricklayer with three kids, and there would be this chap, 'Bow to your partner. Hold hands, advance three paces. Bow. Retire three paces.' Just imagine me with a bricklayer going backwards and forwards! He said, 'If my kids could see me now, they'd never speak to me again!'

When your legs seem made of jelly
and you're squeamish in the belly
and you want to turn about and do a bunk,
for God's sake, kid, don't show it!
Don't let your mateys know it –
You're just suffering from funk, funk, funk.

Robert Service

Before we left England our Chaplain preached several sermons on the effect of danger and suffering on men out here. He said that being constantly in danger of losing one's life made men think of the serious side of life and fly to religion as the only source of comfort. My own experience is quite the contrary. In the bombing raid I was on recently the language was so bad that even the men themselves commented upon it. Men go to their deaths with curses on their lips and religion is never mentioned or thought of. Instead of 'Gone West', being killed is spoken of as being 'Jerked to Jesus'. Why is it? I can only put it down to the fact that life out here is one of continual hardship and suffering, that in war there is no place for a God of Love, no time for the softer emotions, and no inclination to worry about a future when the present is a hell that the devil himself would be proud to reign over.

PRIVATE J. BOWLES
2nd/16th (County of
London) Battalion,
Queen's Westminster
Rifles.

The brutality and inhumanity of war stood in great contrast to what I had heard and read about as a youth. I really wanted to go off to the Front at the beginning of the war because in school we were taught to be super patriots. This was drilled into us – in order to be men we should go off to war and, if necessary, bravely die for Kaiser and Fatherland.

FREIWILLIGER
REINHOLD
SPENGLER,
1st Bavarian Infanterie
Regiment.

When I had joined the army in the spring of 1916 I still carried presumptions that the war would be fought like the 1870 War between Germany and France. Man-to-man combat, for instance. But in the trenches friend and foe alike suffered from the effects of invisible machinery. It was not enough to conquer the enemy. He had to be totally destroyed. The fighting troops of the front lines saw themselves mired hopelessly in this hellish wasteland. Whoever lived through it thanked his good luck. The rest died as 'heroes'. It seemed quite unlikely to me in late 1916 that I should live through it. When you met someone you knew who belonged to a different outfit, he was greeted with the words, 'Well, are you still alive?' It was said humorously but meant in deadly earnest. For a young man who had a long and worthwhile future awaiting him, it was not easy to expect death almost daily. However, after a while I got used to the idea of dying young. Strangely, it had a sort of soothing effect and prevented me from worrying too much. Because of this I gradually lost the terrible fear of being wounded or killed.

Lecture to Officers of the 3rd (City of London) Battalion, (Royal Fusiliers) TF.

I cannot, in this short lecture, go into all the many weaknesses of a man, but will take one thing that in my experience is very rarely ever tackled by officers in Company Training. I mean *fear*.

There is no doubt that the very human characteristics of fear act more powerfully on the feelings of the individual soldier in wartime than any other human emotion and it is very infectious. The soldiers in peacetime never mention fear. It is kept as a sort of skeleton in the cupboard. It seems to be accepted by everyone that to be a soldier means to be a brave man. But what of the soldier, as a class, without *proper training* or without any experience – can he be braver than any other class of man in civil life? Fear in its mild form is present in every human mind, and we could not be without it. We look up a street to see if a taxi is coming for fear of being run over. That is reasonable fear. It is a perfectly legitimate attitude in a soldier. For example, we teach men to take advantage of any cover during an attack, we dig trenches in a defence, in both cases to avoid being shot by the enemy. We apply the emotion of fear to overcome the emotion of surprise, as in good artillery, in good Staff work etc.

Fear is the dread of surprise and the unknown.

I have gone rather fully into this because I feel that it is so important and we must train our men so that they reduce the chance of surprise to a minimum, and when if surprised they know what to do you go a long way to making every man a courageous man. If you instil confidence, make your men believe they shoot better and fight better than the enemy, they will carry all before them.

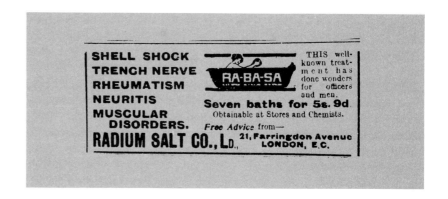

There was one poor little man came to me. He was a half-wit. It was getting on in the war when we were getting very poor material out and he was posted to my Company and he ran away, and he was caught and ran away again, deserted, and he was court-martialled to be shot, and I had to pick, together with my Sergeant-Major, ten men to shoot him, which we did, and one of my Subalterns had to be in charge of the party with a revolver, and he was shot. I wrote to his mother, 'Killed in Action', and I think that's what they were told in every case. One didn't give them details as to how people were killed. I wasn't present at the execution. I didn't want to be. Neither was it a nice job for the ten men. I consulted with my Company Sergeant-Major and he actually picked the ten and I didn't go into the details of how it was done, whether the man was put on a chair or blind-folded, or anything, a mark over his heart – I didn't go into the details at all. I didn't even ask the Subaltern afterwards what happened. It was a horrible thing to have to do, but it had to be done. It had no effect on the men's morale. The morale in the Territorials was there to begin with and we'd got it. It got a bit weaker later on as we got dwindled out by the end of the war. I mean, people came to us from anywhere. They came to the Territorials, but they hadn't got the *esprit de corps* that we had in the early days.

CAPTAIN C. S. SLACK,
MC,
1st/4th Battalion,
East Yorkshire Regiment.

General Routine Order No. 1885 is published for information:

No. 12772 Private A. Botfield, 9th Battalion (Pioneers) Sth. Staffordshire Regt. was tried by FGCM on the following charge:–

'Misbehaving before the enemy in such a manner as to show cowardice'

The accused when proceeding with a party for work in the trenches ran away owing to the bursting of a shell and did not afterwards rejoin the party.

The sentence of the Court was 'to suffer death by being shot'.

The sentence was duly carried out at 5.50 am on 18th October, 1916.

an Entry in the Army War Records of
Deaths 1914–1921

CERTIFIED COPY OF ⬥ AN ENTI

Registration of Births, Deaths and ⬥ Marria

Return of Warrant Officers, Non-Commissioned Officers and Men of *the 18th Bn. The Manchester R*
Killed in Action or who have died whilst on Service Abroad in the War of 1914–1921

Rgtl. No	Rank	Name in Full (Surname First)	Age	Country of Birth
10495	*Private*	INGHAM Albert	24	*England*

An Entry relating to the death of *Albert Ingham*

CERTIFIED to be a true copy of *the certified copy of** an entry made in a Service Departments Registe

Given at the General Register Office, London, under the seal of the said Office, the *11th* da

**If the certificate is given from the
original Register the words "the
certified copy of" are struck out.*

Section 3(2) of the above mentioned Act provides that "The enactments relating to the registration of b
and Northern Ireland (which contain provisions authorising the admission in evidence of, and of extracts
have effect as if the Service Departments Registers were certified copies or duplicate registers transmitted

SAWI 001526

CAUTION:—It is an offence to falsify a certificate or to make or knowingly use a false certificate or a
to the prejudice of any person, or to possess a certificate knowing it to be false without lawful autho

Form A528   Dd. 8924070   1M   287   Mcr(733762)

**TROOPER SYDNEY
CHAPLIN,**
1st/1st Northamptonshire
Yeomanry.

Soon after I joined the Military Police we had to turn out one night and fall in outside the hut. It was very dark and I wondered what it was for. Then along came two of the Police with a prisoner and they stood backs to the hut and we faced them, next came a file of men with an officer and they stood at ease in front of us. We had an old soldier who looked after things at nighttime and he came along with a lighted lantern. Then the APM walked up with a paper in his hand and stood facing the prisoner. The old boy stood at the back of him holding up the lantern to shine over the APM's shoulder. We were called to Attention and the APM began to read: 'Private So-and-So, you have been charged and found guilty of desertion in the face of the enemy. The verdict of the court martial is that you are to be shot at dawn.' It was signed by Sir Douglas Haig.

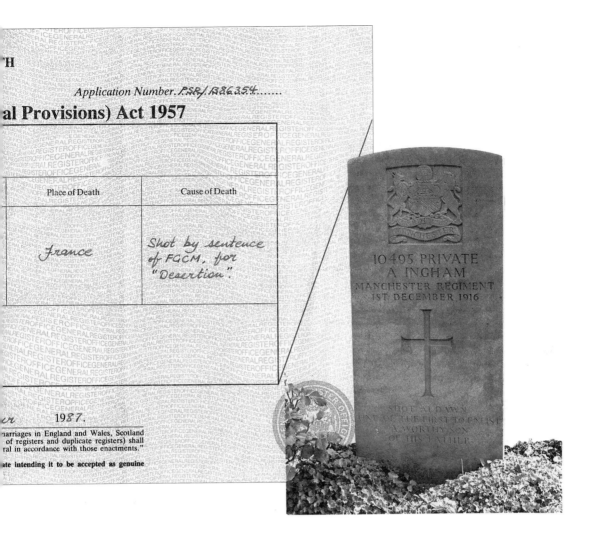

Application Number. PSR/ 126354 ....

al Provisions) Act 1957

Place of Death	Cause of Death
France	*Shot by sentence of FGCM. for "Desertion".*

r 1987.

arriages in England and Wales, Scotland
of registers and duplicate registers) shall
ral in accordance with those enactments."

ate intending it to be accepted as genuine

10495 PRIVATE
A INGHAM
MANCHESTER REGIMENT
1ST DECEMBER 1916

SHOT AT DAWN
ONE OF THE FIRST TO ENLIST
A WORTHY SON
OF HIS FATHER

Next morning the sun was shining and a touch of frost in the air. I
was sent up to the road to stop any traffic and being high up and on
horseback I had a bird's-eye view. I saw the man brought out to the
post and the firing squad march into position, turn right and take up
stand. I heard the report as they fired and saw the smoke from their
rifles. Then they turned and marched off. The officer, with revolver in
hand, inspected the body, then turned away. The dead man was then
taken away in a blanket and buried in the small cemetery in the next
field. It was over. I came down, but it did not seem real.

The next one followed the same pattern, except the APM said,
'Cowardice' – and the man said, 'Never!'

PRIVATE LEONARD
HART,
1st Otago Infantry
Battalion,
5th New Zealand
Reinforcements

Christmas Day 1916   *France.*

Dear Father, Mother and Connie,

We are once more back to the line and feel better after our spell, although mid-winter in France is necessarily accompanied by a good deal of sickness.

Our Christmas Day has turned out wet and cold but most of the chaps seems to be in high spirits, partly, no doubt, on account of the liquid refreshment which can be easily obtained almost anywhere at all in France. The 'Estaminet' (bar) is a feature of the fighting areas of France, and any farmhouse or village where khaki predominates always contains its 'Estaminet' or 'Estaminets' as the case may be. We had some very good plum-duff for dinner today, each man receiving a liberal allowance.

I was sorry to hear of young Jeremy's death, but with such a large number of relatives here some are bound to go. Human life is about the cheapest thing in existence just now and, after the manner of fatalists, we come to regard being alive and well as merely luck. While in billets a short time back I managed to get off for a few hours to visit my old company in the 1st Brigade. I found one of my original Trentham mates still alive and well. He and I are the only ones who have not been either killed or wounded. Out of the original platoon I find that including myself there are still five men out of the fifty who can claim to have come through without a scratch. Unfortunately this is a case of all right 'so far', but the war is not over yet by a good bit.

I will close now hoping that you have all enjoyed a Merry Christmas and will enjoy a Happy New Year.

                              Your affectionate son
                              Len.

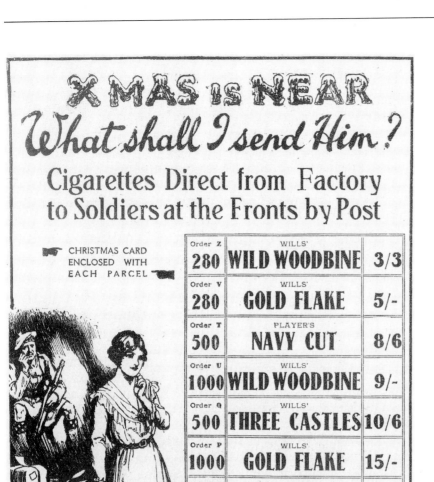

**SHOEING SMITH
C.H. WILLIAMS,**
5th Battalion,
The Oxfordshire and
Buckinghamshire Light
Infantry.

We had our Christmas dinner in Albert in an old sewing-machine factory – the whole battalion together, and the Colonel and the officers came in afterwards. We had beer for our dinner – plenty of it – wine as well, and a good tuck-in to go with it! Roast pork! Beautiful after bully beef! I used to sing one or two bawdy songs. In fact when we were on the march, coming towards the end of the day our Company Officer used to get me up the front and say, 'Come on Williams, give us a song, and get the lads going'. Real bawdy songs they were, but it gave them a laugh and kept them going. Anyway at Christmas we'd all had plenty to drink and the lads had me on to sing. So I gave them a few of my specials. And they always wanted the apple song.

> I once knew a fellow
> his name was Ben,
> He had nine of a family
> (nearly ten!)
> ... Now all you gents
> If you want any more,
> I've an apple up me arse
> And you can have the core!

And that wasn't the worst of it, by any means! I couldn't in all decency repeat what came in the middle. But the lads liked it. They all joined in, and after it was finished our sergeant came up and he said, 'Williams, the Colonel wants to see you!' I thought, 'This is it! Court martial for me.' So I went up to the table where all the officers were, and Colonel Best's sitting there with his jacket undone, smoking a cigar. He says, 'That was a good song, my lad. Do you know any more like that?' I said, 'Well, just a few, Sir.' So he said, 'Well, sing 'em, boy. Sing 'em!' And he gave me a bottle of champagne! That was a night, that was. What with the wine and the beer and champagne, they had to *carry* me back to the billet!

**JÄGER HERMANN
KEYSER,**
9th Jäger Battalion.

24 December, 1916

Dear parents and sister!
Christmas Eve! It is 10 o'clock in the evening. I write you these lines with thoughts of longing for home and days gone by. So much has changed in the past year. The war goes on with no hope for a soon-to-come peace. How ironic that man calls this holiday a time for peace. I can only wish it will happen during the coming year. Nothing would make me happier than to be together with all of you under the Christmas tree. For the first time in my life there is no tree, no singing, nothing.

The company was relieved yesterday, but was sent to occupy a reserve position. They will have no celebration today – maybe tomorrow night or perhaps the next morning. One can only hope. I am sitting here writing by the light of a carbide lamp. This evening I received a parcel, the first of the holiday, from the Turn-Verein [Athletic Association], and it contained a cake and twenty cigarettes. Wasn't that nice? As I write I am nibbling on the cake which tastes quite good. So, now I have described to you my situation on this Holy Evening of 1916.

Yesterday I went to Roulers with a comrade. This city of some 50,000 inhabitants lies one and a half hours' journey away from us by small-gauge rail. In Roulers we went in search of provisions, and bought some bread, doughnuts from Berlin, two pounds of peas and a pound of white flour. The price we were forced to pay was ridiculously high, but there was not much that could be done about it. I have sent some of these things to you along with two nutmegs and two bars of soap. Hopefully you'll receive the package soon.

Now, dear family,
I will close,
sending you my love and best regards.
Hermann.

All night the minnies whinney
As they circle o'er the trees
By many a copse and spinney
They bring man to his knees.

Way down from yonder thicket
The murderous weapon flies,
Lobbing its strange fantastic trails
In circles through the skies.

Like comets in their transit
Piercing the gloom of eve
These thrice winged cylinders of death
The starry heavens cleave.

The many murmured melodies
Of the missile in its flight
Triumph at last in one grand chord,
Strange music of the night!

1917

Same old trenches, same old view,
Same old rats as blooming tame,
Same old dugouts, nothing new,
Same old smell, the very same,
Same old bodies out in front,
Same old strafe from two till four,
Same old scratching, same old hunt,
Same old bloody war.

A. A. Milne

Despite the cost of victory on the Somme, 1917 began with an air of optimism. The troops had advanced on the Western Front. New offensives were afoot; meanwhile, Sir Douglas Haig (whose promotion to Field Marshal was announced on 3rd January) was determined to keep the Front active. Through the months of January and February, in a series of small localised battles, the troops whittled persistently at the enemy line and inched forward to gain a few more yards of mud, to wrest away a few more windswept strongpoints, to win another trench as deep in mud or snow as the trenches from which they jumped off to capture them. Trench raiding was an almost nightly pastime, encouraged as much to keep the troops on their toes as for the prisoners and information they brought back.

But the Germans were far from idle. They too had suffered severely on the Somme and they were short of men. They stood on a huge and awkward salient that bulged northwards from Laon to Arras and took many troops to hold. The ground was lacerated by warfare, and conditions — notably on the Somme — were appalling. Since the previous September they had planned to save manpower by moving back to a shorter, stronger, straighter line behind —* in places as much as twenty-fives miles behind. The 'Siegfried Stellung' was engineered for 'defence in depth', protected by forests of wire many yards deep, the Germans had been building it since the previous September and it was built to be impregnable. In the middle of February they would begin to retire to it.

The barrage opened and we went over through our wire. We got through the best part of No Man's Land and of course Jerry puts his counter-barrage down, but luckily he was overshooting us. I was one of five with Lieutenant-Commander Brown. So we gets in this outpost trench and walk along and come across a tremendous great dugout. There was a hessian curtain hanging at the top of the trench. Pull it to one side and you could just see the dugout at the bottom, thirty-three steps. So he calls out, 'Anyone down there, come out and show yourselves, otherwise there's a grenade coming down.'

With that a Jerry Sergeant-Major comes to the bottom with his hands up. He says, 'Please do not shoot, we have casualties here.' So Brown says, 'Right, we're coming down. Any jiggery-pokery, there'll be more casualties.' Of course, he had his revolver out, followed by the Leading Seaman. I was number three and there was one more behind me. Two men he left up the top. We get down this dugout, there's a sharp turn to the right at the foot of the stairs and there was a chamber twenty feet by eleven easily and, in the middle of this, there was a little table with documents on it. There was a Jerry with a severe thigh wound laying on a stretcher in a corner, a Jerry Sergeant-Major sitting there with two others. It was lit with candles. Brown says to this Jerry Sergeant-Major, 'I want your battalion documents, no hokey-pokey. I want them, or you.' He said to Leach, 'Take his revolver'. Jerry put it on the table. He says, 'Unload it,' so the Leading Seaman shot the bullets out on the floor and he handed it to Lieutenant Brown.

There was a shelf running the length of the dugout and on that there was a box of cigars and I hadn't seen such a big box of cigars in my life! They must have been eighteen inches long, so I take it down, open it and it's full. Lieutenant Brown turned round and he says, 'You don't smoke cigars. I'll have them. You have this'. So he gave me this revolver, a most massive thing. Anyhow, you can't argue the point with your Company Officer so he took my cigars and I had this revolver.

He said to me, 'Search that prisoner there,' and he said to my mate, 'Search that one'. Well, I run my hands over this prisoner and took his haversack off him. In this haversack was a safety razor which I've still got. There's a mark on the blade from Leipzig. There was two candles, a piece of ersatz chocolate, but they were of no interest to me.

Brown stuffs the documents in his pocket. He says, 'Right, we've been here long enough. It's time we were getting back, bring your prisoners.' This Jerry Sergeant-Major tugged his arm. He said, 'Man wounded on the stretcher. Don't leave him.' 'OK,' he says, so these two Jerry prisoners who were able-bodied had to pick up the body and carry it out. When we got out of the trench, we hadn't gone half a dozen yards when Commander Brown says to Leach, 'Do you know where we are!' He says, 'I think we're right, Sir.' This Jerry says, 'No, no, no, no,' and *he* led us to our wire. So that wasn't the first time *he'd* been out there

A/B. J. HAYNES,
Anson Battalion,
Royal Naval Division.

in No Man's Land. Of course, having found our wire, it was no trouble to us to find the opening where we'd got to go in. Jerry never forgot the raid, he was plugging the line all next day. But we got the documents, and we got the prisoners and we got the information they wanted.

PRIVATE L.M.
BALDWIN, MM,
8th (S) Battalion,
East Surrey Regiment.

On 19 February we attacked the enemy from Grandcourt Trench. They occupied Death Valley and Boom Ravine. We captured Boom Ravine with a stiffish fight but not much difficulty. After clearing our own wounded from the Ravine, which was strewn with blood-stained Deutschmarks, we inspected a machine-gun, mounted on a post, ready for swinging round to any position and while we were looking at it our attention was drawn by a young German soldier lying in a 'cubby-hole'. He was one of those who had survived our attack, but he had three machine-gun bullet wounds. The cold weather had congealed the blood, otherwise he might have bled to death. We carried him away under shell fire and my fellow stretcher-bearers suggested 'finishing him off' for our own safety's sake. I said, 'No, we can't do that,' and pointed out that a prisoner of war is entitled to humanity. So off we went, carrying him across the snow with the guns still blazing away. As stretcher-bearers carry no firearms I wondered by what means they would have killed him? But there is always something lying around on the battlefield that could have been used, I suppose. It turned out that the prisoner could speak French and English and he certainly didn't look very comfortable listening to us discussing 'finishing him off'!

We stopped for a rest on the way to the dressing station and during the halt the German boy asked for my home address and promised to send me a souvenir after the war. I had to refuse because finding my address on a German may have implicated me in some way. However, I wrote *his* (Braut Strasse, Bremen) in the back of my small pocket diary. It was 1936 before I came across it and, on an impulse, I wrote to him. I received a reply about a month later from Berlin where he had gone to live. By then he was a Doctor of Economics. In the letter he reminded me that he had promised me a souvenir, and he sent it via a business friend visiting London and staying at the Pall Mall Hotel. 'Bob', as I began to call the Doctor, wanted his gift to be of double value – intrinsic and sentimental. It turned out to be a solid silver cigarette case. Inside one lid is inscribed Bob's brother's name (to whom the cigarette case was given in the first place by his friend Emme at Easter, 1917). *My side reads Robert Liebig to Leonard M. Baldwin who proved to him a friend on February 19th, 1917, Berlin, April 1st, 1936.*

Then he wrote and suggested we should meet and invited me to travel as his guest to Berlin. I went in August 1937 and it was the first of many visits I made through his generosity. But it was the funniest. Stanley Baldwin was Prime Minister at the time and news had got out about our meeting and a facsimile of my letter appeared in the Berlin daily paper. On another page of the same issue appeared, '*Mr Baldwin to visit Berlin*'!

My meeting with Bob in Berlin was reported in various London and local newspapers. The cutting I like best was captioned 'Tell This Story to your Children'. There were posters announcing 'Friendship of Former Enemies' and one paper portrayed me carrying Bob to safety on my back, which I never did. It must have been poetic licence that showed him still holding his rifle! I would have certainly dumped it to lighten the load!

◆

GERMANS RETREAT ON A WIDE FRONT
OUR TROOPS RAPIDLY ADVANCING

◆

We were in the line when we received information one morning that the Germans had fallen back and evacuated the positions they'd held for the winter. The officer came along and ordered me to take a patrol out and see if the Germans were still in occupation in front of us. Well, the previous night, I'd been out on patrol and had went up to the German wire and could hear the Germans were still in occupation and we were fired on, so you can imagine my surprise and consternation when he told me I had to do this. We were wearing trench boots at the time, like Wellington boots right up to the thigh. And I said, 'Well, we can't move in these things out in the open. I'll change into ordinary footwear' – meaning our ankle-boots which were slung round our necks. Well, I made it last as long as I could. In the end our officer was getting furious with me for wasting time, trying to get my trench boots off and my ankle-boots on. The men were doing the same, because we were all very worried about this. Anyhow, we were eventually ready and my instructions to the men were that I would go first. They were to get on the fire-step and if the Germans opened fire, they would return the fire and I would get forward and go by bounds.

I got through the wire and waved them on and we proceeded roughly 300 yards by bounds of about fifty. Eventually, we reached the German

SERGEANT E. COOPER, VC., 12th (S) Battalion, King's Royal Rifle Corps.

trench and it was empty, so we amused ourselves by running up and down and throwing German bombs down the dugouts, making sure that the Germans had already gone, and then I sent a message back that we had occupied the German front line trench and they could now proceed to advance. I thought it was very, very good. Eventually we followed them right up to the Hindenburg Line slowly, forcing them out of a good many positions they took up on the way.

———————◆———————

I do not love you, Mr Hun.
I wish this war had n'er begun,
But now we have you on the run
We'll warm your breeches, Mr Hun.
                    Captain G. Garnett Clarke, Royal Field Artillery

———————◆———————

GENERAL
LUDENDORFF,
My War Memories.

The decision to retreat was not reached without a painful struggle. It implied a confession of weakness bound to raise the *morale* of the enemy and lower our own. But as it was necessary for military reasons, we had no choice; it had to be carried out...

The fact that much property belonging to the inhabitants was destroyed was to be deplored, but it could not be helped. The bulk of the population was transferred eastwards, only a small proportion being collected in certain places, such as Noyon, Ham and Nesle, and provided with rations for several days and left behind. On the one hand it was desirable not to make a present to the enemy of too much fresh strength in the form of recruits and labourers, and on the other we wanted to foist on him as many mouths to feed as possible...

The great retreat began on March 16th, according to plan, and was carried through without a break in a few great stages. The object of GHQ was in general to avoid battle, and to allow the troops time to prepare the Siegfried Line before the enemy reached it in superior force...

The Entente armies followed closely on the heels of our retiring forces and tried to make out that our retreat was a great success for themselves... As a matter of fact they had not gained any military triumph. Thanks also to the false intelligence we had circulated, they had not even interfered with our work of demolition and clearance. The whole movement was a brilliant achievement on the part of both commanders and troops, and is evidence of the careful foresight and work of the German General Staff.

I have been over most of the reconquered country now. In one village a civilian came along in a cart and started dragging box after box out of a filthy pond near a ruined farmhouse, and loading them on his cart. We asked him what he was doing, and he said that when the Germans advanced here in 1914 he had dumped all his cases of champagne in the pond so that they wouldn't find them. They had lain there for two and a half years. He presented us with a case. We did not much fancy the idea of drinking it after lying at the bottom of a dirty pond for so long, but when we opened a bottle in our mess that night it tasted excellent.

MAJOR R. MACLEOD,
  DSO, MC,
C.241 Battery,
Royal Field Artillery.

The Germans seem to have indulged in an orgy of destruction. Houses, and even whole villages, have been blown up and burnt, and nearly all trees have been cut down. The few houses left standing have been thoroughly looted. There may be some military object in destroying villages. The Germans may think that it will delay our offensive if there is nowhere to billet our troops, and we have to get up hutting or other accommodation for them. The systematic destruction of trees has no military object that one can see. In fact, the Germans have provided us with an almost unlimited quantity of firewood, and wood for repair of roads, etc. The fruit trees and trees along roads that they have not had time to cut down have been ringed round so that they will eventually die. The only object seems to be political. They seem to be trying to handicap France so that when the war is over all her resources for some years will be spent in restoring the invaded country, and she will not be able to compete with Germany in trade.

The bad weather, I think, hampers us rather more than the Huns, as we have to advance over the strafed country which has been very much cut up by shell fire.

The Germans have blown up several crossroads, but the success of their object is doubtful as a track round them can be made very quickly.

I am keeping fit. I have not very much work to do, but it takes me a long time to get anywhere now owing to the long distances to be covered.

. . . Permission was requested and given to the inhabitants to return and search the ruins of their houses. They came, and some wept to see the havoc. It seemed that there was nothing for them to do. But every French peasant is a hoarder; all their savings were buried underneath the ruins. There was one old man who unearthed the equivalent of eighty pounds in French gold. He could count himself lucky, for a German trench ran within a few feet of his hiding place.

PRIVATE REG LAWRENCE,
3rd. S. African Infantry Battalion.
South African Brigade.

1 September

Went for a route march through rather pretty country. The Germans have played the game in that they have buried many of our men here. One we passed bore the following simple inscription: *Hier rühen im Gott 17 Britische Kriegern*, or 'Here rest in God 17 British warriors'.

It was a long route march of about 24 kilos. We went to inspect the Butte de Warlencourt, the scene of a particularly unsuccessful attack by some of our men and the DLIs in the Battle of the Somme some months ago. We failed to take the Butte and lost heavily. The ground was battered out of shape and showed signs of the bitter struggle in which our men took the enemy's advanced trenches but were unable to hold them. The 'pimple' which was one of our chief objectives is a large mound of white chalk from which shrapnel bullets could be picked up in handfuls. There were grenades, overcoats, helmets, rifles, lying about in profusion. Over all was the sickly smell which comes from decaying clothing. From one dugout someone pulled out a skeleton with only a pair of German top boots on. I hope somebody buries it.

It was a pleasure to get away from the devastated, shattered and shell-torn area and trench warfare into more open country where the ground, at least, was not muddy and pock-marked with water-filled shell holes. We lived above ground. The type of warfare was more interesting, much more like open than trench-warfare. The shelling was not intense. Most of the German Batteries had been withdrawn behind the Hindenburg Line.

I was posted to the 48th (South Midland) Territorial Division, and was given command of 'A' Battery 240 Brigade.

'A' was an excellent shooting Battery, and in peace time had won the prize for the Territorial Artillery. They had come through the whole of the Battle of the Somme, fortunately with few casualties. The officers and men were good material – the best type of Territorials. But I was not so impressed with their ideas of discipline and administration. Unused to Territorial ways I thought that the NCOs were too familiar with the men. The administration was not very efficient. This was not their fault because in peace time all the administration was done by the permanent staff of Regular Officers and NCOs and the Territorial Officers and NCOs were not trained in it. The officers did not appear to take a grip of their sections, nor the sergeants of their subsections. Orders were given in a conversational tone, almost as if asking a favour, and the men did not jump to them. When I checked an NCO for this and for seeming to be too familiar with some of his men, he said he had to be careful because one of the men in civil life was his foreman and the rest his workmates! In fact, officers and men were often from the same firms and knew each other well, and their sort of discipline was perhaps suitable for the type of war we were then fighting. Maybe I should not have attempted to alter it.

MAJOR R. MACLEOD,
DSO, MC,
Royal Field Artillery.

◆

The troops were preparing for a spring offensive. It was an Anglo-French affair, the plan of the French General Nivelle, to pinch out the great German salient, to attack in three separate areas, drive the Germans inward, and to link up. But the Germans' retirement to what the Allies now named the Hindenburg Line had dislocated his tactics. Nevertheless, despite bickering between the British and French commands, and between the French Command and the French Government, Nivelle did not alter his plans. The British part of the Nivelle Offensive was to break through on a front between Bapaume and Vimy Ridge. Later they called it the Battle of Arras. It was to start on 9 April, Easter Monday.

> *... Deep in water I splashed my way*
> *Up the trench to our bogged front line.*
> *Rain had fallen the whole damned night.*
> *O Jesus, send me a wound today,*
> *And I'll believe in Your bread and wine,*
> *And get my bloody old sins washed white!*
>
> *Siegfried Sassoon*

RIFLEMAN B. F.
ECCLES,
7th (S) Battalion,
The Rifle Brigade.

France,
Easter Sunday 1917.

My dearest Mother,

A strange Easter this, in a strange place. If you could see us you would be more than surprised. You have attended Communion today I know and it will please you to know that I also took the Sacrament. Yes, the best of all services in a place somewhat removed from the surface of the earth in a dim light, big drops of water trickling from the roof on to my head.

It was at 8.30 this morning and the communicants would not number more than twenty. Three rows of us kneeling on stones over which sand bags were laid. In front of me was a Brigadier-General, next a Captain, then a Rifleman. Next to me was another of our gun team, a contented little fellow who always sticks it although he is almost twice my age. In civil life he is a manager of flour mills. Now I must not forget to mention the Altar. Two candles set on a Vickers Gun Chest, the Chaplain's white cloth sat in front with the wine and wafers. Owing to peculiar circumstances, I have had an excellent opportunity of attending service this Easter. On Good Friday, an evening service at 5.30. On Saturday morning communion at 10.30. Then again this morning. (You see we did not expect to be able to attend today, hence the service of Saturday).

Well Mother dear, you can bet I shall be glad to touch civilisation again. Fifteen days now without seeing a shop or civilian. Nothing but ruins. At times the crash, bang, whizz, thump of guns gives one the most awful headache. I have had 10 francs in my pocket for the last three weeks, but no chance of spending it, and there is three weeks pay to come. So, all being well, when another week rolls by we shall make an attempt at a 'spread'.

Now watch the papers.

Well Mother Darling, I must close now. I do not expect to be able to write field cards even, for a day or so. But do not worry about that. I am fit and well and as soon as I can, I will write you a letter. Please tell my little sweetheart that I wished to write to her today but could only get one letter off. You must let her see this letter.

I got your letter of Sunday last and you wondered what I was doing.

Well I will tell you, I was lumbering along one of Fritz's rotten trenches in about a foot of mud. But that night I slept in blankets, so what odds?

Well little Mother, let this Easter cheer you and fill you with a hope that soon all will be at peace once more.

Your most affect. Son,
BURTON.

It is Sunday morning. Behind our farm the valley rises gently in rich meadowland towards the hills. The high plateaux fall away on either side. Thus we have a triangular, flat, sloping depression, and here our Field Service was held. The Chaplain's desk was fixed up under a solitary tree and decorated with flowers and shrubs. What a morning it was! No wind, the sky so blue, the sun shining so warmly.

UNTEROFFIZIER JOHANNES HAAS.

The Chaplain can have been only recently ordained, but there was nothing of the 'pale young Curate' about him! – a thorough officer in walk and bearing. He succeeded in diverting attention from the fine morning to himself. He preached quite a simple, excellent sermon on the divine institution of sacrifice. Then we sang some verses of 'Oh, Wounded Head'. We separated slowly and thoughtfully like the peasants at home, who on Sunday after service go nodding along the road saying, '*Ja, ja*', and then think over their pastor's words as they follow the plough during the week. Good seed had been sown . . .

Arrangements for the service had been shouted with the day's orders, but the instructions did not specify an exact spot, easy to find, and they had not enough enthusiasm to go out and seek for a service.

THE REVEREND J. A. HERBERT BELL, 4th class Chaplain, 1st Battalion Prince of Wales' Own (West Yorks.) Regt.

So I washed out the service but, finding three officers wishing for Communion, I quickly arranged to have one in some part of the buildings of a farm which was close at hand. Its upper storey was in ruins, its ground floor used for cooking etc., its cellar the Officers' Mess and living place for the men. The officers did not welcome my request, thinking that a service would mean a large collection of men, which would tell the enemy, if he looked, that the farm was inhabited, and shells would follow, but I obtained permission to use an outhouse for a Communion. So, in a little cow stall or wheelbarrow shed, about six feet by five, I prepared for my first celebration in the field. I found three empty petrol tins, which I piled on one another for the altar, covered it with a piece of red Japanese silk, hung a crucifix and lighted my solitary candle. The three officers came, and were joined by a private who saw us beginning. They knelt at the open end of the shelter and we carried out the celebration.

**RIFLEMAN RALPH
LANGLEY,**
16th Battalion,
(Church Lads Brigade),
King's Royal Rifle Corps.

Being as how we were in the Church Lads Brigade we were supposed to be very religious. But I don't know! I got hold of two souvenirs. One was a German belt and it's got *Gott Mit Uns* inscribed on it – and that means 'God's with us'. And I also got hold of one of our badges with *Dieu et mon droit* on it, and that more or less meant 'God's on *my* side'. Well, both sides believed that. But it made you think.

**RIFLEMAN FRED
WHITE,**
10th Battalion,
King's Royal Rifle Corps.

The night before we went over the top, the hymn the Padre got us to sing was *Nearer my God to Thee*. Did that make you feel brave? Because it didn't us!

**PRIVATE REG
LAWRENCE,**
3rd. S. African Infantry
Battalion 7
South African Brigade.

Today the Padre preached on the text *Love your enemies, do well to them that do spitefully use you*. Afterwards the Colonel gave us a little heart-to-heart talk on the desirability of remembering that we had bayonets on our rifles and using them accordingly. No encouragement to take prisoners unless they can be of value for information. Dead men tell no tales and eat no rations, etc. ad nauseam. The Church cannot be allowed too much rope lest we lose the war!

◆

A bird lit on the Christ and twittered gay;
Then a breeze passed and shook the ripening corn.
A Red Cross waggon bumped along the track.
Forsaken Jesus dreamed in the desolate day –
Uplifted Jesus, Prince of Peace forsworn –
An observation post for the attack.

Siegfried Sassoon

Somewhere in France, Dear Mother,
Somewhere that I can't tell,
In the midst of the fray
I'm writing to say
That I'm alive and well.
There's some fine big boys from Tipperaree
Somewhere in France with me,
So cheer up, Dear, by next time you hear,
I'll be Somewhere in Germany!

Easter Monday, 9 April
Breakfasted at our assembly area near St Nicholas and proceeded to the attack at 10 a.m. The first attack commenced at 7.30. Prisoners began to appear in large numbers soon after the show began. They must have run to us from 'Zero' itself and they looked delighted when they reached the cage. It was an encouraging sight for our men. The 9th Division carried out the attack in front of us, our job being to pass through them on the Blue or Black line and establish ourselves in the dim distance beyond Fampoux. This we considered a perfectly impossible task and hardly took it seriously, expecting to be switched as a reinforcement somewhere else. But we were wrong. It was a grand success and we gained our objective with very slight losses, taking Fampoux and the 4th German trench system, over 20 guns and about 250 prisoners. Total bag for the Corps about 3,000. The attack seems to have been successful all along the line. It was a most exciting day. To win a battle was a new experience for me. We moved on about 3 p.m., when our troops advanced and we saw them crossing the distant rise as though they were on parade. It was a magnificent sight.

Tuesday 10 April It was much colder today and snow fell. Moved our HQ from the railway cutting to a cellar at l'Abbayette – a ruined farmhouse on the northern outskirts of Athies. Several of us shared a heap of filthy straw. The General has a large double bed in the next cellar – which bed also serves as our mess table!

CAPTAIN R. J. TROUSDELL, 7th Royal Irish Fusiliers, (Attached Brigade HQ).

When zero hour arrived the officer would blow a whistle. If you didn't hear it you saw everybody mounting the parapet, so you did the same and on you went, with the best of luck and a spoonful of rum. On the tenth we went over the top in the second wave and we passed through the first wave when they reached their objective on the Hindenburg Line. We carried on until we reached a network of shallow trenches at the front of Monchy-Le-Preux where we were ordered to stay put and

CORPORAL J. G. MORTIMER MM 10th Battalion The York and Lancaster Regiment we spent the night in these trenches. It was open ground between these trenches and Monchy-Le-Preux. Just after dawn, we got the surprise of our lives when from a copse on our right there emerged the Cavalry. It was a thrilling sight to see them line up in one long line. Then, with the officer and standard-bearer in the centre they set up a yell and set off hell for leather towards Monchy-Le-Preux. We all stood up in the trench and yelled with them. The element of surprise was on their side because they got half-way to Monchy before the Germans realised what was happening – then all hell was let loose and Jerry threw everything he had got at them. They disappeared into the village, where they must have dismounted because groups of about eight to ten horses were brought back to the copse, each group led by one man. They captured Monchy. But at what a price of horses and men!

'The Cavalry came up during the day.... They might as well have stayed away altogether for all the good they did us. We attributed that to the old woman who commanded – not to the troops themselves.

Capt. R. J. Trousdell.

PRIVATE P. J.
BATCHELOR,
Queen's Own Oxfordshire
Hussars.

It was terrible cold and we pegged the horses out in the field in the snow, and we had no hay brought up for them for about three days, and one night I remember we walked the horses about all day till about four o'clock, round and round in a little circle, one after another, to keep them warm and to keep warm yourself. It was about a foot of snow there. We got in an old house with part of the roof on, and we sat down in there. There was a road outside and some lorries went up the road and they'd got some boxes of ammunition in, so our old cook says, 'Here, we'll have some of them, we'll have a fire.' We clambered up the back of these lorries, of course the drivers didn't know anything about it, threw these old boxes out, got about twenty, carried them inside this old house. The cook got his axe and he knocked them up and we sat all round this fire all night and we were warm in front and cold behind. Then we'd turn round and warm our backs. We never had any sleep – there was nowhere to sleep, we'd got no blankets (well, the horses had blankets) and it was wet and snowy. We'd saddle the horses up in the morning and they were so weak they went down with the weight of us. They'd had no grub! Some of the regiments lost a lot of horses up there. Died, they did. Of course, that fizzled out again like all these other attacks. We couldn't get a gap through the line and the cavalry were ordered to go back again. We just went back again to some old village further back.

The funny part about it is that you don't feel things so much going forward. It's when you're being shot at, when you stop, that's when you get the wind up – before you get moving to go over the top and then again when you get to the other side.

RIFLEMAN RALPH
    LANGLEY,
16th Battalion.
(Church Lads Brigade)
King's Royal Rifle Corps.

Of course they got their guns on us when we were going across No Man's Land – and it was such a wide space to go across. I should think it was two thousand yards from where we started – it was certainly a mile – a long distance, bcause the Germans had fallen back towards the Hindenburg Line and we didn't have our noses right up against it. I remember cursing as we were going across this great wide space and thinking that the Higher-ups had put us in to test us. We got tested all right!

It had been snowing all night and we were wet through. We were happy lads! It went on snowing all the time we were advancing, and when we got up towards the German wire, our guns that had been shelling it to smash it up didn't lift soon enough for us. So we laid out there for some minutes, and there was a little Jock officer – he'd only just joined us – and he said, 'Come on, let's get this bloody job over!' Off we went – and just as we got up to the wire the Germans got me through the leg with a bullet. A rifle bullet. You could see them firing at us. And there were machine-guns going too, but being five or ten yards apart they didn't get as many of us as they might have done.

I don't know what the Generals wanted to do that attack for, because it was murder. It was often spoken of between us. They had a job to do, of course, but there were too many lives lost.

*The Hindenburg Line.
Wire, barbed wire! – a
dour and monstrous
serpent round our lives,
and we're like creatures
mesmerised; it glares at us
all day, malignant, sour.*
R. H. Sauter.

CAPTAIN J. M.
MCQUEEN, RAMC,
Sanitation Officer,
15th (Highland) Division.

I got a wire to send up four men to assist the Sanitary Section at St Nicholas in the spraying of dead bodies over the top of the line. I thought to myself when I read this telegram. 'How long are we to suffer from Sanitary Lunatics from home?' I did not believe that there would be more than two gallons of the wretched stuff to spray with, concocted by some silly fool in a laboratory at home and pressed upon more silly asses going by the name of a Sanitary Commission. It is a brutal business, is war. To spray dead bodies with disinfectants is no assistance in wartime. After lying in positions where it is not safe to go out and bury them, the best that can be hoped for is that nature should not be retarded in its process of bacterial dissolution, and nothing should ever be placed on a dead body to prevent a rat eating it. If it cannot be buried, get it down to the state of bleached bones as soon as possible. Disinfectants sprayed on dead bodies by men going over the top after a battle is the height of folly. However, an order is an order, so I chose for this job four unmarried men. If they themselves were left behind with the dead bodies they were spraying, they would not leave a widow, and perhaps children, desolate.

RIFLEMAN B. F.
ECCLES,
7th (S) Battalion,
The Rifle Brigade.

*France,
Monday April 16th 1917.*

My very dear Mother,
I am quite safe and well. I will not say 'in the pink' as I am feeling just a trifle 'war-worn' but a few days rest will soon make me fit again.

I dare say you have guessed from my last letter and the ensuing week's silence that something was on, and now you will have seen the papers. We have been right there. What a Bank Holiday and Easter week! Somehow or other Bank Holidays seem to be big days with us. It has been a rougher do than the Somme although casualties have not been so heavy. It is the blinking weather! Heavy snowstorms on an open battlefield are no 'cop' especially when one is living for four or five days on 'bully and biscuits'. Water was practically napoo so that thirst was an extra addition to our little troubles.

But there again the saying still holds good 'It is an ill wind' etc, for the snow was a godsend to parched throats. Goodness knows how much I ate that night. We were very lucky again, all my pals being safe. We lost one of our team just as we went over the barbed wire but we are still hoping he may turn up. I think I will say, no battalion could have advanced under a Hellish machine-gun fire with such coolness. The way we went forward was as if on parade.

Now, I am thankful to say I went through it quite well. Although I say it myself I kept cool all the time, and was never once troubled with nerves.

This is a great blessing when under fire for one sees cases of fright. And again Mother dear, I must thank you and Dad for your prayers for I believe a fellow has more than luck on his side to win through.

We are now behind the line for a few days. We reached billets after marching all night on top of days without sleep. Our appearance was not exactly civilised! Sunday to Friday without a wash or shave, and all the time in mud holes etc.

So, my dear Mother, just imagine my joy, on arriving at the billet for there awaiting me was a *parcel* and four or five days letters. So I had a feed, then rolled up in my blankets and slept from 5 a.m. to 3.30 p.m.

We then rose, washed, scraped off the thickest mud, had a meal and went to bed again till next morning. Talk about sleeping like a log. But I did not forget to send up a prayer of thanksgiving to God for my safety.

You will remember I told you I was able to attend Holy Communion twice before going up.

Thanks so much for the five-franc note. Since coming down here I have had many cups of coffee. This morning Milner and I bought a couple of fresh eggs each, and we took them to a French woman I know, and she boiled them for us 'Très Bon'.

Now Mother Dearest, I must close. Tell the 'ginger kid' I have got a nice little souvenir of the 'big push' which I want him to hang on my bedroom wall. I am endeavouring to get it through by post.

You will see the owner's name on it. He no longer lives.

Well, goodbye for the present. I shall write again soon. Keep cheerful and smiling, and accept the love of

Your very devoted son,
BURTON.

◆

The Battle of Arras, in the terms of the time, had not been a failure. In many places in the British sector the troops advanced triumphantly on the first day and plugged on doggedly to improve their line over the subsequent weeks and months. The Canadians completed the capture of Vimy Ridge; the Australians broke through the Hindenburg Line to take Bullecourt. But the attacks on the French Front were less successful and it was clear from the start that Nivelle's grand strategic plan had had no chance of succeeding. While Sir Douglas Haig punctiliously continued to fulfil his limited commitment to the French on the Arras Front, he turned his attention to planning the summer campaign in northern Flanders which, he believed, would deal the Germans such a blow that it might possibly end the war. And there was a further reason for optimism. The United States of America had, at long last, declared war on Germany. The Doughboys were coming.

◆ ◆

I joined the Militia after the US declared war, in May 1917. I'd only gone out in 1913, but at the back of my mind was the idea that I owed the country something. If I was going to be an American citizen I should take my part. I don't know what other excuse I had because it isn't that I ever saw any glory in war at all. In ordinary circumstances you'd never have found me near an army camp for the simple reason that I didn't like their spit and polish about things that were not essential. We learnt the hard way. You did squads right and left to put in your time but we never received our ammunition until we got over in France.

SERGEANT R. KNOWLES, No. 99414 164th Infantry, 42nd (Rainbow) Division, US Army.

You went into the camp and then in order to take you out of the State they had to draft you into the regular army. Then we were off to Camp Mills, New York, and then off to France. There wasn't any cameras clicking when we left.

New York had a whole Regiment in our Division. The 165th was from New York, so, naturally, the town was keyed up to a war pitch and when we went there our uniform passed us anywhere, Wiley Satterley and I got acquainted with a couple of girls, so the last night, when we knew we were leaving, we had a date with these girls and I remember we went to a show and bought the girls a box of candy and we went to some place for a supper and the bill was two and a half dollars apiece. I can't remember the name of the show. That's like watching the Lady Godiva parade and remembering what the horse looked like!

We just took away in the night. It was too far for the folks to come so we had no royal send off, we just floated out in the night and slipped out in the fog and that was it. We went from Hoboken.

———————————————◆———————————————

I, Woodrow Wilson, President of the United States of America, do hereby proclaim to all whom it may concern that a state of war exists between the United States and the Imperial German Government ...

———————————————◆ ◆———————————————

Tunnellers all, from the States to Malay
We've mined tin and gold by the ton,
Coal, diamonds, and clay – whatever would pay –
And now we're a-mining the Hun!

Although the Stars and Stripes now flew alongside the flags of the Allies and a token force of Doughboys was already on the way, it would clearly be a long time before America would be in a position to put a large effective army in the field. And the war could not wait. The British Command, disappointed by the partial successes on the Somme and at Arras, both campaigns fought at the instigation of the French, now turned their attention to their own pet project. The plan was to attack from the salient round Ypres, to regain the ports to the north, and to drive the Germans out of Belgium. But first they must drive them from the high ground of the Messines Ridge that ran south from the Ypres Salient. The plans had been in the making for a long time. For more than eighteen months tunnellers, assisted by reluctant dogsbodies of the Infantry, had been burrowing under the Germans' lines and preparing the mines that would blow them off the ridge.

PRIVATE J. BOWLES,
2nd/16th (County of
London) Battalion,
(Queen's Westminster
Rifles).

We left the front line at 4 o'clock and it was nearly eight when we arrived at our dugouts, so you can guess how terrible the marching was through the trenches. After a week in the trenches this was supposed to be our rest. This is how we were treated.

Wednesday. Arrived dugouts 8 o'clock.

Thursday. Called us at 4.30 a.m. Marched us to RE dumping station, gave us planks to carry and marched us to the front line. Here we were split up into parties and sent down mines to carry sacks of earth up a long shaft and empty them on the parapet. It was the most terrible work I have ever been on, and we had to stick it for six hours, and then march all the way back. We were about dead when we got back, not only with the work, but with the march, for the trenches now are in an awful state. The rain continues every day, and in many places we were marching up to our knees in liquid mud. Of course, we worked all day in this state, and then had the same experience coming home.

We arrived home at five in the evening, and the only food we had had was a bit of bread and cheese before starting. 'What can I do for England that does so much for me?' But we made a fire in our dugout, made some stew and were quite happy. I have mentioned mice and rats before but this place licks creation! They go about in swarms and at night they are all over us. And they eat every mortal thing they can get at. We always carry an emergency ration in a bag in our pack. They got in our packs and ate the lot. They ate the pockets from the overcoats that covered us, the laces from my boots and the leather on our equipment, but no one has complained of being bitten. I shall not be sorry when we leave here, for rats in such numbers are abominable.

To return to our work as miners. The day's work mentioned was repeated yesterday. Words fail me to describe it. Three men were compelled to fall out. A word about mines may be interesting. From a sap that joins the firing line a tunnel is dug towards the German lines. In the one in which I was working, a stairway of some thirty rough steps at an angle of 45 degrees led to a chamber where there was an air pump and a windlass. From this chamber a tunnel ran right under the German lines, and down it was the railway with trucks pulled up by a wire on the windlass. It was our job to take the sacks from the trucks, carry them up the steps, take them about 100 yards along a trench and empty them. I was at this same mine yesterday, and at 10 o'clock we were all cleared out. An officer went down and with instruments heard Germans working and talking underneath. They had discovered our mine and were preparing to blow it up for us. What they will do about it I don't know but probably they will tunnel again and get under the Germans. What a game this is, and they call it war. It is not war, it is wholesale butchery, for in a mine they put up to 100 tons of ammonal – enough to blow a thousand men to pieces!

Part of the night we were working on top, quite close to the German lines, with their machine-guns constantly spitting out death and their snipers having a shot when the star lights gave away our position. It is a case of working and ducking all the time until one feels inclined to say, 'Damn it all! Shoot me if you can.'

There was a brilliant moon one night and we worked in a more sheltered spot. Sitting on a sandbag on a beautiful night with machine-guns crackling and the large guns booming, one naturally thinks of home, only a hundred odd miles away and England peacefully slumbering, and your own bed empty waiting for you. 'Now then Sonny, get a move on,' and the picture vanishes and another load of sandbags must be emptied.

It would be pathetic, were it not so absolutely absurd, to count how many people there are who are willing to swear that the Germans have actually mined under our trenches from no other evidence than lying *on* the ground and 'listening' to every blessed overground noise there is. One case we traced to a sentry kicking his heels together twenty yards away. That was last week. The CRE 3 Division traced two other scares, one to a nest of young rats, the second to a loose shutter in a house about 150 yards away which kept on 'dabbing' irregularly in the wind. But I must own that everyone's nerves were at their very worst between midnight and the very welcome dawn.

There is only one way of hearing real underground sounds and that is, dig down about six feet then forward for about ten under your own parapet. Next hang a curtain to shut out noises from your own people who should be sent away for twenty yards or so. Then, at last, lie down and perhaps you'll hear the Germans. If you do, it's time to send for the Corps Travelling Company, but meanwhile you'd better keep on

MAJOR COWAN,
Royal Engineers.

listening, remembering all the time that so long as you *do* hear him you are safe. When he stops work, all you can do is to clear out and wait, ready to rush his crater before he arrives.

Today Harris remarked casually, 'Tulloch has broken into a German mine and is stealing the stuff.' That put the lid on everything and the only thing to be done was to get up there at once and see for myself, and we almost ran the whole way. It was a quiet, still, moonlight night with few shells, so we went across country, getting there about 11 p.m. Apparently about noon some men working under Tulloch in the crater Fritz blew close to our lines last week, found *wood* while they were excavating and sent for him. He broke into the chamber, cut the electric wires and had already removed about three quarters of a ton of high explosive, detonators and all, into our own store. Oh, it was great, and it showed nerve too. I hope he'll get the Cross I mean to recommend him for. We are going to put one of the detonators on to the leads again so that they will test OK – and then try to take a snapshot of Fritz when he presses the button! If we hadn't found the stuff he would have had us rather badly, for we are fortifying the crater meantime.

I went on to Prityman where he agreed to all my proposals, namely a small mine under an advanced German work to be followed five minutes later by a larger under their main parapet. Thereby did I hope to draw Fritz into manning his front line and so make a decent bag and also destroy his main gallery and, with luck, his shaft as well. Low cunning if you like, but this is not war, but merely authorised assassination.

CAPTAIN W. GRANT
GRIEVE,
Royal Engineers.

Although some of the charges were placed in position only on the eve of the attack, the majority had actually been *in situ* for a considerable period – in some cases, over a year! Would they last out, or would the all-pervading dampness penetrate the insulation and cause a short circuit? Had the chambers collapsed, and so fractured the tins, allowing the charge to be saturated and become useless? Would a chance enemy blow wreck a gallery? These and a hundred other such thoughts tormented the Tunnellers, and tended to bestow grey hairs on those in charge.

And so the days dragged on.

More and more guns and troops crowded into the area and filled to overflowing the dugouts which the miners had prepared for them.

At midnight on June 6–7 1917, nineteen huge mines were ready for firing.

The preliminary bombardment, which has thrashed the air for days with its thunder, has now died away. Over the battlefield there is comparative silence – an ominous silence.

Hundreds of pairs of eyes constantly gaze at watches. In the forward trenches the assaulting troops are gathered.

No one who has not undergone the experience can ever know how slowly the minutes before zero can pass.

3.05 a.m. At the firing posts stand officers; their pale faces show unmistakable signs of the strain of suspense. 3.06 a.m. Innumerable watches are consulted. 3.07 a.m. A hasty wipe of clammy hands. 3.08 a.m. Watches are held to the ear. 3.09 a.m. Hands tremble slightly as fingers close around switch and exploder handle; complete silence broken only by laboured breathing. Eyes staring at synchronised watches. Three hours . . . nine minutes . . . fifty-nine seconds . . . ZERO!

The supreme moment at last! With almost the same grim feeling as the soldier plunges his bayonet into the belly of his enemy, the Tunnellers banged in switches and slammed home plungers.

The waiting infantry felt the shocks and heard the rumble of an earthquake. It seemed as if the Messines Ridge got up and shook itself.

All along its flank belched rows of mushroom-shaped masses of debris, flung high into the air. Gradually the masses commenced to disintegrate, as the released gases forced their way through the centres in pillars of flames.

Then along the enemy line rolled dense columns of smoke, tumbling into weird formations as they mounted into the sky, at length opening like a row of giant umbrellas, spreading a dark pall over the yawning, cavernous craters below . . .

PASTOR VAN
WALLEGHEM
(Parish Priest).

7 June – Full moon and a wonderful summer night. My room was very well situated for a good view of the battle. It faced south-east, and there were no houses and very few trees to hinder my view over Wytschaete.

I suddenly witnessed the most gigantic and at the same time chillingly wonderful firework that ever has been lit in Flanders, a true volcano, as if the whole south-east was spewing fire. A few seconds later we could feel the tremor. Like a real earthquake lasting a full minute. At the same time all the guns of the whole Front joined in. What a hellish sound, what an abominable spectacle, thousands of gun-flashes and bangs per minute, beneath a rain of fire and resounding shell and shrapnel explosion. If this were not a human carnage one would call it 'wonderful'. For us onlookers this is nothing, but what must it be for the 100,000 men in that pool of fire.

The noise did not abate; everything shook and trembled and it took me twice as long to shave.

Fourteen people attended my Mass and the altar trembled continuously. After Mass I already observe that the offensive is successful: a procession of horses passes along moving the guns further forward. At 9.30 we hear that Wytschaete and Messines have been taken. Shooting starts again at 3 p.m., but to a lesser degree. After Evensong we go up the Rodeberg for a view of the battlefield. The whole of Wytschaete is naked earth – the village has completely disappeared. The guns from Dickebusch and Mount Kemmel are particularly violent. We see shrapnel shells exploding over Wytschaete and high explosives over St Eloi. A balloon hangs over Mount Kemmel.

Three groups of prisoners have already passed over the Rodeberg, each of approximately 400 men. We see a further group being escorted back. Many of the prisoners did not hide the fact that they were pleased to be out of the war. We learn that Oostaverne (a hamlet half an hour to the east of Wytschaete) has also been captured, and that 3,300 prisoners have been taken.

If you're going back to Blighty
If you're going back to town
In Trafalgar Square
Greet the lions there
Shout 'hello, hello, London'
Give the man in blue a fiver
Kiss the girls, don't be afraid
Tell every Western pet
That she's not forgotten yet
By the boys of the Old Brigade.

Popular song

The Battle of Messines was an outright victory. The Germans had been thrown off the ridge, and the high ground south of the Ypres salient was now in Allied hands. Had they been able to follow up their success by attacking from the salient itself, and with weeks of fine summer weather ahead, they might have pulled off Sir Douglas Haig's grand scheme. At least the weather would have been on their side. But the preparations for the offensive were not yet complete. The troops and the guns had still to concentrate, the French were not ready to take an active part, and in London there were doubts as to whether the offensive should take place at all. Painful memories of the Somme were all too vivid and Lloyd George, who had succeeded Asquith as Prime Minister, genuinely doubted if public opinion would stand another campaign of huge losses in exchange for insignificant gains. While the Cabinet shilly-shallied and the Army discreetly continued with preparations for the offensive, moving troops north to Flanders and stepping up battle training, the weeks of fine weather were passing.

◆

We soon learned that we were marked down for battle, and officers were given three days' leave to Paris. Addresses were handed by those that had been to those that were going and my bit of seeing life cost me £71 for three days. £24 a day seems a lot of money, but we hadn't any immediate use for money. We knew we were going to Ypres and we knew the odds would probably be against us coming out. So, why not see a bit of life, even if it was expensive. I went with another officer and we went to an address near the Eiffel Tower.

When we rang the bell a tow-coloured-haired girl came to the door and invited us in. After we had talked a bit in the lounge she told me to go into a room and say 'how do you do' to some girl who was resting in bed. So I went in and didn't take much notice of the girl in bed, because standing by the dressing-table was a most beautiful girl! So I

CAPTAIN G.D.
HORRIDGE, TD,
1st/5th Battalion,
Lancashire Fusiliers (TF).

hurried out and told Tow-hair that if I was having anyone for a companion for three days it was Cecilie.

Cecilie was eighteen and came from Le Havre. The three days went by in visiting Versailles, the Opera once or twice, going to the best restaurants, buying Cecilie a hat and generally living it up. Cecilie was nice; she had a Major somewhere whom she thought she might be going to marry, and there was a Colonel who kept popping up and trying to get her away from me, but she didn't fall for it. Perhaps he had better luck after I had gone. He was very cross because I suppose he thought that a Colonel had a better right to Cecilie than a mere Captain.

We had to return to the battalion by the midnight train on the third evening. We went to the Opera and when the time came to go to the station, Cecilie said she would like to come to see me off, but if she did, business would cease for the night and she would make no money. I suppose one couldn't blame her, but it put things in the right perspective!

◆

THE BOMBING OF LONDON

The German air raid on London on Saturday has produced much anger in the public mind, and the Government must be prepared to face widespread indignation. After the very serious raid in June, Lord Derby assured the House of Lords, on behalf of the Government and the naval and military authorities, that 'nothing that we can do will be left undone to guard this country against aircraft invasion'. Though he also said, with general assent, that 'the claims of our battle fronts must come first', it was assumed that steps would be taken for the better protection of the capital. The sequel was seen on Saturday. At least twenty German aeroplanes appeared over London. They hovered over London for a considerable time, descending to a much lower altitude than on the last occasion. They left in no great haste, and the four enemy machines which were ultimately brought down were all hit while they were recrossing the sea. Fortunately the casualties, though serious enough, were far fewer than in the June raid, and the damage done was small when compared with the magnitude of the raid. The complaints of London do not arise from fear, and the universal testimony is that the population as a whole remained singularly calm. The instinctive feeling of the people of London rather seems to be that such attacks are a humiliation and that they ought not to be possible at all.

The squadrons which raid London invariably come from aerodromes very near the Belgian coast. On the day that we sweep the invaders from Flanders we shall also be conferring immunity on London.

The Times 9 July, 1917

PRIVATE LEONARD HART,
1st Otago Infantry Battalion,
5th New Zealand Reinforcements

France

Dear Mother, Father and Connie,

I have just returned from my second leave to England and I must say that I enjoyed myself even better than last time if such were possible. Most of the time I spent in travelling in the tubes to different parts of London and seeing all I could and Saturday night went to the Lyceum Theatre and enjoyed the show immensely.

On Sunday morning I went out to Petticoat Lane, and in the afternoon took a train to Richmond. There was an enormous crowd out there, and boating seemed to be the chief pastime. Khaki was, of course, in evidence there as it is in any part of London, but I think that the girls and women must have outnumbered the men by about twenty to one in that particular spot.

On Monday night I went to the Criterion Theatre in Piccadilly, and saw one of the most amusing plays which I have ever seen. My throat was sore with laughing by the time it was over. The play was called *A Little Bit of Fluff* and if ever it should make its appearance in Wellington do not forget to see it.

Tuesday (the fatal day) I was to be seen with full pack up, making my way dejectedly towards Victoria Station at about 6.30 a.m. Men returning from ten glorious days leave are the same as they were when I returned from my last one fifteen months ago. Then, and on this occasion, scarcely a word was spoken in the carriage which conveyed us back to Folkestone – so dejected and downhearted were we all. Well I suppose that all good times must come to an end, but the comparison between sitting in the stalls of the Criterion Theatre, and a day or two after to be trudging through the cursed mud of Flanders is too ludicrous. I have been back two days now. But I can see that it will be a while before some of those pictures of life in London fade away, to give place to uglier, coarser, and more inhuman ones of life out here. A good many of my mates have gone West during those brief ten days away, and things have been very active on our front.

CORPORAL W. H. SHAW
9th (S) Battalion,
Royal Welch Fusiliers.

I got home before Passchendaele started. There was a munitions factory close by, employing about 3,000 men and women and, blow me down, when I got home, my sister told me she was working in the factory. 'Well,' I said, 'why aren't you working?' She said, 'We're on strike.' I said, 'You, what?' She said, 'We're on strike. The men have brought it all up. They want more money,' I said, 'We're getting a shilling a day and you're out on strike!' Lloyd George came down himself to that factory and gave them what they wanted without a quibble and, believe me, when I got back and told the lads what I'd heard and seen – what *they* had to say about it wasn't repeatable.

The windows were boarded up but on some the conductor's bell was still functioning, and, as the boys clambered aboard, one wag inevitably positioned himself on the platform and rang the bell. 'Do you stop at the Savoy Hotel?' It was a favourite joke we could never resist asking, and the reply was always, 'No, sir! Can't afford it!'
Rifn. Joe Hoyles
13th Battalion,
The Rifle Brigade.

The birds were sent back with a small aluminium cylinder containing the message on very fine tracing paper, so that quite a long message could be folded up small, and the lofts were connected by telephone to the Artillery and to Brigade HQ so that they could be passed on very quickly.
Gdsmn. J. H. Worker,
1st Battalion,
Scots Guards.

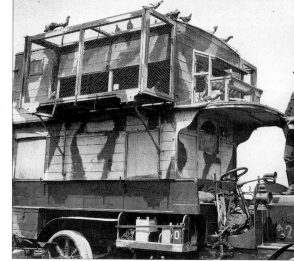

GUARDSMAN J. H. WORKER,
1st Battalion,
Scots Guards.

Boesinghe was the headquarters of the battalion in the line and it was from there that the whole of the activity was directed to preparing the ground and training for the attack which we knew was coming.

I was sent to a school at Army Headquarters and given a course on pigeons. The man in charge of the course was a bird fancier in England and he taught us how to handle the pigeons.

The main purpose was to take the birds up to the battalions in the line. They were changed every twenty-four hours so as to exercise the birds.

The pigeon loft was about a quarter of a mile from Elverdinghe Château along the road towards Woeston. My work was with one other man (we always went up in pairs in case one got wounded) and we had to take baskets of birds up to the headquarters of the battalion in the line.

As a rule, we had four birds in a basket and we took two baskets each. They were camouflaged, because we knew the Germans could see us and it was quite difficult and it took a long time, two to three hours at least, to get up to the Battalion headquarters.

When we got to Battalion Headquarters the birds were handed over to the Battalion Signal Officer and he gave us the birds which had been taken there twenty-four hours before. We took those away and got a little bit away from Battalion Headquarters (so as not to run the risk of giving its position away) and then we put them up into the air and they flew back. That was the exercise and really the training of the birds, so that they knew to get down to the loft as quickly as possible.

Routine messages were often sent down just for practice. The pigeons were vital for communications because when troops went forward they were in front of the signals sections which were bringing up the lines and relaying them, so they needed the birds to send back messages before the communications were established. Then as the Royal Engineers got their lines forward up to the Battalion Headquarters they were able to carry on by telephone, but the lines were continually being cut by shell fire. Runners and orderlies were often wiped out as they crossed the open, and the pigeons were a very useful back-up.

Rouen 15 July, 1917

PRIVATE. REG LAWRENCE,
3rd. S. African Infantry Battalion.
South African Brigade.

We are put through our paces at the Bull Ring – a huge sandy arena about two miles square where Napoleon trained his Army of Occupation before his last attempt to invade England. The instructors gave us a lively time of it with bayonet fighting – 'Gnash-your-teeth-show-the-whites-of-your-eyes-and-look-as-if-you-mean-it!'

We spent a charming day killing straw Germans (with real Kaiser Bill moustaches) suspended by chains. We killed them sitting, lying in trenches, coming out of dugouts, on parade – in every manner in which they could be killed, and *then* we killed them again to make sure they weren't just shamming! We ended our training with a spirited attack on dummy trenches in which we used bayonet, rifle, bomb, gas, smoke screen, boots, teeth and fists. Poison gas, aeroplanes, liquid fire, mines, barbed wire, man traps were used by the opposition. We won!

PRIVATE W. BELL, MM,
9th Battalion,
Army Cyclist Corps.

Directly it was getting dusk the ammunition column would start up and the GS wagons going up into Ypres with the rations for the troops up in the line. Then you could hear the wagon wheels starting on these cobbles, coming up and gradually getting louder and louder when they turned the corner. When the whole column of them was on the cobbles on the straight road into Ypres then old Jerry would open out with his long range guns and he'd get the range and drop shells along the road – one there, and one there, and one there – and then he'd come back again and work back and forwards all the time. All night long that went on until it started the daylight. The road was absolutely a shambles with blood and gore and bits of horses, GS wagons with no wheels on, turned on their side, rations strewn right across the road. It was awful, really awful, and our orders were to shoot the drivers if they refused to stop so we could divide them up, so there was spaces in between. Directly they started to close up it only wanted a shell to drop on one and they'd all get it!

They did panic, you see. You get four mules in the front of a GS wagon and these shells coming over, shrapnel up above, high explosive down below, and the noise! Deafening it was, and horses getting killed and legs cut off, screaming. Of course, the drivers whipping them up, wanted to get away, get off the road, get away from it, as quick as they can. Naturally – it's only human nature, isn't it? Want to get away out of that as fast as you can. Get up into Ypres. Our job was to stop them. It was a rotten job.

We were frightened ourselves. We were as frightened as them. Fear – you've got to be in it to understand what it means – really, fear is any moment to be blown to smithereens. These shells coming over one after another, screeching, one after another. You see, there was no other way, there was no other road into Poperinghe. It was the one straight road and old Jerry had the range of it to a T.

'... *Gas! Gas! Quick, boys – an ecstasy of fumbling, fitting the clumsy helmets just in time, but someone still was yelling out and stumbling and floundering like a man in fire or lime...*'

Wilfred Owen

HERR OTTO HAHN.

After a short time in Berlin, I was transferred to the Bayer Chemical Works in Leverkusen, where I was engaged in the development of a gas that was a mixture of chloromethyl, chloroformate, and phosgene, which was originally merely called an 'admixture'.

Besides this, other new gases, Grünkreuz (green-cross) and Blaukreuz (blue-cross), both mustard gases, were being developed. Blaukreuz was a strong irritant that could partially penetrate gasmasks. Grünkreuz was a typical poison gas, resembling phosgene. When the two substances were used simultaneously – the mixture was called Buntkreuz (motley cross) – those attacked were forced to tear off their gasmasks, leaving themselves exposed to the poison gas.

As a result of continuous work with these highly toxic substances, our minds were so numbed that we no longer had any scruples about the whole thing. Anyway, our enemies had by now adopted our methods, and as they became increasingly successful in this mode of warfare we were no longer exclusively the aggressors, but found ourselves more and more at the receiving end. Another factor was that we front-line observers rarely saw the direct effects of our weapon. Generally all we knew was that the enemy abandoned the positions that had been bombarded with gas shells . . .

CAPTAIN A. F. P. CHRISTISON, MC, 6th (S) Battalion, Queen's Own Cameron Highlanders.

Friday 13 July. The superstitious were saying it was a bad combination, and so it proved to be. C Company under Captain Harry Rowan was on my right, and at about 0800 hours I was going round my forward trench when the Germans started shelling steadily, but with small stuff, and we could not understand why the shells all seemed to be duds. One shell landed in my trench almost beside me and did not burst – just a sort of plop. I felt a burning sensation just above my right knee and heard the man next to me cough and retch. I realised this was something very odd and shouted '*Gas*' and quickly put on my respirator. The gas alarm immediately sounded and, as we were good at our gas drill, only five or six of my Company were gassed. Captain Rowan heard the gas alarm and his men put on respirators. After wearing them for some time in the heat of the morning and no attack developing they thought the original alarm was false as no gas had been smelt. What they did not know was that this was mustard gas, had no smell, and had delayed action. The C Company trenches were saturated with stuff and the whole Company were struck down. By nightfall every officer and man was either dead or in hospital.

We had about eight hours of mustard gas shells, churning into the ground at the side of the battery. I was on duty in the signalling pit, working by a candle and with a mask on. After about six hours, the masks were no good. They'd been neutralized, and we were starting to choke. No. 6 Gun was quite close to the battery pit which was like a shed with a few sandbags on the top of it and a tarpaulin over the doorway, and every time No. 6 Gun went off, it blew out my candle. What with a mask on and doing everything by buzzer, it was rather difficult! By morning, everyone was round the shell holes vomiting and they had to send quite a lot of people out to bring us in. We needed one on each side of us, we were in such a bad way, and they took us back into a trench by the side of a road to wait for transport. The fellows were getting a bit panicky, couldn't get their breath, and I remember saying to myself, 'Hold tight and take no notice,' but breathing was very difficult. Eventually, they brought down a GS wagon, a great big thing, and we got into that. I had terrible cramp in the stomach through vomiting, and as we were going along, the road gradually seemed to fade away. By the time we got to Vlamertinghe we were blind, we couldn't see anything. They led us down into the dressing-station, sat us on a plank and told us, 'Open your mouths'. We waited with our mouths open and suddenly someone shot something like 200 per cent ammonia into your mouth. It nearly knocked the top of your head off. We got bathed and put into bed and I don't remember anything more till I woke up in hospital at the base. It was the 4th Canadian General, and I was there for a long time. Stone blind! I think the worst part was when they opened your eyes to put droplets in them – it was just like boiling water dropping in! Then every day they bathed all the burned spots, and *that* was no joke. I remember my left thigh was nothing but a mass of matter.

CORPORAL H. BALE,
242nd Brigade,
Royal Field Artillery.

... If you could hear, at every jolt, the blood come gargling from the froth-corrupted lungs, obscene as cancer, bitter as the cud of vile incurable sores on innocent tongues, my friend, you would not tell with such high zest to children ardent for some desperate glory, the old Lie: Dulce et decorum est pro patria mori.

Wilfred Owen

WHAT I HAVE SEEN

I have seen 50,000 men in hospital many of them writhing in all the agonies of Hell – and not one complaining.

I have seen thousands of German prisoners being kept out of mischief in cage compounds.

I have seen a thousand silent graves – hundreds of them inscribed simply 'A British Soldier' – on roadside and valley – where, not long ago, they who now rest there fought like mighty heroes for the Right.

I have seen the lads in the trenches.

I have seen the boys in the Rest Camps, and have had many a cheery and heartening chat with them.

I have seen our guns playing upon the enemy lines.

I have seen and taken the salute from brigades of glorious lads marching to the Trenches to put the finishing touch to the Hun.

I have seen the German lines.

I have seen Lords and Labourers, Peers and Peasants, fighting and falling, and resting in silent graves, side by side.

SOMEWHERE IN – HELL!
What I have seen – What I have d.

We had visitors from the outside world. In September 1917 Horatio Bottomley was sent to us by GHQ. We all kowtowed to the little brute, yet despised him intensely – all save the Cinema Sergeant, who on hearing it was Bottomley, said, 'Shall I get my gun?'

He came out to write propaganda; and produced some wonderful stuff. The General took him up to the Gavrelle Switch – some four thousand yards behind the front line and never under fire. "Stand on the step, here, Mr Bottomley, and you will see –" Mr Bottomley crouched in the bottom of the trench and as the General's stick revolved round the compass Mr Bottomley's tin helmet orientated itself below the level of the ground. Yet he insisted on being photographed – many times – and demanded that the official photographer should record that it was within a hundred yards of the enemy. We put him into a gasmask for the purpose of a photograph – and for a moment I had hopes that he would die of apoplexy...

COLONEL W. N. NICHOLSON, CMG, DSO,
15th Highland Division.

WHAT I HAVE LEARNT

And now for what I have learnt. We will have the truth from the trenches at last. *The war is won.* Germany is beaten. On every front she is weakening and weakening – and it is now only a question of the psychological moment to strike. That momentous decision rests with one man – at least, I hope to God it does. If the politicians will kindly keep out of the ring Haig will very soon administer the knock-out blow. *I know what I am saying.* From Field Marshal Commander-in-Chief, right down to the rawest Tommy in the trenches, there is but one spirit – that of absolute optimism and confidence.

Heaven bless the dear boys to whose hands has been entrusted this glorious and sacred task. Heaven cheer the bereaved and the sorrowing. They, too, are bearing the Burden. *All will soon be well.*
Horatio Bottomley, John Bull

at I have learnt – The War is Won!

Dear Horatio,

Since your perilous but little heard-of visit to the 'Jaws of Hell' whose hair-raising horrors you so graphically described, the armies are inspired to greater heights of endurance and all goes well upon the Western Front. During the recent heavy fighting, we chanced upon Major X (we dare not breathe his name) crouched in a shell-hole shaking with fright, his shrapnel helmet rising and falling with his emotion – it was not the Hun Barrage, Horatio, nor yet the devilish chattering of their Machine Guns – no, he was just reading the account of your thrilling adventures and beginning to realise the sickly horrors of war.

Now, Horatio, to the point of this communication. What is being done for the hacking coughs of our gallant men? I have heard a frenzied chorus of coughing far above the din of battle. I have seen Brigadiers so spent with coughing that they could not utter their commands but must sit huddled over some distant fire drinking great draughts of wine to soothe their lacerated throats. One last heart-rending instance – four young officers in our Mess have a passion for crisp oatmeal biscuits. They have coughs. They can no longer eat biscuits. Poor lads.

You cannot, Horatio, have listened to this tale of woe unmoved – hot tears are already coursing down your cheeks. Send us Cough Drops, oh Protector of the Poor, and alleviate our sufferings.

The Mudlark
Troops Newspaper, Royal Naval Division

We put him into a gasmask for the purpose of a photograph – and for a moment I had hopes that he would die of apoplexy...
Col. W. N. Nicholson
CMG, DSO,
15th Highland Division.

WHAT I HAVE DONE

I have been in the First Line Trenches – within 200 yards of the enemy.

I have been in the Reserve lines – which is much more dangerous than the first.

I have been in places where I had to wear a gas-mask and a steel helmet.

I have looked over the parapet and seen the effect of our gunfire.

I have discussed the situation from every possible aspect with men and officers and members of the General Staff.

I have sat alone with Sir Douglas Haig and talked of the great work upon which he is engaged.

I have also had many a conversation with General Sir Arthur Slogget – the wonderful Director-General of Medical Service, to whom we are indebted for the remarkably good health of the troops.

I have spent hours with Priest and Parson, wondering what is the inner spiritual meaning and purport of this great Thing.

Aye, and I have held the hand of the dying – God rest their souls!

O Jesus make it stop

Siegfried Sassoon

◆

CAPTAIN SIEGFRIED SASSOON, MC,
2nd Battalion,
Royal Welch Fusiliers.

. . . I am making this statement as an act of wilful defiance of military authority, because I believe that the war is being deliberately prolonged by those who have the power to end it. I am a soldier, convinced that I am acting on behalf of soldiers. I believe that this war, upon which I entered as a war of defence and liberation, has now become a war of aggression and conquest. I believe that the purposes for which I and my fellow soldiers entered upon this war should have been so clearly stated as to have made it impossible to change them, and that, had this been done, the objects which actuated us would now be attainable by negotiation. I have seen and endured the sufferings of the troops, and I can no longer be a party to prolong these sufferings for ends which I believe to be evil and unjust. I am not protesting against the conduct of the war, but against the political errors and insincerities for which the fighting men are being sacrificed. On behalf of those who are suffering now I make this protest against the deception which is being practised on them: also I believe that I may help to destroy the callous complacency with which the majority of those at home regard the continuance of agonies which they do not share, and which they have not sufficient imagination to realise. . .

(As published in *The Times*, 30 July 1917)

BOBBIE HANMER
to Siegfried Sassoon.

1 War Hospital, Block C 11,
Reading.

. . . What is this damned nonsense I hear from Robert Graves that you have refused to do any more soldiering? For Heaven's sake man don't be such a fool. . .

LADY OTTOLINE MORRELL
to Siegfried Sassoon.

. . . It is *tremendously fine* of you doing it. You will have a hard time of it, and people are sure to say all sorts of foolish things. They always do – but nothing of that sort can really tarnish or dim the value and splendour of such a True Act. Nor rob it of its fruition. Such deeds always bear splendid fruits however much people may carp. . .

5, Raymond Buildings,
Gray's Inn.
10 July 1917

EDWARD MARSH
to Siegfried Sassoon.

My dear Siegfried,

Thank you very much for telling me what you've done. Of course I'm sorry about it, as you expect. As a non-combatant, I should have no sort of right to blame you, even if I wanted to. But I do think you are intellectually wrong – on the facts. We agree that our motives for going to war were not aggressive or acquisitive to start with, and I cannot myself see that they have changed. And it does seem strange to me that you should come to the conclusion that they have, at the very moment when the detached Americans have at last decided that they must come in to safeguard the future of liberty and democracy – and when the demoralised Russian Army seem – after having been bitten with your view – to have seen that they must go on fighting for the sake of their freedom.

I cannot myself see any future for decent civilisation if the end of the war is to leave the Prussian autocracy in any position of credit and trust.

But now dear boy you have thrown your die, and it's too late to argue these points. One thing I beg of you. Don't be more of a martyr than you can help! You have made your protest, and everyone who knows that you aren't the sort of fellow to do it for a stunt must profoundly admire your courage in doing it. But for God's sake stop there. I don't in the least know what 'They' are likely to say or do – but if you find you have a choice between acceptance and further revolt, accept. And don't proselytise. Nothing that you can do will really affect the situation; we *have* to win the war (you must see that) and it's best that we should do it without more waste and friction than are necessary.

Yours,

Eddie

The dead leaves float in the sighing air,
The darkness moves like a curtain drawn.
A veil which the morning sun will tear
From the face of death – We charge at dawn.

Patrick McGill

GREAT ALLIED ATTACK.

YPRES SALIENT WIDENED.

TWO MILES' ADVANCE.

The War : 3rd Year : 383rd Day.
At dawn yesterday began the fourth great battle on the British front this year. From the valley of the Lys to the north, across the reverse slopes of the Messines-Wytschaete ridge, and around Ypres to the Yser Canal, our troops attacked.
Everywhere our objectives were attained.

The Times
1 August, 1917

STORY OF THE BATTLE.

GOOD BEGINNING.

FIRST DAY'S OBJECTS ACHIEVED.

Even after the War Cabinet had given reluctant acquiesence the launch date of the attack had been gradually pushed back. The French were still not ready and towards the end of July the warm days turned to mist with intermittent showers, and bad visibility prevented the Royal Flying Corps from completing essential observations. The preliminary bombardment which had begun on 16 July was prolonged for three more days, and Zero Hour was finally fixed for the morning of 31 July. The Germans were poised ready to meet the attack, and they were well prepared. For two years they had been building a fortress of concrete strongpoints across the ridges beyond the salient, so well camouflaged that they were indetectable from the air, so well-sited and so formidable that they were all but impregnable to troops attacking on the ground. At dawn on 31 July 100,000 troops went over the top. At four o'clock in the afternoon it began to rain. By night they were floundering in the legendary Flanders mud.

◆

To: Lieutenant T. H. Floyd,

Ward 24,
Ontario Military Hospital,
Orpington, Kent.
15 August 1917

Dear Sir,
I have much pleasure in replying to your letter dated August 5th, 1917. I am very pleased indeed to know that you are safe in Blighty. Well, sir, you ask me where I got to when we went over the top. I think you will remember halting and lying down in No Man's Land. Well, as I lay there the time seemed to be long; then I got up and went to the front of the platoon to see what had gone wrong. When I got there I found you had gone on and the remainder of the men had not the sense to follow you. So I led on with the remainder, taking my direction from the compass. I reached the hill and passed Schuler Farm on the right. We started to climb the hill and then a funny thing happened; those already at the top came running back again shouting 'Get back and dig in; they are outflanking us'. I took the warning and retired to a suitable position and got the men digging themselves in. We could see the Boches coming over the ridge like a swarm of bees. When they got nearer we opened machine-gun and rifle fire. All the time this was going on the artillery had ceased firing, and I began to feel a bit down-hearted. Then things quietened down a bit; so I told the lads to make a drink of tea for themselves, which they did gladly enough.
    All the time we could see Fritz preparing for a counter-attack and we knew it had to come. I waited patiently keeping a look-out for them coming. Then men were getting knocked out one by one, until I had

only five; and the Lewis gun had got a bullet through its pinion which rendered it useless. Nothing happened until the evening, and then the bombardment started and we knew we had something to put up with. I sent up an SOS rocket and our artillery opened out, but the shells were dropping short and hitting our men. Then we retired for about fifty yards and took up some shell holes. I looked round and found all my men had vanished. I was amongst some of the Cambridgeshires and Hertfordshires. I really did not know what to do. The artillery became more intense and still our shells were dropping short. There was another sergeant out of the Cambridgeshires in this shell hole with a few men; so I told him I would go back and try and get in touch with the artillery. On my way back I got wounded in the leg, so I rolled into a shell hole. It began to rain and rained heavily all the night. When day broke I found myself covered with clay and mud, and wet through to the skin. I crawled out and looked about me. It was a quiet morning except for a shell bursting now and again, and I could see some men through my glasses, about a mile away, working on a road. I made my way towards them. How I got there I do not know, for I was more dead than alive. I inquired for the dressing-station, which I found after a long walk. I was sent down to the Base to hospital and was sent to England on 6 August.

I am pleased to say that I am feeling much better and my wound is getting on nicely. I hope my letter will find you feeling much better for the rest you have worked so hard for. I saw in the casualty list that the Colonel had died of wounds, the Adjutant killed, 2nd Lt. Gratton missing, Captain Andrews wounded, and Lt. Telfer missing. I think I have told you all the news you require, and hope you enjoy reading it.

With best wishes,
Yours sincerely,
Robert Charles Baldwin, Sgt.

CAPTAIN A. F. P.
CHRISTISON, MC,
6th (S) Battalion,
Queen's Own Cameron
Highlanders.

On Saturday 4 August General Gough who was in command of the 5th Army, inspected our remnant. He remained mounted and said: 'Well done, you did your best. I deplore your losses. I am sure you will all want to avenge their deaths so I am making you up with a large draft so that you can return and avenge your comrades.' A man in the rear shouted angrily: 'You're a bloody butcher'. He rode off taking no notice, but after that he became known in the 5th Army as 'Butcher Gough'.

CORPORAL R. E.
THOMPSON,
13th (S) Battalion,
The Rifle Brigade.

I had my machine-gun team and bombers and riflemen, about fifteen of them, and we were in support to another company that was to take this other pillbox which had been changing hands pretty near every other day. Well, we weren't needed, but when it was all over, the attacking platoon was so weak that I was ordered to supplement them to hold the pillbox. Well, the sergeant of the platoon, he had a little wound in the hand, nothing very much but it wanted attention, and they had lost their officer. We thought between us that it was no good holding the pillbox *from* the pillbox because you can't defend it from the Jerry side, you can only defend it from our side.

We said, 'Well, we'll get out in the bits of trenches on the Jerry side.' There the ground sloped down to a valley about 200 yards across to the German front line, which came out to meet our front line on our left and right. We stayed in there for two or three hours and the sergeant went back to have his wound dressed and he said, 'I'll be back later on when I can'.

I had about ten or twelve of the platoon that were left and my fifteen or sixteen bombers and Lewis gunners, so we got these trenches and we got the Lewis gun in. There was a sort of trench come up through the bank to the pillbox which the Jerries used to use so that we couldn't see them going out and in. We got either side of that and we sat there for three or four hours and nothing happened. Eleven o'clock, twelve o'clock, one o'clock. Nothing happened except for the usual boom, boom of shells going over. We set sentries each end and in the middle and just lay down on the ground to have a doze. Early morning, the chap on the sentry where this trench ran up to this pillbox heard people moving about in front. He woke us all up and we stood there ready and we heard voices, German-speaking! Well, as they approached, about four or five yards away from the trench, we got ready for them and then I challenged them, in German. 'Hande Hoch. Wer da?' As soon as they heard that, they turned round and started running so our chaps started shooting. Killed them both. One had got food, meat and bread, and one had got a coffee pot on his back, a container, the bullet had gone right through him. We turned him over and saved the container and the coffee. We actually all had a cup of coffee!

A quarter of an hour or twenty minutes after that, there was a commotion starting, shelling increasing, and our own front line either side opening up with their rifles, so we knew something was on, and out of the trenches in front of us came about forty or fifty Jerries, coming across the valley to have a go at the pillbox. So we opened up with the Lewis gun on them. I flopped down and started crawling and they got nearer. Then the Jerries opened up with machine-guns either side, covering their own people. They were on to us! They gradually crept nearer and nearer. There was about twenty of them. Well, I was firing my Lewis gun without looking. I was just sticking it over the top and going *Brrrrrrrrrrrr* like the kids do with their toy guns and I wasn't even looking over the top because the Jerries were sweeping along the top with their heavy machine-guns, so the only thing to do was to go *Brrrrrrrrrrr*, like that, and take a chance. Well, they got to about twenty yards of us, I suppose, bombing distance. I'd got about seven or eight chaps left, that's all, out of the whole lot, because the machine-gunners had got them, and there's one London chap, he'd got these bombs, Mills grenades, and he was pulling the pins out and lobbing them over, not looking where they were going, or anything! Well, they got up to within about twenty yards of us and we had no chance, us with seven or eight left and about twenty of *them*! Just then, at the back of us, there was a commotion and the relieving platoon came running down the little trench with the sergeant and took over. Of course, Jerry started hopping back then, when he saw there was a lot more. They saved our bacon. We were nearly done for!

LIEUTENANT H. L. BIRKS,
4th Bttn Tank Corps.

My tank got hit at Poelcapelle. That was an absolute tragedy because I had two brothers in the crew – one was a driver and the other one was a corporal, very fine chap, and the shell that came in and burst inside took his brother's leg off. The worst part of that, strangely enough, was not the brotherhood but the fact that some stretcher-bearers came along and we had to leave the chap with his leg off to the stretcher-bearers and get the rest of the crew back – it was no good losing seven for one. I'll never forget that. His brother was distracted!

We'd moved our tank up to St Julien the afternoon before and camouflaged it, and then we came back at night and had a brew-up there for tea and rum and so forth, and we moved out at 6.15 in the morning. It was a drizzly morning which made it frightfully slippery, one had to be very careful. We went on, and the first thing we saw was another tank bogged beside the road. He was stuck! And then as we came on there was a bend in the road with an enormous tree over it – the Germans had felled these trees all along the road to create an obstacle. You *could* get over them but you were rather inclined to swing round and get into the mud. The Company Commander had got on, he was out of sight, and my driver was a first-class chap, and we got on to this tree and balanced off it, then slid off and away we went on, through the most terrific shell fire, because we'd run into our own barrage plus the German barrage. I'd never before or since experienced anything quite so heavy. I could just see the tail of the tank in front of me, and there was the most almighty crash, and we got a direct hit. That's when the Corporal's brother lost his leg . . . and of course it set fire to the tank.

But the discipline was magnificent. The first thing they did was to put the fire out. I evacuated the crew, they crouched down by the side of the road, absolutely terrified. The next tank came along – it was run by a fellow called 'Rosie' Stevens, and he took all my people on, less the chap without a leg. I told him he couldn't go on because I'd blocked the road with my tank, and his driver turned round on this pivotted run, I don't know how he did it, and we went back about 100 yards and ran, of course, into this tree. The whole of the rest of the Company were stranded there. They'd tried to get off and they'd got into the mud and they were bogged. And 'Rosie' Stevens tried to get round the tree and he got stuck, and so when that happens the crew stand by the tank and the rest clear out. I collected my chaps and we went back to a walking wounded place where they could be attended to; and that was the end of the Poelcapelle business so far as the tanks were concerned. The leading tank had a broken track. Mine was burnt out and the third was stuck. So we never got to the brewery – it remained untapped. It was the last tank show in the salient.

We brought back two wounded chaps in our tank, lying on the floor on either side of the driver's seat, and it was a terrible trip back for those two blokes, because we were lurching over all these felled tree-trunks. It was a case of heave up – *bang*, all the way back, and every time we banged down, those chaps were in agony. I'll never forget their faces.

PRIVATE. J. L. ADDY,
4th Battalion,
Tank Corps.

◆ ◆

'No! Not "For Bravery". They are all brave. It should be inscribed "For Valour".'

Queen Victoria in 1856

People said, 'Now, you must wear a ribbon.' There was a sports shop that sold sporting guns etc. and I said to the lady behind the counter, 'Have you any medal ribbons?' 'Oh, yes. What did you require?' I said, 'The Victoria Cross.' After recovering, she said, 'Well, we haven't any of that ribbon in, but I can get it for you'. Sure enough, on the Wednesday, it was there. The lady said, 'Let me be the first to put it on your breast.' Well, I just stood in front of her and she put it on the right-hand side! Further down the High Street, there was a little photographer. He was stood on the doorstep of his shop and he persuaded me to go in and have my photo taken and so I've got a photo with the VC ribbon on the wrong side!

SGT. E. COOPER, VC,
12th Battalion,
King's Royal Rifle Corps.

On the night of the 15th/16th we moved forward to the Steenbeke and took up our positions on the line of the Steenbeke, ready for the assault next morning. We were the second wave of the attack and the first wave was held up by these blockhouses. We came up with them following the barrage and it was then I realised it was possible to get round the back of this blockhouse and put it out of action.

I was alone at the time, but the men were following me. I'd ordered them to lie down and fire and try and protect me as I rushed forward. When I got to the back of the blockhouse, it was like an old farmhouse and they'd strengthened the inside and demolished the top storey and poured concrete over the lot and it was a very strong position.

I got to the back of this blockhouse and called on them to surrender. I don't know what I said, but they understood. I had the officer's revolver and I'd never had hold of a revolver before. When they eventually decided, the first one came and of course he frightened me to death, and I turned round, pointed the revolver at him and it went off and killed him. Of course, they immediately rushed back into the blockhouse and I had to go through the whole procedure again of getting them out.

Anyhow, they did surrender eventually and we went forward and captured our objective and we stayed there until we were relieved. My officer had been killed and the Company Commander had been killed, Sergeant-Major had been killed and about 30 or 40 men. After I'd captured the blockhouse the Adjutant came up (the Commanding Officer had been wounded at this point) and he saw I was off the line of advance and he started giving me a lecture on the battlefield, on where I should be and asking what I thought I was doing, and I said, 'Well, we've just captured this blockhouse, Sir'. The prisoners were then going back to the rear, and he looked at them and he said, 'You've captured all them?' I said, 'Yes.' And, of course the other battalion who had been held up, they could now come forward, and I suppose they reaffirmed what I told the officer. But I didn't think anything about it at the time. I just thought it was something that everybody would have done in the same position and we carried on with the advance.

When we did actually come out of the trenches there was a parade of the Brigade, what were left of us, and I was brought out in front of the Battalion and the General congratulated me on what I had done, but he said, 'I've a complaint to make about you, Cooper, regarding your treatment of the prisoners'. I was a bit nonplussed. He said, 'One of the officers complained that you kicked him up the pants and clipped him round both the ears.' I recalled then that after I'd killed this first German, the next man out was the officer. In the meantime, I'd put the revolver in my belt and as he came out I stood at the side and as he passed me I clipped him and kicked him, not viciously or anything like that, just, I suppose, excitement. And he'd complained that a sergeant of the British Army should so treat an officer of the Kaiser's Army! But our General wasn't too worried. He said, 'It's a good job he wasn't the *first* one out, wasn't it, Cooper?'

> 'FOR MOST CONSPICUOUS BRAVERY AND INITIATIVE IN ATTACK'
>
> *The London Gazette*

I'd never been home for 16 months and my leave came through and it was usual for the men to go back with the Transport Sergeant when he delivered the rations and the mail. Well, I knew the ground fairly well, so I said to the Sergeant, 'I'm not going to wait for you, I'm going cross-country'. Well, in the meantime, in that very mail he was taking up, there was a notification that I had been awarded the Victoria Cross. It was to appear in Battalion Orders the next morning.

SGT. E. COOPER, VC,
King's Royal Rifle Corps.

I sent a telegram to my parents to tell them I'm in England and would be home this evening. Outside King's Cross Station, there was a YMCA hut so I went in there, had my bun and a cup of tea. I knocked a newspaper on to the floor. As it fell, it opened out. I stooped down to pick it up and I saw the big heading, *Eleven new VCs*. I was in this list!

The first thing that flashed through my mind was, 'What a surprise I'll give my mother when I get home tonight and tell her I've won the VC.'

Of course, in the meantime, my parents *had* got to know that I'd won the Victoria Cross, so, of course, when they knew I was in England, they told Mrs Smith next door and Mrs Jones further up the street and before long everybody in Stockton knew that I was home and they put it on the screen in the pictures that I was coming on the train that evening and when I got home, of course, everybody knew.

At Darlington, I had to change, I had to dash for the train to Stockton, haring along the platform, and somebody threw their arms around me. It was my father! I said, 'Come on, Dad, let's get the train.' It was packed with troops of course. I was sat in one corner and my father in the other and he said, 'Why didn't you tell us?' I said, 'Tell you what, Father?' He said, 'You know.' I said, 'I don't know what you're talking about.' He couldn't contain himself any longer. He said, in front of all the others, 'This is my son and he's won the VC.' The papers in London had told the local press in Stockton that there was a VC in *The London Gazette* and, of course, they'd looked up all the Coopers. They found the address and knocked and my mother answered the door. They said, 'You have a son, Sergeant Cooper?' 'Yes.' 'King's Royal Rifles?' 'Yes.' And, of course, she began to worry then, thinking it was bad news, and she let out a little cry. My sister went to the door and wondered what they were doing, upsetting my mother, and they said, 'We've got good news for you, Mrs Cooper and you've got nothing to worry about. Your son's got the VC.' She didn't know what the VC was! When my father came home for his midday meal, they told him what had happened and he didn't go back to work that day. I think it was the first time he'd ever missed half a day's work in his life. So he'd set off to meet me at Darlington.

When we got to Stockton Station, I was first out of that train and dashed down the subway and there was a Superintendent of Police racing after me. 'Stop!'

I said, 'What's the matter?'

He said, 'The Borough Corporation are here to give you an address of welcome.'

I said, 'I don't want it. I want to get home to my mother.'

They threw the station doors open and of course all the crowd came in and they picked me up and carried me away and that was my home-coming. I was 21. I'd only seen my mother once since I went to France.

ELEVEN NEW VCs

When we went up to the Palace, we sat there, about ten of us, waiting. **SGT. E. COOPER, VC.**
Eventually they came round and said, 'Proceed into the forecourt'. Well,
within minutes there was a Guard of Honour arrived and I looked round
and I saw my mother and father sat just behind us. All the relatives of
the people who had been decorated were there. Then all the Generals
of the London Command came up and talked to us. I said, 'Sir, I'd like
you to tell me what I have to do when I go in front of the King.' 'Well,'
they hummed and haaed. One said, 'Well, what is the King? He's a
Commanding Officer, isn't he? You'll address him as "Sir".' And off
they went. With that, the King appears and he's about twenty paces
away and the medals were on a little table and the Aide-de-Camp reads
out the citation. A Guardsman was first, and I thought, 'Well, if I do
what he does, I can't go far wrong.' So I watched what he did, marched
up and stopped and saluted two or three paces in front of the King, the
King shakes hands and then he has a few words with you. The only
preparation they made was they put a kind of a curtain hook on your
tunic and the King hooked this medal on, and you take two paces back
and salute again and march back to your seat.

Well, the next man to me was a chap called Edwards. He'd gained
his VC about 1,000 yards away from me in the same attack. I didn't
know him, of course, but he'd come straight from France and his
instructions were that he'd meet his wife at Victoria Station at such and
such a time. Anyhow, they missed each other. He'd come straight to the
Palace and he was in a terrible state – of course, hadn't seen his wife!
His name was called out. He gets up to march over to the King, and he
just turned his head to the left and there, at the railings, was his wife,
with her nose through! Well, of course, he broke ranks, dashed over,
and kissed her. Then he realised where he was, came dashing back,
continued his march up to the King. Up in the balcony was the Queen
and all the Royal Family. I just happened to look round to see what my
parents were doing and I saw Queen Mary – she nearly fell over the
balcony! Nothing like that had ever happened before!

Anyhow, when he got up to the King, he told me afterwards, the
King said, 'What's happened there, Edwards?' 'Well, Sir,' he said, 'that
was my wife, Sir. We missed each other at Victoria and I hadn't seen
her for a long time.' and the King said, 'I quite understand. I'd have
done the same myself.' And he carried on with the Investiture.

... The white body of the evening is torn into scarlet,
slashed and gouged and seared into crimson, and hung
ironically with garlands of mist ... And the wind blowing
over London from Flanders has a bitter taste ...

Richard Aldington

The strategic plan behind the Third Battle of Ypres had been to break out of the salient, advance up the low ridges beyond, push forward across the plain and swing north to attack the ports of Ostend and Zeebrugge from the rear in support of an amphibious attack from the sea. But by September the Army, which had been expected to be astride the topmost ridge in a matter of days, was less than half-way to this first objective and it was obvious that the bold strategical plan could not be carried out before the tides and storms of autumn would make it impossible to invade from the seaward side. The plan was abandoned – but not the battle. Encouraged by local successes, the troops inched painfully upwards and onwards through the slough of mud and shell holes. Their objective was now limited to achieving the highest ridge and the capture of the fortifications that had once been the village of Passchendaele.

————————◆————————

PRIVATE REG
LAWRENCE,
3rd S. African Infantry
Battalion,
South African Brigade.

18 September, 1917.

We marched a mile or two along the Ypres road and through Ypres itself — majestic, though in ruins, and silent but for the echoes of marching feet on the stones. There was something unnerving about this silence, broken only by the steady thud of guns. Far away an occasional star shell glimmered for an instant before the inky black swallowed it up. I could not help having misgivings of what was to come and for the first time I felt nervous. We reached the reserve trenches with whole skins, but dog tired, and relieved the Manchester Fusiliers who, poor devils, seemed all of a dither to get away. We had very little sleep as the advanced batteries were only 100 yards behind us and the noise was ear-splitting. They started up before dawn and by the time it was light, the bursts of fire had swelled to one continuous roar as all the batteries along the ridge joined in.

We got everything ready for the fray and made our last wills and testaments. Mine was short and sweet, as I had only about £10 back pay to leave. Brother Geoff's company was posted a few hundred yards in advance of ours and had already suffered a few casualties. In the afternoon he came down to see me. We sat and watched the troops coming up in little columns. Against the skyline they looked like lines of ants. Roscoe remarked that he didn't mind dying if it was sudden, but he hated pain. 'But what about Bunny?' I asked him, and he replied, 'Oh, she'll get over it in time'.

At 10 pip emma we got our marching orders to move up to our jumping-off place. It drizzled mournfully and our spirits sank again as we started slipping in the mud and falling over each other. After keeping fine for seven days it was too bad to rain the night before the attack.

Poor Captain McDonald had slipped into a shell hole on the way up. He was wet and shivering with cold and nerves. He said, 'Lawrence, will you put the company in position for me?' I was only too pleased to take over his job and keep occupied until Zero Hour. I put each platoon on their starting tapes and with muddy shell holes and in the pitch blackness of the night this was no easy matter. At about 3 a.m. I reported to Captain McDonald that the whole company was in position on their attacking line. He thanked me profusely and said goodbye. Poor Captain McDonald, he was in a terrible state of nerves and fear which he seemed unable to fight down. He appeared to dread the coming of the dawn and was apparently convinced that he would fall.

2ND LIEUTENANT
GEOFFREY
LAWRENCE,
1st S. African Infantry
Battalion,
South African Brigade.

After losing our way in the pitch darkness we found the tapes marking our starting point about 2 a.m. and dug ourselves in. In front I could just make out a derelict pillbox tilted at a crazy angle where it had been lifted by a large shell and, on our right, the shadow of the railway embankment running into the darkness in front. Waiting for Zero and the barrage to start I could feel myself drifting away into a great quiet, almost as if I was in church. I kept thinking of the words of the litany – *Good Lord, deliver us. From lightning and tempest, from plague, pestilence and famine, from battle and murder and from sudden death.* Then there was a crash – and like a thousand hurricanes the barrage started.

Puckrin was on his feet first and shouted out 'Come on boys!' There was a sheet of smoke and flame where the barrage was falling and behind it the first lines of men advancing looked larger than human in a ghastly glare of bursting shells. I wondered what would happen to us when we got there, forgetting it was a moving barrage. Just as we started off, Roscoe stopped and turned and shook hands with me. The first few yards we went over were churned up by weeks of shell fire and unburied and half-buried fragments of men simply littered the ground. We passed Geoff with a few men and a Lewis gun stuck in a shell hole. I heard him shout, 'Keep down you fool!'. The Germans were streaming mach-ine-gun fire from the tops of a pillbox. We made for it in short rushes, but about 30 yards from it I saw Roscoe fall sideways into the crater. I ran back to find he was shot under the collar bone. We put on a tourniquet, but he just shook his head. He tried to say something, but I could hear nothing in the fearful din. I knew, though, that it must be about Bunny, his wife. I went off to find some stretcher-bearers, but when I got back I found Puckrin with tears running down his face, and

PRIVATE REG
LAWRENCE

I didn't need a second look to know that Roscoe was dead. We placed his helmet over his face, hiding his twisted lips and his kind eyes and left him with his rifle inverted in the ground at his head – like a gentleman and a soldier.

**2ND LIEUTENANT
GEOFFREY
LAWRENCE**

We all moved off into the dark hell of rattling machine-guns, sparks and whining splinters. Poor Captain McDonald was one of the first to be killed by a burst of machine-gun fire a short distance from our jumping off line. I took cover in a shell hole and signalled to those behind me to follow. I decided to work round the pillbox and so we jumped from shell hole to shell hole to the right and eventually reached my guide-line, the railway leading to Roulers. Here I found a group of our men who had had a shooting match with the enemy and had won. Nearly a dozen were lying dead. Whom should I find amongst our chaps but my brother Reg, who later claimed he had shot five of the Jerries. But not without loss – his friend, Roscoe, was killed beside him.

I went on, with more men now, and came to a dugout on the railway embankment. Here twenty Germans put up their hands in surrender, whilst about ten or more others ran up the line to escape. I fired with my revolver at them, whilst at the same time motioning to the others to get back. With the prisoners we took three machine-guns and I had these marked with chalk '1st. SAI'.

**PRIVATE REG
LAWRENCE**

We picked off the snipers and machine-gunners one by one, until only one grey rat remained. He had two shots at me. I had one and missed him. He had another which was pretty close and, thinking he had made a bull, he showed his white face cautiously over the rim of a trench round the pillbox. I was waiting for it and made no mistake that time. As there were no further signs of activity, Puckrin crept up and dropped a bomb through a loophole. Those that were left came out and surrendered. We counted six round the pillbox, all shot through the head. Another was sitting down and was pretty near the end. I have never seen men so demoralised as the prisoners we took. They surrendered in batches of twenty and more, and one wounded Hun actually *ran* after a batch of prisoners that was leaving for fear he should be left behind.

**2ND LIEUTENANT
GEOFFREY
LAWRENCE**

I had a number of my own men and a few of the Royal Scots. We carried on until we reached our objective. This was difficult going on account of very swampy ground that had been churned up by our heavy artillery fire and three times I sank up to my waist and higher, and would have stayed there if it had not been for the hand my men gave me. Our tempers were up with our losses and I had to restrain my men from shooting the enemy as they came out. I felt sorry for the poor devils and had them sent back.

We passed two Germans (they were hardly more than 17 years of age) clinging to each other and weeping, unable to move apparently. One had most beautiful brown eyes, more like a girl's than a boy. I signed to them to go back with the prisoners, but they could only stare and moan, completely broken by the terrific blast of shell fire that had passed over them.

PRIVATE REG LAWRENCE

The sun rose bloody through the barrage smoke. I had no idea so many had been killed until then. A huge German was lying in a shell hole face downwards, with someone in khaki beside him. Quite near two Scotties were sitting in a shell hole. The older was supporting quite a boy on his lap, holding a cigarette to the boy's lips. From where I stood his head was right against the red ball of the sun, like an aureole round his curly hair. It was just like the pictures of war in the illustrated papers, but in colour. The guns fell briefly silent and on the ridge top the remnants of our Companies joined up to make a solid line. One of our planes came low overhead. We knew already that it would be able to report back that all our objectives had been taken.

On reaching our objective the first thing was to dig in and reorganise our men for the inevitable counter-attack by the enemy. I ran down the line and gave the order for every other man to take out and clean and oil his rifle bolt and, when finished, man the fire-step whilst the other half-section did the same. All the rifles were clogged with flying dust and mud.

2ND LIEUTENANT. GEOFFREY LAWRENCE

The enemy came on, but our rifle fire was so accurate that their attack broke down, and about fifty of them, seeing it was useless, came in and surrendered. There was a good deal of shelling all day and I couldn't help worrying about my brother further to the left in B Company, as they too had had a terrific pasting. Just before midnight two officers at regimental headquarters came up to give Mackie and myself a break. I was quite indignant and thought it was a reflection on us. However, it was the Colonel's kindly assistance for very tired men. We were finally relieved by the Cameron Highlanders in the early hours of the twenty-second.

22 September

Of our Company only thirty-two men answered roll call. Puckrin has shell shock. Engels leg is broken by a shell. Hands is wounded. Roscoe is dead. I am the last and I have no companions left.

PRIVATE REG LAWRENCE

I see no excuse for war, unless it is in defence of home and dear ones. Otherwise it is just legalised murder conducted on a large scale. No one excuses individual murder (which often has just and cogent reasons) while in war you murder a man you have never seen, who has never done you an injury. But, of course, we are fighting for national honour. How absurd! A soldier when he bayonets a man does not nurse the nation's wrongs in his breast.

MUSKETIER HANS
OTTO SCHETTER,
3rd Company, 231st
Reserve Infanterie
Regiment,
50th (German) Reserve
Division.

In the night of 19/20 September we entrain to the front line. Ledeghem, the last station open to traffic, is our unloading stop. Many ammunition columns pass by us toward the front, and the cannonade grows in intensity – giving us a welcome! The enemy is firing fiercely and our own artillery is replying in kind. This morning the British infantry has broken through our first lines at Wilhelmstellung. Often we have to take cover on the side of the highway from the bursting shells. Anxiously I look ahead toward the front line where the shells are bursting with dark smoke clouds. Only stumps are left of the trees, and I try to figure out how I can best get through this hell. I am at watch at the roadside to look for vehicles of Regiment 231. We are moving forward with coffee containers and sacks of bread to our company which has occupied the shell holes and what is left of the trenches – the Flanders position. I am anxiously observing the battleground: concrete bunkers outline the position.

There are no quarters for us, so at night we sleep in a barn on top of potatoes. At 3 a.m. we are awakened and we now move forward in single file on the Menin–Ypres road. On both sides of the highway our batteries are firing and their iron greetings receive prompt reply from the enemy. We have to move fast because it is almost 6 a.m. and we have to reach our front line before daybreak. We reach the Front headquarters from where we are guided to our troops which occupy shell holes 150 metres ahead. The soldiers are reluctantly leaving their shell holes and are not eager for food. The whole earth is ploughed by the exploding shells and the holes are filled with water, and if you do not get killed by the shells

you may drown in the craters. Broken wagons and dead horses are moved to the sides of the road; also, many dead soldiers are here. Seriously wounded who died in the ambulance wagon have been unloaded and their eyes stare at you. Sometimes an arm or a leg is missing. Everybody is rushing, running, trying to escape almost certain death in this hail of enemy shells on the highway, which is the only passage since the fields are flooded shell holes. I breathe easier when we reach our kitchen wagon. Today I have seen the real face of war.

France
19 October, 1917

PRIVATE LEONARD
  HART,
1st Otago Infantry
  Battalion,
5th New Zealand
  Reinforcements

Dear Mother, Father and Connie,
In a postcard which I sent you about a fortnight ago, I mentioned that we were on the eve of a great event. Well that great event is over now, and by some strange act of fortune I have once again come through without a scratch.

For the first time in our brief history as an army the New Zealanders failed in their objective with the most appalling slaughter I have ever seen. My company went into action 180 strong and we came out thirty-two strong. Still, we have nothing to be ashamed of, as our commander afterwards told us that no troops in the world could possibly have taken the position, but this is small comfort when one remembers the hundreds of lives that have been lost and nothing gained. Our brigade received orders to relieve a brigade of Tommies who had two nights previously advanced their positions a distance of two thousand yards. These Tommies had, however, failed to take their last objective and we were going to be put over the top to try and take it. At dusk, we started off in full fighting order.

The weather had for some days been wet and cold and the mud was in places up to the knees. The ground had all been deluged with our shells before being taken from the Germans, and for those five miles leading to our front line trench there was nothing but utter desolation, not a blade of grass, or tree, numerous tanks stuck in the mud, and for the rest, just one shell hole touching another. The only structures which had stood the bombardment in any way at all were the German machine-gun emplacements.

These emplacements are marvellous structures made of concrete with walls often ten feet thick and the concrete reinforced throughout with railway irons and steel bands and bars. The ground was strewn with the corpses of numerous Huns and Tommies. Dead horses and mules lay everywhere, yet no attempt had been made to bury any of them. Well, we at length arrived at our destination – the front line – and relieved the worn-out Tommies. They had not attempted to dig trenches but had simply held the line by occupying a long line of shell holes, two or three men to each hole. Many of them seemed too worn out to walk properly and I don't know how some of them must have got on during their long tramp through the mud back to billets. Each of us had a shovel with him, so we set to work to make some kind of trenches. We were at this point about half-way up one slope of the ridge which in the course of forty-eight hours we were to try and take. The mud was not so bad here owing to the water being able to run away into a swamp at the foot of the ridge. Anyway by daybreak we had dug ourselves in sufficiently and, although wet and covered in mud from head to foot, we felt fit for a feed of bread and bully beef, for breakfast. We stayed in our new trenches all that day and the day following during which it rained off and on, and Fritz kept things lively with his artillery.

At three o'clock on the third morning we received orders to attack the ridge at half-past five. It was pitch dark and raining heavily. When all was ready we were told to lay down and wait the order to charge. Our artillery barrage curtain of fire was to open out at twenty past five and play on the German positions on top of the ridge a hundred and fifty yards ahead of us.

At twenty past five to the second, and with a roar that shook the ground, our guns opened out on the five-mile sector of the advance. Through some blunder our artillery barrage opened up about two hundred yards short of the specified range and thus opened right in the midst of us. It was a truly awful time – our men getting cut to pieces in dozens by our own guns. I heard an officer shout an order to the men to retire a short distance and wait for our barrage to lift. Some, who heard the order, did so. Others, not knowing what to do under the circumstances, stayed where they were, while others advanced towards the German positions, only to be mown down by his deadly rifle and machine-gun fire. At length our barrage lifted and we all once more formed up and made a rush for the ridge.

What was our dismay upon reaching almost to the top of the ridge to find a long line of practically undamaged German concrete machine-gun emplacements with barbed wire entanglements in front of them fully fifty yards deep! The wire had been cut in a few places by our Artillery but only sufficient to allow a few men through at a time. Dozens got hung up in the wire and shot down before their comrades' eyes. It was now broad daylight and what was left of us realised that the day was lost. We accordingly lay down in shell holes or any cover we could get and waited. Any man who showed his head was immediately shot. They were marvellous shots those Huns. We had lost nearly eighty per cent of our strength and gained about three hundred yards of ground in the attempt. This three hundred yards was useless to us for the Germans still held and dominated the ridge.

We hung on all that day and night. There was no one to give us orders, all our officers of the battalion having been killed or wounded. All my Company officers were killed outright – one of them, a son of the Revd Ryburn of Invercargill, was shot dead beside me. The second day after this tragic business, we were surprised to see about half a dozen Huns suddenly appear waving a white flag. They proved to be Red Cross men and they were asking for a truce to take in their wounded and bury their dead. It was a humane and gallant act. Our stretcher-bearers were able to go and take all our wounded from the barbed wire, and we had all the wounded carried out before nightfall. We had not time to bury many of our dead but the wounded should be the only consideration in times like that, but I went out and buried poor Ryburn. My company has come out with no officers, only one sergeant out of seven, one corporal and thirty men. Even then we are not the worst off.

I have just decided to have this letter posted by someone going on leave to England, so I will tell you a few more facts which it would not have been advisable to mention otherwise.

Some terrible blunder has been made. Someone is responsible for that barbed wire not having been broken up by our artillery. Someone is responsible for the opening of our barrage in the midst of us instead of 150 yards ahead of us. Someone else is responsible for those machine-gun emplacements being left practically intact, but the papers will all report another glorious success, and no one except those who actually took part in it will know any different. I will relate to you another little incident or two which never reaches the press, or if it does it is 'censored' in order to deceive the public. This almost unbelievable but perfectly true incident is as follows.

During the night after we had relieved the Tommies prior to our attack on the ridge we were surprised to hear agonised cries of 'Stretcher-bearer', 'Help', 'For God's sake come here' etc. coming from all sides of us. When daylight came some of us, myself included, crawled out to some adjacent shell holes from where the cries were coming and were astonished to find about half a dozen Tommies, badly wounded, some insane, others almost dead with starvation and exposure, lying stuck in the mud and too weak to move. We asked one man who seemed a little better than the others what was the meaning of it, and he said that if we cared to crawl about among the shell holes all round about him we would find dozens more in similar plight. We were dumbfounded, but the awful truth remained, these chaps, wounded in the defence of their country had been callously left to die the most awful of deaths in the half-frozen mud while tens of thousands of able-bodied men were camped within five miles of them behind the lines. All these Tommies (they were mostly men of the York and Lancaster Regiment) had been wounded during their unsuccessful attack on the ridge which we afterwards tried to take, and at the time when we came upon them they must have been lying where they fell in mud and rain for four days and nights. Those that were still alive had subsisted on the rations and water that they had carried with them or else had taken it from dead comrades beside them.

I have seen some pretty rotten sights during the two and a half years of active service, but I must say that this fairly sickened me. We crawled back to our trenches and inside of an hour all our stretcher-bearers were working like the heroes that they were, and in full view of the enemy whom, to his credit, did not fire on them. They worked all day carrying out those Tommies.

Carrying wounded over such country often knee-deep in mud is the most trying work imaginable, and I do not say for a moment that the exhausted Tommies (the survivors of the first attack on Passchendaele Ridge) were physically capable of doing it, but I do say that it was their officers' duty to send back and have fresh men brought up to carry out the wounded that they themselves could not carry. Perhaps they did send back for help, but still the fact remains that nothing was done until our chaps came up, and whoever is responsible for the unnecessary sacrifice of those lives deserves to be shot more than any Hun ever did.

If they had asked for an armistice to carry out their wounded I do not doubt that it would have been granted for the Huns had plenty of wounded to attend to as well as the Tommies. I suppose our armchair leaders call this British stubbornness. If this represents British stubbornness then it is time we called it by a new name. I would suggest callous brutality as a substitute. After reading this do not believe our lying press who tell you that all the brutality of this war is on the Hun's side. The Hun is no angel, we all know, and the granting of an armistice, such as that which we had, is a rare occurrence. The particular regiments who were holding the ridge at the time of our attack are known as '*Jaegers*', but for all the terrific casualties those *Jaegers* inflicted on us, we survivors of Passchendaele Ridge must all admit that they played the game on that occasion at any rate.

We are expecting to move about twenty miles back from here tomorrow where we can get fresh reinforcements and thoroughly reorganised. I shall not be sorry to get on the move.

> With best wishes,
>
> I remain,
> Your affectionate son,
> Len.

Sooner or later the stretcher-bearers would get to you on the Somme, but at Passchendaele the wounded didn't stand an earthly chance. At one aid post a doctor said to the stretcher-bearers, 'Only bring back men we've got a hope of curing. If you get a seriously injured man, leave him to die quietly. Too often you bring men back here and before we can help them they're gone. You're wasting your time and ours.' I thought that was a terrible thing to say. But that was Passchendaele!

RIFLEMAN V. SHAWYER
13th (S) Battalion,
The Rifle Brigade

A stretcher squad consists of four men and you lift the stretcher up and on to the shoulder, and each corner had a man. Now that's the only way you can carry a man properly. But, my God it was hard work, really hard. I mean, the road there was all lumps and bumps. It was being fed with every stone and every old brick that you could think of, and there was no steam-roller rolling it down flat, you know! It was being knocked down with mauls. And carrying over that rough ground is very hard. And of course it's hard on the shoulders. When the conditions got really appalling, it required twelve men to a stretcher, but they couldn't get on the stretcher all at the same time ... you could get six ... one in the middle one side, one the other, and then they would stop and another six men would take over. You see, you're being dragged down in the mud and of course you're plastered in mud yourself. And not only that, they're not fed up like boxers for a contest, they're living on bully beef and water and dog biscuits. No hot meals! Hot meals? Never heard of them.

SERGEANT W. J.
   COLLINS,
Royal Army Medical
   Corps.

What we had was stretchers and the field surgical haversack with the usual bandages, morphia, quarter grain tablets, scissors, plaster, dressings. If I came across a casualty, and it could be dealt with, I always used to use the first field dressing out of the uniform pocket. You ripped the waterproof covering and there was a pad of gauze and an ampoule in it, and all you had to do was to press the ampoule and it crumbled immediately, and the iodine was released all over the pad. And then you put the pad to the wound and bound him up. Every soldier carried one in his jacket, so naturally, to save my dressings in the surgical haversack, the first thing I used was the soldier's own field dressing.

If a fellow was bad, a man who'd lost all colour and was pallid and cold and was perhaps breathing heavily, you'd give him a little morphine. It dissolved immediately. You put it under the tongue, and it was in the blood stream in seconds. And there was always a little bottle of them in the surgical haversack.

I saw a wound there which exceeds the bounds of credibility. A man came in from Hooge trenches. He walked up to me and said, 'Sergeant, there's a doctor here, isn't there? I've got terrible trouble here. I've been wounded here.' So I looked, and I said, 'Oh, Gor blimey!' so I got him in my ambulance and I took him back to Captain Rogers. I said, 'This man's got a rather uncomfortable wound, Sir.' He said, 'What's the matter with him?' I said. 'He's got a shrapnel bullet right in the top of his penis, split it open as if it had been cut equally and *there it's lodged*.' Can you imagine that!

DR BERNARD
GALLAGHER,
U.S. Army, attached
2nd/4th Battalion,
The Gloucestershire
Regiment

Southampton   *Sunday, 7 October 1917*

Went to the station a few nights ago to meet the hospital train load of wounded soldiers for this place, 170 of them. Wounds of every description – legs, arms and eyes gone and bodies peppered with shrapnel. This mournful procession has been going on now for three years here and whereas early in the war the coming of a convoy of wounded soldiers meant the turning out at the station of the whole town, now the natives of the city hardly turn their heads.

In examining the cards which the wounded Tommies bring from France, I found one card signed by Theodore Sweeter of Minneapolis, who was with the 89th Field Ambulance.

The cases at this hospital were all soldiers, largely men who had been wounded in France, with a fair number of gassed cases and men sick with trench fever, nephritis, PUO (pyrexia – fever – of unknown origin), trench foot, heart trouble and 'shell shock'.

Many of the worst gassed patients had lost their voices and developed a chronic cough but those conditions usually improved after a few weeks. In some of the worst, the face and eyes would be so badly burned and swollen that the patient's eyes were completely shut and one would hardly recognise the face as that of a man.

Trench fever cases usually complained of pains in the bones, especially the shin bones, for many weeks after the fever had left. I used to think maybe they were 'slinging the lead' to get out of going back to France, but after having trench fever myself a few months later, I realised that they were not malingering!

Most cases of 'shell shock' seemed fairly normal by the time they got back to England, but I saw two or three patients at the hospital who were wild-eyed and continued to shake and tremble for many days after getting there. No particular treatment was given to them other than rest and quiet.

There is a great difference of opinion about the nature of shell shock, many claiming that it has, in fact no 'nature' at all but is purely a condition of 'scaredness'. Perhaps in a certain number of cases that is so, and no doubt some men malinger or 'sling the lead' as the English call it, on the question of shell shock, but it has always appeared to me from cases I saw in England and later at the front that it was what one might call a 'nerve exhaustion'. Each individual perhaps has a certain amount of 'reserve nerve power', more for some than for others. As this reserve is used up under great stress, such as soldiers pass through in a big battle, some reach their limit sooner than others and develop 'shell-shock', though perhaps no shell has lit particularly close to them.

Rifleman Arthur Russell belonged to the 13th Battalion, KRRs, from my old 111th Brigade and was brought into the ward about a week before I went convalescent. He was, or he had been, a magnificent specimen of manhood, six feet tall. There was not a mark on him, yet he was as helpless as a child. His legs were paralysed, likewise his right arm. He could not raise himself into a sitting position. And he was dumb.

RIFLEMAN H. V. SHAWYER, 13th (S) Battalion, The Rifle Brigade.

I used to think, when I put a lighted cigarette between his lips, that only his eyes were alive. He could not ask for anything, and he spent hours trying to write left-handed on a large sized block of plain paper, no easy task for a right-handed man. His case excited interest among specialists and doctors in our ward, so much so indeed that one morning we saw seven doctors all crowded around his bed, talking, thumping, probing and generally going over him, muscle after muscle and sinew by sinew, all over his body.

When I returned to Netley about a month later I found Russell trying to learn to walk. At best he could only drag one foot behind the other and his useless right arm dangled by his side. His speech was slowly returning, a slow, halting speech, full of stammers, finding some words unpronounceable, followed by long silence, while he searched for other words to replace them. By the time I left Netley to go on sick leave Russell could speak enough to tell us what had happened. It was not a long story but because of his disability, it took a long time to tell as we all sat around the big fireplace in Ward 27B.

A company of his unit (13th Battalion, KRR) was selected for a working party to dig a communication trench and Russell, a stretcher-bearer and first-aid man, was sent along too, in case there were any casualties. It was a bitterly cold night with an easterly wind. By the time the men had been working less than an hour, Russell had become cold, doing nothing – too cold to give first-aid to a casualty if there was one. So going along to a man swinging a pick, Russell took over whilst the other man took a short rest. He worked, driving it into the hard frozen ground, until he began to feel more like a warm-blooded human and less like a dead fish. And then it happened.

The point struck something hard and unyielding as a block of concrete. Immediately, a violent sensation of 'pins and needles' ran up his fingers, his arms, and then down his legs, along his shoulders and into his neck. Russell said he could remember trying to yell but not one word or sound escaped his lips. Then he passed out.

He woke up several days later in a base hospital, a helpless and useless hulk of a man, and in due course came to Netley. His medical chart diagnosed his case as Shock Thrombosis. Massage and electric shock treatment were working wonders on him but I doubt if ever again he became a fully fit man. I *do* know that one of the most pitiful scenes I have ever witnessed occurred when his mother was sent for soon after he arrived at Netley. The poor chap could do nothing to greet her. Only those big staring eyes could function properly and they almost burst from their sockets in the effort he made to force his body to obey his will as it used to do, while his old mother sat there beside him, tears streaming down her face.

This was just one case of the thousands in Netley Hospital. Men with no legs; others without arms; severe head injuries; and equally as bad as any of these, to my mind, the wing of the hospital that housed those terrifying shell shock cases. Where the door jambs were rubber lined; thick felt on window sashes and heavy carpet on floors, everything designed to shut out noise from nervous wrecks. One boy I saw occasionally, although still in his teens, had a head of hair which was a shade whiter every time I met him.

No. 3 Australian CCS,
France, 12/10/17

Mr David Sutherland,

Dear Sir, – I am writing to tell you about your son, Rifleman W. D. Sutherland, 39912. He was brought into this hospital on the 8th, very collapsed, suffering from a severe shell wound in his right arm and chest which penetrated into his lungs, also one of his legs. He was immediately warmed up and made comfortable in bed, but the injury done to his lung had been too severe; he never really picked up at all, and died on the morning of the 11th. I am afraid it is not very much to tell you, but it might be some comfort to his people to know that he was in hospital where he received every possible care and attention, and that he was relieved of all his pain. I told him when he was first brought in not to worry, that I would write and tell you he was wounded, and he was very relieved. He sent his love to everyone and hoped soon to be well enough to write himself. He had no idea at all that he was dying. He was buried today in a military cemetery at 'Nine Elms', near Poperinghe. All his personal belongings will eventually be sent on to you,

I remain, Yours faithfully,

Ida O'Dayer (Sister in Charge)

We had any amount of men who were windy. They are no more frightened than other people. They just unfortunately show it and so they're known as 'windy'. We were coming out of the line at Ypres. There were no trenches there. There was no cover and as you walked back out of the line you walked on a duck-board in full view of anyone who was watching and the morning we were going out Jerry was bombarding the duckboard track and the OC said, 'We'll go in small parties, will you go first with Luxon' – that was the name of the cook – 'and he can get a meal on for the rest of us when we get back.' So we started off. Well, we had a terrible time dodging all these shells. It must have been a quarter of a mile or more before we reached the ruins of a village when we were able to go into the ruins of a house to sit down and get a certain amount of composure.

We hadn't been in many moments when there was a flurry of bodies and a couple of fellows hurtled themselves into our small room – a couple of young officers, 2nd Lieutenants – and when they'd got their breath one said, 'You've saved our lives.' So I said, 'Saved your lives! How?' They said, 'Well, this is our first experience of the line and we didn't know what to do, and so we copied you. Everything you did, we did. When you went into a shell hole, we went into a shell hole. When you went on, we went on. We did precisely what you did!' And Luxon, the windy man, said, 'You did everything I did?' They said, 'Yes.' He said, 'Well, did you shit yourself in that last shell hole?' We all burst out laughing and I don't think Luxon realised it, but he did those young officers a world of good. They could see that it was acceptable to be frightened, to have the 'wind-up' as it was called and yet preserve a sense of humour and get away with it.

CORPORAL A. D. PANKHURST, 56th Division, Royal Field Artillery.

I was frightened out of my life at nighttime. I was jellified, but I was more afraid of people knowing I was afraid – just a sort of bravado – I mustn't show them that I'm afraid – because one of the things that spreads quickest of all is fear. If people in trenches start to shout and scream with fear it spreads like a flame so the best thing is to quieten the bloke, either brain him or, if need be, finish him. Stop it.

One night I was with a runner named Jack Cohen. He was a reasonable soldier but he didn't have an over-sufficiency of pluck. He'd get rattled under shell fire, badly rattled, and we were coming back to this place called Kruisstrat and we were completely lost. We could hear the gas shells coming over – you could tell by the whistle of them, you know – so I said to him, 'Jack, put your helmet on.' 'Are they gas?' And I could feel him trembling, so I said, 'Look, Jackie, we've got to get back to this point. Put your helmet on.' And we put them on and I said, 'Look, make up your mind that we're going to find this road. Make up your mind.' He said, 'I think we'll find it if you'll go in front.' So I said, 'All right. It suits me.' And it was a moonlight night and we'd lost the track

PRIVATE C. MILES, 10th Battalion, Royal Fusiliers.

and I can remember saying then, 'St Anthony, please don't desert me. Let me find the track.' The next thing, I fell over it. A loose duck-board. 'Jack, I've got it!' We were knee-deep in mud then and we got on the track and although it was broken in places, we found the remainder and finally got down to Warrington Road, which was a good strong solid road, made of trees. We were all right then!

◆

Just see what's happening, Worley! Worley rose
And round the angled doorway thrust his nose
And Serjeant Hyde went too to snuff the air.
Then war brought down his fist, and missed the pair!
Yet Hyde was hit by a splinter, the blood came,
And out sprang terrors that he'd striven to tame,
A good man, Hyde, for weeks. I'm blown to bits,
He screams, he screams. Come Bluffer, where's your wits,
Says Worley, Bluffer, you've a blighty, man!
All in the pillbox urged him, here began
His freedom: Think of Eastbourne and your dad,
The poor man lay at length and brief and mad
Flung out his cry of doom; soon ebbed and dumb
He yielded. Worley with a tot of rum
And shouting in his face could not restore him,
The ship of Charon over channel bore him,
All marvelled even on that most deathly day
To see this soul so spirited away.

Edmund Blunden

◆

FIELD-MARSHAL LORD
BIRDWOOD

My men were weak and tired, and when Plumer consulted me I had to advise against any further advance. However, since only one division of my Corps was to be involved in the next stage, and since the other Corps Commanders were in favour of pushing on, Haig decided to do so.

There is little doubt that if the weather had held, and if we had been able to prepare and rehearse our advance as carefully as in the first three stages, we should have been able to take Passchendaele. But the weather defeated us. In that deep, clinging mud neither men nor animals could progress. We made great efforts to avoid 'trench feet' – a complaint officially regarded as a crime and avoidable, though I must confess that I myself succumbed to it. Even though I wore good, thick boots, laced lightly to encourage the circulation, I found that the many hours I had to spend tramping through icy mud turned my feet into blocks of ice, and gradually a couple of toes gave out. I was rather amused when, at one of Plumer's conferences, a somewhat exuberant and opinionated brother Corps Commander came up while I was talking to Plumer, and said, 'I hear Birdie has swollen feet. Let me present him with a brochure I have written on the subject.' Little Plumer put up his eyeglass, as he always did, and murmured, 'Well, that doesn't matter much – at least he doesn't suffer from swollen head!'

I found Monash and Peter Jackson, (GSOI) in a dugout in the ramparts of Ypres, from which they had directed the attack, without either having been to see the ground, before or after the attack which failed disastrously ... If they had been to see they could have saved a good deal of life. Jackson accompanied me up to the line via Kink Corner, where a Brigadier of the Australians was. I don't know how he faced him; the meeting wasn't a very happy one. We had a very nasty reconnaissance through a lot of gas shelling and I found the front quite indefinite. Wounded and dead Australians all over the place and nobody doing anything. I had to organise a line and place the machine-guns myself. No Germans to be seen and no firing (forty-eight hours after the failure). One could walk anywhere in fact. No Australian Brigadier had been up. Hopeless confusion. I found the gun-line so depleted that some sixty per cent only of the guns were firing. They could not be withdrawn owing to mud and congestion. The RA authorities treated all guns in the line as firing. I told my Corps Commander (Currie) so later. I had actually walked them and counted them. Monash and his people should have verified this, as I did. The single road via Potijze to Zillebeke was being mended and used at the same time. Continuously shelled. Casualties in wagons and horses just thrown over the edge into the bottomless shell holes which practically touched anywhere off the road. The gun-lines had a plank road behind them leading off the main road. An endless string of RA were going up day and night with hundreds of rounds of field gun ammunition. Men were falling into shell holes and drowning. I pulled a Highlander out myself. My seven-hour reconnaissance nearly did me in and I was as strong as a horse. No man physically weak could have done it.

I saw that we were being ordered to drive a narrower and narrower wedge into the German line. We might take the crest and so keep the Germans from looking down on us, but we could never keep him away from the crest on either flank and the capture of Passchendaele was tactically useless and strategically more useless. Two barrages were put down, dawn and afternoon, lasting for an hour. Really a terrible affair. The Germans put one down also immediately afterwards, putting less into it than us and going on for half the time. Every attack had been at dawn and several divisions had failed. The whole thing was clear to me after my look. The difficulty was to get the men to the assembly position for a dawn attack. To march through Ypres in the night and assemble

GENERAL SIR EDMUND IRONSIDE.

and attack at dawn was impossible. Two divisions who tried it (one Lawrence's) were hours late and were dissipated by their own fire which had been brought back for some reason when the artillery knew the Infantry were late. You had to get the men through one night and lie all day in shell holes and assemble properly the next night and then attack. This we did successfully. I used one Brigade for work, one to fight and one to leap-frog for the next attack. We built two tracks across the waste of duckboards 1,000 yards each. One up and one down. Done in high wind. Took us four or five days (from memory). The thing that I disliked was the dawn attack with so many men. It was certain the Germans only had posts and no continuous line. I wanted an afternoon attack or night attack by selected men, followed by reinforcement at dawn. I am sure that we should have succeeded.

We got back to Corps HQ, and I took Watson (my Divisional Commander) with me. We found Radcliffe and Currie and some General Officers in the HQ. I told Currie what I had seen, what I thought and asked for only the number of men that he thought he could lose in a dawn attack and guaranteed to take the line he had given us to take. He agreed. Not one of the Corps Staff, even including Radcliffe, had seen conditions. They knew me and knew that I wasn't overcome by battle conditions and knew that I wasn't frightened. As we were talking in came Plumer without Harington. Currie told him the useless mess of the attack and what it would cost the Canadians. He asked for an afternoon attack and told Plumer that the guns were only sixty per cent of what we had been told. This Plumer denied but promised to look into it. He said he didn't like the idea of an afternoon or night attack. He never interrogated me or even said anything to me, though I was the only man in the room who knew the conditions. Plumer knew me well. He told us that he had been ordered to take Passchendaele (as if the very word meant something) and had no option. Then in the middle in came Haig. Currie repeated his story and told Haig that I had been up. Haig never asked a question, but said the attack must take place for political reasons.

There's my story. We had plenty of time to transfer to Cambrai, which as you know was carried out with no reserve at all. Our barrages and the keeping of, say, one Division or one Brigade of the Canadians in Ypres would have kept the Germans (what there were) in the line.

I went up after we had taken Passchendaele and wrote in my diary that we had driven a wedge with a flat point of 1,000 yards into the Boche and could see nothing but desolation in front of us. No sign of anything but a few odd dugouts. No hope of building any communications up front. We buried a steel cable right up to the line and then handed over . . .

(From a private letter dated 29 March 1937)

In the newspapers you read:

'Peacefully they rest on the spot where they have bled and suffered, while the guns roar over their graves, taking vengeance for their heroic death.' And it doesn't occur to anybody that the enemy is also firing; that the shells plunge into the hero's grave; that his bones are mingled with the filth which they scatter to the four winds – and that, after a few weeks, the morass closes over the last resting-place of the soldier.

KANONIER GERHARDT
  GÜRTLER,
111 Bavarian Corps
  Artillerie.

All you hoped for was the next day. It gradually ground you down. We were in a forward position and some sappers were doing repair work on the trench behind us. A shell exploded among them and one of them went up in the air and dropped at my feet. His leg was blown off at the thigh. I knelt down beside him and he whispered, 'Tell mother...', and he was gone, just like that. I went across and looked down into the trench where our chaps were. 'Anybody hit here?' 'No, we're all right.' An officer yelled out to me, 'Come down you damned fool you'll get killed!' I turned to him and I said, 'Who cares?' I'd got to such a state then that I just didn't care whether I got killed the next minute or not.

QMS GORDON FISHER,
1st Hertfordshire
  Regiment

The front line is really an elongated shell hole. In the enormous darkness of the cold quiet night the faint *pop* of a Verey light sounds from the German lines. It ascends and illuminates the ground. In its radiance tree stumps and branches, bare, black, broken on what was once a road, are like bony old women's arms, stretched out to heaven in silent imprecation. Effigies hang on the barbed wire like grotesque figures carried round the streets on Guy Fawkes night. Here and there the ground bulges into a head, booted feet, khaki covered arms. A dead man is lying on his back with his knees up and his arms outstretched as though lazily reclining in a field in the heat of a summer day. The explosion of a distant shell sounds like a gentle tap on a gong ... the thin circles of echo slowly ebb away ...

2ND LIEUTENANT G.D.
  HORRIDGE
1st/5th Battalion
  Lancashire Fusiliers
  (F.F.)

As far as the eye could see was a mass of black mud with shell holes filled with water. Here and there broken duckboards, partly submerged in the quagmire; here and there a horse's carcase sticking out of the water; here and there a corpse. The only sign of life was a rat or two swimming about to find food and a patch of ground. At night a yellow mist hung over the mud; the stench was almost unbearable. When gas shells came over the mist turned to brown. It smelt like violets. The smell of violets was the sign of danger.

PRIVATE H. JEARY,
1st Battalion,
Queen's Royal West Surrey
  Regiment

Spree Farm was hardly a resting place,
In the Nineteen Seventeen year of grace,
It was what was known as a pillar box,
And both Jerry and us had given it socks,
And the boys who mopped up the battle grounds
Found plenty dead Jerries lying around.
By the entrance a hole had been gouged by a 'How'
(Which polite Aussies christened '12-inch cow')
And when that hole was filled in again,
It wasn't with soil – it was Flanders rain.
Then came a dose of snow and ice,
The weather was almost too cold for the lice!
The Howitzer hole froze up like glass –
We slid over it when we wanted to pass,
And dead Jerries stared through with glassy eyes,
As though they were wanting to sympathise
With us who were left on Flanders plain
To endure its Hell all over again

Private A. V. Simpson
7th Duke of Wellington's Regiment

My mother had baked a cake for me and packed it in a parcel, and she'd also put in a packet of disinfectant that would kill lice. It was called Parasitox. It tasted of carbolic, as I found out, because the packet had burst and my cake was covered with this Parasitox – permeated with it. It tasted absolutely foul, but my mother had baked that cake and I couldn't bring myself to throw it away, so piece by piece I ate it, carbolic and all.

Gdsmn. J. Worker, 1st Battalion, Scots Guards.

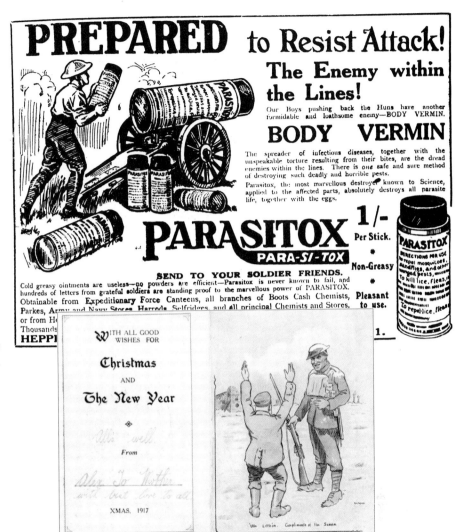

Although the battalion was in the line, we determined to see that Christmas was properly observed. I was elected Master of Ceremonies of B Company. (Few Padres escaped this.) I made friends with the cook, and together we drew up the menu and produced the following remarkable effusion:

XMAS DAY MENU

SOUPE MAÎTRE DE DUGOUT

POISSON PILCHARD DANS LA BOÎTE

BULLE AU BOEUF

POUDING NOEL

The King   Absent Friends

THE REVD S. HINCHLIFFE
Chaplain, 2/6th Battalion, Northumberland Fusiliers.

It's the Duck Board Glide,
It's the Duck Board Slide,
On a cold and frosty night,
For it's over a mile
In single file
Out in the pale moonlight.
It's nippy, slippy,
Bumpy, jumpy,
Shellholes either side,
And when machine guns cough
You can all drop off
That Duck Board Glide.

2nd Lieutenant Sivori Levey,
11th Battalion Prince of Wales' Own (West Yorks.)
Regiment.

THE BROWN FAMILY'S FOUR WAR CHRISTMASES.

France,
28 December 1917.

RIFLEMAN B. F.
ECCLES,
7th (S) Battalion,
The Rifle Brigade.

Dearest Mother, Dad and kids,
This letter will be posted by a chap on leave so here goes:

Before I begin. I am quite well, alive and kicking, happy and 'grateful for life'. So by that you can bet I have had the most exciting run of my existence. Christmas on the Passchendaele Ridge. Yes, and take it from me it is not a nice place to spend one's Christmas Vacation. Fortunately winter had come and everything was icebound which banished the mud.

I was on a bombing post with six others in a shell hole about eight yards long. We were out of touch with the rest, but Fritz did not know exactly where we were. We were so near him we could hear him talking and coughing. It was trying work as we had to be so vigilant. On the night of the 24th I was warned to report to a pillbox (Company Headquarters) as guide. The snow was thick and being moonlight I had several times to throw myself down to avoid the machine-gun bullets, for as you know there are no trenches. Five of us had to find the track to Battalion HQ, which was not too easy seeing the snow had obliterated many landmarks. On our return we were rewarded by a decent tot of rum. On Xmas night, we five had again to set out and report to a place known as 'so-and-so' farm and stay till Boxing night to guide up our relief, a battalion of the Worcesters.

We were not sorry to get out of it for a day, although the journey is so risky. For the cold was pretty keen, and jolly hard to bear especially in a shell hole, where to stand up by day means a bullet through the napper.

More snow on Boxing Day and a brilliant moon. How we cursed that moon.

Consider it. A full moon on a vast waste of snow six inches to a foot deep. And to take a battalion of men over open country in full sight of the enemy. All went well until we had gone two kilos, and appeared on the last ridge, within 600 yards of what is left of Passchendaele. Then we were spotted by Fritz and he opened on us with machine-guns on three sides (the salient is like a horseshoe). We carried on until it became too hot and fellows were drooping over too thickly. Two of my platoon (I mean the platoon I was guiding) were knocked over besides others, so we dropped on the track, and rolled into shell holes. Bullets were whizzing over us a hundred to the minute. We tried to move forward again from shell hole to shell hole, when the platoon behind shouted they had lost their guide. I cried to them to follow me. We were so massed that Fritz properly got the breeze up. He fully thought that we were extending to make an attack, so up went his SOS signal. It was what I had dreaded, for immediately his artillery opened a terrific barrage. Talk about a big slice of Hell! I yelled to the chaps to get flat. I went forward on my hands and knees in the snow and dropped into a shell hole with Ravenhill my fellow Guide, and for fully half an hour we lay with our faces in the snow, while shells did everything but hit us, even though they seemed to burst on the edge of the shell holes. It was the worst half hour I have ever spent. Casualties were heavy and many were the cries of wounded men. In one place no less than four men had their heads blown off.

Then – thank the Lord – our artillery got the wire and they put up such an avalanche of shells on Jerry's lines that he closed up like a wet sack. Then came a respite and a bit of mist arose. I went forward to our lines and we made the relief as well as possible although so many were missing. I met an officer, told him we had got the men up, and he said, 'Grease out of it', which I did. I closed up with some of my old platoon, and we did that three miles out of the danger zone in double quick time.

We had one more narrow escape after, being nearly gassed when a shell hit the track within a few yards of us.

Then at last we reached a zone of safety. Exhausted after living on biscuits, bully etc. for four days, but happy as lords, for after twenty–four days in the Ypres sector our Division had been relieved. We were met by Brigade Officers near St Jean, and a Canteen by the roadside provided hot tea and rum, biscuits and cigs. Then to a camp under canvas until morning. On the 27th, we arose and got the thickest of five days beard off. Then a train journey to our present place sixty miles behind the line near St Omer.

The snow is thick and the frosts are keen, but what matters is we are away from it all again. So we can sing and shout once more.

I may be wrong in telling you all this, but the reason I do is that it is some record of exciting adventure which I never dreamed of.

But here I am, I am not worrying so you need not. I am in the pink, barring being a bit stiff and bruised.

But believe me anything is preferable to that Hell upon earth, Passchendaele Ridge.

So dear people you can play the piano when you read this, and make your minds easy for a bit.

The weather is severe, but we get hardened. We are having our Xmas feed on Sunday, a big pay day. I have plenty of fags, and a fine pipe so I am très bon.

Meanwhile we are nearer the end of the war. I have seen no paper lately but shall get my chance now. I will write Emilla as soon as possible. Tell her she is a dear for sending me such a jolly fine pipe. Meanwhile, the best of wishes for 1918.

May next Christmas be quieter for me. Bank Holidays seem to be Helldays. So Cheero Mother, darling, I enjoyed the Butterscotch within forty yards of Fritz. The socks and gloves reached me just in time.

Fondest love,
Burton.

1918

The company is filled now
With faces strange to see,
And scarce a man of the old men
That lived and fought with me.
I know the drafts are good men,
I know they're doing well,
But they're not the men I slept with
Those nights at la Boisselle.

E. A. McIntosh

The casualties of the Third Battle of Ypres had been huge, morale was low and the question of manpower was now acute. There had been another battle further south at Cambrai where the troops, supported by a large force of the new and faster tanks, had broken through triumphantly – and had been forced to retire through lack of reserves. Lloyd George, violently opposed to Haig's policy of attrition on the Western Front, had diverted several divisions to fight on the Italian–Austrian border, and thus to strike Germany in the back. Despite Haig's earnest representations Lloyd George refused to send more troops to the Western Front. It was now mid-winter and no new moves could be expected before the spring.

BLIMEY!

My Tuesdays are meatless
My Wednesdays are wheatless
I'm getting more eatless each day.
My home it is heatless
My bed it is sheetless
They're all sent to YMCA

My Club Rooms are treatless,
My coffee is sweetless
Each day I get poorer and wiser,
My stockings are feetless,
My trousers are seatless,
My God, but I do hate the Kaiser!

ANITA MOSTYN,
(Daughter of Col. Rowland
Feilding).

Quite suddenly news came that our father was coming home on leave at last. The whole household was jubilant, but there was hardly any food by then (not the kind of food that he would expect and deserve) and very little money.

I remember my mother taking us with her to the shops and standing in a queue for over an hour to get a little extra butter and some cheese on the black market for his supper. We shared her triumph as she came home with a parcel of roasting beef for Father's first dinner. She was so happy that she took us both to meet him off the late troop train from Dover.

I shall never forget Victoria Station with its huge domed glass roof, and the noise of the trains grunting and creaking, and Mother holding tight to our hands in case we were swept away by one of the heavy trolleys which were loaded up with soldiers' bags and haversacks. One of them bumped into a soldier and a girl who were holding each other tightly. The girl was crying and there were tears on the soldier's face too. Mother dragged us away quite crossly. 'Don't stare at people when they are sad,' she said.

Then the great train came steaming into the station, and suddenly my father was there. He had always seemed to me to be one of the cleanest people in the world; if we hugged him he used to say 'Don't touch my collar!' in case our hands were grubby. But there was no need now for this warning. His khaki uniform was crushed and crumpled and there was mud dried on his sleeve. But we all stood and hugged there on Victoria Station. We were all so happy. Someone found a taxi and we bundled in with the huge battered haversack Father had brought with him.

Our cook had dinner all ready, laid out on the dining-room table, delicious roast beef and Yorkshire pudding which she'd made with two of our weekly rationed eggs. Father kept saying, 'Goodness! I had no idea you could still eat as well as this in England.' We sat up late that night to welcome him home and just as we were going up to bed there was the sound of a whistle in the street and a voice shouting, 'Take Cover. Take cover.' My sister started to run upstairs to fetch the Ludo and Snakes and Ladders to take down to the basement. Suddenly Father got red and angry and hurried us downstairs. He said in a funny voice, 'No time now! You can get them tomorrow!' and I remember his shouting crossly to Rose to see who was peeping between the curtains of the landing window to see if the searchlights had found a zeppelin. He even shouted quite crossly to Mother who waited just a moment behind us to put the fireguard in front of the grate.

We couldn't understand a brave man spoiling all the fun like that.

I eventually got my leave pass – fourteen days including travelling time which took me three days from the rail head to get me home to Forgue in Aberdeenshire. The nearest railway station to Forgue was Huntly. My pay for the fourteen days leave was thirty francs which was equivalent to £3. Boat from Calais to Dover, Dover to Victoria Station where our francs were changed into £ s. d. Tube train to King's Cross, night train to Aberdeen. I lay in the corridor most of the way to Edinburgh. (I did think that we would be entitled to a seat but the civvies thought otherwise). At Edinburgh we were treated to free cigs, cups of tea, rolls etc. We had to pay for this south of the border! On arrival at Aberdeen we were welcomed in the real manner – breakfast, clean up, all on the house. I think we deserved it. Spent the day in Aberdeen with my sisters. Train to Huntly at 3 p.m. On arrival at Huntly there was a snowstorm raging, the bus to Forgue not running, so to cover the ten miles to Forgue the only way was to walk it in full marching order, rifle etc. But I was on my way home on the last stage, that was the comforting thing. I wasn't marching to the trenches! Kath my sister decided to accompany me from Aberdeen and she wasn't clad for this journey. I had sent a telegram from London that I was on my way and Mother knew that with the snow there wasn't any conveyance from Huntly to Forgue, with the result that halfway home we were met by Father with a sledge and horse. This was real good! The storm was at its height, so were we glad to see him and he us. A bit of trouble turning this sledge around but eventually we were on our way. That journey I shall never forget. It is as clear in my memory as the day it happened. Our first stop was at Bognie Brae Inn. Mrs Raffan was the innkeeper. Well Father had a good dram. Was he cold! He looked like Santa Claus with his

PRIVATE ALEX BROWNIE,
4th Battalion,
Gordon Highlanders.

beard full of snow. At last home to Chapelhill, Forgue. The road to the old thatched cottage was blocked with snow so we had to take to the fields to get home. Mother was there to meet us. Some home-coming! But was it good!

After something good to eat and drink Mother said, 'It is time you were in bed, Laddie.' I said, 'I am lousy, Mother. I will have to have a wash.' 'Surely you are not lousy?' 'Yes, we all are, all the time.' 'I will have to get the boiler fire on,' she said. There was no bath room in the 'auld hoose'. Bed! And was it good to know that there were no Jerry shells to keep me from sleeping! I awoke next day to a snowstorm and we had to dig ourselves out. It kept me at home for most of my leave but it was good to be home. One thing I did do was to shoot some of the Laird's pheasants – a different target from Jerry. We were glad of the birds for food was getting scarce due to the snow. All roads were blocked for a week.

Mother had one hell of a job to get my clothes clean. She said one day, 'Where are your pants, Alex?' I told her we never wore pants. She wasn't for believing me, so before I returned she had made me a pair – but the first turn into the trenches the pants were done away with. Mother's work had gone for nothing. My leave terminated on 20 January so I was on my way back to join the Battalion. Back to the same bloody fatigues every night.

◆ ◆

We go to the trenches to do night fatigues,
We carry the sandbags and the RE he digs.
We carry the timber from dump to the mine,
Which is usually in the firing line.
We tear through the trench like one in a hunt,
When somebody shouts 'Go steady in front'.
We try to avoid the holes in the ground.
Then suddenly step on a board that's unsound.
We then arrive, after all the excitement,
Then through somebody's order we sling off equipment.
We toil all night from mine head to dump,
And some of the bags are a pretty good lump.
We sometimes slip down, and no words will explain,
The language it causes and also the pain.
We then wait for daybreak, to knock off at five,
Then back to our billet. On rations we thrive.
We get good tea, some bread and some ham,
But goodness knows what's done with the jam.
We still will not worry but take things as lightly,
As they seem to be doing in good old Blighty.
We will still hope for Peace, which we know will bring smiles,
To the writer of this whose name is H. Biles.

H. W. Biles,
2nd Battalion, Royal Sussex Regiment

From the prisoner of war work camp at Tournai we were sent out in small parties to different districts. I had many occupations here, making railways, tramways, emptying coal barges, cleaning streets, removing shells from trucks, carrying German wounded from the trains to hospital. When we were formed up in fours for marching we always made a bargain that whatever a man should have given him it should be shared between the four. Occasionally we got a man who believed in No. 1! Then there was a scramble to be the outside man because passing through the town he was more likely to have things handed to him, which was frequently done by the Belgians. Passing through a village one day a woman stood on the step of her house with a turnip in her hand inviting someone to fetch it. One of the fellows rushed across and was shot through the stomach by the guard for leaving the ranks.

Food was very scarce at this camp. I was taken to the town one day

CORPORAL A. NEWMAN
Prisoner of War

by two Germans to fetch the rations for our men. They consisted of a horse's head (everything complete, eyes etc).

We never took off our clothes to sleep for fear of losing them. (My outfit at this time consisted of an old frock coat which fastened similar to a clergyman's, Italian trousers which reached my knees, old rags for socks and a pair of sabots, size 25, and a schoolboy's cap).

In February of 1918 I was sent to a little place called Troyennes outside Tournai. Our work here chiefly consisted of clearing out all the old barns at farms and spare rooms at houses and putting down clean straw for the German troops coming from the Russian front to prepare for the March offensive against us.

The Germans had suffered losses proportionately greater than the Allies, but the collapse of Russia had released large numbers of men from their Eastern Front. They were well aware that the Allied Forces, now drastically weakened, would very soon be augmented by a large American army. Their only chance was to strike before they got there. They struck with the last of their strength.

When the Germans broke through on 21st March me and my pal, Curly, thought we'd set up a rumour that we was on a forty-eight hours' notice to France and no man could leave the camp. It came back to us so many times during the day that we believed it ourselves. It turned out to be right. When we went on parade the next day, instead of saying, 'Thirteen Platoon, Attention!' the officer said, 'Fifty-six Draft, Attention!' We went down to the Quartermaster's Stores, we got handed out with a gas-mask, field dressing and steel helmet and forbidden to leave the camp.

The next morning, we was lined up about eight o'clock and marched down to the station, and when the train come in we were singing, 'How can I bear to leave you? A Parting Kiss I'll give you.' We were singing that on the station. We arrived in Folkestone at half past two the next morning and marched down to Dover and then we got on the boat for France. There were three boat-loads of us. We was all eighteen – hardly a man of full military age. We stopped several hours for rest in this barracks at Boulogne, then we went on the train to Etaples and there we was under canvas on the sands and we didn't know what was happening. The next morning we were sent down to the Somme from Etaples – Sasseville – pouring with rain. They stood under a barn shouting our names out there. They split us up into Companies and Platoons. I found myself with nobody but myself as I knew in my platoon, and there was an old woman in the farmhouse there and she was looking at us and she spoke in English and she said to the Sergeant-Major, 'What have you got there?' He said, 'Men, soldiers come to fight for their country.' She said, 'No, them's piccaninnies, they should get home with their mother.' He said, 'They've got to fight.' She said, 'Ah! It's not right.'

PRIVATE H. J. HAYNES, 2nd/6th Battalion, The Royal Warwickshire Regiment.

A.D. Nineteen Fifty 'I see the War Babies' Battalion is a coming out'

On Monday the 25th, about noon, we received the order to retire. I and a pal were fast asleep in a bit of a shelter we had made in the parapet, and everyone had gone and left us, when it suddenly dawned upon one of our officers that we had been left and he had made his way back and woke us. Going as fast as our legs would carry us, we soon caught up with the rest of our chaps.

There were three roads, one to the right and one to the left, while the other led straight ahead to a village, (or it had been once). Leading into it was a sunken road with deep dugouts at each side. We knew it as we had passed through the previous Saturday morning. Making our way down this towards the village (the shelling having ceased) one of the Company runners was in front when he got in line with these dugouts. He stopped and stood like a pillar of salt. Then we spotted a German coming out. He upped his rifle, and a German officer at his back started firing his revolver at us, followed by more Jerries with a machine-gun. Some turned and ran back down the road, while some of us clambered up the side of the road and made our way across country with the

PRIVATE W. LOCKEY, 1st Battalion, Nottinghamshire and Derbyshire Regiment, (The Sherwood Foresters).

machine-guns spitting at us. Making our way across country we came upon a road some distance in the rear of the village and came in contact with some more of our battalion who had managed to escape out of the trap. It appears that the Germans had crossed the canal on our right and left, and to quote the words of one of our Generals, he told us that he had given up hopes of ever seeing any of the Sherwoods ever more.

Making our way into a village which was full of our Artillery ready for moving, we came upon some Gunners brewing some tea. Here we rested awhile, one of the Gunners gave us spuds which we prepared, and they were almost ready for eating when the cry that Jerry was entering the further end of the village fell upon our ears, so we made off, climbing the wooded slopes. On our right on reaching the top, we turned and looking back could see the enemy advancing on the village. We enquired where our Company were, but no one could tell us. Going up the road and into the open country, we came across some of our chaps who informed us that Fritz had been knocking hell out of them ever since noon that day and they were now falling back disputing every inch of ground till at last Infantry and Artillery were all jumbled up together while the German guns began pounding us for all their worth. Some of our Artillery with their limbers crossing a ploughed field on our right were hit by a shell, drivers, Gunners and all being blown to bits. As we went we passed an old Frenchman who stood waving his arms and shouting, 'Anglais Soldats no bon!'. That night when the roll was called, there were sixty of us left out of the battalion.

◆

GERMAN ADVANCE CONTINUES

◆

CAPT. C. M. SLACK, MC,
1st/4th Battalion,
East Yorkshire Regiment.

In ten days we went back from St Quentin to Amiens. We were attached to a Brigade commanded by a man called Haig, a cousin of Douglas Haig – Brigadier Haig – and it was a regular mess-up. I retired with the whole of the Fifth Army. By the end of the ten days, the Fifth Army had gone back fifty miles, and we kept doing counter-attacks, take that wood, lose it, take it again, and so on. We kept going backwards and forwards, but it was always one step forward and three back, till we got the other side of the Somme. Later on it did become a rout but it wasn't all of them. There was a tremendous amount of confidence in most of the men, but there were young boys, young men who'd just come out and hadn't got the *esprit de corps*, and they were running away. They didn't care a damn. They didn't mind anything. Rifles gone. I actually had to draw my revolver on an officer.

We were supposed to be doing a counter-attack, and at this time I was Adjutant, and we had attached to us a tank which broke down, and a young officer and a Sergeant with a light machine-gun. They weren't our people, but they were attached to us and there was a regular rout. They'd thrown their rifles away, they'd thrown their equipment away. You couldn't do a thing to stop them. They weren't our own people. We were all mixed up. Anyway, this officer was running away, too. He wasn't running away with staring eyes and he hadn't thrown his light machine-gun away or his revolver, but he was going back. I said, 'Where are *you* going? You're supposed to be over there.' He said, 'I take my orders from General Haig.' I said, 'Yes, *Brigadier*-General Haig, and you're attached to my battalion and I am the Adjutant.' Shortly after that, I found him coming back again, and I drew my revolver. Whether I would have shot him or not I don't know, but I drew my revolver, and at that moment I saw Colonel Thompson, one of the Colonels in our Brigade. I said, 'Colonel, will you talk to this officer?' I told him the story. 'Will you tell him to go back?' And he did, and the officer obeyed him.

Marcelcave
28–30 March, 1918

I found that our men had retreated down the railroad cutting toward the west and had given up the village. That surely was my moment. Should I run away to save myself from capture or worse and leave the men who were crying for help? From a military point of view I imagine the thing to have done was to try to get away, but we had no military training and from the doctor's viewpoint the idea of running in that situation was impossible. I went into the cellars and calmly did what I could for the men.

The German mopping-up squads came into the village.

In a few minutes some officers came along and one of them could talk a little English. They seemed surprised to find an American and could not understand how an American happened to be there. They showed no antagonism, however; their attitude was rather one of curiosity. They said that ambulances would come up to take the wounded back.

We stayed in the cellars all that night and no ambulances came up. The next morning (which was Good Friday) there were more assurances that later in the day the wounded would be hauled back.

A squad of sanitary men came around during the day and I asked the Corporal, who talked fairly good English, for water, and what he said illustrates the propaganda on both sides. He said there were lots of wells around but he would not dare to drink out of them, 'Because you cannot tell, the English may have poisoned them.'

There were some potatoes in a French house over the cellars and I

DR BERNARD GALLAGHER, US Army, attached 2nd/4th Battalion, The Gloucestershire Regiment.

peeled some and boiled them over a fire made on the floor of the cellar, so that that night each man had one boiled potato and nothing else.

Still no ambulance came up. Luckily, I had a bottle containing a lot of quarter grain morphine tablets with me and was able to give them to the men who were suffering acutely from their wounds. The men were dirty and lousy, of course (including myself).

All next day and all next night the English kept up their shell fire and several times shells crashed into the buildings over our heads and brought down debris into the cellars that nearly buried us. Sleep was impossible what with cold and vermin.

On the second morning (Holy Saturday, March 30) it was almost impossible to get in or out of the cellars, for the entrances were piled with rubbish and some of them caved in. Now the Germans said they could *not* send up ambulances because the English were shelling the village so heavily, but that morning I saw three horse ambulances go by to carry down German wounded.

Afternoon came and I had visions of another night there. I was desperate and determined to make an effort to get some care for the men. I walked out in the street and was 'recaptured' by a German soldier. He took me to the very place I wanted to go – a Battalion Headquarters in another cellar. One or two officers there could talk English and I told them my story. It bore fruit, for a machine-gun officer and six or eight men were sent with me and carts were collected to haul the wounded men.

Three or four of them had already died. While we were loading them on carts in the courtyard, shells were dropping all around and I shall never forget that German machine-gun officer. He was very nice and seemed absolutely fearless, for he continued calmly with the work, always smiling, and the closer a shell lit, the 'louder' he smiled. The carts were pulled down the road past the railway station to the old factory where there was a German Dressing Station.

We unloaded the men in the factory cellar which was warm and comfortable. A lot of German stretcher-bearers were there and they had plenty of bully beef and other canned food that the English must have left behind in various storehouses. They had lots of French wine too, and most of them were feeling very cheery and all, of course, were greatly bucked up about the phenomenal progress of their offensive. One big, white-haired young German was feeling particularly good. He helped a great deal about getting our wounded men into the cellar, handling them as gently as he would a baby. Then he warmed up a mess of bully beef and potatoes for us to eat. All the time he kept talking, asserting that he was a Rhinelander ('Ich bin ein Rheinlander') and that he was a good fellow, which seemed to follow seeing that he was a Rhinelander.

After a while, three or four men were loaded in a horse ambulance and I was sent with them. We started back towards the East; I did not know where. The attitude of most of the German soldiers toward me was very courteous, tinged with curiosity. As an example, an old German, who was riding with the driver of the horse ambulance in which our men were riding, insisted on me taking his place in the seat while he walked, for I was an officer and his sense of discipline would not let him ride while I walked.

We twisted along a very bad and muddy road and after an hour or two came to a little village after dark, which was probably La Motte. We got off at a large Dressing Station which was over ground, for there was no shelling here, but in the evening the village was bombed by the English and I saw quite a number of badly wounded Germans brought in.

The Germans in charge here were courteous, gave us something to eat and a place to lie down and sleep for the night. Being an American helped, I think, rather than hindered, for many of them had relatives in America and they certainly manifested no animosity toward me.

SLIGHT BRITISH WITHDRAWAL FROM THE SOMME LINE

SERGEANT E.
DAVIDSON,
Royal Engineers.

We were in Ypres at that time, and without any warning we were shot down to the railway station on to a train and rushed down south to a place called Rosières. We got there on the 22nd, and I was instructed to go and blow up a bridge – of course, it was all a strange area to me, I'd just got off the train. We started off, about four of us with bikes and cases of gun cotton to blow up this bridge and when I got up the road an officer stopped me and wanted to know where I was going. I said I was going to blow up the bridge. He said, 'You're much too late for that. The Germans are already about two miles this side of it. You'd better get in the trench there.' We put our bikes across the road, a silly thing to do but it just made a little bit of an obstacle, and I just became an Infantryman then, straight away. So there and then I ceased to be an RE. I'd only got a couple of my own blokes and I had to take charge of some Infantry chaps. They had a machine-gun and for quite a part of the day we had targets all over the place. The Germans were coming down everywhere and they were so confident that they weren't taking the slightest trouble in concealing themselves.

Letter from SERGEANT
JAMES BLOCKWOOD
TURNER,
Australian Imperial Force.

15 April 1918

Dear Dais,

Well here we are at the other end of France stopping the Hun from getting all he wants, and it has been some shift I can tell you, but it was worth it as we have made a name for ourselves that will never be forgotten in France. Things looked bad when we got the news of the breakthrough and we were a long way from here resting the whole Division, but it was cut short in the middle of the night by the Boss coming and telling us to get going in five minutes, that Fritz had broken through and we had to go and stop him. So into it we went. It seemed so funny when we got close to the place because you would see nothing but Australians going up, and endless streams of broken down looking things coming the other way. They used to say, 'You will meet Jerry before you get to the next village,' at which we all said, 'Good enough. We have come a long way to meet him, and the sooner we meet him by the look of things here, the sooner we will stop his little walk.' Nobody else seemed to be getting in his way! Well we met him right enough and one place they were coming along with their rifles slung over their backs quite happily, and just went up and asked our boys to surrender, as they had been doing with the other lot. The digger just grabbed a little party, and when the officer-in-charge saw the Australian badge on the tunic he nearly had a fit! He spoke English and said, 'Good Gawd, we did not think that there were any Australians here!' Well, the fight started that night and it is a big thing to say but true that the 3rd and 4th Divisions have held the cow, and he has not gained an inch since they got out of the lorries that night; they are magnificent men and it makes you proud to be one of them. We had an English Captain in today, and he was talking to us and we asked him if he thought we had him stopped yet. He said, 'No, we have not, but *you* have, you are the best fighting men the world has ever seen, and I am an Englishman.' So then we thanked him, and the poor cow seemed quite broken up. Our orders were, 'You are not to leave this trench while a man lives' – pretty crude, what! Well, the Hun came, eleven waves of him, which were promptly turned into heaped up dead. The 12th started and out went the 3rd to meet him with cold steel just at sunset. It was a beautiful sight, and meant everything to this end of the line. It was like one man, and all the bayonets glinting in the setting sun, but they soon were put into action – and goodbye the Hun! We beat him back, our little thin line, but my Gawd, they are men. If we only had enough of them, we would be in Berlin in a week I reckon.

We are with the French now and they are fine fellows, and fight like the deuce, and are very fond of our lads since this last 'go'. Oh, it's a great war. There will be a lot to tell you all, if one gets back, and it will seem hard for you to believe, but it may come out all right yet. I hope it does, for our boys' sake. They absolutely saved the place this time. I don't see how it can last much longer and America have done nothing yet, and it's time they did by the same token.

I have not heard from anyone for ages, but I think that is on account of my shifting about so much.

Well, I must close up and get to bed, Roy is already there. He is well. Got the *Punch* you sent. I am just the same old sixpence.

J.B.T.

Villers Brettoneux had been captured by the 15th Australian Brigade on Anzac Day, 1918. The Germans were in there. They'd advanced down and they were within fifteen kilometres, looking right down on Amiens, straight down, and that's a fairly big city. Just on fifteen kilometres, within gun range. They didn't have any heavy guns to shell it from there. They were firing big long-range guns from further back, lobbing only occasional big shells in Amiens and doing a bit of damage. Of necessity, we couldn't tolerate this because while they could shell Amiens they could interfere with the railway service which terminated in Amiens. So the 15th Brigade, they divided – half went to the left, half went to the right – round the back of Villers Brettoneux, and did it at night, and, and, by Jove! They met head on. The road went straight through Villers Brettoneux and they met on that road. They had great fun there. One place there was a Winery, and the Fritzes had found it and it was full of Germans, drunk as owls. Our fellows got in with them. It finished up with Australians and Germans drunk as owls together. Up to their knees in wine in Villers Brettoneux. Then the heads said, 'Where's everybody got to?' They suddenly discovered this Winery and went in, and here was this spectacle. The Fritzes were dragged out by

CAPTAIN F. C. RUSSELL, Australian Imperial Force.

their feet, drunk as lords, and they finished up in the prisoners' compound. The police had to come and put a guard on this place, and that was the end of that. Then they mopped up the town. The line finished just about half a mile beyond Villers Brettoneux. They never got any further. The Fritzes never did get Amiens.

CORPORAL A. D. PANKHURST
56th Division,
Royal Field Artillery.

The OC said to me, 'I want you to go up to the reserve pits – the Germans have attacked and run over our line.' I took my men up with me and we got to a sunken road, and a couple of wounded officers came along and said, 'You can't get through. He's got a machine-gun barrage on the sunken road.' And he was shelling badly and the shells were bursting and the fellows began to get a bit extra windy and I can remember doing a silly thing. I said. 'They can't put a barrage on the sunken road, The trajectory would be such that they'd never get us. We're below the angle of fire.' I got on top – stood on top – and said, 'Look, it's not hurting me. Come on,' and we went and we got through. We got into the pit. I rolled back the camouflage, got the mortar ready, got the bombs ready and I got them to hold my heels, hold me up to the ramp so I could look over the top, and then I saw a sight which I shall never forget. It was the London Scottish advancing in open order with fixed bayonets, just as if they were going for an afternoon walk. They were dropping, dropping, the shells were bursting, the machine-guns were going and they just went on. It was the most awe-inspiring and yet the most wonderful thing I've ever seen, and yet it'd nearly break your heart. And we were the only part of the line to hold on the whole of the 5th Army front. We were the only part that held the line. They took the front line; they might have taken the second line, (they say they came over with spare boots and rations for a week) but we held them.

◆

If you were the only Boche in the trench
And I had the only bomb,
Nothing else would matter in the world that day,
I would blow you up into eternity.
Chamber of Horrors, just made for two,
With nothing to spoil our fun;
There would be such wonderful things to do,
I should get your rifle and bayonet too,
If you were the only Boche in the trench
And I had the only gun.

◆

At Hazebrouck we scrambled out of the lorries at the double, and each man was handed two bandoliers of ammo, and ordered to take up a prone position in a field just outside Meteren on a ridge with a farmhouse in front of us and a big farm building on the left. On the gable end of this farm building hung a large cow bell, with a rope hanging therefrom. This bell kept constantly ringing. There was no one near the rope, so the only conclusion was that snipers' bullets were causing the bell to ring. This indicated that the enemy was within a very short distance. My platoon was ordered to take up a position some fifty yards in front and we lay in a small ditch with a short hedge in front of us.

PRIVATE H. N. JEARY, 1st Battalion, Queen's (Royal West Surrey) Regiment.

Nothing happened until the Saturday morning at daybreak, when we saw two Jerries coming from a farmhouse, and making their way to a Dutch barn some fifty yards away from us. One was carrying two panniers and the other had a box on his shoulder. They put these on the ground and then commenced to scoop up the ground and made a bank in front of the hole. When they had finished two other Jerries came out, one carrying a tripod and the other a Maxim Gun barrel on his shoulder. We watched them fix up the gun and at a given signal we let fire with our rifles at these Jerries, only fifty yards away. Three of them dropped dead and one held his hand to his face which was bleeding terribly.

Jerries by the dozen came from behind slaughtered cattle that lay in the field. I was completely surrounded. I then noticed that my left wrist was bleeding and a bullet had gone through the wooden stock of my rifle. Fortunately it was not much of a wound.

The chap from the gun emplacement with the bleeding face was being helped along by a German stretcher-bearer, and he motioned me to help this wounded bloke. His nose was almost completely shot off. I took hold of his arm and we slowly walked away from the firing zone. I wondered then if they would finish me off, well knowing that I must have been the cause of his wounds and the deaths of the others. I looked to see where the rest of my comrades were and I saw they were all dead or wounded. I was the only one that walked away.

CAPT. C. M. SLACK, MC,
1st/4th Battalion,
East Yorkshire Regiment,
150th Brigade,
50th Division.

The Germans started up again, an aftermath of the big retreat, and we had to rush up to the River Lys and it was at this time that the orders came out, 'No retreat. Whatever happens, no retreat. Stay where you are. You must not retreat.' Our battalion had two companies in the front line, about three or four hundred yards back from the banks of the Lys and two in reserve. Battalion HQ was a few hundred yards behind them in a big shell hole with a bit of corrugated iron over the top. There was Major Jackson, there was my assistant and a clerk and the RSM, five of us in this shell hole, alongside a road that ran right down from Estaires to the River Lys, more or less a farm road. We were just on the side of it and on the other side was a ditch. Then the Germans got over. They threw bridges over the Lys, and they just mopped up those two front line companies, wiped them out. Well, they were nearly all new little boys out from England, only been out a few days, only heard rifles fired on the ranges in England. They were annihilated, either bayoneted or shot. We were shooting from our little shell hole. They got round on our right and we shot them and they got round on our left, and then when we realised that our two companies had been wiped out, we still had the orders, *Hold on at all costs. No retirement.* 'But', we thought, 'the battalion is nearly wiped out and there's only five of us. Let's get on to this road and run like Hell back to our own troops.' We should have had to run between the Germans on either side of us, but we were going to do that. It was far better than staying where we were, and a running target *is* difficult to hit, and so the other four got out on to this road, prepared to run like Hell and I stayed behind, pulling mud down on the shell hole, in order to bury the orders I'd got from Brigade and Division, (I didn't want them to get into the enemy's hands if I got hit or caught) and then I got out of the shell hole on to the road and I looked round to the right to see how far the other fellows had got back, and there was a squad of Germans a matter of a few feet from me. There they were! Well, it was no use me running. They signalled to me to take my pack off, which I did, and then I went to get my shaving gear out — but, 'Nein, nein, nein, leave that pack alone'. So I didn't argue. I saw my own people standing with their hands up. I felt lousy! Awful! I felt an absolute swine. There was no blame whatever. I couldn't have done anything else, but my morale had gone. I felt absolutely awful.

We were herded back over the Lys, and I had a wrist watch on and one of the German soldiers said, 'We want that watch,' and I said, 'No, you can't have it. My lass gave it to me.' And I appealed to a German officer and he was very decent and he told these German Privates off and I've still got the watch. After that we went to a cage, just a wire netting cage it was. There was a hut in it and the officers were all bunged in there and the Other Ranks were put in the yard outside in the barbed wire. I felt, 'Well, at least I've come through in the end.' I didn't feel that I'd been a coward. I *knew* I hadn't.

◆

OUR TROOPS IN GOOD HEART AND FIGHTING SPLENDIDLY

◆

Our own position was on the banks of the La Bassée Canal, and it was a very quiet part of the line, so much so that the civilians were still living there. We were very friendly with all the people round about until 9 April. We knew that the battle had started, and we wondered if our turn would come, then about four o'clock in the morning all hell let loose. We hadn't known a bombardment like it before. I was in the top bunk and I reached for my trousers, trying to get them on as fast as I could to get out and get to the place where the Colonel was. There was a trench leading to a house where the Colonel was, and we dashed as quickly as we could and we jumped into this trench. Just on the canal there was a French barge guarded by two French soldiers. I don't know what their job was, but these Frenchmen must have thought that we were Germans when we came running, and they said, 'Mercy, Comrade, Nous Français, pas Anglais!' As much as to say, 'We're Frenchmen. Don't kill us! If they're English, kill *them*!' I took a running kick at one of them, I was so furious, even in my hurry.

We were sent out very early to contact the batteries. We went round all the batteries, taking messages to them. When I got back, later on in the morning, a man came up. A civilian I knew by sight. He was bleeding on his neck, crying, hysterical. He says, 'Venez avec moi, Monsieur. Venez avec moi. Madame est morte et les enfants. Venez avec moi.' Well, I was in a quandary really. The shells were coming over like I don't know what, and I thought, 'Well, if they're all dead, what's the point of going with him?' But I thought it was possible that one at least was living, out of the lot of them, and he was begging, 'Venez avec moi, Monsieur,' and tugging at me. So I asked one chap if he'd come over

GUNNER GEORGE
  WORSLEY,
276th Brigade,
Royal Field Artillery,
(2nd West Lancashire
  Brigade).

with me with him. He said, 'Oh, no. I'm not going. I have to cook the officers' breakfast and I haven't time to go and look at your dead people.' In the midst of all that confusion! Well, I turned away from him in disgust, and I got one chap and he said, 'Yes, I'll come with you,' and then I got our young American doctor and he said, 'Yes, I'll come.' So the three of us set off with this French chap. He lived in a cottage about a hundred yards away. Halfway there the other chap said, 'I'm off back. I can't stick it – all these shells flying overhead'. So just the American and I got there.

The front door was open and his wife was laid in the hallway dead with a child who looked about five or six. They were shrapnel bullets. They'd pierced the roof of the house and then all the bullets had gone into everything. Of course, the look of death was accentuated by the plaster on the faces. It was dreadful really. The French chap fell down to kissing her and mauling her about and everything and he said, 'Encore là. Encore là.' He was pointing inside. Of course, the French always have these shutters at the window, so it was black dark in the interior, and we struck matches – it was all we could do. Strike matches. Of course, our fingers were a bit shaky. And there was an old man in the corner with his arms stretched out round three children. And when we touched them they were all stone dead. Every one of them were dead. The shell had burst as it came through the roof, and the shrapnel went everywhere. In that confined space they'd no chance. I really think it was one of our own prematures. There weren't many shells of such light calibre falling from the German side as far back as where we were.

Well, the Frenchman was still crying over his wife so we pulled him up to take him back and when we got outside he made a dive for the canal! Wanted to do himself in! His body was in the water and we grabbed hold of his legs and dragged him out, and we shook him like a terrier shaking a rat. When he'd pulled himself together, we pointed which way to go (the shells were dropping all this time) and he went off. Later he came back with an old farm muck-out cart and he took his wife and the three children away. But he left the old man who'd died with his arms round his children and our chaps buried him there.

<table>
<tr><td>

LANCE-CORPORAL DAVID WATSON,
11th Battalion,
Royal Scots.

</td><td>

I'd been home in hospital and I'd just been sent back to Battalion Reserve when the 21 March do started, so we were shoved back to France straight away. We landed at the base at Etaples. It was known as the Bull Ring and the discipline there was terrible. But what a difference I saw in it in April '18. You could more or less do as you liked at Etaples then. It was just a staging-post. You were in and away, and we were staggering about really – trying to find our units. The Retreat was on. We eventually picked up the 11th Royal Scots in Ridge Wood, not far from Dickebusch and the following day we went up the line at Ypres. I had a young lad with me as a Signaller, Andrew Meek

</td></tr>
</table>

of Bathgate, the first time he was out, and he was keen. He was a West Lothian miner and he was as keen as mustard. We got into a dugout, telephone post – wires running everywhere, and really it was quiet. Andrew says, 'This is cushy!' So I agreed with him it was quiet. Then all of a sudden we heard feet running along the duckboards. The Signal Officer popped his head in through the double curtain. 'Dismantle your instruments. Tear out all your wires and cut as many as you can and run like steam down to the train.' There was a light railway that had brought us up and the train was standing down there fully loaded with the whole of the battalion except ourselves. He'd forgotten where he had posted us! So I looked out. Gosh, the Verey lights were all round us, almost in a half circle. So I said, 'Look, we haven't time to cut wires but we'll tear them apart.' And we ran like blazes down and the train was on the move before we jumped on to it! The Germans were at our backs. They were on our heels!

CORPORAL A.D.
PANKHURST,
56th Division,
Royal Field Artillery.

I'd always looked forward to my twenty-first birthday because in the early 1900s it was traditional on twenty-first birthdays that the twenty-first boy would be given a nice pocket wallet with silver mounts, a silver cigarette case, a silver watch chain perhaps and a silver matchbox to hang on the watch chain. He had lovely things which I always coveted. Well, my twenty-first birthday was in front of Arras. We were going to attack in the morning and that evening we were in a barn and on my leave I'd brought back a small portable gramophone. That was in the very early days of the portable gramophone. It was a Decca and I'd brought back about a dozen records, mostly of musical comedy, and I could sing some of the songs I heard there now, and we were playing this gramophone. It started shelling and an ammunition convoy that passed through the village was hit and it all blew up. We had to evacuate our barn and we spent the night in the open. It rained heavily. I woke up in the early morning, finding myself practically covered with water in the shell hole, but too tired to move, but we went up into the line and took part in the battle. At the end of the day we went back and I thought I'd go into the barn where we were to try to recover any property. The whole roof had gone. The floor above us had completely gone but I managed to climb up on to one of the joists, and by good fortune my gramophone was perched on the joists, so when the floor collapsed the gramophone remained there. I got across to it. It was covered with the dirt, straw rubble that the walls were made of and I blew it off the record and cleaned it as well as I could. Well, the gramophone started, to my great surprise. It played 'The End of a Perfect Day'. That was the record! People may think I'm making it up, but it's perfectly true. That was my twenty-first birthday. April the ninth, 1918.

A special effort must be made to replace promptly the serious losses in guns, machine-guns and ammunition which are resulting from the great battle now in progress.

I rely upon everyone concerned in the manufacture of munitions to put forward their best efforts. There should, therefore, be no cessation of this work during the Easter holidays....
Minister of Munitions

If we lost—

ORDER OF THE DAY

11 April, 1918

To All Ranks of the British Forces in France.

Three weeks ago today the enemy began his terrific attacks against us on a fifty-mile front. His objects are to separate us from the French, to take the Channel ports and destroy the British Army.

In spite of throwing already 106 divisions into the battle and enduring the most reckless sacrifice of human life, he has as yet made little progress towards his goals.

We owe this to the determined fighting and self-sacrifice of our troops. Words fail me to express the admiration which I feel for the splendid resistance offered by all ranks of our Army under the most trying circumstances.

Many amongst us now are tired. To those I would say that victory will belong to the side which holds out the longest. The French Army is moving rapidly and in great force to our support.

There is no other course open to us but to fight it out! Every position must be held to the last man: there must be no retirement. With our backs to the wall, and believing in the justice of our cause, each one of us must fight on to the end. The safety of our homes and the freedom of mankind alike depend on the conduct of each one of us at this critical moment.

D. Haig
Field-Marshal

> LLOYD GEORGE TO THE UNITED STATES OF AMERICA
> We are at the crisis of the war. Attacked by an immense superiority of German troops, our Army has been forced to retire. The retirement has been carried out methodically before the pressure of a steady succession of fresh German reserves, which are suffering enormous losses.
>
> The situation is being faced with splendid courage and resolution. The dogged pluck of our troops has for the moment checked the ceaseless onrush of the enemy, and the French have joined in the struggle; but this battle, the greatest and most momentous in the history of the world, is only just beginning.
>
> Throughout it the French and British are buoyed with the knowledge that the great Republic of the West will neglect no effort which can hasten its troops and ships to Europe. In war time is vital. It is impossible to exaggerate the importance of getting American reinforcements across the Atlantic in the shortest possible space of time.
>
> *The Times, 29 March*

◆ ◆

... we're booked for the Great Adventure, we're pledged for the Real Romance; We'll find ourselves or we'll lose ourselves somewhere in giddy old France ...

Robert Service

SERGEANT PHELPS HARDING,
306th Infantry Regiment, 77th Division, American Expeditionary Force.

Camp Upton, N.Y., 29 March, 1918.

Dear Dad,

I just wrote Mother that the regiment is almost ready to leave for France – in fact, it is liable to go any day. I thought it better to tell her a little ahead than to write hurriedly at the last minute, although I know that the news will be quite a blow. Her letter is going on the same mail as this.

This letter is addressed to you at the Vermont for strategic reasons – to avoid Mother seeing it. I simply want to tell you that we were secretly,

OVER THERE ~ 1918

several weeks ago, practically given our preference as to whether we would rather serve here or abroad. That's what I came into the fight for, and I want to see it through. Don't tell Mother that I had an opportunity to stay here, for I know that it would make her feel badly that I did not stay. I am just telling you so that if anything should happen to me you will know that I met the danger of my own free will, and with a full knowledge of what to expect in the fighting on the other side. I'm mighty glad I have the chance to go over and do my share – and I know you are glad to have me go.

As I said before, we are just about ready to leave, and it is rumoured that we will sail before the week ends. My recommendation for a commission has been made, and it is just a question of red tape and a need of officers before I get my 2nd Lieutenancy. That is the only rank given out of this camp. Considering the number of older men and non-commissioned officers in the school, I believe I have done fairly well, for I stand pretty high on the official list, although I do not know the exact number.

Now I'll close. I'll write you again before we leave, even if I have to leave a card here for one of the other men to send.

Lots of love,
PHELPS.

When the war broke out, there was a divided opinion. The general feeling was that we would have to go in there eventually, but in order for our President to do anything it had to be an Act of Congress. We happened to be in a strong German settlement.

SERGEANT ROGER KNOWLES,
164th Infantry,
42nd (Rainbow) Division,
US Army.

There was one fellow there, Peter Farrell. He was a German, in fact he had served in the German Army and in this little town of Calumet it was ninety per cent German, so Pete could shoot off his mouth a little bit and, 'Oh! They won't last long, once they get up against us Prussian soldiers, it's murder to send them out there.' He had plenty of support in the German community and we had to keep quiet, you know.

The English-speaking people were all on the side of the English. The German people of course were all for Germany.

In Calumet it got around so that you weren't allowed to speak German over the telephone, it got quite an anti-German feeling, after the lists of casualties started coming back, then people realised that we were at war and it was a deadly game. Anyone of German parentage there who had German leanings were singled out. The sinking of the *Lusitania* probably turned a lot of people against the Germans, but if you were living, as I was, practically in Germany, why, I've an idea, although they wouldn't express it, the *Lusitania* should have stayed home. It shouldn't have been in there in the first place. It depends whose dog is getting shot how far your sympathies were.

283

F. W. GRASER,
10th Field Artillery,
US Army.

A big percentage of the American boys had German blood. I was fifty per cent German. My grandfather came to the States from Germany in 1840 when he was 20. It was always said that he came to avoid going in the German Army – then he had to fight in the Civil War. He met my grandmother over here and she was full-blooded German too. At that time St Louis was more or less a German colony, and my father was very much against me going into the service. He felt more loyalty to Germany than he did to Britain. But my mother was a native American from generations back, and I felt myself to be an American. Patriotic. So I told my father I *was* going, and that was that.

I left on the last day of February, 1918, and we did some more training in France and then we went into the line on 13 July. We were told that we had information that the Germans were going to start a big drive at midnight of 14 July because they figured that the French would be celebrating Bastille Day and wouldn't be in a good state to defend themselves. So the object was to put over a counter-barrage starting at 6 o'clock on the fourteenth – and we put over *some* barrage. We put it over for six hours. Of course they were retaliating and we were getting it hot. Those shells! There were so many of them between our firing and theirs coming back on us that if you wanted to talk to someone you'd have to put your mouth up to his ear and yell at the top of your voice. That went on for six hours, and it dimmed the Germans' drive so much that they didn't come over in full strength.

I was on communications between our battery and our Battalion Headquarters which were further back, running lines out in the open. The only dugout was for the top officers. During that first night our battery telephone was in an old farmhouse, and we had decided that we would put our blankets down in this farmhouse and the ones who ranked topmost put their blankets at the back of the house. Being lower ranking I had mine in a room at the front. It quieted down a little bit in the morning and after running lines all night I came in to rest up a little bit. I went upstairs and looked in my room and there was a hole about eight or ten inches in diameter – one hole in the entire building! – and my blankets where I'd made my bed were shredded. From then on, all my life I've figured, why, I'm living on grace. I never worried from that time on. It gave me the feeling that if it's intended you'll be there, you'll *be* there! They gave us lectures in the USA, and they quoted statistics. A certain percentage would be wounded and have to go home, a certain percentage would be killed. But they led us to expect that the odds were all in favour of getting back home safe and sound. We took some powerful casualties though. We figured their statistics were somewhat optimistic.

The Battery Commander was a First Lieutenant. He was a man who'd been kicked out of West Point for fighting, but when the war started he went back in. He was a very brilliant man, a big Irishman by the name of Pat Kelly, and he did something I thought was one of the smartest things. We noticed that an aeroplane would go overhead with French markings (captured I guess) and every time it did we would catch shelling pretty bad. So Kelly had a brilliant idea. When we'd got in there we'd had no chance to put camouflage up, so our guns were in the open, and where you walk around the guns there are paths and from the air, why, you're marked! So what he did, he moved the guns over just by their own width and put up camouflage and used the same trails as he did before, but with the camouflage over the guns in the new position. Of course, from the air, he figured, it looked as if our place had been evacuated. But we went right on using the same location and we had not much trouble after that. I thought that was one of the smartest things we did.

There was a British Brigadier in charge of their training who warned us of all probable pitfalls. He advised us to take the line that we were demonstrating British methods as a matter of interest without the slightest suggestion that our audience might profit from what they saw.

CAPTAIN A. O.
POLLARD, VC,
Honourable Artillery
Company.

There was tragedy in their self-sufficiency. They had to pay very dearly for their mistakes when they came up against such an intrepid and experienced fighter as Fritz. The two Divisions to which I was temporarily attached were decimated in their first action.

It was the officers who were to blame, not the men. The men were a magnificent set of fellows, big and husky – to use their own word. Their officers let them down. They were too full of their own importance, too jealous that we might confuse their lack of knowledge with inefficiency.

Our main item was a demonstration of a 'Platoon in the Attack,' which we carried out strictly in accordance with the official pamphlet issued on the subject. At this period of the war the platoon was considered as the principal unit of the Army. It was self-contained, consisting of four sections. A Lewis gun section, with two guns. A section of rifle grenadiers who were also bombers, and two sections of rifle and bayonet men. An army in miniature, the Lewis guns supplying covering machine-gun fire; the rifle grenadiers acting as artillery; and the riflemen making the infantry assault.

My friend Edward Holder, the 'Ox', usually gave the demonstration as it was his platoon. On the day in question our audience consisted of an American regiment. The men sat round on the grass in the form of a horseshoe, the Ox standing in the middle and explaining what was happening. First of all the attack was carried out by numbers to a whistle, the Ox from time to time stopping the advance to explain each strategical manoeuvre. Afterwards a spectacular display was carried out with ball cartridges, the rifle grenadiers firing live bombs and putting up a smoke screen. The men were drilled to the minute and the result was a masterpiece of co-ordination between different arms.

The Brigadier rode up whilst this show was in progress and joined the group of officers where I was enlarging on the Ox's commentary. I was receiving a sneering reception, the general opinion being that American troops would storm their objective without bothering about such fads as covering fire and barrages, etc.

'In any case it doesn't require much training or practice to do a show like that,' commented one officer.

The Brigadier was on him like a knife.

'Very well,' he snapped. 'I should like one of your platoons to give us a demonstration immediately.'

The result was a complete fiasco. The men were willing enough but they simply did not understand what they were trying to do. I strolled round to where the Lewis gunners were stationed on one flank. They were trying to fit the magazine on to the gun upside down! The riflemen were shooting indiscriminately in every direction whilst I decided to keep as far away from the bombers as possible. I should not have been in the least surprised had there been one or two casualties. When they had finished the General let them have it hot and strong, pointing out what would have happened had they been facing a real enemy. After that we had a somewhat better reception . . .

I now found myself Officer in Charge 7th Camerons (Training Battalion), a skeleton unit forming to help train the 119th Regiment National Guard, USA Forces just arriving in France. Three Battalions with auxiliary units, all on British scales of equipment and transport. We found them keen but green. We were allotted the 3rd battalion whose men spoke mostly Swedish, Hungarian and German.

CAPTAIN A. F. P. CHRISTISON, MC, 6th (S) Battalion, Queen's Own Cameron Highlanders.

Route marches on cobbled roads are nobody's cup of tea and ill-fitting British Army issue boots caused many sore feet. On one occasion on a very hot day a big Swede fell out. I was riding with his Company Commander who rode back and said, 'Hike'. The Swede pointed to his boots and said, 'No can hike no more'. To my surprise, the Company Commander trotted forward to the Battalion Commander and together they returned to the big Swede. 'Hike' said his CO. 'Me can hike no more,' said the Swede. Both officers then rode off and returned with the Colonel of the whole Regiment, a hoary old Virginian dugout who wore a sword, spurs about four inches long and carried two ivory-handled pistols in his belt. 'You there,' he said, 'get up and hike.' He got the same reply. Slowly, the old Colonel drew a pistol, cocked it, and pointed it at the Swede. 'Hike,' he bellowed, 'if you don't get up and hike, I'll shoot.' 'I guess you can shoot, Colonel, I ain't going to hike.' Whereupon the Colonel replaced his pistol and ordered the man to be picked up by the following ambulance. He turned to me and said, 'You can allus tell a shirker!!'

One evening I had to give a lecture on 'The Attack' to the whole Regiment's Officers in the Town Hall, Yeuse. I mugged up the Army's official pamphlet and duly held forth, adding a few personal experiences and lessons. When I had ended the old Colonel, dressed more like a Sheriff than a Colonel, heaved himself up on the platform and said, 'Gentlemen, I'd like youse all to accord the Scottish Major a hearty vote of thanks for his verra interesting lecture'. Then he shook his finger and went on, 'but I'd have youse guys remember the British have been trying these tactics for near four years and they ain't done much damn good!'

◆ ◆

KAISER'S DREAM

There's a rumour now current, though strange it may seem,
Of the German Emperor's wonderful dream –
Being tired of War, he lay down in bed,
And amongst other things, dreamt that he had gone dead
And in a deep coffin, lying in state
With his cold waxed features frozen with hate
He wasn't long dead, when he found to his cost
That his map of the next world and his passports were lost.

So leaving this earth, to Heaven he went straight,
Jauntily strutting right up to the gate.
But the Look-Out angel, in voice strong and clear,
Said, 'Begone, Kaiser Wilhelm, we don't want you here.'
'Well,' thought Wilhelm, 'that's very uncivil,'
Does he mean I must go straightaway to the Devil?'
So he turned on his heels and off he did go,
Running full speed to the regions below.

But when he got there he was filled with dismay,
For whilst waiting outside he heard Old Nick say
To his imps, 'Now look here boys, I give you all warning
I'm expecting the Kaiser down here this morning
But don't let him in, for to me it is clear
We are far too good for the mongrel down here.
If he gets in, there will be the dickens to pay
For bad as I am, he is worse any day.'

'Oh Satan, dear friend,' the Emperor cried.
'Excuse me for listening, whilst waiting outside.
If you don't let me in, then where can I go?'
'Indeed,' said the Devil, 'I really don't know.'
'Oh do let me in, I am feeling quite cold,
If it's money you want, I have plenty of gold.
Just give me a corner, no matter how hot.'
'No,' said the Devil, 'certainly not.'

'We don't let apartments for riches or pelf.
Here's some sulphur and matches, make a Hell for yourself.'
Then he kicked Wilhelm out, and he vanished in smoke
And just at that moment the Kaiser awoke.
He jumped out of bed in a shivering sweat
And said, 'Gosh! What a dream, I shall never forget
That I won't go to Heaven, I know very well
But it's awful hard lines to be kicked out of Hell.'

Private F. W. Laver

GUNNER B. O. STOKES,
13th Battery,
New Zealand Field
    Artillery,
3rd Brigade.

France,
29 July, 1918.

My Dearest Mum and Dad,

Two years ago today! Well, perhaps I shouldn't recall that day, the day I waved farewell to you all, for how long I did not know. But somehow I cannot let the day pass by without writing you a little note. Two years ago, I was keen to be away and anxious to follow the rest of our NZ boys to the Front, But today after two years I recall some of the experiences I have had. Experiences one never thinks of until face to face with them. How little we knew of what we were coming to when we left NZ, but we never let the future worry us in those days – not that we do now.

And now after two years I am still found in France with the war still raging, and me, well, perhaps just as keen to get away home again, as I was to get here. Not exactly keen to run away from the war, but just longing for a glimpse of home and dear ones.

This evening I have been reading the short note of cheer Dad wrote me and gave to me just before we sailed. I still have it with me, and I often read that short note so full of help too. Then there is the little Testament Mother gave me. I have always carried it with me and the priceless treasures it contains.

Today I am entitled to wear three blue chevrons for service overseas. One for the day I left NZ, and one for each year's service. So, you see, I'm an old 'sojer' boy now, far too old a soldier, I think.

I am keeping A1 just now. I'm still at the guns, still strafing the 'Beastly Boche'. Lots of love to Gran, Chris and Sid and fondest love and kisses to your own dear selves. God Bless and keep you.

Your loving son,
BERT.

XXXXXXXXXXXXX

SERGEANT S. CHAPLIN,
Military Mounted Police,
15th Division.

After their terrible time in holding up the German advance at Arras, the move to this small mining town must have been a wonderful relief to the survivors. Except for a salvo of shells at odd times which mostly went over it was quiet and how nice to see people going about their daily tasks. The troops were able to take things easier as the line was also quiet and they were also able to have a drink in one of the small cafés when off duty. One café, small and clean, belonged to a man who was serving in the French Army so his young wife who had a baby about a year old, and Grandmère, kept the place going. It was popular with the troops and the baby came in for a lot of fuss from them. I looked in one day to see the baby cradled in the arms of a bearded Highlander who was quietly singing to it whilst Madame served out the drinks.

One afternoon I was on duty in the main street. The cafés were closed, everything quiet. I went to the rear of this café to the toilet, and as I was walking back I heard voices coming from the kitchen. So I went to the door, opened it and stepped inside. Silence. Grandmère sat by the fire. Madame sat in a chair nursing the baby and four NCOs sat at the table with a drink each. Grandmère looked as if she were going to faint at the sight of a Military Policeman. Madame was white-faced and the others just looked. Now, one of the things we were told during training as MPs was to use your own discretion. But our APM didn't believe in this. We had orders to report any breaking of Divisional Orders, no matter how small, and put the offenders on a charge. So here were two Sergeants, one Sergeant-Major, one Quartermaster, having a drink after the café was closed. All I had to do was to take their names and numbers. They would then be charged and tried, which could probably mean loss of rank or seniority. Also I knew as soon as I put in my report our APM would have the place put out of bounds and that would be disastrous for Madame. I saw that these chaps had just come out of the trenches and I could imagine what a treat it was for them to have a drink. So I looked at Madame and said, 'Is your front door closed?' 'Yes,' she said. 'Right, now it's eighteen minutes after time and I would advise you to keep your door locked in case any thirsty Jocks come out of the trenches and want a drink. Someone might hear them talking.' I then asked Grandmère if she was well and she managed a little smile as she answered yes. As I turned to leave I remarked, 'Watch your step. You never know who is around outside.' Then I went back to my beat.

Did I do right?!!

Things settled down to a quiet normal life again. In July we were behind the line. Our cook in charge of our galley there, he was a Tynesider. He was an untidy, scruffy individual but a likeable chap, you couldn't help but like him and to us he never seemed to have any fear. If Jerry happened to start shelling he'd never take cover. We was behind this big ridge and I can't with any certainty say where it was, but it was open country. Six Jerry planes come over. Well, the cook had his old field kitchen brewing up tea and he must have been spotted because these planes circled round at a tremendous height about half a dozen times. I expect he'd seen the smoke from the old field kitchen. He started shelling again. We dived for cover. The old cook – it was a warm day, he'd got his tunic off and it was hanging on a post about six yards from the kitchen itself and *he* took cover. Luckily he did because the next shell landed right under the old field kitchen and up it went in splinters. The shelling finished as quick as it started. The cook was one of the first out and he goes and picks up his tunic. It's just like a colander. More than that. He says, 'Ah! You bloody bastards! But I wasn't in it, was I?'

SERGEANT C. W. HAYNES, 13th Battalion, The Sherwood Foresters, (Notts. and Derby Regiment).

My first trips in a balloon were with a young Lieutenant quite new to me. On descent he would sit on the side of the basket – a stupid practice as I had seen, by two years of ground work, how pockets of high wind would suddenly throw the balloon about. True enough it happened – on descent one day, when we were down to about five hundred feet, we came into high wind. The balloon lurched and the officer fell back into the basket, knocked into me and, in falling, kicked a valuable German instrument over into the air. It crashed on the ground, in pieces. We were both on the carpet and were sent back to the line, which had settled down. The German advance had been stopped.

I was told to report to No. 23 Section near Abeele. The Commanding Officer made me very welcome, also the NCOs, but they warned me to give Captain Machin a wide berth. I soon found out he was very strict, his discipline was the cause of some of the dislike among the NCOs. But he turned out to be my finest instructor, and his example was a great help to me.

My first flight was with the Commanding Officer, who gave the general outline of the German occupation. Dranoutre village was wiped out. Locre Church, just inside our lines, was burning, the village itself was slowly being wiped out by shell fire, it was like seeing my own home village in ruins.

OBSERVER BERNARD OLIVER, No. 23 Balloon Section, Royal Flying Corps.

When I was a young boy, I had a slight stammer in my speech and this returned under stress. Now our Commanding Officer had a very bad stammer. (Later I understood he had been badly shell shocked.) However, I wished he would not take me up with him. Sure enough, we had an urgent call to give a map reference of a German gun firing on one of our gun sites. The map reference was found, but the CO, with the telephone in his hand, just could not say a word. In his depair, he handed the phone to me. I was speechless. You can imagine how I felt!

My turn came to fly with Captain Machin and up we went about four thousand feet. Suddenly a mighty crash and a flash of an exploding shell very close. Captain coolly remarked, 'That's the German gun on rails – 9.2 weighs a ton, find and tell me when to expect the shell burst and report any damage to us, I'll carry on with the observation.' At intervals the gun fired, time of flight, twenty-seven seconds. I gave the Captain roughly where the shell burst and damage, if any. My word, he didn't bat an eyelid, another of these Public School boys!

Major Cochran, MC, from Company Headquarters, phoned us with the warning of trouble ahead. The winch below reported very high tension on the cable. Reluctantly Captain Machin told the winch to haul us down, as we were still being shelled. The winch, owing to the tension, was unable to haul us down, so the crew resorted to the spider. This was a pulley which fitted around the cable. The crew could walk us down. The slow operation started. When we were down to about 1,000 feet hardly any wind blew so the balloon crumpled up and down we came. The basket fell on a clump of trees, through which the basket landed gently on the ground, with us safely hanging above. After climbing from the balloon, we walked a distance away from the escaping gas and had a smoke. It seemed a long wait before the crew arrived. I shall never forget how they very cautiously looked in the basket to see the state of the bodies, which they assumed they would find within. We had vanished – it was not Easter Sunday. This was my first flight with Captain Machin.

The officer who flew with me on the next flight, we will call Officer No. 3. Soon after reaching our observation height about 4,000/5,000 feet, we were informed on the telephone to look out for Richthofen's flying circus, who had attacked one of us. Very soon we noticed the fourth one north of us in flames, then the third one went down. It was a cloudy day so the planes could easily hide. All was quiet for a while, we settled down and got to work. Suddenly machine-gun bullets were flying all around in all directions. I saw one of the red-marked planes of Richthofen's, very close to us. Looking to my officer for orders to get out, I found myself alone! Not another Easter Sunday! Like a shot, I was over the side, closed my eyes and dropped into space. On my downward journey I opened my eyes and, behold, the pilot of the plane was flying very close to me waving his hand. I gladly waved back. I landed on the edge of a hop field.

As I was heavier than Officer No. 3, I had passed him on the way down. He landed in a stream of dirty water and the wind in the chute carried him quite a way through it. Yes! I think I may have smiled a little to see him! A motor car from the section soon picked us up and No. 3 Officer said, on arriving back at camp, 'You heard me tell you to jump?' 'Yes, Sir,' I replied.

On Bastille Day, 14 July, 1918, they were going to have a parade in Paris. The British Army was represented by a Company from the Guards, a Company from the Colonials, a Company from the Royal Scots, being the 1st Foot, and a Company of The Queen's, being the 2nd Foot. Right! I'd to take a relief up. The old Sergeant-Major come along and he said to us, 'You know you're going to Paris. You behave yourselves. You know your drill, you know what to do,' he said. 'But, first off,' he said, 'You're going to have a week with the Irish Guards' Sergeant-Major.' He said, 'Don't think they can show you anything. You're The Queen's, and remember that! You'll be drilled under the Regimental Sergeant-Major, crowns on each arm, but don't forget you're The Queen's!'

PRIVATE W. LUFF, DCM,
1st Battalion,
The Queen's (Royal West
Surrey) Regiment.

We landed in Paris, got from the station to a bridge, Pont Alexandre, crossed that and then we went down the Champs Elysées. We passed the Petit Palace and we got to the Grande Palace and that's where we were billeted. Our beds were on the balconies and we were billeted with the French, of course. You came down in the morning, you could bring a bucket if you wanted. Red wine! You could have as much red wine as you liked. Anyway, the food we had there wasn't so wonderful. There was stew most of the time and floating about was mangel worzel. We were only there for three days. We marched off and got into order, of course. The Yanks, obviously, were the first, then us. Marched past – Salute! We were marched back to our billets and we were all given Champagne – a bottle between two. We were free then to go out. Standing along on the bridge were about six good-time girls. 'Hallo Tommy! Hallo Tommy!' One man said. 'Don't listen to them! Come on!' So, we paraded around the town, just took in the sights. I saw the Notre-Dame. One thing I do remember about the streets of Paris, they were very wide and the horse cabbies had top hats. We roamed around for three days. At the end of the three days, when we were due to entrain and go back, there were quite a number of people in the Guardroom, Scotsmen without kilts. They had frocks on and all sorts of things! There was *nine* Queen's missing. We never *did* find them!! We went back without them! And that was *my* experience of Paris, in July 1918.

Steadfast and strong is the Tommy of England,
Gallant and gay is the Poilu of France;
We've been asleep, but thank God, we're awake now!
Frenchmen and Englishmen, give us a chance.

Give us a chance! we stand for the right, too!
Give us a chance! we know how to fight, too!
Brothers of England and comrades of France,
Give us a chance!

Laura E. Richards

SERGEANT ROGER KNOWLES,
168th Infantry Regiment, 42nd (Rainbow) Division, US Army.

We were up on the Champagne front, the wheat was just ripening, it was in July, and this Major Worthington, he was an excitable sort of a fellow, he came there and he wanted us to go to a place where the Infantry had been held up. It was a road, sunken in places and that afforded cover, because the Germans were taking advantage of all the natural cover they could get and he wanted us to go and take these machine-guns out. You know, at the Front, you didn't give a damn what insignia was on their shoulder, I mean, it was what was in their head that counted, and I was just ornery, and I suppose it gave me courage, and he wanted me to take the Stokes Mortar boys out there and blow up this machine-gun. I said, 'That's something for the Artillery. We can't get close enough in a wheat field. We're just sacrificing the men.' Anyway, he blew up something – insinuated that we lacked the courage. I said, 'It isn't that. I'll go over with you, Major, whenever you're ready, but I will *not* go until I've had an order from my Lieutenant,' so then Lieutenant Peterson came round – I think it probably cost him his 1st Lieutenancy, but he said, 'No, I have a bunch of men here trained for a special job. It's foolish to send them out there when you have your Artillery.' Well, this Major, he didn't like to have his tail feathers plucked, but, anyway, we didn't go out there.

But our Lieutenant, he used to tell us when we were going, 'Roger, I don't want any casualties if you can help it. You never won a war with a bunch of dead heroes,' so that's what we kind of kept in mind. And to do our job and still be alive to do the next job; those are the things that you learn the hard way.

SCHÜTZE EMIL AMANN,
2nd Company, 75th Machine-gun Abteilung, attached to the 28th (Baden) Division.

Between 2 and 5 June, 1918, the Americans appeared for the first time on the Marne front in divisional strength. At the time, my unit was located near Licy Farm in the area of Belleau Wood. The Yankees had much courage – but little experience – and they paid dearly during the first days of fighting on the Marne. There were Americans in the front line who hollered at us in German: 'Ergebt euch! Schmeisst die Knarren weg!' (Surrender! Throw your guns away!) But the result was different.

It only made us Germans angry. If one was well trained and could depend on his rifle or machine-gun, he could take a chance and let the enemy come close, especially if he was angry. The Americans suffered many casualties for another reason. Instead of leaving three to five metres between each man in an attack, they bunched together. When I saw my first five or six American prisoners, they were all six feet or more tall, well fed with red cheeks. They were the perfect picture of health compared to us pale, skinny and hungry Germans.

Dear Mother,
The two enclosed pieces of propaganda were dropped from Boche planes when I was in the front line.

I got the torn paper before it touched the ground – it landed just inside our wire. Both papers are good examples of Boche attempts to break the morale of our troops. Please keep them for me.

Lots of love,
PHELPS.

SERGEANT PHELPS
HARDING,
306th Infantry Regiment,
77th Division,
American Expeditionary
Force.

NEVER SAY DIE!

Don't die until you have to!

What business have you to die for France, for Alsace-Lorraine, or for England in France?

Isn't it better anyhow to live than to die, no matter for how 'glorious' a cause? Isn't it better to live and come back to the old folks at home, than to rot in the shell holes and trenches of France?

You have had to hear many high falutin words about 'liberty', 'humanity' and 'making the world safe for democracy', but honest now, aren't these catch words, merely sugar coating to the bitter pill of making you spend wretched months far from home? Do you really believe those German soldier boys in their faded grey uniforms on the other side of 'No Man's Land' are hot in the trail of your liberties?

Just like you, they want the war to end with honour so they can go back to their home folks. All they want is a chance to live and let live.

And so, if it should happen to you to fall into their hands you will find that they will treat you fair enough on the principle of 'live and let live'. Why run any more chances than you have to; you might as well be a free boarder in Germany till the war is over. *You don't want to die till you have to!*

> **HELP STOP THE WAR.**
>
> The only way to stop the war is to stop fighting. That's easy. Just quit it and slip across 'No Man's Land' and join the bunch that's taking it easy there waiting to be exchanged and taken home. There is no disgrace in that. That bunch of American prisoners will be welcomed just as warmly as you who stick it out in these infernal trenches. Get wise and get over the top.
>
> There is nothing in the glory of keeping up the war. Just think of the increasing taxes you will have to pay; the longer the war lasts the larger those taxes at home will be. Get wise and get over!
>
> Wake up and stop the war! You can if you want to. Your government does not mean to stop the war for years to come, and the years are going to be long and dreary. You better come over while the going is good.

DR. BERNARD
GALLAGHER,
US Army, attached
2nd/4th Battalion,
The Gloucestershire
Regiment.

The attitude of the Germans towards me when I was a prisoner is rather hard to explain. I was treated with considerable courtesy, but it was a kind of curiosity, for they never quite knew what to make of me. Most of them had never seen an American before and they did not quite see how I happened to be up there with the English – I think they doubted a little my story that I was an American doctor serving with the English. The old Major in charge spoke very good English and was certainly fine to me. When I told him that I lived in Minnesota, he said, 'That is where the Mayo Clinic is located, at Rochester, is it not? If you ever get back to Rochester, tell the doctors there that I have often translated their articles from English into German for the German medical journals.' He was not a bit vindictive, but often talked to me about the war and his big question, like all the rest of them, was, 'Why did America come into the war?' They could not see that it was any of our business, and when I talked to them about the submarines, the intriguing with Mexico, etc, they would only wave their hands and say that had nothing to do with it – we had loaned money to the Allies and had come in for fear we would lose it. In other words, we went to war for money. Only a few weeks before I had had vigorous arguments with English officers, who maintained that we stayed *out* of the war for money, which only proves that a great deal depends on the point of view.

There were two or three Chaplains around there, and two of them were fine, but one was a red-faced Prussian with a 'Hindenburg scowl'. When he learned that I was an American he flew into a rage, flung his hands and shouted like a maniac, 'Why did America come into the war?', etc, etc. All in German, of course, but I understood him perfectly well. I replied to him calmly, "When my country goes to war, so do I!" He bellowed some more and I walked away. Later, when he learned that I was a doctor taking care of the British wounded, he seemed a little ashamed and tried to be sociable, but I pretended not to see him when he came around after that. It seemed queer that the only abuse I should get should come from a Chaplain.

The attitude of the soldiers was good. Nearly all of them seemed to have uncles running breweries in Milwaukee or Cincinnati and were anxious to tell me about it and to tell me how they wanted to get to America after the war. Three months to the end of the war was the figure they all had. They expected to occupy Paris in six weeks and to conclude the war in three months – with victory for Germany, of course. All were highly elated with the success of their attack, and yet amongst the officers, I thought I could detect a feeling of uncertainty – a feeling that they sort of realised that their victories were empty and costly, leading them further into the enemy's country and then stopping nowhere. They pretended not to fear America's entrance into the war, for the U-Boats would not allow many of our troops to come. Their manner was extremely confident and arrogant on the surface, but behind it all they were worried and realised, I am sure, that it could not go on much further and that they must win in a hurry or all was lost, for their resources were nearly exhausted.

Everything that Germany had done during the war was justified on the grounds of 'military necessity'. A young German Quartermaster, Michael Baptist, who had been a teacher at Augsburg in Germany and spoke a little English, often talked to me, and one day I asked him if the Germans believed in treaties, and he said that of course they did. Then I asked him how about their treaty with Belgium and about Von Bethman-Hollweg calling a treaty a scrap of paper. He thought Chancellor Hollweg was very undiplomatic to call it a 'scrap of paper' – admitted that they had a treaty with Belgium which ordinarily should have been lived up to, but drew the analogy of a garden with a sign, 'No trespassing'. A man is surrounded by enemies on three sides who are chasing him and the only way out is across the garden. That was the position of Germany in regard to Belgium, he asserted. Three enemies – England, France and Russia – were about to attack – and under the circumstances, Germany was justified in invading Belgium just as the man would be justified in crossing the forbidden garden to avoid his enemies. I could not quite see the parallel, but it seemed to be a 'military necessity' which justified the act.

We rested in the sheltered hollow,
Kinsells quipped a Cockney joke,
We called for more
While we waited tense for Zero;
A shell fell near, the barrage broke
With rising roar.

Kinsell's head was gently nodding
Blood and brains were pumping out
In the bright sun.
The whistle blew, our sergeant leading
Swept away our fears and doubt,
To meet the Hun.

The scene was set for us to rush
One hundred yards or so away,
As I recall:
A small affair in the Great Push
To clear the wood where Jerry lay;
And end it all.

Ligny Thilloy – August 27th 1918.

FIRST CONTEMPTIBLE : "D'you remember halting here on the retreat, George?"
SECOND DITTO: "Can't call it to mind, somehow. Was it that little village in the wood there down by the river, or was it that place with the cathedral and all them factories?"

8 August was the black day of the German Army in the history of this war.

GEN. LUDENDORFF
My War Memories.

... Early on 8 August, in a dense fog, rendered still thicker by artificial means, the English, mainly with Australian and Canadian divisions, and the French attacked between Albert and Moreuil with strong squadrons of tanks, but otherwise in no great superiority. Between the Somme and the Luce they penetrated deep into our positions. The divisions in line at that point allowed themselves to be completely overwhelmed. Divisional staffs were surprised in their headquarters by enemy tanks. The breach very soon extended across the Luce stream; the troops that were still gallantly resisting at Moreuil were rolled up.

... By the early hours of the forenoon of 8 August I had already gained a complete impression of the situation. It was a very gloomy one.

Six or seven divisions which could certainly be described as battle-worthy had been completely broken. Three or four others, together with the remnants of the battered divisions, were available for closing the broad gap between Bray and Roye.

The situation was uncommonly serious. The report of the Staff Officer I had sent to the battlefield as to the condition of those divisions which had met the first shock of the attack on the 8th, perturbed me deeply ... I was told of deeds of glorious valour but also of behaviour which, I openly confess, I should not have thought possible in the German Army; whole bodies of our men had surrendered to single troopers, or isolated squadrons. Retiring troops, meeting a fresh division going bravely into action, had shouted out things like 'Blackleg', and 'You're prolonging the war', expressions that were to be heard again later. The officers in many places had lost their influence and allowed themselves to be swept along with the rest. A battalion commander from the front, who came out with a draft from home shortly before 8 August, attributed this to the spirit of insubordination and the atmosphere which the men brought back with them from home. Everything I had feared and, of which I had so often given warning, had here, in one place, become a reality. Our war machine was no longer efficient.

... The Entente began the great offensive, the final battle of the world war, and carried it through with increasing vigour, as our decline became more apparent.

We were preparing to leave Briastre as the battle approached, but one German said, 'Madame nix partie. Les Anglais venir'. Others said, 'Tommies kom!' etc. We went to bed, but towards morning the can-

MADAME LEGRAND
WILLERVAL.

nonade redoubled and we went down to the cellar and stayed there most of the day, because the fighting was very near. Towards midnight, when it became quieter, we went upstairs to bed. We were still in bed when we heard a tremendous noise outside and voices speaking with a strange intonation. A soldier in khaki came into my room, smiling broadly and said, 'Bonn' jour, Madam!' He was English!

We left Briastre reluctantly, because shells were falling, even on the road we had to go along, but the English led us across the fields and into the trenches where we were sheltered. They helped us carry our baskets. They wanted to get us away out of gun-fire range and we eventually arrived at a camp filled with carts and beautiful horses with harnesses shining like the sun. All the soldiers we met said, 'Bonn'jour, Madame! Comment allez-vo?' They offered us food and at first we took it gratefully. We were soon absolutely gorged, but we couldn't refuse, we had to go on eating, because they were so pressing and good-hearted. Then at five o'clock ever so many soldiers offered us tea! The roads were broken and very bad. As we got further away from the bombarded zone, my small grandson, Edouard, after many stumbles, climbed up on a gun carriage. When we at last arrived two kilometres from Caudry, we flopped down to rest with other refugees who told us that an English officer had promised a vehicle to take them into the town. It was evening, and it had begun to rain when a wagon drawn by two superb black horses came up to take us to the Hotel de Ville in Caudry. From there we were taken to the hospice where they made up makeshift beds in a sort of wash-house. But there, at last we could breathe again. We were saved! No more Germans. No more artillery.

SERGEANT HARRY BARTLETT,
293rd (Army) Brigade,
Royal Field Artillery.

All the men were quartered at the farm in barns, outhouses etc. The officers were accommodated at the farmhouse to which the rightful owners had returned. We sergeants had nearly half a mile to go for our own billet, a farmhouse, still uninhabited. We had ample room to spread ourselves here. There was little furniture left, a table and a few chairs. Upstairs, the Germans had fitted out the room with the usual timber and wire netting bunks. There was no front door, it had been removed by the Germans we imagined. A stream separated us from a large village, about three quarters of a mile away.

The first night we were there Hammond and I went to the estaminet to see what was doing in the shape of a drink. Our rum wasn't exhausted, but we went on a voyage of discovery to see what was doing.

The poor woman at the estaminet was in tears. Quite a number of men had been there. She had nothing to sell. What was worse, she had next to nothing to eat. A number of little ones clustered round her, all looking nearly starved. She herself was as thin as a rake. We knew little French and she no English, for, of course, she had been in occupied German territory ever since the early days of the war.

Bit by bit we discovered that the woman didn't know where her husband was. He was fighting with the French Army, but whether he was dead or alive or a prisoner she didn't know. She hadn't heard from him for years. The estaminet had been her only means of support. It was patronised by the Germans, but latterly she had been unable to get supplies and had been forced to work in the fields.

Old Hammond was touched, I could see. So was I. We couldn't do much but we did what we could. First to the Sergeants Mess to get a bit of spare grub, sugar, tea, tinned milk, bully, bread and Quaker Oats. Back we went with them. The Quaker Oats presented the most difficulty. We had to show her how to cook them. We locked the door and we set to and gave the kids and the woman a good feed. She seemed a bit scared at first, thought we were after her I think. The youngsters were not afraid of us. Eventually when she found we didn't want to maul her about she was quite pleased to see the youngsters enjoying a meal, and she had some herself. Poor frightened creature! I'll warrant those old Germans had led her a hell of a life. We had an idea we could help her still further and asked her if we could look over the place to see if there was room for men. We had the whole section in their new quarters by the next night. The men were pleased, but they worried the poor woman at first. She seemed to think it wasn't good enough for them. There was very little furniture and they slept on the floors of the rooms. This really worried Madame.

Although our arrangement put money in her way, there was nothing to buy in the neighbourhood. Apart from the supplies brought into the area for the British Army, there were no foodstuffs at all. The shops had no stocks.

In March 1918 our retreat had taken us straight across a series of the old Somme trenches. These had been bridged by the Sappers with temporary wooden bridges of doubtful strength and just wide enough to take the gun wheels. Any mistake at one of these bridges would have been disastrous – for a gunwheel dropped in a trench would have blocked the whole road. However, with the Hun behind us and perhaps not too far at that, the driving was superb. No body, nor horse, put a foot wrong. But when we were advancing across the Canal du Nord in September our route went across a large open field in which there was *one* solitary shell hole. One of the guns managed to put a wheel into that shell hole! Such is the difference between withdrawing with the threat of a German bayonet behind you and advancing against crumbling opposition.

CAPTAIN T. E. H. HELBY, 59th Siege Battery, Royal Garrison Artillery.

Today I have been a good deal amongst German prisoners, who are collected in the different cages behind the lines. Souvenirs can be had in the way of money, rings, watches, decorations and so forth. Of money and rings I got a good few in exchange for a few cigarettes, of course in

PRIVATE ADRIAN HART, New Zealand Engineers

the majority of cases the best of the souvenirs are taken off them before they get back to us. Many of them give quite freely of what they have, and a good many speak fairly good English. Certainly they seem to be well contented to be finished with the war and well they might.

RHEIMS FREED

GEN. GOURAUD'S GREAT VICTORY

ENEMY FLUNG BACK ON 25 MILES FRONT

The Times,
7 October 1918

Special Order of the Day by Field-Marshal Sir Douglas Haig. ... Less than six months after the launching of the great German offensive which was to have cut the Allied Front in two, the Allied Armies are everywhere today advancing victoriously side by side over the same battlefields on which by the courage and steadfastness of their defence they broke the enemy's assaults. Yet more has been done. Already we have pressed beyond our old battle lines of 1917 and have made a wide breach in the enemy's strongest defences.

... My thanks are due to all ranks of the fighting forces for their indomitable spirit in defence and their boldness in attack, to all Commanders and their Staff Officers, under whose able direction such great results have been attained, and also to all those whose unsparing labours behind the actual fighting line have contributed essentially to our common success.

To have commanded this splendid Army, which, at a time of grave crisis, has so nobly done its duty, fills me with pride. We have passed through many dark days together. Please God these will never return. The enemy has now spent his effort, and I rely confidently upon each one of you to turn to full advantage the opportunity which your skill, courage, and resolution have created.

10 September

ALL THE OLD GROUND REGAINED

CRUMBLING GERMAN DEFENCE

LIEUTENANT PHELPS HARDING,
306th Infantry Regiment,
77th Division,
American Expeditionary Force.

Dear Christine,

The last time I wrote you I was in Paris, having received my Commission and about ready to start for my new Division. Since then I have covered a lot of territory, both in lorries and on foot, and I have passed over a battlefield that has but recently been the scene of some mighty hard fighting – some that my new Division and people of New York will long remember.

My orders took me first to Château Thierry. You have probably read about the fighting in that city. The place is pretty badly banged up from shell fire, but not as badly as most of the smaller villages beyond it. The Huns tore things up in great shape – statues, ornaments and pictures in homes were broken and cut up as if by a band of plundering outlaws. From Château Thierry my trail led toward the Ourcq River, which our men had to cross under heavy machine-gun fire and artillery shelling. Beyond was open country. You will see what a tough proposition it was when you read the casualty list for the few days when the Boche were retreating. They retreated, but they put up a stiff resistance with machine-guns, artillery and planes – and taking machine-gun nests is a real man's job.

I found my Division by the Ourcq, having been relieved, and spent three days in camp with it. The men were pretty tired, and of course they felt the loss of their comrades. I realized this latter point best when censoring their letters. It is mighty hard for a boy to write home to his mother and tell her that his brother has been killed. I read two such letters in the first batch I censored. Each writer tried to tell how painless the death was, and how bravely the brother met it – but in each case I imagine the mother will think only of her loss, and not of the fact that her boy died a true American.

◆

'THE BOYS'

Washington, Sept. 14 – Telegraphing his congratulations to General Pershing, President Wilson asked that his grateful and affectionate thanks should be conveyed to all concerned in the St Mihiel victory.

The President says: 'The boys have done what we expected of them and done it in the way we most admire. We are deeply proud of them and their Chief.'

LIEUTENANT PHELPS
HARDING,
306th Infantry Regiment,
77th Division,
American Expeditionary
Force.

22 September, 1918.

Dear Christine,

My last letter was written just before we commenced the St Mihiel offensive, which began September 12th. I am writing this letter in what was then German occupied territory, sixteen kilometers from our original front line.

When the Division left the Chateau Thierry front we thought we were bound for a rest camp, for the organisation was badly in need of both rest and replacements. Then the order came to move. We marched by night and slept in the daytime, arriving at our position back of the front line after several nights of pretty hard going – hard because the rain fell almost continuously, the roads were bad, the traffic heavy. Our stopping places at the end of each march were thick woods. It is no fun moving into thick, wet woods in the dark, and trying to find places to sleep.

The last night the rain and wind were fierce – I had to be careful not to lose my platoon, the night was so dark and the marching conditions so bad. We moved to within about a kilometre of our line, my battalion being in support of the regiment, and took cover in an old drainage ditch. Wet? Rather!

At exactly 1 a.m., the artillery cut loose. It seemed as if all the artillery in France had suddenly opened up. The sky was red with big flashes, the air seemed full of Empire State Expresses, and the explosion of the heavier shells made the ground tremble. It was a wonderful and awe-inspiring sight.

At 5 a.m., the assault troops went over the top. We followed in the third wave. First we passed batteries that had been shoved right up to our lines – 75s firing like six-shooters. Ahead of us French tanks were ploughing along like big bugs, standing on their beam ends at times as they crossed the trenches or unusually bad ground. Our first line went too fast for them, but they did a lot of good work in breaking up machine-gun nests and in taking villages. Our boys in front just couldn't wait for them, even to smash the wire.

Before we had gone far prisoners began to come in first by twos and threes, then by platoons and companies. We took 13,000 Boche that day. We passed dead men of both armies, but many more Boche than Americans. I was surprised at the indifference I felt toward dead Americans – they seemed a perfectly natural thing to come across, and I felt absolutely no shudder go down my back as I would have had I seen the same thing a year ago.

We kept on going forward until we reached the crest of a hill, and here the shelling became so heavy that we made ourselves as small as possible in ditches and holes. Shells were striking all around us, and too close for comfort. A big 'dud' – a shell that failed to explode – landed in the middle of my platoon and hit a man from the Engineers on the thigh, practically taking his leg off and tearing him up pretty badly. He died in a short time. The company at our right had sixteen casualties from this shell fire, but we, apparently being better duckers, came out without a scratch except for the Engineer who had happened to take cover with us.

After taking the shelling for possibly twenty minutes our artillery spotted the Boche batteries, which were either destroyed or withdrew, permitting us to move forward again. After this the Boche did not make much of a stand. His artillery was apparently too busy moving homeward to bother about fighting.

The first day we covered nearly sixteen kilometres, reaching our objective on scheduled time. It was pretty hard work, for the going was often bad, even after leaving the front line area. It was up and down hill, and at a fairly fast pace. That night we slept on a hillside, and since then we have been moving around slightly, digging in each time, and acting as a reserve for the troops ahead who, with Engineers, are making a line of trenches and putting up wire, placing machine-guns and doing everything necessary to give the Boche a warm reception if he attempts a counter-attack.

In this recent drive, our artillery moved almost as rapidly as our Infantry – sometimes faster than our kitchens and wagon trains – and a Boche battery would hardly open up before a plane would go over it, signal the battery location, and presto! American shells would drop on it. The Boche may not have had much respect for the American Army a few months ago, but from what prisoners say now, we are about as welcome as the proverbial skunk at a lawn party!

Just one more item before I end this letter and go to inspect my platoon. We had expected to be relieved before now, but yesterday news arrived that changed all our plans. Probably my battalion will go into the new line in a day or so, possibly to stay there for a fairly long period. We may even move forward again – no one knows definitely. Anyway, you may not hear from me for a couple of weeks or so – longer, if we push on toward Berlin.

'The British casualties were exceptionally light on Thursday. The prisoners taken by the British and the French now number 17,000, with over 200 guns (including a railway gun of heavy calibre), large numbers of machine-guns and trench mortars, and "immense quantities" of stores and material – including "a complete railway train and other rolling stock".'

CORPORAL A. NEWMAN,
Prisoner of War.

The prisoners were got out at 4 a.m., and told to pack hurriedly (we were not aware at the time that our lads were advancing and we had to retreat). Belgian farm wagons were commandeered for German baggage. Then pieces of rope were tied to the wagons and we acted as horses! In this way we travelled all day and night.

At 4 a.m. next morning we rested. I slept with my head on a doorstep in a passage and at seven in the morning we took to the road again. In this way we travelled to Brussels, doing seventy miles in four days.

◆

ALLIES' GREAT DAY

OSTEND, LILLE AND DOUAI TAKEN

The Times, 18 October 1918

> **AUSTRIA GOES OUT**
>
> **ARMISTICE AT 3 TODAY**
>
> **THE ISOLATION OF GERMANY**
>
> *4 November 1918*

On 9 November, Germany, lacking any firm guidance, bereft of all will, robbed of her princes, collapsed like a house of cards. All that we had lived for, all that we had bled four long years to maintain, was gone. We no longer had a native land of which we might be proud. Order in state and society vanished. All authority disappeared. Chaos. Bolshevism, terror, un-German in name and nature, make their entry into the German Fatherland. Soldiers' and Workmen's Councils, an institution prepared in long, systematic underground work, were now established. Men had worked at this who might by service at the Front have secured a successful issue of the war, but who had been dubbed 'indispensable' or had deserted.

The bulk of the troops in depots, among whom the idea of revolt had long been gaining ground, went over to the side of the revolutionaries.

On the fighting front in the west, Soldiers' Councils, with approval from high quarters, could not be formed fast enough.

The new rulers and their *bourgeois* camp followers abandoned all resistance, and without a shred of authority signed our unconditional capitulation to a merciless enemy.

GENERAL LUDENDORF
My War Memories

On the ninth all Batteries were relieved by the 42nd Divisional Artillery and orders were issued to march to Quièvy to rejoin the Division. We moved on 11 November – Armistice Day, and we heard the announcement of the Armistice when we were still in the Forest de Mormal on a cheerless, dismal, cold misty day. There was no cheering or demonstration. We were all tired in body and mind, fresh from the tragic fields of battle, and this momentous announcement was too vast in its consequences to be appreciated or accepted with wild excitement. We trekked out of the wood on this dreary day in silence. We read in the papers of the tremendous celebrations in London and Paris, but could not bring ourselves to raise even a cheer. The only feeling we had was one of great relief.

GUNNER B. O. STOKES,
13th Battery,
New Zealand Field
Artillery.

Official Communiqué,
11 November, 1918.

TO ALL TROOPS

ELEVEN o'clock to-day, November 11, troops will stand fast on the positions reached at the hour named. The line of outposts will be established, and reported to Army Headquarters. The remainder of the troops will be collected ready to meet any emergency. All military precautions will be preserved, and there will be no communication with the enemy. Further instructions will be issued. Acknowledge.

◆

GUNNER. A. D.
PANKHURST,
56th Division,
Royal Field Artillery,
(Trench Mortars).

We were working towards Mons when the war finished, and moving about so we had trouble getting fed. On the night of 10 November we'd had no rations and our last food had been the midday meal of the day before, so I went off to try to find a source of supply. I walked for about an hour until I came to a small village where there was a chateau that was Divisional Headquarters and I went in and saw a staff officer and told him the position. He said, 'Right, I'll see to it.'

While I was waiting I saw a noticeboard nailed to a tree on a patch of grass outside the château and I struck a match to read it – for it was dark by now – and I read that an Armistice would be declared at 11 o'clock next day. This officer was as good as his word, because soon a GS wagon drove up, laden with food, and I got on it and off we went. We got back to the ammunition dump in the early hours of the morning and when they'd unloaded the food I roused the cook and said, 'I've got some food. Get up and make a meal.' He set to and made a bully beef stew, and when we sat down to our dinner it was breaking dawn. When we'd nearly finished the food I said to them casually, 'The war's over at 11 o'clock this morning.' Somebody said, 'Yeah?' Somebody else said, 'Go on!' They just went on eating! There was no jumping for joy or dancing around. We were so war weary that we were just ready to accept whatever came. When I read of the dancing in the fountains in Trafalgar Square and men riding on top of taxi-cabs going down the Strand and the Maficking that went on in Blighty, my mind always goes back to us few men and the quiet way *we* took the news.

It was different in France. Near the dump there was an old couple in a small farm, and we'd been there to try and get something to eat and they didn't have a thing in the house – not a crumb! So later that morning I took them a share of our rations – a tin of milk, a tin of butter, a tin of bully beef, some bread, some tea. Someone had got hold of a copy of the *Continental Daily Mail* and on the front page was the announcement of the Armistice. I showed it to them and they just sat rocking back and forwards in their chairs with tears rolling down their faces. They'd been in occupied territory for practically the whole of the war and they were virtually beaten, just resigned to whatever would happen to them. I shall always remember that old couple. They must have suffered so much, not to have shown some glimmer of happiness.

On 10 November, my gun team was moving forward with a troop of the 12th Lancers. We came to a farm on the road towards the Belgian village of Sevry and we went up and knocked on the front door. A woman opened it and was very surprised to see us. She put her fingers to her lips and, pointing inside, said, 'Boche!' When we went in, the Germans left by the back door, leaving their breakfast behind them on the table. They ran as fast as they could across the orchard and left us to eat their breakfast which was one black loaf, one tin of fat pork, a dixie of coffee made of burnt wheat. We shared it and went on to some crossroads about half a mile nearer the village. We found that it had been tunnelled ready to blow up, so we took up our positions about fifty yards back. We had been there for about an hour when a German patrol, nine in all, came, intending to blow the crossroad up. I shouted, 'Eh up' and let fly with one pannier of bullets into the whole patrol. They ran in all directions, dropping the sticks of explosives. In the afternoon we were relieved by a Battalion of the Manchester Regiment. We went back to Solre le Chateau and we were billeted for the night in a German bread store. We had to sleep on stacks of black bread with rats running all over the place. The next morning we got up to see our Officer coming down the street in his shirt and braces with a barrel of beer on a big French wheelbarrow. He came into the billet and said 'Come on lads, the war will be over at 11 o'clock.' When the French folks heard, out came the flags and wine, beer, all sorts, and everybody got totally pickled.

PRIVATE FRANK J. H. DUNK,
No. 3 Platoon,
7th (S) Battalion,
Queen's Own Royal West Kent Regiment.

> **BRITISH TAKE MONS.**
>
> **CROWNING TRIUMPH IN LAST HOURS OF THE WAR**

Now this bloody war is over
Oh how happy I shall be,
When I get my civvy clothes on
No more soldiering for me.
Only just one more Reveille
Only one more night parade,
Only one more kit inspection,
Then we're marching home again.

Heavy loads will then be fewer,
Guards, fatigues will be no more,
We'll be spooning with the wenches,
As we did in days of yore.
NCO's will then be navvies,
Privates own their motor cars,
No more 'sirring' and saluting,
No more tea in two-pound jars.

◆

> **GERMANY SURRENDERS. OFFICIAL.**
>
> The Prime Minister made the following announcement today:
>
> The Armistice was signed at Five o'clock this morning and hostilities are to cease on all fronts at 11 a.m. today.

◆

MAUDE CRA'STER   I went to the Red Cross Depot as usual this morning and we were told the Armistice had been signed ... Someone came and said the King would speak from Buckingham Palace – then the question was, would we be in time if we went there? A few of us flew into our coats and rushed out to find a taxi. Of course we didn't get one but we hailed a growler and four of us got into that. He put us down at Buckingham Palace where the mass was already terrifying, but a friend and myself were loath to go back, and a happy idea struck me. Just where we got out of the cab a taxi was standing, with two ladies and a man. I asked if Mrs C. and I could get up by the driver; they said, 'Of course,' so there we were, happily seated out of the crowd. We gave the man half a crown, so he was quite decent to us – and we were in full view of the balcony!

I can't tell you *what* the sight was! Lorries crammed with men and women all with flags – people crammed on the top of taxis and inside too. Large Government motors with hospital nurses, WAACs and WRENs and soldiers, and the *mass* of all kinds on their feet. There we all waited. Presently there was a great to-do, for mounted policemen pushed the crowd in front of them to let the bands through to the Quadrangle.

Directly the bands got into position, they struck up 'God Save the King', and he and the Queen, Princess Mary, the Duke of Connaught and Princess Patricia appeared on the balcony. I think Queen Alexandra was there too. The roar as they appeared was one roll and everyone sang with the bands. Then the King said something – but of course we couldn't hear – and then the band played 'All People that on Earth do Dwell', and everyone sang again. Then the band struck up 'Home Sweet Home', and it was this that touched the crowd really. It was solemnly sung, almost with a sob, and I felt it a moment never to be forgotten.

After that the English reserve gave way and they sang 'For He's a Jolly Good Fellow!' Then 'Tipperary' was played and after that the different Anthems – and then again everyone sang with the bands, 'Now thank we All Our God'. After that the National Anthem was played again and the cheers roared and roared, and the Royal Family went in . . .

To: **CORPORAL A. D. PANKHURST,** 56th Division, Royal Field Artillery, (Trench Mortar Battery).

My Dear Arthur,

Jolly pleased with your letter this morning. Isn't everything ripping! I am so happy!! You can imagine what a relief it was to know the Armistice was signed. When the first maroon went off (at 11 a.m.) there was one big cheer. Everywhere closed down and no more work was done that day. Then the town was thronged with thousands of people giving vent to their feelings and it was a wonderful sight. I only wished you had been here to have witnessed it – or rather joined in. Every vehicle was chartered, private cars, taxis, down to a brewer's dray, including buses, government lorries of every description, and were packed with people making merry with rattles, bells, anything that made a noise. The great place was to sit on the top of the taxi, also it was to see who could wear the most flags! No class distinction, Army etiquette, officers and men were one, and everyone's most awfully happy. I saw an officer changing hats with a sailor and a well-dressed woman in beautiful furs hugging the Colonials in a procession! There was such a lot of amusement, a greengrocer's cart going down the Strand was commandeered, heaps of people scrambling on, the poor driver – an old man – looked as though he thought the world was coming to an end and sat helplessly gazing at the 'young wimmen' and comparing them to his day, gave it up as a bad job and drove on, while his companions pelted people with his Brussel sprouts. One officer getting into a taxi had a fresh herring smack on the side of his face, while some scrambled on to the top and danced, some sat on the step, the back, and even the mud-guard. One incident amused me very much. One girl of our Corps was driving a car down Bedford Street, and had some Colonials with her. Another car going along the Strand with more Colonials and RAF girls in, was noticed by them – one girl in particular they fancied, so they drove their car into the RAF, sprang out, collared the girl of their choice, the others trying to keep her back, but they won, carried her back, 'pitched' her into their car and drove off with her amidst a din of applause. It is really impossible to describe it. Towards night it rained and even that did not disperse the crowds. It was carried on for a week, with fireworks and bonfires, in the Square, as you will see by the papers. Everywhere still looks awfully jolly with plenty of flags flying.

When do you think you'll be home for good? And what about leave? We are all well and waiting keenly for you to come home.

Much love,

MARIE.

There was a tremendous atmosphere of excitement and elation. In the evening of Armistice Day we went to the Alhambra and we had the most awful job to get to the theatre through the crowds. It was 'The Bing Boys', with George Robey and Violet Lorraine, but the audience was so excited and so uproarious that after a time the show stopped completely. They couldn't go on with it! They put a big screen up on the stage and flashed pictures on it of all the Allies – I hadn't realised the enormous number of Allies we had until then! We were standing in the back row of the stalls – everyone was standing up, the theatre was mad – and right over the back of me, leaning over, were endless Australians and New Zealanders. They were going wild, and every time one of our foreign Allies came on the screen they shouted 'Who won this bloody war?' And they all roared 'Britain!' Every single time. They never applauded anybody. They were quite, quite wild!

AUDREY GEIDT

11 November – Monday
Cold and raining. Runner in at 10.30 with order to cease firing at 11.00 a.m. Firing continued and we stood by. 306th Machine-Gun Company on my right lost twelve men at 10.55, when a high explosive landed in their position. At 11.00 sharp the shelling ceased on both sides and we don't know what to say. Captain came up and told us that the war was over. We were dumbfounded and finally came to and cheered – and it went down the line like wildfire. I reported Jones' death and marked his grave. Captain conducted a prayer and cried like a baby. Built a big

SERGEANT T. GRADY,
US Army

fire and dried our clothes and the bully beef tasted like turkey. We told the new boys our tales and about the battles and they were heavy listeners. Other teams returned from outposts and we celebrated by burning captured ammunition and everything that would burn.

GUNNER G. WORSLEY,
276th Brigade,
Royal Field Artillery.

The first we knew was when a Colonel we'd got was driving round in a car shouting to everybody, 'They've asked for an Armistice! They've asked for an Armistice!' Then, at 11 o'clock on the day itself a trumpeter came round and sounded the 'Cease Fire', quite dramatically. I remember doing a cartwheel and I said to myself, 'I'm alive! It's all over and I'm alive!'

We went into the house of a French woman. We found her in the kitchen, furiously pulling up all the flagstones in the stone floor to find a bicycle she'd taken to pieces and hidden from the Germans all through the war. She was a woman of great spirit. She actually didn't think the war should be over. She kept shouting, 'Berlin! Berlin!' and pointing, as much as to say we'd given up too soon. The Germans had been sleeping there the night before. She shouted, 'Pas fini! Revanche! Revanche!' She wanted revenge. I said, 'Mais peutêtre je suis mort' – you know, I might get killed. She says, 'Sanfairyann', meaning that didn't matter. I said, 'Sanfairyann be buggered! *I'm alive*. The war's over. That's good enough for me!'

◆

No more marching, no more doubling
In the morn at six fifteen
No more pushing blooming barrows,
No more digging out latrines.
No more Sergeants getting shirty,
No more bread like granite rock
No more rising at five thirty,
And Lights Out at ten o'clock.

No more asking when we're marching
'Please Sir, may we have a drink?'
Or because we drop a shovel
No more putting in the clink.
No more 'shunning-as-you-were-ing'
No work for a bob a day.
When next the country has a war on
We'll find a job that brings more pay.

◆

KING'S MESSAGES
TO THE FORCES

THE VICTORY WON FOR
JUSTICE AND RIGHT

France.   GUNNER B. O. STOKES,
18 November 1918   New Zealand Field
                     Artillery.

My Dearest Mum & Dad and all,
Hurrah for our side! Can you realise hostilities have ceased? I'm sure I can't. It seems too wonderful to believe, yet here there is no excitement, no celebrations, and everything is going on in the same old way. We still have horses and guns to look after, but of course we miss the screeching and screaming of the 'old gentleman's' shells. Really though, the army has taken the happenings of the past few weeks in a calm and subdued manner. Not even a cheer was raised when first we heard the official news. But away deep down there is the knowledge that soon we shall be seeing the home shores appearing on the horizon, and that is what the signing of the Armistice means to us. It means home. We are now at a village called Quesnoy near Caudry, south-east of Cambrai. We are having a good time here, but the sooner we get rid of horses, harness and guns the better. We will then realise the war is *finis*. The main question now is when are we going to get home.

You may now address me Bombardier B. O. Stokes. While I was on leave I was promoted Bombardier, so what do you think of me now, a one-stripe artist? The war has just lasted long enough for me to get a stripe. After two years in France my turn has come round!

Lots & lots of love & kisses to all. Soon I'll be marching home again, so cheero Mum, Dad, Chris & Sid.

          Au Revoir
                    Your ever loving boy
                    Bert xxx
                    xxxxx

P.S. 30 Nov. Sorry have not been able to post this letter before, we are on our way to Germany now and are near Bavai about 5 kilos from the Belgian border.

CORPORAL A.
NEWMAN,
Prisoner of War.

13 November. We rose early and was surprised to find no German Guards left. They left a note in the hall saying we were to make our way to Tournai or Ath which was the boundary our troops had to keep to for seven days, giving the Germans time to evacuate. We started off early in the morning with nothing to eat and we were feeling very hungry. The last day in Brussels we were given a spoonful of jam and during our first day's march turnips we got from a field constituted our food for three days. We walked all this day and arrived at Ath about 8.30 p.m. I hardly know how I did the last few miles, but about four miles out of this town we met one of our despatch riders, and the sight of khaki cheered us up. At Ath we were told to go to the Town Major who would find us sleeping accommodation but I felt I could walk no more and went with two of my friends into a factory and slept on bags of shavings and although our lads cooked supper for us, we were too far gone to get up for it. Next morning saw us lined up for breakfast early. We were given a piece of ham, bread and butter and tea. What a feed! I had seen nothing like it for ages.

COLONEL W. N.
NICHOLSON,
Suffolk Regiment,
Staff Officer attached,
15 Highland Division.

The Armistice was timed to commence at 11 a.m. on 11 November and till that hour there was heavy firing from the German lines. A German machine-gun remained in action the whole morning opposite our lines. Just before 11 a.m., a thousand rounds were fired from it in a practically ceaseless burst. At five minutes to eleven the machine-gunner got up, took off his hat to us, and walked away.

At 11 a.m., there came great cheering from the German lines; and the village church bells rang. But on our side there were only a few shouts. I had heard more for a rum ration. The match was over; it had been a damned bad game.

CORPORAL O. W.
FLOWERS,
Motor Transport Section,
Army Service Corps.

I was with the 8-inch Howitzers and we got to the point when we were too slow. The troops was going pretty quickly following after the Germans and we couldn't keep up, so it was left to the field guns to finish it and we pulled out into fields on the roadside near Lille, between Roubaix and Tourcoing. When we heard the Armistice was signed we thought we'd have a bit of fun. There was a lot of small dumps about, ammunition and Verey lights, so we set them alight – firing shots into them, and then of course you only wanted one to go up and all the rest went. We had a real Guy Fawkes. The officers never interfered, but a bit later I was with the lads round the lorries and we was all jostling together, talking, having a bit of sport because all work had finished, and the officer came across to me. He says, 'Flowers, I want to have a word with you.' I thought it was about this stuff we'd blown up. He said, 'Come across to my office' and he linked me – and that struck such a note in my head, because I was only a corporal and there was this officer linking me with his arm!

As we got to the door of the office, he says, 'Have you had any letter from your wife of late?' I said, 'Yes, I had one yesterday, on the 10th.' Now my wife worked in munitions and in this letter she told me she was taking time off to go and nurse her mother who was bad with influenza. The officer said, 'Did she say anything about feeling poorly?' Now that influenza was raging and it dawned on me immediately what he was going to say. I said, 'Now don't go and tell me what I'm thinking.' 'I'm afraid I am,' he says, 'I've got a telegram here. She passed away.' Well, I just swooned into his arms. He sat me in a chair in his office and he made me take a drink of whisky. 'Now,' he says, 'I'm going to leave you here entirely on your own for a while and I'm going off to get your leave through.' I couldn't even thank him, because I was just – out! I thought what a day it was for this to happen. Now that we can be sure we're going to get home – because there hadn't been a day in the last four years that we dared say that, and now it looked as if we were all safe and going to see our homes again, now *this* has come.

I was on the boat next day – and of course, the leave boat, with the war being over, it was all jollificating, all the lads excited. But I ran into one chap leaning over the rail. I thought he was sick at first, and then I saw he was weeping. I put my hand on his shoulder and said, 'What's the matter, Chum?' And he pulled a telegram out of his pocket and showed me. Same thing! So I pulled mine out and says, 'There's a pair of us!' We stuck together, not knowing where to go, what corner to get into to get out of it all. Broken down. I've had some journeys in my life, but I never had one like that one. To think I'd gone the four years without a scratch except a bit of gas, and got to the end of the war and then to lose her. It took me a day to get down to Boulogne, another day to get across to London and a day to make my way up to Yorkshire, and by the time I got home she'd been buried three days.

◆

People said when we enlisted,
Fame and medals we should win,
But the fame is in the Guard Room,
And the medals made of tin.
Now we've finished with the Kaiser,
At the Empire we shall sing
The Battalion National Anthem
Twice a night. God Save the King!

LAST HOURS OF THE WAR
REVOLUTION IN GERMANY

Naval Mutiny Spreads to Hamburg and Many other Ports.

LEUTNANT FRITZ NAGEL,
Reserve Feldartillerie
Regiment Nr. 18.

The German naval officers intended to go out and go down fighting. When orders were given to the stokers to fire up the boilers, they refused. The crews were quite unwilling to sacrifice their lives in this useless gesture. For the first time in German history, seamen refused to obey their officers and fights broke out on several ships. The revolution was on, spreading very quickly to the Army.

What worried me most was the terrible news reaching us from home. Drunken soldiers roamed the streets. Even the police were reported to have joined the revolution. Some of these reports were exaggerated, but we did not know it then. The people at home were terrified.

At this time, while all discipline apparently had collapsed, so-called 'Soviet Soldiers' and Navy Councils' were formed under the leadership of the worst elements. One of their main objects seemed to be getting rid of those officers they hated.

I must say that the men of the revolutionary council treated me with respect and after a long palaver, asked me if I would lead them home. They realised we would obtain food and petrol only if we marched as a unit. They promised to obey and did so.

All 'K' Flak batteries in our sector decided to march together – ten officers and 193 men. The march home ordinarily would have been a depressing affair. The weather was cold and rainy. The population knew that its territory would be occupied by American and French armies marching a few miles behind us. In spite of this the people were cheerful and did their best for us. Some towns and villages had erected welcome signs across the roads. But the tremendous joy and relief that the war finally had come to an end dominated our emotions completely.

'When they ask what you did in the war, Bill, just remember you delivered Belgium.'

CAPTAIN C. M. SLACK, MC,
1st/4th Battalion,
East Yorkshire Regiment.
(Prisoner of War)

We eventually finished up in the barracks in Cologne, about three hundred of us, and not much food except what came in our parcels, and then the Armistice came along.

Then a few days after that they were still blowing the bugle for us to go out on parade – but we didn't. We said, 'No, we've won the war. We're not going to parade any more.' One day a fellow called Hicks, a Gunner Officer, said to me, 'Look here, Slack, we've won the war, will you walk round Cologne with me?' I said, 'Yes,' and we polished our buttons up and walked straight out past the sentry. Although we'd won the war the sentries were still there. We went out past the sentry. 'Halt!' 'It's all right, we're coming back.' We went on slowly, half expecting to get one in the back. We went into the cathedral and stayed there for about half an hour and nothing happened, no hue and cry, and we came out and crossed the Hohenzollern Bridge and back to the camp and that was that.

We'd seen some of the Germans coming back, the unconquered heroes, and they came back with their donkey carts and their goats and all sorts of things. A regular rabble, shouting and waving to the crowds who were cheering them on, banners across the road, 'Welcome home to our unconquered heroes!'

A day or two after that, four officers went down to the station with their suitcases and asked for four tickets for London and they were told, 'We're sorry, but the lines are broken,' and so they came back to the camp.

Even though we were prisoners, we were paid. They gave us money and it had been debited against our account and it was accumulating all the time and there were three hundred of us. The senior officers went to the Cologne Authorities and said, 'Look here, can't we contact a boat?' so we chartered a boat down the Rhine. We stopped at Dusseldorf for the first night and some of the people put up at hotels. I put up at the equivalent of the YMCA, and about three in the morning a policeman was shaking my shoulder. 'Get back to the ship. They're rioting in the town.' Dusseldorf was a red place and they were going to burn all the hotels and places where these British officers were, so we got back into our ship, sailed on to Rotterdam, and there the British Authorities took us over. The next day they put us on their own boat and we landed in Hull, my old home town, a fortnight after the Armistice. We were the first people home. We came on our own. We just came!

On 22 November we reached the Rhine bridge near Kaiserslautern. Dirty and sloppy looking revolutionary soldiers wearing red armbands stopped us and refused to let us cross the bridge. They feared our cannons as well as the thought that our whole outfit would join the counter-revolutionary army rumoured to be forming beyond the Rhine. They were quite orderly and polite, but I really did not care what happened to the guns. According to the Armistice conditions, the guns were to be surrendered and turned over officially to the French or Armistice commissions at some assembly point anyway. I agreed to let these men have the guns against proper receipt for two motorised flak guns, two trucks and one passenger automobile. After these formalities were over, we parked the vehicles on the west side of the Rhine and then proceeded on foot to the other side of the bridge. I shook hands with every man and dismissed them with instructions to get home the best way they could. That was the end of the war for me.

LEUTNANT FRITZ NAGEL,
Reserve Feldartillerie,
Regiment Nr. 18.

LIEUTENANT FRANK
MOYLAN,
2nd/7th (City of London)
Battalion.
(Prisoner of War)

By that time I was up on the Baltic. There was an interpreter there named Franck, a Saxon Artilleryman. He spoke English well, but he got jailed for supplying some of the prisoners with something or other in exchange for cigarettes or soap. The ninth of November came and he appeared with some other blokes on the scene and put the camp Commandant in the gaol. Franck told us that he was now the president of the Soldiers' and Sailors' Council. They put the red flag up and opened the gates, but there was nowhere for us to go, so we stayed there.

We left about a month after, about the eighth or ninth of December, and that Saxon Private came with us on the train to Danzig. When we got to Danzig, there were two ships, two cruisers, *Coventry* and *Centaur*, and two Danish ships, and the British troops got on one, and the French got on the other, and we had bread rolls and eggs and butter. (We hadn't had butter for months.) There was a crowd on the quayside and there was so much bread that we started throwing rolls – well, the Germans were starving – and there was a man in a fur coat and he had a fishing net. Some of the bread had fallen into the water and he was getting it out with a net. A man in a big fur coat!

The two British cruisers both put their searchlights on, crossed, one flying a French tricolour and the other one the Union jack, and they played their searchlights on each other's flags and the band on one of the quays played, 'The Watch on the Rhine'. As the ship left, that Saxon Private shouted out, 'Let bygones be bygones', and that was the end!

◆

THE BOYS ARE COMING HOME

Every day they are returning from the war, these men who have faced death countless times on the land and sea, and in the air, in the defence of their homes and yours – what are you doing to show your gratitude and appreciation? What are you doing to help these men confronted with the difficult problem of regaining their footing in civil life?

Show your appreciation in a practical way.

It is so easy to praise, cheer, wave flags, but the men who have fought for you don't want empty condolences, and to offer them charity is an insult. They want a chance to become useful civilians again – they want to make good in commerce and industry as they made good in the Army and Navy.

THE KING'S FUND FOR THE DISABLED

We embarked on the *France* for Dover – great excitement on reaching here! Being Sunday, many people awaited us and we were the first batch of prisoners to reach England. The Prince of Wales met us and entertained us to a feed in the Station Hall. He gave a fine speech on behalf of the King (who regretted he could not attend). The King sent us (846 of us in all) a parcel containing pipe tobacco, cigarettes, chocolate and toffee. From here we were conveyed in private motors to the North Wall camp. The streets along the way were lined with enthusiastic crowds and they greeted us wildly. Each man was given a hospital bed with wool mattress. Oh, the joy! We spent three days here getting the necessary papers and passing the doctor, then went by special train to Birmingham. We arrived here about 4 p.m. No reception! No one knew who we were. A man asked me if I had come on leave! But the next day the Lord Mayor had the police band at New Street Station to welcome the next batch – supposed to be the first prisoners home!

CORPORAL A. NEWMAN

We were given two months' sick leave, then had to return to Shoreham-by-Sea for demobilisation. Thus ended my three and a half years as a Soldier of the King.

I was nursing the wounded French soldiers in Dr Blake's hospital on the Rue Puccini in Paris, and my favourite was my friend Boillose, nineteen years old, right leg and left arm amputated. He had black hair and red rosy cheeks.

SISTER NELL BRINK, US Base Hospital No. 27, (University of Pittsburgh).

I went down to the Medicine Chef, as they call him, and told him it was our last day in Paris and I said, 'I just have one ambition before I leave, I'd like to take my friend Boillose out, with your permission, I'd like to take him for a walk in the Bois, I would also like to take him down to Rumpelmyers. I think it would be a nice treat for him, you know', and of course, they were all delighted, anything you would do for a Frenchman, you know. OK, I went downstairs, and I got the wheelchair, put him in the wheelchair, took him out. He was *not* over-enthusiastic, but he was satisfied. They were so used to accepting, the French were, after four years. They were pretty stoical, but he had had so many operations, and just the odour of ether alone, without an operation, just suddenly going through the corridor, he'd turn pale, sick, you know.

In the Bois, it was lovely, really, the French people saw us in American uniforms and said, 'There's Americans,' and gave him a flower and put it in a buttonhole.

And then I went and called a taxi and we got Boillose in. We went up to Rumpelmyers. It was the nicest thing in the world, really. We were getting out of the taxi and he got up on his leg, and before we got to the doors – they had the big swinging doors, very difficult for him to get through – it was as if somebody pressed a button and the doors opened up, just like that. I didn't know what to order for Boillose, because I'm no drinking woman, myself, but I thought he ought to have champagne, so I looked over the menu where they had all the drinks, and what I ordered was a great long champagne drink and it was full of fruit. It was nice. It was nice for the occasion, you know. So we had that and we took our time, and the waitress came over and was so nice to Boillose, and then we had tea and got back in another taxi. He enjoyed it in his own way, I suppose. But he didn't say much. Very stoical. Didn't smile or anything. So, OK, I took him back to his ward and said, 'Au Revoir.' We were sleeping on the top floor in the same building where we were nursing. So, after I'd packed my things, I said to my friend, 'I'm going down to see how Boillose's getting along for the night.' So I went down and there he was, sitting in a chair in the middle of this one ward, surrounded with the Frenchmen, and he was telling them the whole story and they were having a real gay time. It was the cutest thing in the world.

SERGEANT TOM BRADY
US Army

24 April – Thursday

Passed through the 'Narrows' 7.30. Far Rockaway and Coney Island looked good. Decks were jammed with troops. Small boats carrying girls came out to meet us. Major-General came out to welcome us. The big Staten Island Ferry, *Mayor Gaynor* – 'The Mayor's Committee of Welcome' – came out loaded to capacity, with friends and relatives, and the Police Band played some snappy music. There were other boats and tugs loaded with friends. Some carried placards, displaying the name of some boy on board. Passed 'Liberty' and steamed up the river to Pier 54. People working in the big office buildings waved flags and threw out ticker tape. Took three hours to dock. Red Cross nurses lined the pier and a Marine Band played 'There Will Be a Hot Time etc.', 'How Dry I Am' and other old songs, and the boys yelled themselves hoarse. Pulled into the big shed and we received some real lemon pie, coffee and chocolate from the Red Cross. Piled on to a ferry and went down round the Battery and up the North River to the Long Island Railroad. We received a rousing welcome all along. Every steamboat saluted us with their siren horns and bells. The Red Cross put over another barrage of apples, sponge cake and milk. Boarded electric trains and there is some difference betwixt these and the 'Hommes and Chevaux'. A pretty young miss ran out and planted a nice big kiss on a Company 'D' man, only to find out that it was a case of mistaken identity. Another fainted when she met her son. There was a mixture of tears, laughter and whooping and it looked like a 'free for all' as the 'Sweeties' clashed with their heroes. The boys are like a bunch of kids and feel very jubilant. Lieutenant Gorham's wife blew in, and she put an awful barrage of kisses over. I can see now why he shaved off his moustache.

14 May – Wednesday
Up 5.30. Rolled packs. Fell out 6.45. Called the check.

16 May – Friday
Turned in our blankets. Received our discharge and pay 4.00 p.m. Hired a car and beat it to Boston – toot sweet. Just caught the last train home. Finis!!!

A GASSED AND WOUNDED TERRIER

There has just left Liverpool for America a West Highland terrier which was presented by the Black Watch to the first contingents of American troops. The dog, which is called 'Tytus' has taken part in three pushes. He was gassed at St Mihiel, and wounded by shrapnel, but has been nursed back to health and is going to the United States to be exhibited during a YMCA campaign.

The Times, 17 October 1918

F. W. GRASER,
10 Field Artillery,
US Army.

By the time we got back to the States it was so long after the war was over that they hardly knew we'd returned. They wanted seasoned troops to go into Germany, so they took the 1st, 2nd, 3rd Divisions and 46th Division, because they were seasoned and the others hadn't had any action. They sent them back – didn't need them – and some of them just turned around practically as soon as they got off the boat, and went back home. They were the ones that marched down 42nd Street and got all the acclamation. When we came home, why, we just got on the train and went to camp, got on another train and headed home. And when I got back ten months after the Armistice I found that the boys who were in the National Guard outfits, who'd done nothing but guard duty in Paris, were running the American Legion and having a gay old time! They were the ones who got all the bouquets.

◆ ◆

Here dead we lie because we did not choose
To live and shame the land from which we sprung.
Life, to be sure, is nothing much to lose;
But young men think it is, and we were young.

A. E. Housman.

Extract from the Diary of
FIELD-MARSHAL SIR
HENRY WILSON, GCB,
KOB, CB, DSO.

4 October, 1920

Dean Ryle (Westminster Abbey) came to see me with a proposal which greatly pleased me. He wants to exhume the body of a private soldier (not identified) in France and bury it with full honours in Westminster Abbey putting a plain stone over it saying something to the effect 'Here lies the body of an unknown British soldier who died for his King and Country etc.'

I suggested some other word being used than 'soldier' as then this would cover the Navy and Air Force and he agreed. I told him he must ask the King who returns from Balmoral on Friday. He suggested 11 November. for the day.

From BRIG-GEN. L. J.
WYATT,
GOC British Troops,
   France and Flanders,
   1920, and Director of the
   War Graves
   Commission.

To the Editor of the Daily Telegraph

Sir,

From time to time accounts have been published purporting to relate how and by whom the Unknown Warrior's body was selected in France for burial in Westminster Abbey on Nov. 11, 19 years ago. I should like to give here the authentic account of what took place.

In October I received a notification from the War Office that King George V had approved the suggestion and the proposal that the burial should be in Westminster Abbey on Nov. 11. I issued instructions that the body of a British soldier, which it would be impossible to identify, should be brought in from each of the four battle areas – the Aisne, the Somme, Arras and Ypres, on the night of Nov. 7 and placed in the chapel of St Pol. The party bringing each body was to return at once to its area, so that there should be no chance of their knowing on which the choice fell.

Reporting to my headquarters office at St Pol, at midnight on Nov. 7, Col. Gell, one of my staff, announced that the bodies were in the chapel and the men who had brought them had gone... The four bodies lay on stretchers, each covered by a Union Jack; in front of the altar was the shell of the coffin which had been sent from England to receive the remains. I selected one, and with the assistance of Col. Gell, placed it in the shell; we screwed down the lid. The other bodies were removed and reburied in the military cemetery outside my headquarters at St Pol.

I had no idea even of the area from which the body I selected had come; no one else can know it... The shell, under escort was sent to Boulogne... The next morning, carried by the pall-bearers who were selected from NCOs of the British and Dominion troops it was placed on a French military wagon and taken to Boulogne Quay where a British destroyer was waiting... Six barrels of earth from the Ypres Salient were put on board to be placed in the tomb at Westminster Abbey so that the body should rest in the soil on which so many of our troops gave up their lives...

Then HMS *Verdun* moved off, a guard of honour of Bluejackets at 'the Present', carrying that symbol which for so many years, and especially during the last few months, has meant so much to us all.

Yours Etc.
L. J. Wyatt.

Kirkby Lonsdale, Nov. 1939.

ENGLAND HONOURS ITS UNKNOWN DEAD

Scenes at the Cenotaph and in Westminster Abbey

THE WARRIOR LAID TO REST

Great silent crowds watched yesterday's supremely impressive tribute paid to an unknown 'common soldier.'

The unveiling of the Cenotaph in Whitehall by the King, the procession thence to Westminster, and the service in the great national Abbey were of deep significance, but most impressive of all was the two minutes' universal silence.

'THE MAN WHO WON THE WAR'

By Our Special Representative

With the first round of the salute came the faint sound of martial music. The cortège had left Victoria and at a slow march was wending its way westward. Then the brass instruments died away and there came the low wailing music of the bagpipes.

A small company of soldiers in khaki came first, then the massed bands, and following them the pipers.

And then there came the gun-carriage bearing the Unknown and Unnamed Warrior.

Army officers of high rank marched on one side, on the other marched high rank Naval officers, but it was not they whom the crowd had come to honour.

Other contingents of sailors, marines, and sailors in khaki followed and, finally, a great procession of ex-Servicemen in mufti. Within ten minutes the funeral procession had passed and, making its way down Constitution Hill, vanished into the low-lying mist.

AT THE CENOTAPH

When the first stroke of Big Ben sounded over Whitehall, the King, standing in the middle of the road, surrounded by Admirals and Field-Marshals, turned southwards to face the Cenotaph.

Behind the King, the gun-carriage, bearing the coffin, draped with the Union Jack was drawn across the road.

THE MOURNING THRONG

Windows and roofs were crowded with spectators, and on the pavements below stood the dense throngs of the bereaved, to whom alone this part of Whitehall was open.

Women were loaded with flowers, chiefly white chrysanthemums, and the faces of many revealed the sweet and bitter stresses of unforgettable emotions.

THE UNVEILING

On the last stroke of eleven, the King pressed a knob on the top of a little pedestal erected in the road, and the two great Union Jacks that draped the Cenotaph fell to the ground.

At the same moment the King raised his cap. Bareheaded and silent, he stood in the midst of this vast gathering of the silent people.

At the end of the Two Minutes, the bands struck up, and the choir led the singing of 'O God, our help in ages past,' while the drums, draped in black, rolled low thunder in the intervals.

IN THE ABBEY

Through the guard of honour of VCs, past the massed mourning of the widows and mothers of the fallen, they carried him – this representative of the Common People; the Man Who Won the War; this Unknown British Warrior.

The Burial Service was read. The earth from the soil of France was scattered on the coffin by the King.

As we stood there in silence while the muffled drums began to whisper, as it were, myriads of miles away, and grew and grew into the sound of a rushing mighty wind, the stone atrocities faded, the vulgarity and bad taste were forgotten, the pomp and circumstance forgiven.

There remained only the clear sunlight streaming through the pale windows of the Abbey, only the splendid proportions of the mighty Gothic church. And in our ears there sounded, not the strains of the 'Recessional,' but the crash and thunder of battle under a windswept sky, and the trumpets' promise of a cleaner and a sweeter day.

Daily Herald,
12 November 1920

Beautiful flowers and masses of laurel surround the last resting-place of the Unknown, and many of these tributes bear pathetic inscriptions.

At eight o'clock the people stood eight deep in a double line from the Cenotaph to Trafalgar Square. From here the queue stretched down Northumberland Avenue to the Embankment and along the Embankment to Westminster. From there it doubled back to Trafalgar Square.

These were no mere sightseers, these men and women slowly moving along in that great pilgrimage, tired and drooping with the long waiting. They were the mothers and the fathers and the wives and the children of the great army of the dead.

There were old mothers in dingy black, down whose furrowed cheeks the tears trickled; there were young women who carried in their arms the little ones grown sleepy on the long trail.

And all along the way the air was heavy with the pungent earthy odour of white chrysanthemums and the strong sweetness of the lilies that so many of the pilgrims carried.

At last, through the mist, the noble lines of the Cenotaph appeared, now standing twelve feet deep in flowers. Here the policemen gently marshalled the pilgrims into double file, and with bowed heads they passed, the men with bare heads, and the women, many of them with their faces buried in their handkerchiefs.

At either end of the enclosed space more flowers were banked high, and then were piled higher and higher as woman after woman, and here and there a child stooped to add their tribute. Many of the women, bowed and broken, were overcome with weeping as they were led away.

Daily Herald,
12 November 1920

It did not seem an Unknown Warrior whose body came on a gun-carriage down Whitehall where we were waiting for him. He was known to us all. It was one of 'our boys' – not warriors – as we called them in the days of darkness lit by faith... To some women, weeping a little in the crowd after an all-night vigil, he was their own boy who went missing one day and was never found till now... To many men wearing ribbons and badges on civil clothes, he was a familiar figure, one of their comrades...

It was the steel helmet – the old 'tin hat' – lying there on the crimson of the flag, which revealed him instantly, not as a mythical warrior, aloof from common humanity, a shadowy type of national pride and martial glory, but as one of those fellows dressed in the drab of khaki, stained by mud and grease, who went into the dirty ditches with this steel hat on his head...

Philip Gibbs
Daily Chronicle, 12 November 1920

We knew him over there, in his billets, grousing... We knew him at his sports, and on the road 'going up' – tramp! tramp! tramp! tramp! – through squelching mud or the thick dust of passing traffic, along the long straight roads with their uneven, exasperating pavé between the rows of splintered trees, whistling perhaps, or halted for rest by the wayside, leaning his heavy pack against a tree-trunk or a hump of earth, grousing still, and breaking off with a laugh to help his mate.

The Times,
12 November 1920.

PATHETIC TRIBUTES

Close by the King's massive offering there lay a small wreath of laurel and flowers, to which was attached this touching dedication:

'In loving remembrance of our darling, Jim Cook, who answered his country's call at the early age of thirteen years and ten months, and laid his life down at seventeen years of age. Ever remembered by Dad and Mam, Brothers and Sisters at home and abroad.'

Another bore this touching inscription:—

'From "Little Mother" (unable to be present) to her only child, "Somewhere in France".'

Yet another sorrowing 'Little Mother' had inscribed her offering:—' "Somewhere in France." We will remember thee in the mornings, and in the night season we will not forget.'

Daily Herald, 13 November 1920

What candles may be held to speed them all?
Not in the hands of boys, but in their eyes
Shall shine the holy glimmers of good-byes.
The pallor of girls' brows shall be their pall;
Their flowers the tenderness of patient minds,
And each slow dusk a drawing-down of blinds.

Wilfred Owen.

EMPIRE'S SACRIFICE: OUR 658,705 DEAD

The people of the Empire see figures that will cause them to bow their heads in proud grief at the Noble Sacrifice of our Great Dead; and our hearts go out to those Mothers and Fathers, Wives and children whose splendid menfolk have by their selflessness opened wide the Portals of a New World.

Honour to the Immortal Dead – that great white company of shining souls who gave their youth that the World might grow old in Peace.

In the House of Commons yesterday our total war casualties were announced as follows:—

	Officers	Other Ranks
Killed	37,876	620,829
Wounded	92,644	1,939,478
Missing and Prisoners	12,094	347,051

Thus the grand total of casualties is 3,049,972.
Honour to the splendid living who have endured so much for Britain!
Homage to those who have been maimed in Freedom's Cause!
Honour to those who have lived with unconquerable spirit in the grim shadows of prison camp and slavery!
Daily Mirror
20 November 1918

The casualty figures were revised (upwards) several times after the end of the war. Although it has never been possible to come to an unequivocally precise figure, the 1922 computation is generally regarded as coming closest to being accurate.

They ask me where I've been,
And what I've done and seen.
But what can I reply
Who know it wasn't I,
But someone just like me,
Who went across the sea
And with my head and hands
Killed men in foreign lands ...
Though I must bear the blame,
Because he bore my name.

Wilfrid Gibson.

Yesterday I visited the battlefield of last year. The place was scarcely recognisable. Instead of a wilderness of ground torn up by shell, a perfect desolation of earth without a sign of vegetation, the ground was a garden of wild flowers and tall grasses. Nature had certainly hidden the ghastly scene under a veil of many colours. I was specially struck by a cross to an unknown British warrior which stood up like a sentinel over the vast cemetery of the fallen in last year's battle, now hidden under the dense vegetation. Most remarkable of all was the appearance of many thousands of white butterflies which fluttered round this solitary grave. You can have no conception of the strange sensation that this host of little fluttering creatures gave me. It was as if the souls of the dead soldiers had come to haunt the spot where so many fell. It was so eerie to see them, the only living things in that wilderness of flowers. And the silence! Not a sound, not even the rustling of a breeze through the grass. It was so still that it seemed as if one could almost hear the beat of the butterflies' wings. Indeed, there was nothing to disturb the eternal slumber of this unknown who was sleeping his last sleep where he fell. A contrast indeed to the hideous crash of battle of a short year ago.

From a British officer at the Front.

OFFICER, well educated, capable organiser and administrator, wide secretarial experience, keen, energetic, tactful, good horseman, experienced athlete, desires post as secretary or secretary-manager; home or abroad; excellent references.

MISS KATHLEEN GIBB I was engaged to a dear boy who joined up when he was eighteen and came through (as we thought at the time) without a scratch. He used to tell me about his life in the trenches (Passchendaele, the Somme, Mons). Some time after, my fiancé was taken ill, recovered, but the illness recurred and was diagnosed as consumption, or tuberculosis. Then the doctors realised it was caused through being gassed twice during the conflict, it had eaten away one lung and was affecting the other. At that time there was no cure for TB. He died after four years, just faded away. I was broken-hearted. He had no war pension as it was too late to apply. When I think I could have been a happy grandmother today if it hadn't been for that terrible war.

◆

INFANTRY OFFICER (23) seeks POST as private secretary. Public school education. Highest references.

In 1916 I went into Corbie with a limber and two horses and I saw an officer sitting very uncomfortably on a horse. The animal was throwing its head up, and dancing around. The officer called to me and said, 'Is anything wrong? This horse is usually very quiet to ride.' I told him to dismount and the first thing I found the bit had been pulled up tight in the horse's mouth and the curb chain was also too tight. So I slacked the curb and dropped the bit and by then the horse was quite docile. He thanked me and we had a talk. Then he said, 'I would like to be able to have a drink with you, but that's against orders.' So he handed me a ten-franc note and said, 'Drink my health,' and shook hands.

TROOPER SYDNEY CHAPLIN, 1st Northamptonshire Yeomanry.

In 1923, I was still without regular work (just odd jobs when I could get them) when I was told that the Corps of Commissionaires were interviewing ex-Servicemen in London. So I managed to scrape enough to pay for a return ticket to London and enough to pay for expenses. I was interviewed by a Major who took my particulars, checked my discharge papers, then informed me that owing to the amount of applications it would be a very long while before they could offer me a post. So that was it.

I had a walk round and eventually sat on a seat on the Embankment. I must have dozed off, because it was dark when I woke up, so I decided to stay put until the morning. I woke as the dawn was breaking, and what a sight it was. All the seats were full of old soldiers in all sorts of dress – mostly khaki – and a lot more were lying on the steps, some wrapped up in old newspapers. Men who had fought in the trenches, now unwanted and left to starve, were all huddled together. I was on the end of a seat, so I eased my fingers into my pocket to get a cigarette, as I did not want to wake the chap who was leaning against me, then I managed to light up. 'That smells good,' said the voice of the man I thought was asleep. I recognised him at once. I handed him a cigarette and said, 'Would you like a light, Major?' 'Good Lord! You, Corporal!' We stood up and looked at each other. 'Well, what about a spot of tea?' I said. He just spread out his hands and said, 'I am flat broke.' So I took him to a coffee stall and we had a mug of tea and two slices of bread and dripping each. The Major told me he had been caught out by one of the many crooks who were battening on to old soldiers. These offered shares in a business, producing false books, and when the money had been paid over they just disappeared. All his money had gone. However, he was to see one of his old junior officers that day and he was hoping to get a break. After an argument, I persuaded him to accept a few cigarettes and a shilling to carry him over.

I spent the day looking for work, but there were no vacancies anywhere. Finally I went into a cinema for a rest in the threepenny seats. It was dark when I came out and started to walk to St Pancras Station for the night train. As I was passing a shop doorway, I heard someone crying. I stopped and looked in and saw a man wearing an Army greatcoat with a turban on his head and a tray suspended from his neck with lucky charms on it. Another, unwanted after three years in the trenches. He and his wife were penniless when some crook offered him a chance to earn money easy if he could find five shillings. His wife pawned her wedding ring to get it, and in return he got a tray, a turban and a dozen or so lucky charms to sell at sixpence each. What a hope! Now after a day without anything to eat or drink he was broken-hearted at the thought of going home to his wife without a penny. He was an ex-Company Sergeant-Major. I sorted my cash out (one shilling and tenpence), gave him the bob and a fag. Then I carried on to the station, spent my tenpence at the coffee stall and got the train home.

It didn't last forever, but it lasted long enough. By 1930 I was happily married and in regular employment. One day I was returning from London to the Midlands by train. We pulled into Luton Station and stopped alongside a stationary train heading for London and in the first class compartment opposite I saw a well-dressed man smoking a cigar and reading a newspaper. Suddenly he looked up, the next moment down came both windows, and we clasped hands. It was the Major. He said, 'Corporal, you brought me luck. I found friends and a position that day I met you, and I have never looked back. And you?' 'Fine,' I said. At that moment his train moved out. We waved. I never knew his name.

◆

> COMMANDER, R.N. retired, aged 44, married, shortly demobilised, exceptional experience, executive officer of ships for many years, 2 years in command, total abstainer. WANTS WORK. Moderate salary.

◆

TROOPER G. HUGGINS,
D Squadron,
Queen's Own Oxfordshire
Hussars.

I left for home in February 1919, and the worst thing was leaving my horse behind. He was a lovely old chap. His name was Billy.

We were told if anyone wished to buy their horses to clip their initials on the horse's rump and give our names in and we would be notified when they were being sold. It must have been three months later I got notice to say he was being sold at Tattersalls. I was back home working on the farm and my father gave me the money. I put it in my pocket (and it was a tidy sum), I took the saddle and bridle and went up on the train to London and got to Tattersalls good and early to look for him before the sale. He found *me*! As I was looking round I heard a horse give a nutter, and I turned round. There he was. I said, 'Hello, Billy', and I walked up and he gave another nutter and rubbed his nose up and down my chest. That was at least three months after I'd last seen him. I gave fifty guineas for him – a *lot* of money then, but I'd have given more if need be. I took him back in the guard's van in the train, saddled him up at the station and rode him home. My mother was waiting at the door to see if I'd got him. Oh, he was a beauty! We'd been right through the whole war together and all he'd got was a little bit of shrapnel on his nose once. I could go to any field he was in and call, 'Come on, Billy,' and he'd come galloping up to me. We had him for years and years, and he had a good life on the farm, did old Billy. He ended his days in clover.

My husband only got home after the end of the war and he was so ill. Malaria. He was in the Scottish Horse and he'd been in Gallipoli and Egypt. I hadn't seen him for four years. My little girl was three and a bit and he'd never seen her. He came home straight off a hospital ship and he was so weary and unwell he went straight to bed. I said to Connie, 'Go in and see your Daddy.' She was very shy of him, but she went and stood at the bedroom door. I said, 'Well, say something to Daddy.' She said, 'My Mummy's made scones for you.' He just looked at her. He was too ill, too tired to speak. We lived with my family for a while. We'd had a war wedding before he left, so we didn't have a house of our own. After a few months we were given a railway carriage to live in. That was the Home for Heroes. It was the best they could do. So we started our married life in a converted railway carriage.

MRS I. MCNICOL

Us fellows, it took us years to get over it. Years! Long after when you were working, married, had kids, you'd be lying in bed with your wife and you'd see it all before you. Couldn't sleep. Couldn't lie still. Many's and many's the time I've got up and tramped the streets till it came daylight. Walking, walking – anything to get away from your thoughts. And many's the time I've met other fellows that were out there doing exactly the same thing. That went on for years, that did.

RIFLEMAN FRED WHITE, 10th Battalion, King's Royal Rifle Corps.

Mind you, they were a wonderful generation . . . let's face it, there were we, at the beginning of the war, the regular soldier, tough, hardened from India and South Africa, and then the 1st Army, Kitchener's . . . grand men they were. I watched a battalion of them march into battle on the Somme in 1916, and I thought to myself, 'My God! What a wonderful lot of chaps'. Fine physically, good, well set up, good marching . . . it was a good generation. It's a great pity it was decimated.

SERGEANT W.J. COLLINS, Royal Army Medical Corps.

Letters are anxiously awaited from the following N.C.O.'s and men, or news from comrades regarding them:—

302003 Cpl. A. E. W. WHITE, B Co., 8 Plat., London Regt. (missing Aug. 16). Mrs. White (mother), 3, Glentham Road, Castlenau, Barnes, inquires.

233837 (8511) Pte. F. SPENCELEY, D Co., 15 Plat., London Regt. (missing June 15-16). Mrs. Spenceley (wife), 40 Mildmay Street, Mildmay Park, N.1, inquires.

280091 Pte. H. B. COX, D Co., 15 Plat., London Regt. (missing Aug. 16). Mrs. Cox (mother), 29, Harvist Road, Holloway, N.7, inquires.

302863 Rfm. RAYMOND W. WHITE, A. Co., 2 Plat., London Regt. (missing Aug. 16). Mr. G. White (father), "Merven" 7, Gordon Road, Sevenoaks, inquiries.

51449 Pte. G. W. BANGS, 1 Co., 4 Plat., Royal Fusiliers (missing Apl. 23). Mrs. Bangs (wife), 33, Shakespeare Avenue, Harlesden, N.W.10, inquires.

315141 Rfm. F. GILES, A Co., 2 Plat., London Regt. (Missing Aug. 15-16). Mrs. Giles (mother), 45, Kempshead Road, Albany Road, Camberwell, London, S.E., inquires.

293583 (7228) Pte. H. F. SLY, D Co., 13 Plat., London Regt. (Missing,

4, Culvers Way,
Carshalton,
Surrey.

13 November 1924

To the Editor of The Ypres Times.

Dear Sir,
   My son was killed in Ypres Sector on about the 20 October, 1917, with the 14th Warwickshire Regiment at a place called Polderhoek Château, Gheluvelt. No. 29893, Private John Billett. I should be glad to hear from any of your readers if they know anything about him.
   I remain, Yours sincerely,
   H. Billett (late Sergeant of the SLI).

Lord Plumer of Messines,
at the unveiling of the Menin Gate, 1927.

One of the most tragic features of the Great War was the number of casualties reported as 'missing, believed killed'.

To their relatives there must have been added to their grief a tinge of bitterness and a feeling that everything possible had not been done to recover their loved ones' bodies and give them reverent burial ... when peace came, and the last ray of hope had been extinguished, the void seemed deeper and the outlook more forlorn for those who had no grave to visit, no place where they could lay tokens of loving remembrance ... and it was resolved that here at Ypres, where so many of the missing are known to have fallen, there should be erected a memorial worthy of them which should give expression to the nation's gratitude for their sacrifice and their sympathy with those who mourned them. A memorial has been erected which, in its simple grandeur, fulfils this object, and now it can be said of each one in whose honour we are assembled here today:

'He is not missing; he is here!'

◆ ◆

June 16.) Mr. W. Sly, 199, Piccadilly, London, W., inquires.

21940 Pte. T. PADGHAM, D Do., R.W. Surrey Regt. (Missing Sept. 20–22). Mrs. Sleigh (mother), 79, Stonebridge Road, South Tottenham, London, N., inquires.

232482 (5518) Pte. E. G. HIGGINS, C Co., 12 Plat. London Regt. (missing June 15). Mrs. Higgins (mother), 49, Belmont Road, Ilford, Essex, inquires.

62992 Pte. F. F. BUCK-LAND, 2 Co., Royal Fusiliers (missing Oct. 4). Mrs. Buckland (wife), 87, Lancaster Street, Newington, Causeway, S.E.1, inquires.

231938 (4778) Pte. S. S. LOWE, B Co., 5 Plat., L.M.G., London Regt. (missing Aug. 16). Mrs. Lowe, 3, Berkeley Street, Lambeth, S.E., inquires.

20907 Pte. A. KERSHAW, A Co., 1 Plat. E. Surrey Regt. (missing Aug. 9). Mrs. Kershaw (mother), 36, Carlyle Avenue, Stonebridge Park, Harlesden, N.W. 10, inquires.

G21188 Pte. A. RANBOUX, D Co., 15 Plat., E. Kent Regt. (w. and m. Oct. 12). Mrs. Ranboux (wife), 131, Gt. Titchfield Street, London, W.1, inquires.

3896 Rfm. GEORGE HINDS, B Co., 5 Plat., L.G.S., London Regt. Q.W.R. (Missing July 1/16). Mrs. Hinds (mother), 8, Corfton Road, Ealing, London, W.,

ACKNOWLEDGEMENTS

I would like to acknowledge my debt to the following people without whose much-appreciated assistance this book would not be possible.

Corporal Jason Addy,
  4th Battalion, Tank Corps.
Captain A. V. L. B. Agius,
  1/3 City of London Battalion,
  The London Regiment.
Schütze Emil Amann,
  75 Machine-gun Abteilung,
  28 Baden Division. (*German*)
Private L. M. Baldwin,
  8th Battalion, East Surrey
  Regiment.
Corporal H. Bale,
  Royal Field Artillery.
Lieutenant G. Barber,
  1st Battalion, Queen's Own
  Cameron Highlanders.
Sergeant Harry Bartlett,
  Royal Field Artillery.
Private Percy Batchelor,
  Queen's Own Oxfordshire
  Hussars.
Private H. Baverstock,
  1st Canterbury Battalion,
  New Zealand Division.
Sergeant H. Biles,
  2nd Battalion, Royal Sussex
  Regiment.
Padre J. A. Herbert Bell,
  4th Class Chaplain.
Private W. G. Bell, MM
  Army Cyclist Corps.
Gemeiner Ernst Bergner,
  143rd Infantry Regiment.
  (*German*)
Lieutenant H. L. Birks,
  Tank Corps.

Private Charles Blane,
  2nd Battalion, King's Own
  Scottish Borderers.
Lance Sergeant, J. L. Bouch,
  1st Battalion, Coldstream Guards.
Private J. Bowles,
  2/16 (County of London)
  Battalion,
  Queen's Westminster Rifles.
Sergeant T. Brady,
  United States Army.
Sister Nell Brink,
  United States Army Nurse.
Sergeant S. V. Britten,
  13th Battalion, Royal Highlanders
  of Canada.
Lieutenant E. H. T. Broadwood,
  1st Battalion, The Norfolk
  Regiment.
Sergeant B. J. Brookes,
  1/16 Queen's Westminster Rifles,
  County of London Regiment.
Private Alex Brownie,
  4th Battalion, Gordon
  Highlanders.
Trooper Sydney Chaplin,
  1st Northamptonshire Yeomanry
Captain Bagot Chester,
  3rd Queen Alexandra's Own Gurkha
  Rifles, (The Sirmoor Rifles).
Major-General (then Captain)
  A. F. P. Christison,
  6th Battalion, Queen's Own
  Cameron Highlanders.
Captain G. Garnett Clarke,
  Royal Field Artillery.

Corporal P. J. Clarke,
  13th (S) Battalion, The Rifle
  Brigade.
Company Sergeant Major J. Coggins,
  4th Battalion, Oxfordshire and
  Buckinghamshire Light Infantry.
Private Jack Cole,
  2nd Battalion, The
  Worcestershire Regiment.
Sergeant C. Coles,
  1st Battalion, Coldstream Guards.
Sergeant W. J. Collins,
  Royal Army Medical Corps.
Sergeant E. Cooper, VC,
  12th (S) Battalion, The King's
  Royal Rifle Corps.
Major J. Cowan,
  Royal Engineers.
Rifleman J. Cross,
  13th (S) Battalion, The Rifle
  Brigade.
2nd Lieutenant W. Cushing,
  9th (S) Battalion, The Norfolk
  Regiment.
Sapper E. Davidson,
  Royal Engineers.
Corporal Harold Diffey,
  15th (S) Battalion, (1st London
  Welsh) Royal Welsh Fusiliers.
Captain H. M. Dillon,
  2nd Battalion, Oxfordshire and
  Buckinghamshire Light Infantry.
2nd Lieutenant C. Drummond,
  Royal Field Artillery.
Bombardier Alex Dunbar,
  Royal Field Artillery.

Private F. J. H. Dunk,
  7th (S) Battalion, Royal West
  Kent Regiment.
Rifleman Burton Eccles,
  7th (S) Battalion, The Rifle
  Brigade.
Gunner R. Elwes,
  Royal Garrison Artillery.
Private Harry Fellowes,
  12th (S) Battalion,
  Northumberland Fusiliers.
Sergeant G. Fisher,
  1st Battalion, The Hertfordshire
  Regiment.
Corporal O. W. Flowers,
  Motor Transport Section,
  Army Service Corps.
Private S. Fraser,
  Honourable Artillery Company.
Dr. B. Gallaher, United States Army.
Mrs Audrey Geidt.
Miss Kathleen Gibb.
Captain Alan Goring,
  6th Battalion, The Yorkshire
  Regiment.
Sergeant Tom Grady,
  United States Army.
Sergeant F. W. Graser,
  10th Field Artillery,
  United States Army.
Padre Eric Green,
  Army Chaplain's Department.
Kanonier Gerhardt Gurtler,
  111th Bavarian Corps Artillerie.
  (German)
Sergeant Phelps Harding,
  306th Infantry Regiment, United
  States Army.
Private L. Hart,
  1st Otago Infantry Battalion,
  5th New Zealand Reinforcements.
Sergeant W. Hay,
  9th Battalion, The Royal Scots.
Private Horace Haynes,
  2/6 (TF) Battalion,
  Royal Warwickshie Regiment.
Able Seaman J. Haynes,
  Anson Battalion,
  Royal Naval Division.
Gefreiter Fritz Heinemann,
  165th Infantry Regiment.
  (German)
Captain T. E. H. Helby,
  59th Siege Battery,
  Royal Garrison Artillery.

Lieutenant H. S. S. Henderson,
  1st Battalion, Prince of Wales'
  Own,
  (West Yorkshire Regiment).
Mrs Lily Henry.
Corporal W. Holbrook,
  4th Battalion, Royal Fusiliers.
Rifleman Stanley Hopkins,
  18th Battalion, The London
  Regiment
  (London Irish Rifles).
Lieutenant George Horridge,
  1/5 (TF) Battalion, Lancashire
  Fusiliers.
Legionnaire Harry Houghton,
  2nd Regiment,
  French Foreign Legion.
Trooper G. Huggins,
  Queen's Own Oxfordshire
  Hussars.
Private H. Jeary,
  3rd Battalion, The Queen's,
  (Royal West Surrey Regiment).
Jaeger Herman Keyser,
  9th Jaeger Battalion. (German)
Sergeant R. Knowles,
  16th Infantry Regiment,
  42nd (Rainbow) Division,
  United States Army.
Sergeant Gottfried Kreibohm,
  Lehr Infantry Regiment.
  (German).
Rifleman H. Ralph Langley,
  16th (S) Battalion, (Church Lads'
  Brigade),
  King's Royal Rifle Corps.
Lieutenant Geoffrey Lawrence,
  1st South African Infantry
  Battalion.
Private Reg Lawrence,
  3rd South African Infantry
  Battalion.
Corporal A. L. Lee,
  A Battalion,
  Tank Corps.
Private W. Lockey,
  1st Battalion, The Sherwood
  Foresters
  (Notts. and Derby Regiment).
Private F. Longbottom
  2nd Battalion, Duke of
  Wellington's
  (West Riding Regiment).
Private Ernest Lowe,
  13th (S) Battalion, Royal Fusiliers.

Corporal John Lucy,
  2nd Battalion, Princess Victoria's
  (Royal Irish Fusiliers).
Private W. Luff,
  3rd Battalion, The Queen's
  (Royal West Surrey Regiment).
Captain R. MacDonald,
  7th Battalion, Queen's Own
  Cameron Highlanders.
Rifleman J. McArthur,
  13th (S) Battalion,
  The Rifle Brigade.
Captain Bryden McKinnell,
  10th (Scottish) Battalion,
  King's Liverpool Regiment.
2nd Lieutenant J. Macleod,
  Queen's Own Cameron
  Highlanders.
Lieutenant R. A. Macleod,
  Royal Field Artillery.
Private W. T. Manewell,
  1st Battalion, Royal West Kent
  Regiment.
Captain Maurice Mascall,
  Royal Garrison Artillery
  (Mountain Regiment).
Trooper P. Mason,
  9th (S) Battalion, (Yorkshire
  Hussars Yeomanry)
  West Yorkshire Regiment.
Unteroffizier P. Melber,
  1st Machine-gun Company,
  28th Ersatz Infantry Regiment.
  (German)
Private C. Miles,
  10th (S) Battalion, Royal
  Fusiliers.
Private Ivor Morgan,
  16th Battalion (Cardiff Pals)
  The Welsh Regiment.
Corporal J. G. Mortimer, MM,
  10th (S) Battalion,
  The York and Lancaster
  Regiment.
Mrs Anita Mostyn.
Lieutenant Frank Moylan,
  2/7 Battalion. (TF) City of
  London Battalion,
  Royal Fusiliers.
Able Seaman Joseph Murray,
  Hood Battalion,
  Royal Naval Division.
Lieutenant J. Naylor,
  Royal Field Artillery.
Leutnant Johannes Niemann,

Leutnant Johannes Niemann, *cont.*
133rd Royal Saxon Regiment
(*German*).
Private W.H. Nixon,
2nd Battalion, The Cheshire
Regiment.
Corporal T. North,
1st Battalion, The Lincolnshire
Regiment.
Observer Bernard Oliver,
23rd Balloon Section,
Royal Flying Corps.
Corporal A. D. Pankhurst,
Royal Field Artillery
(Trench Mortars).
Private W. Parker,
12th Battalion, (Sheffield Pals)
York & Lancaster Regiment.
Captain C. J. Paterson,
1st Battalion, South Wales
Borderers.
Colonel H. C. Rees,
2nd Battalion, The Welsh
Regiment.
Gefreiter Heinrich Renzing,
88th Infantry Regiment. (*German*)
Lieutenant Ewart Richardson,
4th Battalion, Prince of Wales'
Own
(Yorkshire Regiment).
Corporal C. R. Russell,
1/14 (County of London)
Battalion,
London Scottish.
Captain F. C. Russell,
22nd Battalion, A.I.F.
Cadet Sydney Savage,
Oundle School O.T.C.

Musketier Hans Schetter,
231st Reserve Infantry Regiment,
50th Reserve Division. (*German*)
Corporal W. H. Shaw,
9th Battalion, Royal Welsh
Fusiliers.
Rifleman H. V. Shawyer,
13th (S) Battalion, The Rifle
Brigade.
Private A. V. Simpson,
2/6 Battalion, Duke of
Wellington's,
(West Riding Regiment).
Captain C. S. Slack,
4th Battalion, East Yorkshire
Regiment.
Gunner Herbet Smith,
5th Battery,
Royal Field Artillery.
Freiwilliger Rheinhold Spengler,
1st Bavarian Infantry Regiment.
(*German*)
Private Carson Stewart,
7th (S) Battalion, Queen's Own
Cameron Highlanders.
Gunner B. O. Stokes,
13th Battery,
New Zealand Field Artillery.
Lieutenant L. A. Strange,
Royal Flying Corps.
Major T. D. H. Stubbs,
Royal Field Artillery.
Gunner Norman Tennant,
245th Battery,
Royal Field Artillery.
Corporal R. E. Thompson,
13th (S) Battalion,
The Rifle Brigade.

Private A. Thomson,
7th Battalion, The Royal Scots.
Lieutenant K. F. B. Tower,
4th Royal Fusiliers.
Captain R. J. Trousdell,
1st Battalion Princess Victoria's
(Royal Irish Fusiliers).
Private James B. Turner,
A.I.F.
Lance-Corporal David Watson,
11th Battalion, The Royal Scots.
Sergeant J. Watson,
8th (S) Battalion,
Northumberland Fusiliers.
Rifleman Fred White,
10th (S) Battalion. King's Royal
Rifle Corps.
Captain T. A. White.
13th Battalion, A.I.F.
Madame Legrand Willerval.
Shoeing Smith C. H. Williams,
Oxfordshire and
Buckinghamshire Light Infantry.
Guardsman J. H. Worker,
1st Battalion, Scots Guards.
Rifleman W. Worrell,
12th Battalion,
The Rifle Brigade.
Gunner G. Worsley,
Royal Field Artillery.
2nd Lieutenant J. D. Wyatt,
2nd Battalion, The Yorkshire
Regiment.
Sergeant J. E. Yates,
6th Battalion, Prince of Wales'
Own,
(West Yorkshire Regiment).

My sincere thanks to the many people who have so kindly made available private accounts, letters, diaries and other written records, too numerous to specify, of soldiers who served in the Great War: Mrs Nora Brookes, widow of Sergeant Bernard Brookes; Mrs Eileen Brandon, neice of Rifleman Bert Bailey; Malcolm Drummond, son of Brigadier Cyril Drummond; Mrs Alice Timothy, USA, daughter of Sergeant Tom Grady; in Australia, Graham and Vivien Riches; in New Zealand Roger Hart, son of Private Leonard Hart and nephew of Adrian Hart; Colonel Jim Trousdell, son of Captain R.J. Trousdell; Mrs J. Griffiths for the diary of Lieutenant Ewart Richardson; Richard Baumgartner, USA, for generously contributing and translating a large number of German accounts from his own archive and for permission to quote from his book *Fritz*; The San Diego Group, also in USA; Mr Reginald Lawrence, South Africa, for his brother's diary as well as his own; Mrs Anita Mostyn, daughter of Colonel Rowland Feilding; the estate of Esmée Mascal; Dr William Gallaher, USA, son of Dr Bernard Gallaher; Mrs K. Hill, daughter of Major T.D.H. Stubbs; my old friend Norman Tennant for his wartime drawings; Captain Mike Haslam for permission to use his material on the Chilwell munitions factory; Corporal A.V. Simpson; Mrs H.L.S. Dodd, daughter of Brigadier-General H.C. Rees; Major A.R.S. Tower, son of Lieutenant-Colonel K.F.B. Tower, MC; Mr J.H. Wyatt, son of 2nd Lieutenant J.D. Wyatt; Harrods Ltd of Knightsbridge; Lt-Colonel A.A. Fairrie at Regimental HQ, The Queen's Own Cameron Highlanders; Brigadier J.M. Cubiss at Regimental HQ, The Prince of Wales' Own Regiment of Yorkshire; John Callcut of the Newdigate Society, the Public Record Office, and lastly, but very far least, The Imperial War Museum who, as always, put their resources unstintingly at my disposal.

My particular thanks go to John Peters who owns a large collection of old gramophone records and generously sent me tapes of forgotten wartime songs, a number of which he will find in this book.

I hope that I have overlooked nobody, though many people have been so consistently generous in sending me documents over the years that I fear this may be the case. I hope that anyone whose name has been omitted will forgive me and will regard the inclusion of the material they supplied as an indication of its value as well as my appreciation.

Selecting the items which would cover varying aspects and a wide spectrum of the attitudes of those who fought or lived through the Great War, and incorporating them in a book which would chronologically follow the course of the war itself, entailed reading literally millions of words in transcripts, memoirs, letters, diaries, and wallowing in oceans of paper. My grateful thanks must go to Josephine Brooks who spent literally months slaving over a temperamental photocopier making copies of fragile and valuable documents, to Alma Woodroff who somehow managed to solve the jigsaw puzzle of a thousand or more extracts and produced an immaculate manuscript, to John Woodroff for checking units, facts and figures with his customary zeal, and to all three of them, for their very considerable help in collating a mountain of disparate material into sequence and order.

Shirley Seaton's role is acknowledged on the title page but I would like to add a word of personal thanks for her assiduity in pursuing some challenging lines of enquiry, for many useful ideas and suggestions, and for coming up with some marvellous serendipities which made no small contribution to the scope of the book.

The publishers wish to thank the following for permission to reproduce extracts from material to which they hold the copyright:

W.M. Heinemann: "From 'W' Beach", Geoffrey Dearmer.
John Murray: "Domum", Charles Scott-Moncrieff; "In the Morning", Patrick MacGill.
Peters, Fraser & Dunlop Group: "The Pillbox", Edmund Blunden.
Sidgwick & Jackson: "The Dead", Rupert Brooke.
Penguin Books: Untitled poem by Patrick Shaw Stewart.
Faber & Faber: "The Glory of Women", "Stand to Good Friday Morning", "Died of Wounds", Siegfried Sassoon; *Unwilling Passenger*, Capt. Arthur Osburn; Siegfired Sassoon Diaries 1915–1918.
Curtis Brown (originally published by Methuen): "Gold Braid", A.A. Milne.
Hogarth Press: "Dulce et Decorum Est", Wilfred Owen.
The Bodley Head: "Farewell", E.A. McIntosh; *3 Chevrons*, Major H.F. Bidder.

Society of Authors representing estate: "Here dead we Lie", A. E Housman.
Macmillan & Co: "Back", Wilfred Gibson.
The Elmfield Press: *A French soldier's Diary*, Henri Desagneaux.
Jonathan Cape: *A Brass Hat In No Man's Land*, Brig. Gen. Crozier; *Behind the Lines*, Col. Nicholson.
George Allen and Unwin Ltd: *The Supreme Command*, Vol. 1, Lord Hankey; "Sunsets", Richard Aldington.
Hutchinson & Co Ltd: *My War Memoirs*, General Ludendorff Vol. 1; *Fireater*, Capt. A. O. Pollard.
Estate of Robert Service: "Funk", Robert Service.
The Medici Society: *War Letters To a Wife*, Col. Roland Feilding.
Seeley Service & Co/Leo Cooper: for permission to reproduce an edited extract from *The First Hundred Thousand*, Ian Hay.
Mrs J. F. Lisle: "Death's Men", W. J. Turner.

Every effort has been made to contact the copyright owners of quoted material, and the publishers wish to apologise for any inaccuracies or omissions to the above list.

The Imperial War Museum: (Back cover, 48, 51, 57, 74, 79, 112, 127 (bottom), 132, 141, 142, 147 (top), 152, 156, 158 (top & bottom), 166, 169, 171, 174, 179, 186, 196, 200, 202, 204–5, 209, 213, 218 (top & bottom), 220, 221, 225, 242, 256, 266, 271, 279, 290 (top & bottom), 302, 306, 309, 327); Hulton Picture Library (10, 40 (bottom), 127 (top), 227, 275, 286, 294, 311, 328, 332, 336); Mansell Collection (7, 15, 26, 27, 28, 39, 53, 102–3, 243, 288); John Frost Historical Newspaper Collection (end papers, 13, 45, 62, 70, 86, 125, 187, 258); British Library Newspaper Library (30, 40 (top), 114, 182, 257 (top), 281); Syndication International (14, 15, 22, 33, 35, 313); John Woodroff (end papers, 29, 234, 262, 329); Liddell Hart Centre for Military Archives, King's College, London (95, 98, 100, 121); Bettmann Archives (207, 322); Illustrated London News Picture Library (81, 92); *Punch* (115, 298); Malcolm Brown (42, 153); Keystone Collection (165, 299); National Museum of Labour History (177); The Brooke Trustees and King's College Library, Cambridge (72); Harrods Ltd. (50); Lt-Colonel W.G. Taylor (147). The design of the death certificate is Crown copyright and is reproduced with the permission of Her Majesty's Stationery Office (184–5).

INDEX

Names of contributors are in italics.